TEACHING OF INTELLECT

Intellectual property (IP) comprises not only the valuable economic assets of private firms, but also the social and cultural assets of society. The potential impact of intellectual property assets is so great that it is certain to have a considerable effect on national and international economic development in the future. Despite this, the area of IP education is relatively new to many academic institutions, and principles and methods in teaching IP are still evolving.

Against this backdrop, a number of internationally renowned professors and practitioners share their teaching techniques in their particular fields of expertise, including what they consider should be taught in terms of coursework. The result is a valuable handbook for teachers and those wishing to get up to speed on international IP issues.

YO TAKAGI is an executive director at the World Intellectual Property Organisation, in charge of strategic planning and policy development and the WIPO Worldwide Academy.

LARRY ALLMAN is a senior counsellor of the World Intellectual Property Organisation.

MPAZI A. SINJELA is dean of the Worldwide Academy of the World Intellectual Property Organisation.

TEACHING OF INTELLECTUAL PROPERTY

PRINCIPLES AND METHODS

EDITED BY
YO TAKAGI
LARRY ALLMAN
MPAZI A. SINJELA

CAMBRIDGE UNIVERSITY PRESS
Cambridge, New York, Melbourne, Madrid, Cape Town, Singapore, São Paulo, Delhi

Cambridge University Press
The Edinburgh Building, Cambridge CB2 8RU, UK

Published in the United States of America by Cambridge University Press, New York

www.cambridge.org
Information on this title: www.cambridge.org/9780521716468

© World Intellectual Property Organization 2008

This publication is in copyright. Subject to statutory exception
and to the provisions of relevant collective licensing agreements,
no reproduction of any part may take place without
the written permission of Cambridge University Press.

First published 2008
Reprinted 2008

Printed in the United Kingdom at the University Press, Cambridge

A catalogue record for this publication is available from the British Library

ISBN 978-0-521-71646-8 paperback

Cambridge University Press has no responsibility for the persistence or
accuracy of URLs for external or third-party internet websites referred to
in this book, and does not guarantee that any content on such
websites is, or will remain, accurate or appropriate.

CONTENTS

Notes on contributors	vii
List of abbreviations	xii
Table of figures	xiv
Foreword	xvi
KAMIL IDRIS, *WIPO Director General*	

1	Recent trends and challenges in teaching intellectual property	1
	LARRY ALLMAN, MPAZI SINJELA AND YO TAKAGI	
2	Teaching patents	13
	JOSEPH STRAUS	
3	Teaching copyright and related rights	33
	MIHÁLY FICSOR	
4	Teaching trademark law	63
	JEREMY PHILLIPS	
5	Teaching industrial design law	84
	WILLIAM T. FRYER III	
6	Teaching intellectual property, unfair competition and anti-trust law	130
	THOMAS COTTIER AND CHRISTOPHE GERMANN	
7	Teaching the economics of intellectual property rights in the global economy	166
	KEITH E. MASKUS	
8	Teaching intellectual property in a business school	185
	SUSANNA H.S. LEONG	
9	Teaching IP practical skills for practitioners and attorneys	212
	HEINZ GODDAR	

10	Teaching intellectual property to non-law students RUTH SOETENDORP	230
11	Using the new technologies in teaching intellectual property (distance learning) PHILIP GRIFFITH	268
12	Teaching current trends and future developments in intellectual property CHARLES R. MCMANIS	299

Index   320

CONTRIBUTORS

Larry Allman is a senior counsellor at the World Intellectual Property Organization (WIPO) and is currently working on a publication documenting the history of WIPO from 1992 to 2007. He has worked at WIPO since March of 1995 in several capacities, including in the Copyright Department, in the Strategic Planning unit, in the WIPO Worldwide Academy, and on Special Projects. Prior to WIPO, he was a practicing lawyer in Los Angeles, California.

Thomas Cottier is managing director of the World Trade Institute and professor of European and International Economics Law at the University of Berne and dean of the Faculty of Law. He directs a national research programme on trade law and policy. Educated at the Universities of Berne and Michigan (Ann Arbor) he was a research fellow at Cambridge University, and taught at the University of St. Gallen and Neuchâtel prior to his appointment as a full professor at the University of Berne in 1994. He served on the Swiss negotiating team of the Uruguay Round from 1986 to 1993 as chief negotiator on TRIPS. He held several positions in the Swiss External Economic Affairs Department and was the deputy-director general of the Swiss Intellectual Property Office.

Mihály Ficsor is president of the Hungarian Copyright Council. From 1977 to 1985, he was director general of the Hungarian Copyright Bureau (ARTISJUS). Between 1985 and 1999, Dr. Ficsor worked, first, as director and, then, from 1992 as assistant director general of the World Intellectual Property Organization (WIPO) in charge of copyright and related rights. He is recognized as having played a decisive role in the preparation, negotiation and adoption of the so-called "Internet Treaties": the WIPO Copyright Treaty (WCT) and the WIPO Performances and Phonograms Treaty (WPPT). His book on the two Treaties and the Internet has become a widely used copyright treatise.

William T. Fryer III is a professor at the University of Baltimore School of Law, Baltimore, Maryland, USA where he teaches intellectual property (IP) law courses. He represented the American Bar Association, IP Law Section at all the meetings of experts and at the 1999 Diplomatic Conference on the Geneva Act of the Hague Agreement Concerning the International Registration of Industrial Designs. A book he has published recently describes the history of this treaty development and its operation. His website www.fryer.com is a source of documents and original articles on industrial design protection and contains a detailed CV.

Christophe Germann is an attorney at law admitted to the bar of Geneva and authorized to practice in Switzerland and in the European Union, and lecturer on the international intellectual property law system at the Institute for European and International Economic Public Law of the University of Berne Law School. He also acts as alternate leader of the research project on international trade regulations addressing special and differential treatment, variable geometry and regionalism in the framework of the Swiss National Science Foundation's programme "National Centres of Competence in Research". In parallel, he currently participates in the post-doctoral "Max Weber Fellowship" program of the European University Institute of Florence where he is researching in the area of trade-related cultural diversity laws and policies.

Heinz Goddar is a German patent attorney and European patent and trademark attorney, partner in Boehmert & Boehmert and in Forrester & Boehmert, Munich. He has a PhD in physics. Dr. Goddar is an associate judge at the German Federal Court of Justice and a senior advisor to IIC, Berlin. He teaches patent and licensing law as an honorary professor at the University of Bremen, as a lecturer at CEIPI, Strasbourg, and MIPLC, Munich. He is a visiting professor at the Universities of Santa Clara, Washington, and Seattle, the National ChengChi University, Taipei, and the Tokai University, Tokyo. He is a past president of LES International and of LES Germany.

Philip Griffith is professor of law and the associate dean (Teaching and Learning) at the faculty of law in the University of Technology, Sydney. He has researched, taught, published and engaged in policy debate and reform in the field of intellectual property since 1972. He led the development, design and delivery of specialist postgraduate intellectual property courses, delivered nationally and internationally through online teaching programs at UTS. He has also been involved in the development of intellectual property education in Asia with particular interests in Hong Kong, Korea, Indonesia, Thailand, Vietnam, Pakistan and, most recently, in the People's Republic of China.

Susanna H.S. Leong is an associate professor at the NUS Business School, National University of Singapore and is an advocate and solicitor of the Supreme Court of Singapore. She received her LL.B (Hons) from the National University of Singapore and her LL.M from the University of London, University College London. She teaches business-related law courses such as contract, sale of goods and intellectual property to undergraduate and graduate business students. Her research interests are in intellectual property and technology-related laws. She is the academic director of the NUS-PKU International MBA program, a senior fellow at the Intellectual Property Academy of Singapore, a member of WIPO Arbitration and Mediation Centre's Domain Name Panel and a member of the Regional Centre for Arbitration, Kuala Lumpur (RCAKL) Panel.

Keith E. Maskus is Stanford Calderwood professor of economics at the University of Colorado, Boulder, USA. He has been a lead economist at the World Bank and is also a research fellow at the Institute for International Economics. He has been a visiting professor at the University of Adelaide and the University of Bocconi, and a visiting scholar at the China Center for Economic Research at Peking University. He is the author of *Intellectual Property Rights in the Global Economy* and co-editor of *International Public Goods and the Transfer of Technology under a Globalized Intellectual Property Regime*, published by Cambridge University Press. He recently wrote a paper calling for fundamental reform in US patent policy.

Charles R. McManis is the Thomas and Karole Green professor of law and director of the Intellectual Property & Technology Law Program at Washington University in St. Louis, Missouri, USA. He received his B.A. degree from Birmingham-Southern College in 1964, and both his M.A. (in Philosophy) and J.D. degrees from Duke University in 1972. During 1993 and 1994, Professor McManis was Fulbright fellow at the International Intellectual Property Training Institute in Taejon, Republic of Korea. He has served as a WIPO consultant in India, Republic of Korea, and Oman, and in 2002 he presented a paper at a joint WIPO/UPOV symposium, on the co-existence of patents and plant breeders' rights, in Geneva, Switzerland. His books include *Intellectual Property & Unfair Competition in a Nutshell* (fifth edition), *Licensing Intellectual Property in the*

Information Age (co-author, the second edition, 2005) and *Biodiversity and the Law: Intellectual Property, Biotechnology and Traditional Knowledge* (editor, 2007).

Jeremy Phillips is research director, Intellectual Property Institute, London; visiting Professor, University College London; intellectual property consultant, Slaughter and May solicitors; co-founder, the IPKat weblog; editor, *The Journal of Intellectual Property Law & Practice*; and editor, *The European Trade Mark Reports*.

Mpazi Sinjela is dean of the WIPO Worldwide Academy. He holds a JSD (Doctor of Laws) and an LL.M (Master of Laws) from Yale Law School (USA), and an LL.B (Bachelor of Laws), School of Law, University of Zambia. He is a co-director and professor for the LL.M degree in the intellectual property program (organized by the University of Turin (Italy) with the WIPO Worldwide Academy); visiting professor, Intellectual Property Law and Human Rights Law Program (jointly offered by the Raoul Wallenberg Institute), the University of Lund (Sweden) and the WIPO Worldwide Academy. He previously served as senior legal officer at the United Nations, New York and the University of Zambia School of Law.

Ruth Soetendorp is a graduate of Bournemouth, Southampton and London Universities' law schools. Her award in 2001 of a UK National Teaching Fellowship recognised her work on IPR education in the non-law curriculum, developed through consultancy projects with the UK Patent Office, EPO, WIPO and private companies. Her research has brought her face to face with engineering faculties in Europe, Australia, Japan, China, Russia and India. She is co-author of interactive resources designed to facilitate self-managed learning of IPR. She was founding convenor of the Society of Legal Scholars' legal education section, and leads the education subgroup of the UK Intellectual Property Awareness Network.

Joseph Straus is Dr. jur., Dres. h.c. professor of law (Universities of Munich and Ljubljana), director Max Planck Institute for Intellectual Property, Competition and Tax Law, Munich, chair of the Managing Board, Munich Intellectual Property Law Center, and Marshall B. Coyne visiting professor, George Washington University Law School, Washington DC. Born 1938 in Trieste/Italy, Dipl. in Law 1962 University of Ljubljana, Dr. jur. 1968, University of Munich, Habilitation 1986 University of Ljubljana. Private Practice 1966–1974, since then Max Planck Institute. He has published about 300 works in the field of intellectual property law and has provided consultations to various national and international institutions. He has also actively participated in projects in many national and international organizations.

Yo Takagi is an executive director at WIPO in charge of strategic planning and policy development and the WIPO Worldwide Academy. Before joining WIPO in 1994, he worked in the government of Japan as a patent examiner, legal advisor and delegate for the negotiation of the TRIPS Agreement and for various meetings at WIPO. He studied chemical engineering at the University of Kyoto.

ABBREVIATIONS

Andean	Subregional Integration Agreement of the Andean Group Countries (also known as the Cartagena Agreement and the Andean Pact)
ARIPO	African Regional Intellectual Property Organization
Bangui Agreement	Bangui Agreement on the Creation of an African Intellectual Property Organization (OAPI)
Budapest Treaty	Budapest Treaty on the International Recognition of the Deposit of Microorganisms for the Purposes of Patent Procedure
CAFC	US Court of Appeals for the Federal Circuit
CBD	Convention on Biological Diversity
CGIAR	Consultative Group on International Agricultural Research
CISAC	International Confederation of Societies of Authors and Composers
DNS	Domain Name System
DRM	Digital rights management
EAPO	Eurasian Patent Office
EPC	European Patent Convention
FAO	Food and Agriculture Organization
FDI	Foreign Direct Investment
FIA	International Federation of Actors
FIM	International Federation of Musicians
GATS	General Agreement on Trade in Services
GATT	General Agreement on Tariffs and Trade
GPL	General Public License
Harare Protocol	Harare Protocol on Patents and Industrial Designs within the Framework of the African Regional Intellectual Property Organization (ARIPO)
IFRRO	International Federation of Reproduction Rights Organizations

ABBREVIATIONS

IFPI	International Federation of the Phonographic Industry
INTA	International Trademark Association
IP	Intellectual property
IPR	Intellectual property rights
ITT	International technology transfer
LDCs	Least developed countries
MTA	Material transfer agreement
NAFTA	North American Free Trade Agreement
OAPI	African Intellectual Property Organization
OHIM	Office for Harmonization in the Internal Market
Paris Convention	Paris Convention for the Protection of Industrial Property
PCT	Patent Cooperation Treaty
PLT	Patent Law Treaty
R&D	Research and development
RMI	Rights management information
TCE	Traditional cultural expression
TPM	Technological protection measure
TRIMS	Agreement on Trade-Related Investment Measures
TRIPS	Agreement on Trade-Related Aspects of Intellectual Property Rights
UNESCO	United Nations Educational, Scientific and Cultural Organization
UPOV Convention	International Convention for the Protection of New Varieties of Plants
USPTO	United States Patent and Trademark Office
WCT	WIPO Copyright Treaty
WIPO Convention	Convention Establishing the World Intellectual Property Organization
WPPT	WIPO Performers and Phonograms Treaty
WTO	World Trade Organization

FIGURES

Figure 1:	International registration DM/062739 for a basket	88
Figure 2:	International registration DM/053603 for a chair	89
Figure 3:	International registration DM/067464 for scissors	91
Figure 4:	International registration DM/066970 for a motorcycle	94
Figure 5:	International registration DM/052645 for a camera	96
Figure 6:	Geneva Act of the Hague Agreement Operation	109
Figure 7:	Operation of an industrial design registration, non-novelty examination system	114
Figure 8:	Basic operation of a design registration novelty examination system	115
Figure 9:	Basic operation of the EU Community Design system	119
Figure 10:	US Design Patent 1440 (page 1 of 3 pages), patented July 16, 1861, inventors: J. Gorman, G. Thurber & L. Dexter, Jr.	121
Figure 11:	Illustration diagram from *Gorman* design patent US Supreme Court Opinion, 81 U.S. 511 (1871)	122
Figure 12	Basic access–innovation trade-off in IPRs	172
Figure 13:	Relationship between patent rights and per-capita GNP	173
Figure 14:	ARM Holdings PLC pre-eminent global semiconductor IP supplier	234
Figure 15:	Faculties involved in interdisciplinary teaching and research	236
Figure 16:	Contents of the graduate IP tool box	239
Figure 17:	Laboratory write up topics at Valdosta	241
Figure 18:	Osaka Institute of Technology IP Major in intellectual property syllabus	241
Figure 19:	International IP law in multinational companies syllabus (China)	242

Figure 20:	IP questions prospective employees need to consider	245
Figure 21:	Kolb's learning cycle	246
Figure 22:	Abstract of patent number GB 1 588 932	249
Figure 23:	The IP law student and non-law student client advice letter	251
Figure 24:	An undergraduate IP curriculum map	254
Figure 25:	Bloom's Taxonomy	258
Figure 26:	Devising learning outcomes for IP in a non-law course	259
Figure 27:	A time-limited introduction to intellectual property	261
Figure 28:	Reasons for reluctance to teach IP to non-lawyers	264

FOREWORD

Intellectual property is an increasingly important generator of economic, social and cultural growth and development. A clear understanding of the intellectual property system has, therefore, become a necessity for all those associated with creative and innovative endeavor – from policy-makers and business executives to educators and archivists, as well as artists and inventors themselves. A solid grasp of the mechanics of the system and a keen awareness of its enormous potential and power are key in leveraging the opportunities it offers – at all levels.

It is for these reasons that enhancing intellectual property education, in order to meet the growing need for informed and effective personnel trained in the field, has become one of the main challenges of the World Intellectual Property Organization (WIPO). In 1998, the WIPO Worldwide Academy took up the task of implementing the Organization's new program of intellectual property education, geared to human resource development. Since then, the scope, content and diversity of that program has expanded considerably, including the holding of several global symposia, often in collaboration with like-minded institutions, to examine intellectual property education and encourage the sharing, at international level, of the valuable experience in the field acquired by academics around the world.

In 2005, speakers at one of those symposia encouraged the Academy to consider preparing a publication that would showcase the best in intellectual property curricula and teaching methods. This book, the fruit of almost two years of preparation, is the response to that challenge. It brings together the knowledge and wisdom of some of the most eminent and respected educators and practitioners in the intellectual property field, who draw on their many years of personal experience in intellectual property education at the very highest level.

The purpose of this book is to enable those experts to explain their teaching techniques in their particular field of expertise, including setting out what they consider should be taught in terms of coursework based on "best practices." The result is a publication with thoughtful, well-written, scholarly input from all contributors, which, it is hoped, will serve intellectual property education well for many years to come.

I would like to express WIPO's great appreciation to each of these authors for the time, effort and skill they have put into making this publication possible. I also wish to thank my colleagues Larry Allman, Julie English, Lesley Sherwood, Mpazi Sinjela, and Yo Takagi for their contributions in bringing the project to fruition.

I hope the readers of this book will find it stimulating, useful and practical. Enhancing intellectual property education so that it is more effective, responsive, and accessible, will benefit all countries of the world and heighten the effectiveness of the intellectual property system as a tool for development.

KAMIL IDRIS
Director General
World Intellectual Property Organization
Geneva, Switzerland

1

Recent trends and challenges in teaching intellectual property

LARRY ALLMAN
MPAZI SINJELA
YO TAKAGI

Intellectual property education in the past

For many decades, intellectual property (IP) was the exclusive domain of a small number of specialist lawyers, who had generally acquired their IP expertise from working in IP-based companies or representing clients with IP-related problems. At best they might have had an introductory IP course during their legal studies. Such was the state of IP education until relatively recently.

On-the-job training was, therefore, necessary to supplement the limited opportunities to learn about IP offered by academic institutions. One such avenue has been national and regional IP offices (Patent Office, Trademark Office, Copyright Office), particularly those where the relevant laws require substantive examination of patent applications and/or administrative appeals. Those offices often set up internal training facilities to provide IP-specific courses for their staff, often to very specialized levels. The training was initially for primary education in IP, after which the trained staff was deployed to specific functions within the office, for further on the job training. In some countries, after several years of services at an IP office, a number of such trained staff have left to join law firms or other IP-related businesses. This means that IP training programs at IP offices have contributed to the development of IP skilled human resources by constantly supplying experienced experts to the private sector.

Though one could argue that this rather ad hoc form of IP education used to be sufficient, the acceleration in the use of the IP system and the importance IP has attained, on a global scale, has created a demand for more and better trained IP professionals, far beyond that which this rather limited approach could provide. While the following sections will illustrate the extent of that demand and how an attempt is being made to address lacunae in meeting it, it is clear that opportunities for IP education are still limited both in the scope, beneficiaries and availability of IP programs.

IP issues have, for decades, been researched and discussed, on many occasions and in many different contexts, including national debates on revising and updating national IP laws, and debates in national and international fora on international IP treaties and conventions. WIPO, in cooperation with governments and IP-related non-governmental organizations,[1] has provided assistance to academia and other IP institutions in their research and education activities and programs in the IP field. For example, as far back as 1981, WIPO's assistance resulted in the establishment of the International Association for the Advancement of Teaching and Research in IP (ATRIP),[2] whose members consist of IP professors and researchers from all over the world.

Recent changes in IP education

With the acceleration in the globalization of a world economy that is becoming increasingly knowledge-based, in the last decades, IP was recognized as a trade-related issue. With the adoption of the World Trade Organization (WTO) Agreement on Trade-Related Aspects of Intellectual Property Rights (the TRIPS Agreement),[3] the obligations arising from its implementation prompted a comprehensive review of national IP legislation. This process awakened policy-makers in government and in the business sector to the increasing role of IP in development. The increasing prominence of IP on the national and international scenes has also had a significant impact on the way IP is taught and on the content of what is taught.

The following statistics demonstrate the magnitude of the changes that have taken place in the ever-evolving and expanding relationship between IP and the world economy. In the 1980s, an estimated 40 per cent of the total assets of private corporations in the United States of America consisted of intangible assets. Today, that percentage has increased to approximately 70 per cent.[4] The number of patent applications filed worldwide increased from 884,400 in 1985 to 1,599,000 in 2004. This rate of growth is about 5 per cent annual growth rate, which is comparable to the overall

---

[1] www.wipo.int/treaties/en/general/.   [2] www.atrip.org/.
[3] www.wto.org/english/tratop_e/trips_e/trips_e.htm.
[4] Kamil Idris, *IP– A Power Tool for Economic Growth*, Chapter 3, "Intellectual Property, Knowledge and Wealth Creation", WIPO Publication No. 888 (www.wipo.int/about-wipo/en/dgo/wipo_pub_888/wipo_pub_888_index.htm).

increase in economic activity (as measured by the world growth of GDP). Use of the patent system internationally has increased markedly in recent years. This can be seen by the increase (an average of 7.4 per cent a year since 1995) in patent filings with national patent offices by non-residents of the country of filing and in the dramatic increase in patent filings in countries such as Brazil, China, India, the Republic of Korea and Mexico. Though the use of the patent system remains highly concentrated in five patent offices (United States of America, Japan, Republic of Korea, China and the European Patent Office) accounting for 75 per cent of all patent applications and 74 per cent of all patents granted, the recent surge in the use of the patent system in emerging economies is impressive.[5]

The growing impact of IP has also become a central topic of discussion in various media. It is now perceived as one of several factors that are key to a healthy and successful economy and "wealth ... will increasingly gravitate to those countries who get three basic things right: the infrastructure to connect ... ; the right education programs and knowledge skills to empower more of their people to innovate and do value-added work on that platform; and, finally, the right governance – that is, the right tax policies, the right investment and trade laws, the right support for research, the right intellectual property laws, and, most of all, the right inspirational leadership – to enhance and manage the flow with the flat world."[6] According to one expert, IP is one of "[f]our interconnected features of the modern market economy that are of decisive importance, especially for any discussion of global economic integration alongside with the corporation, innovation and the role and functioning of financial markets and ... [G]iven the role of innovation, intellectual property is not a marginal feature of the property-rights regime of a modern market economy, but its core. It is the most important example of property that only a powerful state can protect."[7]

IP education at university level

Students from a wide range of disciplines, including business, law, fine arts, engineering, the sciences, and journalism, could benefit from IP

---

[5] WIPO Patent Report 2006 (www.wipo.int/ipstats/en/statistics/patents/patent_report_2006.html#P70_1820).
[6] Thomas L. Friedman, *The World is Flat*, Chapter 8: "The Quiet Crisis", published with updates by Penguin Books (2006).
[7] Martin Wolf, *Why Globalization Works*, Chapter 4: "The Magic of the Market", published by Yale University Press (2004).

education; and many teaching programs should include IP in their curricula. A WIPO Worldwide Academy survey indicated that, in many countries, three programs stand out as most commonly including IP in their coursework.

First, basic law degree programs offer IP courses that give students a general understanding of the philosophy and application of IP law. Even law students who do not intend to specialize in IP should be made familiar with the basic rights that are protected by IP law. Most basic university training programs in the law faculty include courses in commercial law and property law, as well as courses dealing with civil and criminal procedures, together with whatever array and level of basic IP courses it might provide. Some specialized post-graduate (LL.M) programs, including specialized IP–LL.M degree programs typically provide a more comprehensive, specialized knowledge of the theory and practice of IP law.

Second, some business schools have introduced IP courses. Although IP does not yet feature significantly in the curriculum of most economics faculties, almost all business programs (B.A. and M.B.A.) include some overview of the subject. It is important for students who hope to go into business or government to have a basic understanding of the role that IP plays in the modern concepts and day-to-day realities of economics and trade.

Third, in some faculties of science and engineering, general aspects of IP are taught, since the need for students in these disciplines to understand the role of IP in the context of R&D and technology project management is being increasingly recognized. Engineering faculites, for example, are including such topics as the acquisition and management of IP rights (in particular patents). An increasing number of faculties of science and engineering have realized the need for expanded collaboration with industry. To facilitate such collaboration, further mutually shared goals and objectives and safeguard their interests, some universities have established an internal body to be in charge of the management of their IP. The Technology Licensing Office (TLO) facilitates the collaboration between universities and industry, monitors the results, and often adds value to those collaborations through licensing, co-financing and strategic transactional assistance with key players from industry. This trend, and the evolving role of the TLO, also encourages the expansion of basic, and even advanced, IP courses within the faculties of engineering and science, where the results of those collaborations are most visible.[8]

---

[8] Kamil Idris, *IP– A Power Tool for Economic Growth*, Chapter 4: "Patents, Research and Development, and New Technologies", WIPO Publication No. 888.

It is difficult to estimate the number of universities in the world where IP is taught, due to the absence of reliable data, but a preliminary estimate by the WIPO Worldwide Academy indicates there are some 700 of them, with most of their IP courses being centered in the law faculty. IP courses are elective and often fairly brief. The majority of universities with IP courses on their curricula offer only general IP programs primarily focusing on the nature and extent of the rights which are protectible under IP law, and the impact and role of IP in the context of the knowledge-based, globalized economy.

However, some countries offer more specialized and comprehensive IP courses. For example, in the United States of America, there are some 20 IP-specialized LL.M. programs. In Japan, a few technical universities have started to offer a year-long IP course in conjunction with other technology-related disciplines such as the management of technology (MOT). In France, several universities have compulsory IP courses in the science faculty. Recent trends suggest that more universities will include IP courses in their curricula, while existing IP courses will continue to expand, particularly in countries where IP activities have grown. For example, in China, the Ministry of Education has officially encouraged universities to set up Masters and Ph.D programs in IP law or IP management. As a result, at least sixteen universities now offer IP courses, including five universities where courses are taught at their law school dedicated to IP.[9]

Challenges facing universities

The results of a sampling of some twenty universities around the world – designed to pinpoint the current constraints and challenges faced by academic institutions in the area of IP education – indicated problems in: updating programs to keep up with dynamic and rapid changes taking place in IP laws; obtaining up-to-date materials necessary for the teaching of emerging IP issues; and enhancing the curriculum to make it suitable for an interdisciplinary approach in which IP is taught in the light of its increasing role in such fields as business, commerce, science and engineering.

On June 30 and July 1, 2005, WIPO hosted an International Symposium on IP Education and Research, at which the authors of several of the chapters of this book participated as panelists.[10] The panelists made the following recommendations regarding the above problems:

---

[9] Information provided by Prof. Shengli Zheng, IPSchool, Peking University, China.
[10] www.wipo.int/meetings/en/details.jsp?meeting_id=8083.

- encourage and advocate at the highest policy level the strengthening of governmental support for IP education and research in the context of development;
- help developing countries establish institutional bases (e.g. IP research centers) and more effective mechanisms to collect and disseminate current and relevant documentation for IP education and research (IP libraries);
- develop the inter-disciplinary nature of IP in curricula, and to bring other partners, such as those in the field of economics, business management, engineering, science and technology, culture, environment and sociology into that process;
- conduct IP research from a national strategic perspective to facilitate national debate and policy formulation in developing countries;
- start IP education at an early stage with a view to fostering a culture which respects creativity and which strives to curb IP abuses;
- explore various new and different sources of funding to enhance IP education and research;
- provide IP researchers in developing countries with opportunities to publish their work, both in their country, and externally;
- conduct joint research operations involving researchers from both developed and developing counties, in an attempt to find common grounds for the further development of the IP system;
- develop a range of models of IP curricula tailored to the needs of different target groups such as engineers and business managers; and
- develop mechanisms allowing universities to collaborate internationally through, for example, teacher and student exchange programs to promote sharing of teaching materials and useful information about IP issues.

The recommendations require further debate at the national level, because there is no "one-size-fits-all" solution and the background, development and needs of each country differ markedly. For instance, the quality of an IP education program depends on the availability and quality of the IP lecturers available to teach it. Ideally, good IP education should be provided by full-time university faculty members who have specific expertise in one or more aspects of IP. However, many universities do not have such specialists available, and IP education depends on professors who take an interest in the IP field, in addition to their main specialty. In some countries, practicing lawyers give part of their time to teach IP courses. Referred to as "adjunct professors", in the United States of America, these "outside" lecturers provide an effective and economical way of building a comprehensive and high-quality IP program. Adjunct professors can bring the benefit of many different areas of expertise to a university program and provide a breadth of expertise that would not otherwise be available to a university.

However, in many countries where practicing and experienced IP lawyers are still scarce, different solutions need to be explored to meet the strong demand for IP teachers. There is no quick fix: IP education and research needs to receive enough political attention and support, including financial assistance, to enable universities to produce a national core of IP resource persons, with the intention of their becoming IP lecturers some day. Proactive government policies would make it possible to include more IP courses in the programs of national universities. The creation of a critical mass of IP educators, and the momentum associated with that process, would then encourage other universities to benefit from the initial steps already taken. The creation – in parallel – of a training center for government staff responsible for IP rights registration in the national IP Office, and the eventual expansion of the training center into a national IP Academy or Training Centre (which could offer training programs also to IP practitioners) would also contribute to IP education through the exchange of IP resource persons, teaching materials, and IP knowledge at a practical on-the-job level.

The new IP paradigm and its impact on IP education

Given that results from most innovative and creative activities now have some form of IP protection, and given that a well-functioning IP regime is one of the most crucial factors for success in an increasingly knowledge-based economy, the need for awareness and knowledge about IP is no longer limited to lawyers and technical specialists.

In the field of copyright and creativity, consider merely the fact that millions of Internet users are now potential creators of copyright and related rights works, "[t]he success of advanced economies is increasingly dependent not on their physical capital, but on their capacity to mobilize their citizens' brainpower."[11] Many newspapers featured the growing popularity of a website "YouTube" as one of the most significant events in 2006. The website allows a large number of users to post video clips of their own creation which are susceptible of copyright protection.

[11] "The Battle for Brainpower, A Survey of Talent", *The Economist*, October 7, 2006.

In the field of patents and innovation, the patent attorney has always needed to understand the science and technology of the invention, the IP of which he has been engaged to protect. Now, however, the scientist working in the R&D lab must also have a similar level of awareness of IP and what IP rights might arise from his scientific endeavors, for purposes of, for example, determining the ownership of IP rights, downstream benefit-sharing, research co-financing with other scientists or organizations, product development and marketing, and licensing and follow-on products. All of these patent-related considerations are best handled with the assistance of IP professionals (best if locally available in the country, however small in number) and also working with the scientists involved. Such a collaboration at an early stage is critical for effective IP management leading to successful product development and exploitation.

The challenge of producing more and better qualified IP professionals and a more IP-conscious workforce needs to be seen now in the new context of a greatly expanded awareness of the use, value and potential of IP – what might be referred to as a "new IP paradigm." The new IP paradigm, where IP knowledge is necessary at many different levels of enterprise, government, activities of creativity and innovation, and in other stakeholders, is most obvious, and most effective, if IP education can be designed to cater to and support diversified needs in an inter-disciplinary manner. This is the context which is at the very center of the accelerating need for more and better educated IP professionals and IP workers.

While an increasing number of countries have taken a dynamic approach to modernizing their IP legislation and national IP policies, the approach to updating and enhancing IP education has often been slow. It is hoped that the authorities responsible for national education systems and those in academia will look closely into this. In the meantime, in industry and companies, where IP rights are increasingly involved in the crafting of management decisions and overall policy, the pace and nature of changes is much faster. Some private corporations proactively participate in and support IP education by providing financial contributions to IP courses and programs in developing countries.[12] The participation of the private sector in IP education could contribute to meeting recent needs for an inter-disciplinary approach to IP which should benefit from various and actual experience in the management of IP assets.

Ongoing efforts to improve IP education could also be greatly assisted if international cooperation to forge greater partnerships and more effective

---

[12] www.china.org.cn/english/culture/93464.htm, visited on March 2, 2006.

strategic cooperation among academic and educational institutions, companies and governments were strengthened. The WIPO Worldwide Academy made a first step towards the institutionalizing of international cooperation for IP education by launching a global network of IP Academies.[13]

Lifelong IP education

The need for IP education is no longer limited to university students and specialist IP practitioners. Introducing young students, early on, to the concepts and principles of the IP system and its incentives and infrastructure can pay dividends later. An effective and interesting introduction to IP allows children to see where their creativity can lead them and how their dreams and imaginings can result in actual products and services. At the same time, it teaches them to respect both the original work of others, and their own original work. It also teaches respect in general, and gives them a sense of what current business is about and lessons in how the power of human intellect, innovation and creativity can drive the economy in a sustainable manner.[14]

Specially designed teaching programs which enable business executives and other adult groups to obtain basic or additional IP skills as well as up-to-date knowledge about emerging IP issues applicable to their business activities and career management, have all increased in response to the current dynamic evolution of IP. In some countries, more refresher courses are offered by organizations of IP professionals to their members who wish to obtain additional skills. More business schools are offering IP specialized courses which are now attended also by business managers. Some companies have included IP courses in the corporate educational program to ensure that all researchers, engineers, and managers contributing to the generation and exploitation of the corporate IP assets should fully understand and follow the corporate IP strategy and policies.

Teaching methods, materials and the Internet

A comprehensive, detailed syllabus covering the entire course should be presented to the students in advance. A syllabus is a list (with some

---

[13] WIPO Press Release UPD/2007/290 at www.wipo.int/pressroom/en/articles/2007/article_0022.html.
[14] Kamil Idris and Hisamitsu Arai, *Intellectual Property-Conscious Nation*, Chapter 5: "Improved Education for the Next Generation", WIPO Publication No. 988 (www.wipo.int/about-wipo/en/dgo/wipo_pub_988/index.html).

explanations) of the topics to be presented in the course, and the reading materials which correspond with each topic. An effective syllabus might separate the topics to be covered in the class in outline form, list the days on which each topic will be covered, and give the names of authors, titles and page numbers of the reading materials. A syllabus provides a coherent outline of the course, giving the students in advance an idea of the topics to be covered, and giving them in retrospect a guide for reviewing what they have, or should have, learned in the course. In scheduling topics for the various class sessions, the amount of time spent on each subject should correspond with the relevance, importance or difficulty of the subject. However, some advanced subjects should only be mentioned in passing and should be left for more advanced courses, or self learning according to the student's needs or interest. This publication includes advice and ideas from our very experienced authors on setting a syllabus. Some selected curricula are also posted on the WIPO Worldwide Academy's website for reference.[15]

In the case of general courses (i.e. basic, broadly focused courses which are designed to give an overview of the various fields of intellectual property), it is important to stimulate the interest of students and allow them to understand better that IP is highly relevant to their daily life. As often is the case, strictly legal aspects of IP are not always easy to digest. An effective technique in an introductory course is to present specific facts concerning current topics involving IP, connecting those topics to how and in what ways they might manifest or impact the daily lives of the students, and thereby hopefully interest the students a bit more – those students might even decide on some specialty focus in IP for their career as a result of that course.

In preparing teaching materials, those used by other lecturers can be a starting point for a new IP lecturer. Today, enormous amounts of information are made available through the Internet. In giving reading assignments, students should be encouraged to search for relevant resources themselves, using the Internet and other appropriate sources. For specific thematic surveys, a number of portals focusing on IP issues and websites dedicated to IP subjects are also useful in locating the most relevant and up to date resources (for example, in addition to the WIPO website itself,[16] the WIPO website offers links to other IP-related organizations[17]).

---

[15] www.wipo.int/academy/en/teaching/sample_curricula/index.html.
[16] www.wipo.int/portal/index.html.en.
[17] www.wipo.int/members/en/organizations.jsp.

WIPO has posted a number of resources which could be used as IP teaching materials, both in general, and in specialized, courses. For example, the *WIPO IP Handbook: Policy, Law and Use*, WIPO Publication No.489 (E)[18] and *IP – A Power Tool for Economic Growth*, WIPO Publication No. 888 (E)[19] are now made available on the WIPO website for free downloading.

Different methods of IP education lend themselves to different situations. At a faculty of law in common law countries, the traditional "case method" of teaching would tend to be used. The teaching materials employed in this method are based on the principles of the common law, with its overlay of statutes and administrative regulations and interpretive judicial decisions. An alternative approach is the "problem-solving method" of teaching, where a particular set of circumstances which raise specific legal problems will be presented and the students are then asked to apply the relevant principles of law to analyze and solve those problems. At business schools with an IP curriculum, case studies have been used to good effect, as they give clear description of actual business situations involving IP. At a faculty of engineering and/or science, however, patent documents often can be useful materials in helping to develop practical skills that will allow students to make use of patent information in their future careers; to provide useful assistance regarding their own inventions to the patent attorneys who are drafting patent applications; and possibly, further downstream, to facilitate their involvement in activities such as litigation and licensing.

Finally, the advent and growth of the Internet has also allowed students to take distance learning courses in almost all subjects and areas of learning, and that certainly includes IP education. The WIPO Worldwide Academy is a pioneer and now provides several general and advanced IP courses through its distance learning facilities.[20]

The purpose of this book

This book is intended to meet the growing demand for expert advice on IP teaching and education, and to address problems identified by IP experts concerning the shortage of IP education resources, including the compilation of best practices in IP teaching. The principles and methods

---

[18] www.wipo.int/about-ip/en/iprm/.
[19] www.wipo.int/about-wipo/en/dgo/wipo_pub_888/index_wipo_pub_888.html.
[20] www.wipo.int/academy/en/courses/distance_learning/.

applicable to the teaching of IP are examined and discussed by authors whose experience, training and wisdom in IP and IP-related subjects are widely recognized and well-proven. By setting out what elements of the subject matter, in the view of each author, should be taught in a best practices course, the book allows the reader to benefit from the advice and experience of some of the most experienced experts in IP education, and to be empowered to prepare and enhance their own IP education programs. This book is not intended to harmonize or standardize the way in which IP should be taught. It aims to facilitate the process of IP teaching for each teacher and assist in efforts to prepare tailor-made programs which best fit the needs of the targeted students.

In preparing this publication, WIPO requested authors to follow, to the extent possible, the following structure:

– Introduction and overview;
– Challenges in this subject;
– Identification of target audience;
– Subject matter curriculum;
– Approaches and methods to teach in this area (including any problem areas);
– Materials, references, cases and other sources of assistance;
– Future trends; and
– Conclusions.

Each of the chapters in this book can stand alone, i.e. each chapter could be a separate publication. The totality of all chapters, and the scope of knowledge and practical IP experience offered herein, makes this book invaluable for new IP teachers, for IP law students, for non-law IP students, for business, economics, science and technology students and for all others who may need or want to understand what constitutes a best practices IP education, or just a specific IP subject.

One of the recommendations made by the experts at the WIPO Symposium on IP Education and Research was to develop models of IP curricula tailored to the needs of different target groups, such as engineers and business managers. It is hoped that this publication will contribute to the joint efforts of many academic and educational institutions to address that specific need, as well as all the problems and challenges inherent in expanding IP education and making it more effective, more relevant and more widely available to all students who need or want it.

2

Teaching patents

JOSEPH STRAUS

Introduction and overview

Among intellectual property rights, patents, as exclusive rights of exploitation with blocking effects, occupy a prominent place and are characterized by many peculiarities: they reveal the closest link to most advanced technological and scientific developments; they play a crucial role in the innovation process as an incentive to invent, innovate and invest in high risk research and development (R&D); and they are an important factor in international economic relations. Whereas the importance of patents in all these respects is not disputed, much controversy exists whether their respective economic impact is beneficial and if so, for whom.

As far as the results of the most advanced scientific and technical developments, such as DNA-sequences, embryonic stem cells, gene therapy, genetically modified plants or animals, or computer software and business methods, are concerned, the question arises whether they are eligible for patent protection, and if eligible, under which conditions. Moreover, does patent law take into account aspects of ethics, protection of human, animal or plant life, or health and the environment? Does, and if so how does, the law resolve the tension between the patent as an exclusive right with blocking effects, often misleadingly called "monopoly," on the one hand, and competition, a fundamental pillar of the market economy, on the other? In other words, how are patents treated by anti-trust law?

Finally, how can one protect patents internationally? Which instruments of international public law serve patent protection and, what is their economic impact? Can patents be internationally viewed as a means of technology transfer, incentives for foreign direct investment (FDI) and genuine innovation activities, or as a means for exploiting foreign markets and maximizing profits of foreign patent holders, who as a rule hold the majority of patents granted in a given country?

Thus, teaching patents does not only involve teaching national, regional and international substantive patent law, patent granting and revocation, as well as enforcement proceedings, but requires a holistic approach: making the modern technologies understandable, critically reflecting the economic impact of patents as exclusive rights, and presenting and analyzing the respective national and international legal network.

Challenges in this subject

Patents are exclusive rights aimed at protecting inventions, i.e. instructions how to solve problems by technical means.[1] Discussing patenting of subject matters such as DNA sequences, genetically modified plants etc., requires some basic understanding of genetic engineering techniques, that of monoclonal antibodies, some understanding of hybridoma technology for their production, and that of computer software, including some basic understanding of software development. For instance, in the case of the much discussed patenting of DNA sequences or entire genes, without a certain basic understanding of recombinant DNA technology and genetics in general, one may not be able to explain why, in view of the multifunctionality of genes, product patents on DNA sequences, rightly or wrongly, may be seen as a problem. As a rule, the efforts necessary to acquire such basic knowledge are within acceptable limits, but a certain readiness to learn and understand the technology at hand is required.

Not less challenging is the necessity to understand and properly impart the economics of the patent system as a genuine incentive to invent and innovate and as an integral part of the new world economic order, established in 1994 under the auspices of the World Trade Organization (WTO). In this respect, it is essential to understand that the General Agreement on Tariffs and Trade (GATT 1994), the General Agreement on Trade in Services (GATS), the Agreement on Trade Related Investment Measures (TRIMS) and the Agreement on Trade Related Aspects of Intellectual Property Rights (TRIPS) are to be viewed as an inseparable whole, which is aimed at the mutual opening of markets, i.e. for commodities as well as intangibles. As empirical evidence demonstrates, this new world economic order has since 1995 also worked if not primarily

---

[1] In its well-known "Red Dove" decision of 1969, the German Federal Supreme Court defined the invention as: "a teaching to methodically utilize controllable natural forces to achieve a causal perceivable result:" 1 *IIC* 136, at 138 (1970).

then at least substantially to the benefit of newly industrialized and a number of developing countries.[2] This in turn means that teaching patents also requires some basic understanding of IP-linked economics and the readiness to monitor national and international economic developments, including collecting, analyzing and comparing empirical, i.e. statistical data, which relate, for instance, to patent applications, patents granted, national investment in R&D, FDI, growth of gross national product (GDP), etc.

Identification of target audience

Patents are taught at law schools as well as many schools of engineering, chemistry, etc. The students attending patent law courses at law schools are not necessarily only law students, but can well be students of chemistry, biology or other natural or technical sciences, depending on the study order of the respective university. Moreover, one has to realize that law students in Europe and many parts of the world have no technical background, whereas their counterparts in other parts of the world, especially in the United States of America not only have completed a technical education at the undergraduate level, but very often are Ph.D. holders in various areas of science, who have chosen to enroll in law and earn a Juris Doctor (J.D.) at the postgraduate stage.

Apart from teaching patents in the framework of ordinary courses at university level, patents are also often taught at the postgraduate level, such as Master of Law (LL.M) courses, where students again may have different backgrounds. Depending on whether the addressed students have a purely technical education and are interested in becoming patent attorneys or employees of industry or patent offices, or, as in some countries like Germany, specialized patent judges, or are "ordinary" law students, the emphasis of the teaching may vary. Whereas in the case of purely technically oriented students, taking patent courses either at technical universities or at postgraduate specialization level, details of substantive patent law and details of patent granting and revocation proceedings as well as, but already to a lesser extent, the enforcement of patent rights, will stay in the forefront, and will require the inclusion in the curriculum of such topics as claim drafting, priority claiming or

---

[2] See J. Straus, "The Impact of the New World Order on Economic Development – The Role of Intellectual Property Rights" *The John Marshall Review of Intellectual Property Law* vol. 6.1 (2006).

dealing with provisional, divisional and continuation in part applications. In the case of students of law, the focus will be less on technicalities of patent prosecution, but more on enforcement, international aspects and on economic and general patent policy (national and international) issues.

Subject matter curriculum

Patents, as other intellectual property rights, relate to intangible, ubiquitous creations of the human mind that can be used at the same time and at any place. International aspects of acquiring and enforcing patents, therefore, have to be addressed in any patent course. However, different approaches can be chosen in this regard. In view of the historical development and the impact, which international and regional conventions and treaties, such as the Paris Convention for the Protection of Industrial Property of 1883, the Patent Cooperation Treaty of 1970 (PCT), the European Patent Convention of 1973 (EPC) and the Agreement on Trade Related Aspects of Intellectual Property Rights of 1994 (TRIPS), have had on national patent laws, one can deal with the international patent-related legal network at an early stage of the course. The disadvantage of this approach is the fact that students still lack basic patent law knowledge. Shifting the presentation of the international legal network more to, or even entirely to the end of, the course, on the other hand, makes it necessary to address specific international patent law aspects randomly and in parallel with the presentation of national patent law.

As emphasized, patents form part of "intellectual property," which according to Article 2(viii) of the Convention Establishing the World Intellectual Property Organization of 1967 (WIPO Convention), "include rights relating to literary, artistic and scientific works, performances of performing artists, phonograms and broadcasts, scientific discoveries, industrial designs, trademarks, servicemarks and commercial names and designations, protection against unfair competition, and all other rights resulting from intellectual activity in the industrial, scientific, literary or artistic fields." Inventions, to which patents relate, and other subject matters of intellectual property, covered by copyright, neighboring rights, designs, tradenames and trademarks, plant variety certificates etc., have some characteristics in common but differ in many others. This is also reflected by the respective rights' design, especially scope and reach of protection. For a proper understanding of the functioning of the patent system and its role in the context of intellectual property rights, and beyond, consequently every patent course should address the interrelationship of patents with other intellectual property rights at the very beginning.

Patents have proven to be a powerful instrument of economic policy since they succeeded the medieval privileges, first granted by English kings in the fourteenth century. A brief review of the historical development of patent law, since the adoption of the Venetian Inventor's Statute in 1474, the English Statute of Monopolies of 1623/24, the United States 1790 and 1793, as well as the French 1791 and 1793 Patent Acts, seems advisable. This review should not be used only to present descriptively the historical development, but to reflect on the underlying rationale behind the respective decisions of the law-maker and the economic impact those decisions have had on the development of national economies. One should use this review, irrespective of obvious time constraints, also to address such aspects of historical development as the introduction of product patent protection for pharmaceuticals in Italy and Japan, or of patent protection in general in the modern Peoples' Republic of China. Moreover, the attempt should be made to clarify the international implications of patent protection and the necessity for international solutions.

Since the development of modern patent laws is closely linked to the development of international treaties, preference is given here to an early presentation of the basic principles and mechanisms of the Paris Convention for the Protection of Industrial Property, such as the principles of territoriality, national treatment and minimum rights, with particular emphasis on the complex priority right rules, the rule on the independence of national patents and the rules on compulsory licenses.

This should be followed by a presentation of the Patent Cooperation Treaty, a substantial improvement of the international mechanisms for protecting patents, and its advantages, as compared with the Paris Convention, should be elaborated.

Subsequently, the question should be addressed of existing regional treaties serving a central patent-granting procedure, such as the European Patent Convention (EPC), the Bangui Agreement on the Creation of an African Intellectual Property Organization (OAPI) of 1977, the Harare Protocol on Patents and Industrial Designs within the Framework of the African Intellectual Property Organization (ARIPO) of 1982, and the Eurasian Patent Convention of 1994, in force for certain member states of the former Soviet Union. Depending on where the course is taught, the focus may be more on the much used (some close to 200,000 applications in 2005) and highly developed EPC or some other treaties. Moreover, such conventions as the Budapest Treaty on the International Recognition of the Deposit of Microorganisms for the Purposes of Patent Procedure of 1977, the Patent Law Treaty (PLT) of 2000, and the International Convention for the Protection of New Varieties of Plants (UPOV Convention) of 1961 should be, at least briefly, explained. Here again, even in a course on patents, depending on where that course is taught, some specific attention should be paid to the plant varieties protection.

Any presentation of international legal mechanisms dealing with patents would, however, be incomplete and seriously deficient without an in-depth presentation of the principles, objectives, specific patent-related rules and enforcement provisions of the TRIPS Agreement. With the adoption of the TRIPS Agreement, after more than 100 years of international negotiations and discussions, for the very first time internationally binding protection standards for patents have been introduced. Those standards relate to subject matter eligible for patent protection, content, scope, limitations and the term of protection, as well as enforcement measures and dispute resolution.

The general introduction to patent law may conclude with a brief comment on the overall economic aims of patent protection as originally summarized by the US/Austrian economist Fritz Machlup:[3] namely, to recognize intellectual property rights of the inventor, to reward the inventor for her useful services for the society, to give incentives to the inventor and the industry to invent, invest, and innovate, and to provide incentives for early disclosure and dissemination of technical knowledge.

Before starting teaching substantive and procedural aspects of patent law, reference has to be made to the sources of the applicable law in the country at hand. In other words, to the Patent Act currently in force, including, if any, implementing regulations, examination guidelines etc., and international and regional treaties to which the respective country is a party, as for instance, the Paris Convention, PCT, TRIPS or PLT etc., the principles and mechanisms of which will already have been presented.

Substantive patent law teaching starts with a detailed discussion of the subject matter eligible for patent protection, i.e. the definition of the patentable invention, on the one hand, and, on the other, of non-patentable achievements and creations of the human mind, such as discoveries and

---

[3] *An Economic Review of the Patent System*, Study for the United States Senate, Washington D.C., 1959.

scientific theories, mathematical methods, aesthetic creations, methods for performing mental arts, business methods or computer programs.

Depending on the respective national and/or regional statutory and case law, the subject matter eligible for patent protection may well vary from country to country and region. On the one hand, the EPC and many national patent laws contain a catalogue of human creations specifically either placed outside the subject matter eligible for patent protection, as is the case, for instance, with scientific discoveries and theories, business methods and computer programs, or do not question their invention quality, but exclude them for various reasons, as for instance in the case of therapeutic, surgical and diagnostic methods as well as plant and animal varieties. The US patent law, on the other hand, does not contain any specific exclusionary provisions. The US Supreme Court in the widely known *Chakrabarty* decision of 1980, specifically clarified that under US statutory law, the patentable subject matter includes "anything under the sun that is made by man."[4] At the same time, the US Supreme Court did not question the ethical issues which genetic engineering as technology raises, but stated that they are to be resolved in the respective regulatory laws and not by patent law. The EPC and national patent laws following suit, on the other hand, exclude from patentability inventions, the exploitation of which would be contrary to *ordre public* or morality. The question may be raised whether the rules at hand are in compliance with the mandatory international standards as set forth in the TRIPS Agreement. It is, however, important that the reasons for those differences are discussed and well understood. Depending on the target audience, more time may/should be spent for discussing differences between patentable inventions and nonpatentable discoveries, exemplified by addressing, for example, the patentability of natural substances isolated from complex natural environment, where students of chemistry or biology are addressed, or computer programs, in the case of students of informatics etc. Irrespective of where the course is taught, there should be some comparative law analysis in this context, for instance, by making references to the solutions adopted in the European Directive on the Legal Protection of Biotechnological Inventions of 1998,[5] or solutions applied in the Andean Pact countries.[6] Advantages and disadvantages of those solutions should be discussed.

---

[4] *Diamond* v. *Chakrabarty*, 447 U.S. 303, at 309 (1980).
[5] Directive 98/44/EC of the European Parliament and the Council of 6 July 1998, OJ ECL 213/13 of 30.7.98.
[6] E.g. Art. 6b of Decision 344, which stipulates that substances pre-existing in nature and their replications are not an "invention."

Once the subject matter, potentially eligible for patent protection, i.e. the notion of invention, has been defined and well understood, the specific patentability requirements, namely that of novelty, inventive step (non-obviousness), industrial application (utility) and enabling disclosure should be explained in some detail.

No matter who the audience is, solid knowledge and understanding of all patentability requirements are essential. Therefore, when discussing the novelty requirement, all details regarding relevant prior art, including prior rights, i.e. earlier filed, not yet published applications, as well as non-prejudicial disclosures, are to be addressed and discussed. Moreover, the method by which novelty is to be examined, namely based on a comparison of all elements of the invention with elements of the prior art which has been disclosed in an individual and enabling manner (1:1 comparison), and the yardstick to be applied, namely the skills and understanding of an average expert ("the person skilled in the art"), must be explained.

Irrespective of the country where the course is taught, the fundamental differences between the *first-to-invent* system of the US and the *first-to-file* system applied by the rest of the world, have to be explained. Because the US is an important market for every inventor, the impact of the US first-to-invent principle on the rest of the world has to be addressed. No matter where, e.g., in Brazil, Japan, Kenya or the US, the person who invented first, and can prove that fact, is entitled to the US patent, even if with a weaker filing priority. Thus, evidence, such as laboratory protocols, witnesses etc., of no importance in a first-to-file system, may play a crucial role to establish the date of invention and thus, for the US, the priority date, i.e. the date at which the invention may not have formed part of the prior art, may not have been anticipated. In view of considerable differences as regards non-prejudicial disclosures, i.e. availability or non-availability of a grace period, some additional discussion on this topic combined with warnings regarding the negative, mostly detrimental impact of pre-filing publications should be given. It is equally important to specifically address other differences as regards the relevant prior art of various patent systems. Such differences exist especially between US patent law on the one hand and the EPC, Chinese and Japanese patent laws on the other.

Much attention has to be paid to the discussion of the patentability requirement of inventive step, i.e. the fact that an invention in order to be patentable, may not be obvious to a person skilled in the art in view of the prior art at the relevant date. First, the underlying rationale for this, originally a requirement developed by case law in the US, United Kingdom and Germany, should be explained and, subsequently, the main differences as compared with the requirement of novelty emphasized. Whereas the person skilled in the art as yardstick remains the same, the comparison at hand uses a so-called *mosaic method*, i.e. the invention for which protection is sought is faced with a combination of the relevant prior art documents. The latter, i.e. the prior art, which has to be considered as the comparison's basis, may vary from system to system. Whereas in some systems, as for instance that of the US, so-called prior rights form part of the relevant prior art to be taken into account for the inventive step/non-obviousness test; in other systems, for instance under the EPC, they do not. Also the stringency of the applied substantive tests reveals a broad range: from the very liberal, much criticized, of the USPTO (US Patent and Trademark Office), to the more rigid of the European Patent Office (EPO).

Except in the area of biotechnological inventions, the patentability requirement of industrial applicability or utility, meaning that the invention, according to its nature, can be made or used (in a technological sense) in any kind of industry, should be understood in its broadest sense. Having regard to the rising importance of biotechnological, especially genomic, inventions also for developing countries, it is most advisable to include in the discussion the solutions adopted, for instance, in the Utility Examination Guidelines of the USPTO,[7] namely the requirement that the invention reveals a utility which is substantial, specific and credible.

Finally, as an international mandatory patentability requirement,[8] the obligation of the applicant should be discussed, namely that the invention must be disclosed in the application in a manner sufficiently clear and complete for the invention to be carried out by a person skilled in the art (requirement of sufficiency/enabling disclosure). Here reference is to be made to the possibility that a WTO member may also require the applicant to indicate the *best mode* for carrying out the invention known to the inventor at the filing or the priority date. Even more than in case of utility, biotechnology inventions may also cause specific problems as regards enabling disclosure; because micro-organisms and other inventions related to biological material often cannot be carried out by an expert exclusively based on written description, but require access to claimed sample material, special rules have been developed in this regard, first, by the courts and then, by legislative measures, such as the EPC and the European

---

[7] 66 Fed. Reg. 1092, 1098 (January 5, 2001), at www.uspto.gov/web/com/sollnotices/utilexguide.pdf.
[8] It should be noted that the TRIPS Agreement neither defines relevant prior art nor the terms "novelty" and "inventive step," but specifically sets out the notion of enabling disclosure (Art. 29).

Directive on the Legal Protection of Biotechnological Inventions, on deposit and release of micro-organisms and other biological material in depositories accessible to the public. The regime of international recognition of such depositories is set forth in the already mentioned Budapest Treaty (1977). Depending on the target audience, specific problems of depositing, for instance, hybridoma cell lines producing monoclonal antibodies, or plasmids and viruses as DNA-sequences carrying vectors etc., should be adequately presented and discussed.

It seems appropriate to continue the course by moving to the entitlement to patent protection. Whereas under all patent laws this right is, in principle, conferred on the inventor or co-inventors, a problem, however, arises and its solution may vary considerably from country to country, when the invention at hand is made by an employee (or employees) in the course of employment, i.e. a service invention. Where special rules on employees' inventions exist, be it as separate laws, be it as rules implemented, for instance, in the respective patent laws, they should be presented and their economic impact on innovation addressed. Bearing in mind the rising importance of academic/university research results for innovation, special rules dealing with ownership in such inventions, if any, should, depending on the target audience, be properly dealt with.

In this context, moral and property right's aspects of the inventor have to be clarified and distinguished from the patent right. Because of their far reaching impact on the rights of the inventor, which should not be confused with those of an applicant or patent holder, the differences between the *first-to-invent* and the *first-to-file* system have also to be addressed. Attention should be paid to the often complicated issue of co-inventorship and that of applicable law in case co-inventors were members of an international team, and, possibly, subject to different jurisdictions.

As already alluded to above, one has to distinguish between the right to the invention and the right to the patent. Once the entitlement to the patent has been clarified, the technicalities of patent application, especially its content, as prescribed by the respective national law, for instance under the PCT and EPC, have to be discussed. Statutory provisions, including implementing regulations, are quite specific in this respect and, as a rule, need little comment. There is, however, one very important exception, namely claims.

Claims drafting, eventually determining the scope of protection of the patent, is a high art which requires in-depth understanding of the technical teaching for which patent protection is to be sought, and considerable linguistic skills. Thus, depending on the target audience, great emphasis may/should be put on this activity, where future patent attorneys are addressed. For law students, it may suffice to explain different claim categories, i.e. main, independent and dependent claims, and their mechanisms and significance.

Depending on the subject matter of the invention at issue, patent claims may relate to products, for instance a mechanical device or a chemical substance, or to processes or methods, for instance for the production of a chemical substance, measurement, sorting etc., or to both, i.e. to a product and the method of its production. Here also the so-called "product-by-process-claim," i.e. claims relating to products, defining the product by describing the method of its production, for instance "substance x obtainable by. . ." have to be discussed. Such claims in some jurisdictions are allowed only if the respective product, for instance a macro-molecular substance, cannot be precisely defined by the usual parameters, such as molecular weight etc.

Once the class has been familiarized with all the details of the patent application, patent granting procedures should be presented. Whereas it is clear that procedural rules of the respective national patent law should receive primary attention, the procedures under the PCT and, in view of the global activities of patentees, under regional treaties such as the EPC, should not be entirely ignored. Here, references to implementing regulations, examination guidelines and other official instructions may provide important information, including information concerning fees, representation etc.

Patent granting procedures have to be understood in the broadest sense, i.e., including, where applicable, all aspects of opposition and appeal proceedings, no matter whether they are taken care of by the patent office or judicial bodies (i.e. courts) or semi-judicial bodies, such as Boards of Appeal of the European Patent Office.

At the end of successful patent prosecution, a patent is granted; thus, there is time to explore its legal nature, its effects, as well as the scope of protection and its limitations, if any.

A patent is a subjective, absolute (effective against anybody – *erga omnes*) property right with blocking effects, meaning that it is, as a rule, effective also against independent inventors. However, a patent is not a license to use the patented invention. Thus, the use of the patented invention is only allowed if it is in compliance with the respective regulatory laws, such as on animal welfare, protection of the environment or marketing of pharmaceutical products, and if it does not violate rights of third parties, for instance patents with a better priority.

Much attention should be paid to the effects of the patent right, i.e. the rights it confers on the patent owner in case of a product and/or process patent, respectively. As a consequence of TRIPS, a product patent confers on its owner the exclusive right to prevent third parties not having the owner's consent from acts of making, using, offering for sale, selling or importing the product for these purposes. In case of a process patent, the owner would have the exclusive right to prevent third parties not having his/her consent from using the process and from using, offering for sale, selling, or importing for these purposes at least the product obtained directly by that process. Here, the differences between "product-by-process-claims" on the one hand, and the protection of a direct product of a patented process, on the other hand, should be discussed. Moreover, the distinction between direct and contributory infringement is to be explained and the respective requirements considered.

In order to balance the effects of the patent right as an exclusive right, especially in order to enable further development and improvement of the patented technology, but, under certain conditions also its commercial exploitation, exceptions to or limitations of the rights conferred by a patent may be provided by the respective patent law. Whether those exceptions are provided for experimental use purposes, or in favor of prior users or farmers, or as compulsory licenses for commercial exploitation, they are subject to mandatory TRIPS standards. In all patent courses, all of these aspects should be discussed in some detail, including the much-debated treatment of the so-called research tools.

Another important limitation of the patent right, which has attracted and still attracts much international attention and to which considerable attention should be paid, is the exhaustion of the patent right. The differences between national, regional and international exhaustion of the patent right should be explained and the various solutions either set out in statutes or developed by case law presented and their respective economic impact analyzed and discussed. The legal regime under the TRIPS Agreement should also be included in this discussion, especially after the adoption of the Doha Declaration of the WTO Ministers Conference of 2001.[9]

One, if not *the* key issue of patent law, is how to determine the extent of the protection conferred by the patent. In patent litigation a finding of

---

[9] Declaration on the TRIPS Agreement and Public Health of November 14, 2001, Doc. WT/MIN(01)/DEC/W/2.

infringement by a device depends on whether the features of the alleged infringing device are covered by the claims of the respective patent. How important the claims and their interpretation are in this respect is best reflected by the comment made by the legendary late Judge Giles S. Rich of the US Court of Appeals for the Federal Circuit (CAFC), who emphasized that "the name of the game is the claim."[10]

Although a general consensus internationally exists that the extent of protection should be commensurate with the inventor's contribution to the state of the art, and that claims interpretation should take into account, on the one hand, the legitimate interests of the inventor to be adequately rewarded, and on the other hand the interest of the public at large and of competitors in legal certainty, i.e. to rely on patent claims, determination of the extent of patent protection in case law varies from country to country, even among, for instance, countries parties to the EPC. Notwithstanding the patent law of the country in which the class is taught, the class should be made aware that the extent of the protection may go beyond that which is literally covered by the claims, as interpreted or construed by the court, and may encompass also the so-called *equivalents*. The term equivalent, for example, as interpreted by the United States Supreme Court, refers to a product or process of an alleged infringer which performs "substantially the same function in substantially the same way to obtain the same result."[11] The rationale behind this move of the US Supreme Court, and to a certain extent similar holdings of the courts of many other countries, is the intent to prevent fraud on a patent, i.e. to counteract insignificant modifications into the claimed invention in order to escape literal infringement. It is essential, however, not only to discuss differences in the case law approaches, for instance those of UK,[12] German,[13] Japanese[14] and US courts,[15] but also to refer to the generally accepted limitations of extending patent protection beyond literal wording of the

---

[10] "The Extent of the Protection and Interpretation of Claims – American Perspectives", 21 *IIC* 497 et seq., at 499, 501 (1990).

[11] US Supreme Court in *Graver Tank v. Linde Air Products Co.*, 339 U.S. 605, at 608.

[12] See e.g. House of Lords decision in *Kirin-Amgen Inc and others v. Hoechst Marion Roussel Ltd. and others*, [2005] R.P.C. 9.

[13] See e.g. decisions of the German Federal Supreme Court in cases *Moulded Curbstone (Formstein)*, 18 *IIC* 795 (1987), and *Plastic Pipe (Kunststoffrohrteil)*, 34 *IIC* 302 (2003).

[14] Decision of the Supreme Court of Japan in the case *Tsubakimoto Seiki K.K. v. THK K.K.*, known also under *Ball Line Spline Bearing III*, 30 *IIC* 443 (1999).

[15] See e.g. the US Supreme Court decisions in *Graver Tank v. Linde Air Products Co.*, 339 U.S. 605, *Warner-Jenkinson Co. v. Hilton Davis Chem. Co.*, 520 U.S. 17 (1997), *Festo Corp. v. Shoketsu Kinzoku Kogyo Kabushiki Co.*, 522 U.S. 735 (2002).

claims, whether it is called "doctrine of equivalence" or "purposive patent claim construction." For example, such limitations mean that no protection could have been obtained for technologies known to the art or their obvious variants. Another example is a principle known in US law as the public dedication doctrine that is, no protection is extended to subject matter disclosed within a patent but not expressly claimed. Because of its practical importance and widely differing solutions in comparative law, the role of prosecution history for the interpretation of claims should also be briefly addressed.

Prior to presenting the possible defenses of a potential patent infringer, remedies for patent infringement, namely permanent and preliminary injunctions, damages, as well as related issues of evidence should be dealt with. The presentation of the solutions applied under the national law should be accompanied by references to the existing respective mandatory standards of the TRIPS Agreement.

As to the defenses of an accused infringer, first the possibilities that exist to initiate an invalidation/revocation proceeding against the claimed patent and the conditions and procedures under which they can take place should be presented.

The course should end with a presentation and discussion of the court's competency – jurisdiction in patent granting and revocation proceedings, as well as in proceedings regarding patent infringement.

Patents may be assigned or licensed. Dealing with various aspects, especially of licensing, including anti-trust issues, is not necessarily part of patent law teaching, but is usually the subject matter of a specialized course. However, depending on the entire curriculum of the respective school, it may be advisable to include into the patent course also some basics on licensing.

Approaches and methods to teach in this area

Teaching patents purely from the books is not only a somewhat boring exercise, but also a deficient one. More than in other areas of law, the essence of patents and the mechanisms of the complex patent system, practically always involving problems of technology and international law, can only be adequately understood and the students' interest in the subject matter kept alert, if the teaching does not focus entirely on discussing statutory solutions and their doctrinal interpretation, but also concentrates to a large extent on the case law. The value of including a focus on case law lies not merely in the reporting of facts, but, more importantly, in the opportunity it provides for critical analysis, barked up, where possible and appropriate by attending oral court hearings in infringement and/or revocation cases.

Discussion of cases is essential for a number of reasons. Most cases, even those involving disputes over the right to Paris Union priority, or infringement, as well as those in which novelty or inventive step tests are the subject, require good knowledge and understanding of the patent at hand, which in turn requires the students to make themselves familiar with and understand the technology involved. The reading and the discussion of cases provides students, especially those without scientific or technical backgrounds, with the necessary understanding of the respective technology and its specific problems. At the same time, those with technical and scientific backgrounds, who by and large are not used to the more abstract way of thinking and writing, which lawyers, especially in Continental Europe carefully nourish, receive the opportunity to have doctrinal comments, statements and observations directly linked to real-life facts.

In this context, it may be added and emphasized that the court techniques of decision drafting and decision making also vary considerably from jurisdiction to jurisdiction. Whereas, for instance, French courts tend to the highest degree of abstraction, common law courts, especially UK courts, are at the opposite end of the range, with German and Dutch courts, for instance, in between. Thus, notwithstanding the obvious necessity to familiarize students with the case law of domestic courts, for educational reasons it seems advisable to use one or two decisions of a UK or US court to demonstrate all the scientific and technical problems involved in a complex patent litigation, as well as the solutions found and their specific rationale.

This method is particularly rewarding in problem areas, such as for instance the very controversial patenting of human genes. An analysis and discussion of the already mentioned UK House of Lords decision in *Kirin-Amgen and others* v. *Hoechst Marion Roussel Ltd. and others* of October 2004[16] will provide students with all the information necessary to make even a layman understand the technique of genetic engineering, i.e. how foreign DNA sequences are transferred into host organisms, where they are responsible for the expression of the targeted protein,[17] or

---

[16] [2005] R.P.C. 9.
[17] Especially if the extensive decision of the UK Court of Appeals is considered in parallel [2003] R.P.C. 31, and even more so if the course also discusses the House of Lords decision in *Biogen Int.* v. *Medeva plc.*, [1997] R.P.C. 1, to which the Court explicitly referred.

how an inactive endogenous gene can be activated – "switched on" – in its natural environment by using a phenomenon called "homologous recombination," i.e. by inserting into the non-coding region of the DNA, upstream of the region, coding for, in the case at hand, the hormone Erythropoietin (EPO) exogenous DNA. Apart from learning the technology and getting acquainted with the so-called "race for Erythropoietin," students will also receive remarkable lessons on the practical application of the novelty requirement in general, and in respect to the so-called "product-by-process" claims more specifically, and, last but not least, they will not only learn how UK courts determine the extent of patent protection and the historic development of their approach, but also how German and other European courts deal with that issue and why the House of Lords does not entirely concur with them, but is nevertheless of the opinion that its approach is in line with the rules of the EPC controlling the extent of the protection of European patents, which are binding for all national courts of the countries who are party to the EPC. Despite the length of such decisions, which present a challenge for students and for the teacher, whose course is usually subject to considerable time constraints, discussions of such cases have always been a rewarding experience.

Materials, references

Ideally, for students and teachers, a patent law textbook and a complementary book on patent cases should be available. Ideally, they should cover the national patent law as well as the key aspects of international (Paris Convention, PCT, TRIPS) as well as the pertinent regional (EPC, NAFTA, Eurasian Patent, ARIPO, OAPI, Andean Pact, etc.) patent law aspects. In the broader area of intellectual property, that idea has been successfully realized by Professor William Cornish with his books *Intellectual Property: Patents, Copyright, Trade Marks and Allied Rights*,[18] and *Cases and Materials on Intellectual Property*.[19] Quite apart from the declared ambition of Cornish's book, to "encourage the study of the terrain as a whole, since one of the dangers we face is from experts whose knowledge is confined to a single segment" (p. vi), thus going well beyond teaching patents, these books would also be beyond the financial reach of most students. A similar observation may be made in

---

[18] Fifth Edition by Cornish and David Llewelyn, Thomson, Sweet & Maxwell, London 2003.
[19] Fourth Edition, Thomson, Sweet & Maxwell, London 2003.

respect of the comprehensive textbook of Roger E. Schechter and John R. Thomas, *Intellectual Property, The Law of Copyrights, Patents and Trademarks*.[20]

In some countries, especially in the US and Germany, suitable textbooks such as for instance that of Janice M. Mueller, *An Introduction to Patent Law*,[21] and that of Roger E. Schechter and John R. Thomas, *Principles of Patent Law*,[22] in the US, and Rudolf Kraßer, *Patentrecht, Ein Lehr- und Handbuch*,[23] in Germany, exist and can be well used as teaching material; however, in most countries, such suitable materials rarely exist.

Even in a (nearly) ideal case of having a very good patent law case book available, it seems, however, advisable to prepare a comprehensive reader, which should faithfully reflect the actual subject matter of the course, i.e. the syllabus. The experience shows that a reader, in which PowerPoint presentations of the discussed subject matter are complemented with the most prominent and typical court decisions, offers the teacher a good opportunity to outline the problem, briefly present the statutory solution and its interpretation by courts and subsequently analyze these matters and discuss their rationale with the students, ideally using "soft" Socratic methods, i.e. leading them through the respective decisions by asking well-structured questions.

Preparing his own reader (or materials) has the clear advantage that the teacher can compose it exactly to his needs and plans. In support, additional reading can always be assigned. For the purpose of facilitating the students in their preparation of seminar works, the reader should also contain a bibliography indicating the pertinent statutory materials and the most important books and law journals, in which articles on patents and court decisions of interest are regularly published.

It goes entirely beyond the task of this contribution even to attempt to provide a comprehensive, let alone a (nearly) complete bibliography of works on patents. The only aim of the list provided in the annexed Selected Bibliography is to help those who teach patent law to gather information on the state of patent law in a given country based on a very selective sample of more recent publications. It should be emphasized here that it is essential to provide teachers and students with online access to journals and court decisions. This should be viewed as an obvious responsibility of every educational institution.

---

[20] Thomson, West, St. Paul 2003.
[21] Second Edition, Aspen Publishers, New York 2006.
[22] Thomson, West, St. Paul 2004.
[23] Fifth Edition, C.H. Beck, Munich 2004.

Future trends

As to the future trends of teaching patents, one can predict that the importance of electronic access to all sorts of information, in particular to patents, published patent applications, files of patent offices, in some countries even to court proceedings files, as well as to law and scientific journals, will increase and provide for further progress in teaching methods.

Provided that the respective schools and other education institutions, as well as students, will be equipped according to the latest state of the art technology, teaching materials and teaching methods in the class could reach a new dimension. Readers and other materials will be stored on students' laptops, teachers will demonstrate the course of patent granting proceedings, for instance, by inspecting office or court files from the classroom or viewing oral hearings at the opposition division of the patent office via video conference, etc.

Distance learning, to which no reference has been made in this chapter so far, will for sure become more important than it already is.

In many countries, for sure, most of this will remain for long a vision and a kind of a dream, probably even at universities in the developed world. All persons involved in teaching patents, as a subject matter practically inseparable from technology and its developments, should feel obliged to demonstrate in practice, i.e. in all of their teaching activities, how close to technology they are and how important it is that technological innovation and patents are viewed and understood as an organic whole.

Conclusions

The economic importance of patents has increased enormously during the last two decades. This is evidenced not only by continuously growing numbers of patent applications filed and patents granted worldwide, but also by data relating for instance, to royalties paid for patent licenses, or to the role that patents have played and continue to play for start-up companies in cutting edge areas of technology. This observation does not only apply to developed countries, but is true also for a number of newly industrialized or developing countries, like Brazil, China, India, Mexico and others.

In contrast to the ever rising economic importance of patents, for quite a while teaching patents at universities and other institutions of higher education in most countries remained either a privilege of some schools, which had a longstanding tradition in this area, very often linked to their location, for instance at the seat of the national Patent Office or a similar authority, or was a stepchild of a school's curriculum. Luckily, things began to change some time ago. At last, it has been realized that skills in the complex area of patents are essential not only for the business success of a company, but also for the performance of a national economy at large as well.

The message should be that a firm, as well as a national economy, can only successfully act if it can use the same detailed, tactical knowledge and negotiating skills in patents as its competitors in other firms, as well as at state levels. Only then can one negotiate licensing agreements, defend one's own patent rights or attack potential infringers of those rights, or, not least, defend oneself against unjustified attacks by patent owners on an equal footing. Nobody, whether a firm or a state, no matter whether developed or developing, can afford any more the luxury to be less knowledgeable or even ignorant in this complex and important field of law. Expenditures for infrastructure and human resources necessary for teaching patent law should be understood as an essential and good investment in the future wellbeing of nations. Saving money in this area could well result in its loss in the future – not a recipe for success.

Selected bibliography

Adelman, Martin J., *Patent Law Perspectives*, 2nd edn, Matthew Bender, New York 2005 (loose leaf)

Bercovitz Rodrígues-Cano, Alberto, *Apuntes de derecho mercantil*, 6th edn, Cizur Menor (Navarra), Thomson Aranzadi 2005

Carvalho, Nuno Pires, *The TRIPS Regime of Patent Rights*, 2nd edn, Kluwer Law International, The Hague 2005

China Intellectual Property Law Guide, Kluwer Law International, The Hague 2005

Chisum, Donald S., *Patents, A Treatise on the Law of Patentability, Validity and Infringement*, 15 vols., LexisNexis (loose leaf)

Cornish, William and Llewelyn, David, *Intellectual Property: Patents, Copyright, Trade Marks and Allied Rights*, 5th edn, Thomson, Sweet & Maxwell, London 2003

Gervais, Daniel, *The TRIPS Agreement, Drafting History and Analysis*, 2nd edn, Thomson, Sweet & Maxwell, London 2003

Grubb, Philip W., *Patents for Chemicals, Pharmaceuticals and Biotechnology*, 4th edn, Oxford University Press, Oxford 2004

Jaenichen, H.-R., McDonell, L.A., Haley, J.F., *From Clones to Claims, The European Patent Office's Case Law on the Patentability of Biotechnology Invention*, 3rd edn, Carl Heymanns, Cologne, Berlin, Bonn, Munich 2002

Kieff, F. Scott and Nack, Ralph (eds.), *International, United States and European Intellectual Property, Selected Source Material*, Aspen Publishers, New York 2006

Kraßer, Rudolph, *Patentrecht*, 5th edn., C.H. Beck Publishers, Munich 2004

Mueller, Janice M., *An Introduction to Patent Law*, 2nd edn, Aspen Publishers, New York 2006

Patterson, Gerald, *The European Patent System, The Law and Practice of the European Patent Convention*, 2nd edn., Sweet & Maxwell, London 2000

Schechter, Roger E. and Thomas, John R., *Principles of Patent Law*, Thomson & West, St. Paul 2004

Singer, Margarete and Stauder, Dieter (eds.), *European Patent Convention*, 3 vols. 3rd edn, Thomson, Sweet & Maxwell and Heymanns Publishers, Cologne, Berlin, Bonn, Munich 2003

Terrell *On the Law of Patents*, 16th edn, Thomson, Sweet & Maxwell, London 2006

Thomas, John R., *Pharmaceutical Patent Law*, BNA Inc., Washington D.C. 2005

Vanzetti, Adriano and Di Cataldo, Vincenzo, *Manuale di diritto industriale*, 5th ed., Giufrè Editore, Milan 2005

Vivant, Michel, *Le droit des brevets*, 2nd edn, Dalloz, Paris 2005

3

Teaching copyright and related rights

MIHÁLY FICSOR

Introduction

Around the middle of the last century, the importance of copyright within both undergraduate and postgraduate courses was relatively modest. In the undergraduate curricula – where it extended, if at all, to intellectual property rights in general, and to copyright, in particular – only a couple of hours were devoted to these rights. As regards copyright, this usually consisted of an outline of the social-political justification of copyright protection, the identification of the applicable national law and international treaties (in general, only the Berne Convention), a listing of moral rights and economic rights along with the exceptions to, and limitations of, the latter rights, a reference to the term of protection, some discussion about copyright contracts and a brief description of the available enforcement measures.

Since that time, there have been accelerating developments in and around the field of copyright. These have included: the recognition of related (or "neighboring") rights in the Rome Convention and in more national laws; the advent of a number of new technologies for the creation and use of works and objects of related rights; the emergence of widespread piracy as a result of the ever easier and more perfect reproduction technologies; the extension of copyright protection to new categories of works (such as computer programs, databases and videogames); the growing importance of copyright industries for national economies and international trade, reflected, inter alia, in the TRIPS Agreement; and the spectacular success of digital technology and the Internet with a number of challenges for copyright and related rights, leading to the adoption of the WIPO "Internet Treaties" (WIPO Copyright Treaty (WCT) and the WIPO Performers and Phonograms Treaty (WPPT)).

The accelerating developments and increasing challenges have required a number of adaptations in the international regulation and national laws on copyright and related rights, as well as in the practice of applying the existing norms. This has consisted in the recognition of new rights and the prescription of new means of protection, and, at the same time, in the regulation of exceptions and limitations in a way that the existing balance can be maintained.

The need for creating and maintaining an appropriate balance has emerged for different reasons. Since the 1960s, developing countries have repeatedly pointed out that they need preferential treatment for their educational and research programs, as well as some kind of intellectual protection for their artistic folklore; their demands have received new emphasis recently in the Program of WIPO. The international copyright norms, since the very first Act of the Berne Convention, have been based on the principle of a due balance between the public interest in providing adequate protection as an indispensable means of promoting the creation, protection and availability of valuable works and objects of related rights, on the one hand, and other public interests – including the respect for certain basic human rights and freedoms – on the other hand. With the advent of computer and digital technology and the Internet, certain completely new kinds of issues concerning the balancing of interests have arisen that were unimaginable before. Those issues include the "interoparability" or "reverse engineering" of computer programs, the interface between technological protection measures and exceptions to copyright, and the protection of privacy in connection with the application of digital rights management.

Also, some "alternative," collaborative systems have appeared recently that are, in principle, based in copyright but which offer broad, free uses of literary and artistic work, such as the free software movement, the open source initiative, the creative commons licenses, the Wikipedia online encyclopedia, etc. Some of these are ideology-based, while others serve rather as parts of new business models.

In view of the increasing importance and growing complexity of copyright and related rights in the knowledge-based economy, it seems obvious that this branch of intellectual property rights now deserves much more attention and a substantially broader timeframe in both undergraduate and postgraduate curricula than before.

This chapter on teaching copyright and related rights is divided into two parts. The first part outlines those topics that seem indispensable elements of general undergraduate teaching, while the second part contains modules, as examples, that may be the objects of either specialized courses or postgraduate programs.

Neither in the case of the undergraduate course, nor in the case of the modules for special courses and postgraduate programs is any specific timeframe indicated in the number of hours to be devoted to the various elements. The time needed for the presentation and discussion of the various topics obviously is determined by the intensity and the thoroughness with which they are dealt, and on certain methodology aspects (such as whether mainly statutory law is described or also case law is analyzed in a more intensive way, or whether contractual practices and enforcement measures are dealt with more in detail), which in turn depend on the profile and the teaching traditions of the university or postgraduate institution concerned. Nevertheless, if an estimation has to be given, it seems that the required timeframe of the undergraduate course is between 12 and 14 hours, while the modules for special courses or postgraduate programs is between 10 and 20 hours, depending on the aspects mentioned above.

As can be seen below, the undergraduate course includes twelve items, while the specific modules contain ten items. This is in harmony with the above indication of the possible timeframes. The presentation of each of the items requires at least one hour, but, if more thoroughly discussed, it may take longer.

Undergraduate course

The role of copyright in economic, social and cultural development

The discussion of this topic should extend to copyright and related rights as incentives for creativity and access to works and to other cultural and information products; to the economic importance of copyright; and to copyright and cultural diversity.

It is necessary to emphasize the basic differences between the more pragmatic "socialcontract"-type justification of copyright in the common law system, and its human-rights foundations in the civil law system. It is also important to point out the tentative signs of convergence recently appearing between the two systems (see, for example, certain provisions of the TRIPS Agreement serving as bridges between the two systems, or the converging elements in the *Rural* v. *Feist*[1] decision of the US Supreme Court and in the provisions of the EU Directives regarding the criteria of

---

[1] *Feist Publications, Inc.* v. *Rural Tel. Serv. Co.*, 499 U.S. 340 (1991).

copyright protection of certain specific categories of works (computer programs, databases, photographic works)).

As regards the economic importance of copyright, reference should be made to recent national studies, preferably those which have been carried out on the basis of the harmonized methodology worked out by WIPO. The growing importance of the copyright industries for economic growth, GDP, employment and foreign trade should be particularly emphasized.

It should be pointed out that the absence of effective protection of copyright and related rights, including those of foreign owners of rights, may lead to the inundation of national cultural markets by cheap – sometimes pirated – foreign products, and that this, in turn, may undermine domestic creativity and production, national identity and cultural diversity.

Copyright and Human Rights

First, Article 27(2) of the Universal Declaration of Human Rights[2] should be analyzed. That article contains the basic provision concerning authors' rights ("right to protection of the moral and material interests resulting from any scientific, literary and artistic production") in harmony with Article 17 on the right to property, along with the principle that "[n]o one shall be arbitrarily deprived of his property."

These should then be compared with those provisions of the Universal Declaration which may require balancing with copyright, in particular, with Article 19 on the freedom of opinion and expression and the freedom of access to information; Article 26 on the right to education, and with Article 27(1) on the right to participate in cultural life, to enjoy the arts and to share in scientific advancement. In this connection, it is also necessary to refer to Article 29 of the Universal Declaration which states that "[i]n the exercise of his rights and freedoms, everyone shall be subject only to such limitations as are determined by law solely for the purpose of securing due recognition and respect for the rights and freedoms of others and of meeting the just requirements of morality, public order and the general welfare in a democratic society."

It should be emphasized that the provisions of the international copyright and related rights treaties (in particular, the Berne Convention, the TRIPS Agreement, the WCT and the WPPT) and the regional regulations

---

[2] On December 1, 1948, the United Nations General Assembly adopted and proclaimed the Universal Declaration of Human Rights.

and national laws duly implementing them, offer appropriate conditions for adequate balancing with the various rights and freedoms mentioned above (on the basis of the principles of idea-expression and information-presentation dichotomies, the specific exceptions recognized in view of fundamental public interests, and the "three-step test" etc.).

Copyright and competition

First of all, it should be pointed out that intellectual property rights – and thus also copyright and related rights – do not necessarily grant a market power to the owners of rights or lead to monopolies unduly restricting competition. On the contrary, the creation and production of new works and objects of related rights normally increase competition and broaden consumer choice. In this aspect, the objectives of copyright law and competition law converge.

Also in this context, it is necessary to refer to the idea-expression and information-presentation dichotomies, as serving as a basis for reasonable competition.

At the same time, those cases should be discussed where there may be tensions and even conflicts between the actual way of exercising exclusive rights, and competition rules. How legislation and case law (including the varied practice of the European Court of Justice) handle these possible tensions and conflicts should be reviewed.

The following topics should be covered:

(i) the possible conflicts emerging when copyright protection – to be applied basically to cultural products – might have an undesirably chilling effect on the markets of utilitarian products (with reference to the specific problems in respect of the protection of works of applied arts/industrial designs);
(ii) the way the interoperability of computer programs may be guaranteed (see, for example, the relevant provisions of the EU Computer Programs Directive[3]);
(iii) the interface between standardization and copyright;
(iv) misuse of monopoly position by not respecting the principle of information-presentation dichotomy (see, for example, the *Magill*[4] case in the European Court of Justice); and

---

[3] Council Directive 91/250/EEC of 14 May 1991 on the legal protection of computer programmes as amended by Council Directive 93/98/EEC of 29 October 1993.
[4] *Radio Telefis Eirann v. Commission* [Magill], C-241/91P ECJ [April 6, 1995].

(v) the justified *de facto* or *de iure* monopoly position of collective management organizations and the legal means to prevent the misuse thereof.

Legal sources of copyright and related Rights: International treaties, regional rules and national laws

This area should include a general description of the three "layers" of the present international norms: (i) the Berne Convention and the Rome Convention; (ii) the TRIPS Agreement; and (iii) the WIPO "Internet Treaties," extending to their history, relationships, principles and basic norms. Brief reference should be made also to the Phonograms Convention and the Satellites Convention, where appropriate.

Regional norms should also be described, in particular in those countries (member countries of the EU, countries party to NAFTA or the Cartagena Agreement, etc.) where they are relevant.

Finally, the applicable national laws should be described. In this context, it should be discussed (i) how international norms and regional rules are implemented at national level; (ii) the relationship between the constitution, the civil code, certain specific laws, on the one hand, and the law on copyright and related rights on the other hand; and (iii) the role of case law.

Copyright and trade: the TRIPS Agreement

The negotiation history of the TRIPS Agreement[5] in the Uruguay Round should be reviewed briefly. The relationship between the Berne Convention and the Rome Convention, on the one hand, and the TRIPS Agreement, on the other hand, should be presented.

Articles 3 and 4 of the TRIPS Agreement, on the principles on national treatment and most-favored-nation treatment principles, should be analyzed by pointing out that, as regards related rights, the obligation to grant national treatment is more limited than under the Rome Convention.

When dealing with Articles 7 and 8 on "Objectives" and "Principles," it should be emphasized that they mainly relate to "technological innovation," "transfer of technology," "technological knowledge," "technological

---

[5] Agreement on Trade-Related Aspects of Intellectual Property Rights adopted as Annex 1C of the Marrakesh Agreement Establishing the World Trade Organization (WTO).

development" and, thus, basically to industrial property rights; but, that, nevertheless, they also state the need for balancing rights and obligations, as well as the importance of taking into account certain public interests, and that the latter aspects are also relevant for copyright and related rights. It should be pointed out that these aspects may and should be duly taken into account in the framework of the application of the "three-step test" provided for in Article 13 of the TRIPS Agreement.

Section 2 of the TRIPS Agreement (Articles 9 to 14) on copyright and related rights should be described and analyzed in comparison with the provisions of the Berne Convention and the Rome Convention (inclusion of existing provisions by reference or otherwise, interpretative provisions and the few new obligations). Only a brief review of Part III on the provisions on enforcement of rights should be offered here (enforcement of rights is covered later, see p. 43 below). It should be stressed what kind of improvement the inclusion of detailed norms on enforcement in the international regulation of intellectual property rights has brought about.

Finally, the WTO dispute settlement system should be described, with a brief analysis of those dispute settlement cases which directly or indirectly concern copyright and related rights.

Copyright in the digital, networked environment; the WIPO "Internet Treaties"

The impact of digital technology, and in particular of the Internet, should be outlined. The preparatory work at the international level (at WIPO and in the "Berne Protocol"[6] and the "New Instrument"[7]) and at regional and national levels should be reviewed.

It should be emphasized that the provisions of the WCT and the WPPT: (i) reflect the recognition that, although some modifications are necessary in the international norms, there is no need for fundamental changes; (ii) are well-balanced, flexible, and duly take into account the legitimate interests of all the countries with different levels of development and of all major stakeholders; (iii) if duly implemented, are not burdensome in economic or legislative terms; and (iv) mainly consist of clarifications about the application of existing international norms

---

[6] WIPO Committee of Experts on a Possible Protocol to the Berne Convention preparing the instrument which became the WCT.
[7] WIPO Committee of Experts on a Possible New Instrument on the Rights of Performers and Producers of Phonograms preparing the instrument which became the WPPT.

(certain adaptations of these norms to the new conditions, and the truly new obligations provided in them – on technological measures and rights management information – do not mean an extension of the scope of protection either, but only new means for the exercise and enforcement of rights that are indispensable for the fulfillment of the objectives of copyright in the new environment).

The WCT and the WPPT may be characterized as the most up-to-date international treaties which, as regards substantive copyright norms, basically contain: (i) what is provided in the Berne Convention and Rome Convention; (ii) plus what is provided for in the TRIPS Agreement; and (iii) plus what was necessary to be included on the basis of the so-called "digital agenda."

The review of the results of the "digital agenda" should extend to: (i) the application of the right of reproduction in the digital environment (see, for example, the way it is regulated in Articles 2 and 5(1) and (5) of the Information Society Directive of the EU[8]); (ii) the right of making available to the public; (iii) the application of exceptions and limitation in the new environment; and (iv) the rules concerning technological measures and rights management information.

Summary of the substantive elements of copyright protection

The summary should extend to the basic principles (national treatment, independence of protection, formality-free protection), the coverage of protection (idea–expression and information–presentation dichotomies, originality, the question of fixation, main categories of works, works that may be excluded from protection), moral rights, economic rights, and the terms of protection.

Summary of the Main Substantive Elements of Related Rights

The summary should be similar to that outlined above concerning copyright: national treatment (emphasizing the difference between the Rome Convention, on the one hand, and the TRIPS Agreement and the WPPT, on the other); "minimum formality" under the Rome Convention, formality-free protection under the TRIPS Agreement and the WPPT;

---

[8] Directive 2001/29/EC of the European Parliament and of the Council of May 22, 2001 on the harmonization of certain aspects of copyright and related rights in the information society.

categories of related rights recognized at the international level (the rights of performers, producers of phonograms and broadcasting organizations), possible further categories recognized at regional and national levels (the rights of publishers in "published editions," producers of "first fixation of a film" and the *sui generis* rights of database makers); moral rights of performers, economic rights.

Balancing of interests: Exceptions and limitations

The summary of the substantive elements of copyright and related rights outlined, above, only becomes complete with this item of the program.

It should include the description of the specific exceptions and limitations allowed under the international norms, possible regional norms and the corresponding provisions in national laws, as well as the concepts and practical application of the "fair use"/"fair dealing" doctrines. It will be necessary to point out the differences between the various categories of exceptions and limitations from the viewpoint of their social-political and legal justifications (balancing with other basic rights and freedoms and with certain specific public interests, responding to market failures, etc.).

The questions of the interpretation and practical application of the "three-step test" as provided for in Article 9(2) of the Berne Convention, Article 13 of the TRIPS Agreement, Article 10 of the WCT and Article 16 of the WPPT should be discussed in detail.

Special attention should be paid to the "interface" between the protection of technological measures, on the one hand, and exceptions and limitations, on the other hand, with detailed description of the different solutions to guarantee the maintenance of an adequate balance of interests (specific statutory exceptions, regular administrative reviews, mediation/arbitration systems) and their practical application.

Copyright and developing countries: Preferential treatment, protection of folklore

As the title indicates, two main topics should be covered under this item: preferential treatment for developing countries, and the protection of folklore. It is to be noted that the issue of the protection of folklore (or, to use other terms, "expressions of folklore" or "traditional cultural expressions" (TCEs)) is not restricted to developing countries. Nevertheless, it seems justified to deal with it under this item, at least for two reasons: first, folklore in developing countries is still a living tradition and an important form of creativity and cultural production, much more than in industrialized countries; and, second, due to this, developing countries are in the frontline to demand adequate intellectual-property-type protection for expressions of folklore/TCEs.

As regards preferential treatment, it should be discussed how this issue emerged at the 1967 Stockholm conference to revise the Berne Convention, and how it was settled at that time in a protocol, and then, at the 1971 Paris revision conference in the Appendix to the Convention. The compulsory licensing system provided in the Appendix should be described, pointing out the reasons for which it has not, in general, been used, in practice.

WIPO's efforts to take into account and promote the special interests of developing countries in international norm-setting (referring, in particular, to the preparation of the "Internet Treaties") and in its development cooperation programs should be reviewed. The debates and programs concerning the "WIPO Development Agenda"[9] initiated in 2004 should be described.

Reference should be made also to the preferential provisions for developing countries (in particular for least-developed countries (LDCs)) in the WTO-TRIPS system and to the ongoing WTO negotiations.[10]

As far as the protection of folklore is concerned, it should be explained how the 1967 Stockholm revision conference tried to settle this issue in the new Article 15(4) of the Berne Convention, including the reasons for which this was not a true solution in practice (referring to the difficulties in applying certain basic concepts of copyright, such as "authorship," "work," "originality," and certain norms, such as the one on a *post mortem auctoris* term of protection, to folklore creations).

The presentation should extend to an analysis of (i) the WIPO–UNESCO Model Provisions adopted in 1982 on a *sui generis* system for the protection of "expressions of folklore";[11] (ii) the national laws – in particular those of many African countries – which provide for copyright or *sui generis* protection of folklore creations; and (iii) the reasons for which the attempt at transforming the principles and provisions of the Model Provisions into an international treaty failed in 1984.

It should be described how the consideration of the issues of intellectual protection of folklore was launched again at the WIPO–UNESCO

---

[9] See WIPO Press Release WIPO/PR/2006/461 at www.wipo.int/pressroom/en/.
[10] The Doha Development Round of WTO negotiations launched in Doha in 2001, with subsequent ministerial meetings in Cancún in 2003 and in Hong Kong in 2005.
[11] See www.wipo.int/tk/en/folklore.

World Forum on the Protection of Folklore held in Phuket, Thailand,[12] in 1997, and what kinds of positive results the various WIPO projects – and, in particular, the preparatory work in the Intergovernmental Committee on Intellectual Property and Genetic Resources, Traditional Knowledge and Folklore[13] – have brought about so far.

Individual exercise and collective management of rights

As regards individual contracts based on exclusive rights, reference should be made to the different approaches of the common law system (with greater emphasis on contractual freedom) and the civil law system (with a trend of more intensive legislative interventions, in particular, in favor of authors and performers regarded as weaker parties in contractual negotiations). The impact of general civil law legislation and case law on copyright contracts and their interpretation and application should also be analyzed.

Some typical licensing models should be presented (book and music publishing, film production, creation and use of computer programs).

The discussion of the item should also extend to a review and analysis of free software/open source (GPL, etc.) and creative commons licenses.

Finally, the collective management of copyright and related rights should be discussed (typical fields of application; voluntary, extended and mandatory models; basic principles of licensing; collection and distribution of remuneration; governmental control where appropriate; etc.).

Enforcement of rights

The differences between the WIPO-administered treaties and the TRIPS Agreement should be recalled from this viewpoint.

The presentation of the topic should be based on the description and analysis of the provisions of Part III of the TRIPS Agreement.

The need for specific norms against optical-disc and Internet piracy, and for the regulation of the liability of Internet service providers (along with an adequate notice-and-take-down system) should be discussed, and examples of the practical application of such norms should be offered. Reference should also be made to the newly emerging issues

---

[12] See UNESCO WIPO World Forum on the Protection of Folklore, Phuket, Thailand, April 8 to 10, 1997, WIPO publication No. 758 (E/F/S).   [13] See www.wipo.int/tk/en

concerning the liability of "software providers" and to some related court cases (*Grokster*,[14] *Kazaa*,[15] etc.).

Special courses/Postgraduate programs

As regards special courses, seminars and postgraduate programs, many different programs may be construed depending on the special features and teaching strategy of a given university or academic institution. It would not be possible to present all the possible variants in the framework of this chapter. Below, four examples are offered for such possible courses and programs. The first three of them (A to C) – communication-related rights, information technology and copyright and collective management – cover those topics which, at present, are particularly timely, while the fourth one (D) is more practice-oriented, which is quite typical in the case of such courses and programs.

There are overlaps between the above-outlined undergraduate program and these four special courses/postgraduate programs. This is inevitable since, in the case of the former, the basic issues are presented in more general terms, while under the latter ones, in addition to the specific questions, partly the same issues are also discussed, but in much more detail. Furthermore, there are also certain overlaps among the four specific programs, since they are not constructed to be taken one after the other by the same students, but rather as alternatives, and it follows from the nature of the four topics themselves that there are connections between them.

The topics of the special courses/postgraduate modules are presented in a simpler way than those of the program of the undergraduate course above – simply in the form of a list of issues to be dealt with – since the level of details makes the questions to be covered quite self-evident.

A. "Performing/communication rights" and the "making available" right in the field of copyright and related rights

1. *Review of the international norms on "performing/communication rights" and the "making available" right* (the right of public performance, the right of broadcasting and the rights concerning the retransmission of

---

[14] *MGM Studios, Inc. v. Grokster, Ltd.* 545 U.S. 913 (2005).
[15] *Universal Music Australia Pty Ltd v. Sharman License Holding Ltd* [2005] FCA 1242 (5 September 2005).

broadcast works; the right of communication to the public by cable; and the right of making available to the public).

2. *Basic concepts requiring interpretation* (the concepts of "public" and "[communication] to the public"; differing concepts of "communication to the public" under the international copyright and related rights instruments; the concept of "broadcasting," in particular concerning satellite television and encrypted programs; the "emission theory" and the "communication theory"; and simultaneous and unchanged cable retransmission of broadcast programs and "cable-originated" programs).

3. *Individual exercise and collective management of "performing/communication rights"* ("grand rights" and "small rights"; exercise of "grand rights" in dramatic and dramatico-musical works through direct licensing, through agencies, and through "partial" collective management; and collective management of "small rights" in non-dramatic musical works).

4. *Right of broadcasting* (the relevant provisions of the Berne Convention, the Rome Convention, the TRIPS Agreement, the WCT, the WPPT, regional rules and national laws; Article 11*bis*(2) of the Berne Convention on the application of "conditions": non-voluntary licenses and mandatory collective management; broadcasting of live performances under the Rome Convention and the WPPT; and right of performers and producers to a single remuneration for broadcasting and communication to the public of phonograms published for commercial purposes under Article 12 and 16 of the Rome Convention and Article 15 of the WPPT).

5. *Communication to the public by cable* ("cable-originated" programs and retransmission of broadcast programs in the field of copyright and related rights; collective management of cable retransmission rights; and mandatory collective management, for example, under the EU Satellite and Cable Directive[16]).

6. *The rights of broadcasters and cablecasters* (the relevant provisions of the Rome Convention, the TRIPS Agreement, regional rules and national laws; and the proposed WIPO Treaty on the Protection of Broadcasting Organizations).

7. *Webcasting and simulcasting* (webcasting and simulcasting from the viewpoint of copyright and the rights of performers and phonogram producers; collective management schemes; and the issues of webcasting and

---

[16] Council Directive 93/83/EEC of September 27, 1993 on the coordination of certain rules concerning copyright and rights related to copyright applicable to satellite broadcasting and cable retransmission.

simulcasting discussed during the preparation of the proposed WIPO Treaty on the Protection of Broadcasting Organizations).

8. *The right of making available to the public* (the "umbrella solution"; differences between the relevant provisions of the WCT and the WPPT; new situation – in contrast with non-interactive performing/communication rights – concerning the choice between individual exercise and collective management of rights; the role of digital rights management (DRM) (technical protection measures (TPMs) and rights management information (RMI)) in the exercise of the right of making available to the public; and the relevant norms in the WCT, the WPPT, regional rules and national laws).

9. *Collective management of "performing/communication rights" and the "making available" right in the field of copyright* (differences between the exercise of "small" and "grand" "performing/communication rights"; voluntary, "extended," "presumption-based" and mandatory collective management; and main principles and functions).

10. *Collective management of "performing/communication rights" and the "making available" right in the field of related rights* (differences between the rights of performers and producers of phonograms, on the one hand, and the rights of broadcasters, on the other, from the viewpoint of collective management; organizational models; types of bilateral contracts; and main functions and principles).

B. Information technology and copyright

1. *Copyright protection of computer programs* (the relevant provisions of the TRIPS Agreement, the WCT, regional regulations (such as the EU Computer Programs Directive) and national laws; operational systems – application software; source code – object code; exceptions and limitations; and legal conditions of "decompilation" (reverse engineering)).

2. *Business models for the development and use of computer programs* (free software as ideology; open source software as business model; open source versus proprietary software; "shared source"; and open standards and interoperability).

3. *Copyright and* sui generis *protection of databases* (the relevant provisions of the TRIPS Agreement, the WCT and the EU Databases Directive; the conditions of copyright protection; *sui generis* protection of databases; and the failed attempt of working out a WIPO Databases Treaty).

4. *The impact of digital technology and the Internet on copyright and related rights; the "Internet Treaties"* (opportunities and challenges; the preparatory work and the main features of the WCT and the WPPT; adherence; and implementation).

5. *The application of the right of reproduction in the digital environment* (digitization as an act of reproduction; electronic storage of works and objects of related rights as an act of reproduction; and temporary copies: protection and exceptions).

6. *The right of "making available to the public"* (the emergence of the "umbrella solution"; communication-type and distribution-type interactive transmissions; the principle of "relative freedom of legal characterization"; differences between the WCT and the WPPT concerning the provisions on the right of making available; and basic forms of implementation).

7. *Exceptions and limitations in the digital, networked environment* (extension of the application of the three-step test to all economic rights under the WCT and the WPPT; the Agreed Statement to Article 10 of the WCT and its interpretation; and adaptation of the exceptions for educational (in particular, concerning "distance learning") and library purposes and for private copying to the digital environment).

8. *Copyright and the p2p systems* (centralized and decentralized p2p systems; liability of "system providers," "software providers," "content providers" and end users; and major lawsuits: *Napster;*[17] *Grokster; Kazaa,* etc.).

9. *DRM: technological protection measures (TPMs) and rights management information (RMI)* (the relevant provisions of the WCT and the WPPT; access control TPMs and rights control TPMs; defense line to be built in the stage of manufacture, importation and distribution of illegal circumvention devices and of commercial services; "interface" between TPMs and exceptions; and application of the norms on RMI).

10. *Liability of service providers* (the concepts of service and access providers; general conditions to enjoy "safe harbor" provisions against certain sanctions and remedies; special rules concerning mere conduit, caching, hosting and location tools/hyperlinks; and notice and take down procedures).

C. *Collective management of copyright and related rights*

1. *The rational of collective management* (where collective management is justified and where it is not justified; the difference between

---

[17] *A & M Records, Inc.* v. *Napster, Inc.*, 239 F. 3d 1004 (9th Cir. 2001).

exclusive rights and rights to remuneration from this viewpoint; the freedom of choice of exclusive rights owners; and main functions of collective management organizations).

2. *Voluntary, "presumption-based," "extended" and mandatory collective management systems* (the relevant norms of the international treaties; the meaning of "determining/imposing conditions" for the exercise of exclusive rights under Articles 11*bis*(2) and 13(1) of the Berne Convention; cases where mandatory collective management is allowed; "presumption-based" systems and their legal nature; and the conditions of the application of "extended" collective management).

3. *Elements of a full-fledged collective management system* (legal forms of authorization by owners of rights; bilateral agreements with foreign organizations; documentation of the repertoire; blanket licensing; per-use licenses; monitoring of uses; collection of remuneration; and distribution of remuneration, legal conditions of deductions for cultural and social purposes).

4. *Organizational models* (private associations or governmental organizations; one organization or separate organizations for the management of various rights of various categories of owners of rights; one organization or several organizations for the management of the same rights of the same category of owners of rights; "coalitions" of collective management organizations; and internal organizational structures of collective management organizations).

5. *Review of the main fields of collective management organizations* ("performing/communication rights" in musical works; "mechanical rights"; "performing/communication rights" in dramatic, and dramatico-musical works; "Rome Article 12" rights of performers and producers of phonograms; levy-based right to remuneration for private copying; reprographic reproduction rights; resale right (*droit de suite*); and cable retransmission rights).

6. *Basic models: collective management of "performing/communication rights" and the "making available" rights in musical works* (collective management of "performing/communication rights" in the traditional, analog environment; collective management of "performing/communication rights" and the "making available" right in the digital, networked environment; and the role of CISAC[18]).

7. *Basic models: collective management of reprographic rights* (collective management of the right of reproduction concerning photocopying;

---

[18] International Confederation of Societies of Authors and Composers (CISAC).

collective management of rights through reprographic rights organizations (RROs) in the digital, networked environment; the role of IFRRO[19]).

8. *Basic models: collective management of the rights of performers and producers of phonograms* (collective management of traditional "Rome Article 12 rights"; collective management of the rights of performers and producers of phonograms in the digital, networked environment; "simulcasting" and "webcasting" licenses of phonogram producers; "residual rights" of performers; the role of FIM,[20] FIA[21] and IFPI[22]).

9. *Basic models: collective management of the right to remuneration for private copying* (the relevant provisions of the international instruments, regional regulations (such as Article 5(2)(b) and (5) of the EU Information Society Directive[23]) and national laws; "levies" as a basis for remuneration; legal entities and physical persons obligated to pay remuneration; organizational models (an existing organization acting also on behalf of others or a new organization acting on behalf of all the interested categories of owners of rights); distribution of remuneration; and application of the principle of national treatment).

10. *The role of the government; dispute settlement* (statutory regulation of the establishment and operation of collective management organizations; licensing, accreditation, registration; supervision of the activities of collective management organizations; and approval of tariffs or mediation/arbitration between collective management organizations and users).

D. Copyright and related rights in practice

1. *Review of specific rules concerning different categories of works and specific aspects of exercising rights therein* (*literary works*: publishing on paper and in electronic form in the different publishing sectors and the related contractual system; reprographic reproduction rights and their collective management; public lending rights; *musical works*: music publishing; "performing/communication rights" and the "making available" right; "mechanical rights"; levy systems for private copying and their "interface" with TPMs; collective management; *dramatic and dramatico-musical works*: the protection of dramatic works proper and their original theatrical presentations; individual contracts, agencies, "partial" collective management; and *audiovisual works*: authorship and original ownership; the

---

[19] International Federation of Reproduction Rights Organizations (IFFRO).
[20] International Federation of Musicians (FIM).
[21] International Federation of Actors (FIA).
[22] International Federation of the Phonographic Industry (IFPI).   [23] See note. 8 above

status of producers and directors; the status of pre-existing works used, and the works specifically created, for audiovisual works; contractual system; sequence of markets; territorial division of rights; "related rights" of producers of "videograms" of the makers of "first fixations of films").

2. *Review of specific rules concerning different categories of works and specific aspects of exercising rights therein; continuation* (*works of fine arts*: right of exhibition; relationship between copyright and the ownership of the original or copies; resale right and its exercise/collective management; *photographic works*: artistic and "amateur" photos: application of the originality test; use as illustrations; exploitation on the basis of photo "databases" and through the Internet; *architectural works*: different status of technical and artistic elements; special considerations in the application of the moral right of integrity and the economic right of adaptation; and *works of applied arts*: various national systems for their delimitation with works of fine arts; relationship with the protection of industrial designs).

3. *Review of specific rules concerning different categories of works and specific aspects of exercising rights therein; continuation* (*computer programs*: operational systems and application programs; source code and object code; criteria of protection; free software/open source software and proprietary software; contractual models; specific exceptions – in particular for "decompilation" – and the conditions of their application; *databases*: criteria of protection; relationship between the protection of databases themselves and the components of their contents; *sui generis* rights of database makers; *multimedia*: collective management systems for the creation of multimedia productions; definition and differing legal characterizations of multimedia productions; and *web-pages*: protected elements of web-pages; "framing" and "deep-linking").

4. *Review of related rights* (*rights of performers*: live performances: key role of contractual arrangements; fixation of phonograms: exclusivity agreements and recording contracts; right to remuneration for broadcasting/communication to the public of phonograms and for private copying and the "residual" rental right; collective management of these rights; audiovisual performers: the status of featured actors and "extras"; *rights of producers of phonograms*: reproduction, distribution and rental rights; right to remuneration for broadcasting/communication to the public of phonograms and for private copying; collective management of these rights; making available/distribution through the Internet on the basis of DRM systems; "interface" between DRM (TPMs) and exceptions; and *rights of broadcasting organizations*: terrestrial and satellite broadcasting;

encrypted programs and their protection; applicable law in case of direct broadcasting by satellite; satellite-to-cable systems, retransmission rights: cable- and simulcasting).

5. *Exercise of copyright and related rights: free dissemination* (public domain; works excluded from copyright protection; free use of works and objects of related rights on the basis of exceptions; advertisement- and subsidy-based dissemination; free availability of certain categories of works or parts thereof through the Internet; free software/open source software; "creative commons"; and "orphan works").

6. *Exercise of copyright and related rights: individual licensing* (individual contracts as typical form of exercising exclusive rights; licensing through agencies; "catalogue licensing"; assignment of rights and licenses; exclusive licenses and non-exclusive licenses; general rules of contracts and the role of civil codes; typical contractual forms; and more detailed analysis of publishing contracts as the "prototype" of copyright contracts).

7. *Exercise of copyright and related rights: collective management* (the contractual system of the three elements of fully fledged collective management: (i) "upstream": mandate given to collective management organizations by owners of rights, (ii) bilateral representation contracts between collective management organizations, and (iii) "downstream": licenses for users; special features of the various forms of collective management; management of mere rights to remuneration, in particular such a right for private copying based on "levies"; government accreditation/licensing/registration and control; models for the settlement of disputes between collective management organizations and users; and special licensing systems for Internet uses).

8. *The application of DRM (TPMs and RMI)* (protection of access-control and rights-control TPMs; protection against the manufacture, importation and distribution of illegal devices and commercial services; main forms of existing TPM systems; exceptions to the protection of TPMs; interface between TPMs and certain "public-interest" exceptions; dispute settlement models; and standard digital identifiers and the question of interoperability).

9. *Liability of service providers and "software providers"* (liability and "safe harbors"; the general and specific conditions of "safe harbors": mere conduit, caching, hosting, location tools/hyperlinks; notice-and-take down systems; new developments concerning the liability of "software providers"; and analysis of recent cases: *Grokster, Kazaa*, etc.).

10. *Enforcement of rights* (procedural requirements, presumptions of ownership, evidence; injunctions; identification of illegal copies: the

"sampling method"; calculation of damages; actual, statutory and "punitive" damages; the requirements and conditions of provisional – in particular *ex parte* – measures; special requirements related to border measures; seizure and subsequent measures regarding infringing copies and material and implements used for the making of such copies; and the application of criminal sanctions: the concepts of "piracy" and "commercial scale," the level of sanctions necessary to provide a deterrent effect).

Future trends

Growing economic and social importance of copyright and related rights

In the knowledge-based economy, with the widening role of copyright-based industries, the economic and social importance of copyright will further increase. The recent studies completed on the basis of the harmonized WIPO methodology indicate that the contribution of the so-called copyright industries to national economies and international trade is growing in a spectacular manner.

Beyond the economic statistics, the impact of intellectual property-related achievements on many important aspects of human life and social development should also be taken into account. It should be seen that the general political importance of the protection of intellectual property rights, including copyright, is also increasing. In many fields, no well-founded strategic decisions may be taken, no truly workable economic and social projects may be prepared, without duly taking into account the relevant intellectual property considerations.

All this should be duly reflected in the teaching programs of universities and other teaching fora, and the projects of research institutions, in the form of more time and attention devoted to these aspects.

Broadening the interface between copyright and other disciplines, theories and principles

The extension of the impact of copyright to ever more aspects of human life and social activities inevitably broadens the scope of issues where it is not sufficient to take into account intellectual property considerations alone. It is therefore equally important to examine the effects of the application of copyright and related rights in and with respect to other fields.

New issues have emerged concerning the relationship between the protection and exercise of copyright and related rights, on the one hand, and human rights areas, such as the protection of privacy, the freedom of expression or the right to have access to fundamental information, on the other hand. This relationship should be reconsidered and more harmoniously regulated.

This may have a double effect on research and teaching in the field of copyright. First, it is ever more evident that any kind of isolationist approach to copyright issues is untenable. The emphasis on the theoretical foundations of copyright and related rights is indispensable, including the well-established principles of copyright and related rights laws. However, those copyright components should be constantly compared and reconciled with the principles and theoretical and practical considerations of other branches of law, and with other important disciplines, such as economics, sociology, ethics or technology-oriented studies. Second, there should be an appropriate reaction on the copyright side of this broadening interface, in that copyright considerations should be duly taken into account.

The recognition of the necessity of this kind of interrelationship and interaction should have an impact on research projects, and should lead to modifications in teaching programs, not only in the field of legal and economic studies, but also in the field of the other disciplines concerned.

More attention required for limitations and exceptions

With the growing importance and broadening field of application of copyright and related rights, the question of limitations and exceptions to these rights emerges with greater emphasis. In the regulation of the protection of rights, not only the interests of owners of rights but also the interests of users and of the public at large should be duly taken into account. The justification for some of the limitations and exceptions may be found, inter alia, in those other branches of the legal system or in the principles of other disciplines which – as discussed above – have a close interface with the intellectual property system.

Under these conditions, the identification of those limitations and exceptions that are truly justified is an important task for copyright researchers and teachers. They should promote the establishment of an appropriate balance of interests. In this context, one quite frequent theoretical error should be avoided; namely, addressing the issues of limitations and exceptions in such a way that copyright and related rights as pure private rights are confronted with "public interests." This is a theoretical error since an adequate protection of copyright and related rights, due to its indispensable role in promoting the creation and dissemination of valuable works and other productions, is also important to the public interest. Therefore, in the future consideration of such issues, it should be seen that, when it comes to the balancing of interests, this public interest associated with the creation and dissemination of valuable works etc., should be balanced with the other public interests (both aspects must also take into account the important private interests involved).

Intellectual property and the protection of rights and interests related to traditional knowledge and folklore

Another result of the growing importance and broadening scope of the broadening application of intellectual property rights is that the protection of rights and interests concerning traditional knowledge and artistic folklore has also received greater attention recently.

Researchers and teachers in the field of intellectual property must avoid any kind of elitism in neglecting as irrelevant these emerging traditional knowledge and artistic folklore issues. There are some indispensable questions which should be dealt with for the sake of establishing a well-balanced system of protection for all aspects of intellectual creativity and inventiveness.

Three aspects deserve particular attention in this area: first, the applicability of existing international, regional and national norms for the protection of traditional knowledge and folklore; second, the possible need for introducing some new forms of protection; and, third, the coexistence of the privileges and interests of members of the communities in which such knowledge and artistic creations have been developed and are maintained, with the rights and interests of those who – through adaptation or further development of the relevant knowledge and creative expressions – may obtain intellectual property rights.

Better harmony between theory and practice

It may be said that intellectual property, including copyright, is too serious a matter to leave it just to professors. This is not a denial of the need for an appropriate theoretical justification of intellectual property, but rather a warning against any idea that intellectual property regulation might be based merely on some deductions from age-old theories and principles. "L'art pour l'art" speculative studies and theory-production (on the basis of a consideration that "although it perfectly works in practice one should check whether it also works in theory") have never been less necessary.

With due respect to the indispensable theoretical foundations of copyright and related rights, research and teaching in this field should have a practical orientation. Pragmatism should not come into conflict with some basic underlying values and principles; however, it is equally important that dogmatism should not create any obstacle to the establishment and operation of workable and well-balanced systems and solutions, in harmony with the interests of both rights owners and users, and of society at large.

Contracts and copyright

Recently, at least at the international level, attention has been paid mainly to the harmonization of substantive norms (on what kinds of objects, what kinds of rights should be granted, with what kinds of limitations and exceptions, and under what kinds of conditions) and to enhancing the effectiveness of the enforcement mechanism. In the teaching programs and research projects, however, great attention should also be devoted to such aspects as the system of contracts, its regulation and practical application.

In this area, the knowledge of researchers and teachers is particularly indispensable, taking into account the fact that the international conventions and treaties on copyright and related rights, in general, do not regulate contractual aspects; therefore, the study and evaluation of the various national contract systems are necessary tasks.

Studies and projects in this field should address such issues as:

(i) the desirable level of contractual freedom, on the one hand, and the possible legislative intervention into some contractual aspects, on the other hand, including the issue of transferability of exclusive rights (it is becoming ever clearer that these issues may not – and should not – be settled through a mere "deductive" method, merely on the basis of some theories, such as the monistic or dualistic theory; a pragmatic approach is needed which takes into account the negotiating strength of the partners in these contracts, the nature of works involved, as well as the object and objective of the contracts);

(ii) standards and best practices in respect of the conclusion of the most important types of contracts;
(iii) the question of the validity, if any, of "stipulating around" the limitations of, and exceptions to, copyright and related rights;
(iv) the question of validity of "shrink-wrap" and "click-on" contracts; and
(v) the various aspects of online licensing, in general.

Collective management of copyright and related rights

Collective management has become recently a frequently applied form of exercising copyright and related rights. It also has an important role in the digital, networked environment.

There are at least three aspects in this field which will deserve attention in teaching programs and research projects. First, the description and categorization of the various collective management schemes (which is in itself a challenging task, taking into account the ever more numerous different forms of management); second, the analysis of the normative issues; namely the issues of compatibility of the various management systems with the international norms and regional and national regulations (in this context, studies should be directed towards, inter alia, in which cases it is allowed to prescribe mandatory collective management of rights, and under what conditions national legislation may provide for an extended effect of collective management); and, third, dealing with the know-how, or how-to-do aspects, that is, with the methodology of the establishment and operation of efficient collective management systems.

Globalization trends

The globalization of the economy, and of trade and information systems, poses major challenges to the copyright system. It is becoming more important than ever that national and regional regulations and institutions should be interoperable. This may be achieved by more intensive harmonization of the relevant norms and/or through appropriate adaptation and application of the principles of private international law.

In the program of WIPO, this recognition is duly reflected. Recent results of various WIPO projects indicate that there is a realistic prospect of achieving this ambitious objective. Also, the kind of international "case law" emerging from the WTO panel findings may contribute to growing harmonization.

Researchers and teachers should not be satisfied with the mere description of the differences that still exist between the various legal systems in the field of intellectual property, in particular between the civil law and common law systems. Efforts must be made to eliminate or, at least, reduce, step by step, dogmatic barriers between these systems, and to effect a true, fundamental harmonization.

In parallel with this, new inventive solutions are needed in the field of private international law (concerning choice of law, applicable law and the recognition and enforcement of "foreign" court decisions, etc.). It seems that, in many of these cases, a functional approach may have a better chance of success than the traditional categorical approach.

Enforcement of rights

One of the important new features of the regulation of intellectual property rights in the TRIPS Agreement is that it also includes detailed norms on the requirements and means of enforcement of rights.

The issues of the application of the enforcement provisions form an important new dimension for research and teaching. This new dimension should extend not only to the theoretical aspects, to the questions of interpretation, and to the different legal means of implementation of the enforcement provisions, but also to the issues of practical application, such as methodology, best practices, investigation tactics and the like.

The questions of the enforcement of intellectual property rights on the Internet and similar future networks will be particularly exciting aspects of enforcement-related studies. Special attention should be devoted to the issues of the liability of service, access and software providers, and, in general, to the questions of contributory liability.

The widening overlap between industrial property and copyright

The differences in the justification – and some basic principles and categories (such as novelty versus originality, idea orientation versus expression orientation, formalities as conditions of protection versus formality free protection) – of industrial property rights, on the one hand, and copyright and related rights, on the other hand, will (and should) certainly survive amidst the accelerating new developments which are impacting intellectual property rights. Differences do and will exist between the various sub-branches of these two basic branches of intellectual property. There are, however, at least two converging trends which deserve special attention.

First, there is a widening borderline area between the two main branches of intellectual property – industrial property and copyright (including related rights) – where both of them may be applied (although not necessarily in the same cases or in the same aspects).

The overlap between the protection of works of applied art and the protection of industrial designs has existed, and has been taken into account, for a long time with quite extensive flexibility at the level of international norms, and with broadly differing national solutions. The new forms of computer-related creations, however, have raised a number of new and, as far as their impact is concerned, much more important overlap issues. The possible double protection of computer programs by patents and by copyright is one of the obvious examples. Recently, the possibility of an overlap has also emerged, at least in theory, in respect of biological (DNS) data.

Second, there is a growing number of common issues of industrial property and copyright. It is sufficient here to refer to the joint regulation of enforcement requirements in the TRIPS Agreement, as well as to the common issues raised by electronic commerce, the Internet, and globalization trends.

As a consequence, one can also see some converging trends in the institutional structure. At the international level, the WTO is an obvious example, but the recent and ongoing institutional reforms of WIPO may equally be considered as a manifestation of this trend. At regional and national level, some organizational changes are also taking place which reflect the recognition of both the importance of intellectual property and the need for a smoother harmonization of strategic planning and political-level decision making with respect to all branches and sub-branches of intellectual property.

In this respect, research and teaching seem to have two tasks: first, to study the conditions and consequences of the coexistence of industrial property and copyright protection, and, where appropriate, to work out legal solutions to avoid certain undesirable consequences (as happened a long time ago concerning the "traditional" overlap between works of applied art and industrial designs); second, to follow developments in the field of institutional convergence and suggest, where necessary, appropriate organizational structures (paying due attention, however, at the same time, to guarantees for maintaining justified differences between the two basic branches of intellectual property).

Developing and least developed countries

The reason for which the problems of these countries are mentioned at the end of this outline of future trends is not that they are regarded as less important. Just the opposite: it is due to the fact that they are of key importance, and because many issues discussed above emerge with even greater emphasis in these countries than in the industrialized countries.

These special aspects need special treatment and special responses if the international community wants to achieve the objective that intellectual property may function appropriately and smoothly in the globalized world. This recognition is fully reflected in the program of WIPO, and it also has an important impact on the WTO negotiations.

Researchers and teachers seem to have a double responsibility in this field. First, they have to identify those special conditions and requirements of developing and least developed countries in respect of copyright rules and institutions which require specific legal and/or economic measures. Second, they have to contribute to the ambitious program of WIPO, and, in particular, the WIPO Academy, to establish research and teaching infrastructures and groups of essential researchers and teachers in (or readily available to) these countries.

Conclusion

In summary, it may be stated that the issues concerning the protection of copyright and related rights have become more complex and also more important from the viewpoint of economic, social and cultural development. The exercise and enforcement of these rights has multiple impacts in respect of many areas of human activities, and therefore, there is a need for a proper balance between the various private and public interests involved. This trend may become even stronger with the spectacular technological developments which we are witnessing, and in particular with the ever more widespread use of global information systems.

The recognition of these trends should have an impact on teaching and research activities, and should result in an increase of time and resources devoted to copyright and related rights in university curricula and research projects.

Selected bibliography

General political and economic aspects

1. Kamil Idris: "Intellectual Property – a Power Tool for Economic Growth," WIPO publication No. 888 and No. CD888
2. Kamil Idris and Hisamitsu Arai: "The Intellectual Property-Conscious Nation: Mapping the Path from Developing to Developed," WIPO publication No. 988
3. Shahid Alikhan: "Socio-Economic Benefits of Intellectual Property Protection in Developing Countries," WIPO publication No. 454
4. "The New Millennium Intellectual Property and the Least Developed Countries" (Compendium of the proceedings of the High-Level Interregional Roundtable on Intellectual Property for the LDCs), WIPO publication No. 766
5. Dimiter Gantchev (ed.): "Guide on Surveying the Economic Contribution of the Copyright-Based Industries," WIPO publication No. 893
6. "WIPO Intellectual Property Handbook: Policy, Law and Use," WIPO publication No. 489

Treaties, records, guides

7. Mihály Ficsor: "Guide to the Copyright and Related Rights Treaties Administered by WIPO and Glossary of Copyright and Related Rights Terms," WIPO publication No. 891
8. Berne Convention for the Protection of Literary and Artistic Works, WIPO publication No. 287
9. "Records of the Intellectual Property Conference of Stockholm," WIPO publication No. 311
10. Arpad Bogsch: "1886 – Berne Convention Centenary – 1986," WIPO publication No. 877
11. Claude Masouyé: "Guide to the Berne Convention" (1978), WIPO publication No. 615
12. Mihály Ficsor: "Guide to the Substantive Provisions of the Berne Convention" (2003), in WIPO publication No. 891
13. Rome Convention – International Convention for the Protection of Performers, Producers of Phonograms and Broadcasting Organizations, WIPO publication No. 328
14. Claude Masouyé: "Guide to the Rome Convention" (1981), in WIPO publication No. 617
15. Mihály Ficsor: "Guide to the Substantive Provisions of the Rome Convention" (2003), in WIPO publication No. 891

16. Convention for the Protection of Producers of Phonograms Against Unauthorized Duplication of Their Phonograms, WIPO publication No. 288
17. Claude Masouyé: "Guide to the Phonograms Convention" (1981), in WIPO publication No. 617
18. Mihály Ficsor: "Guide to the Substantive Provisions of the Phonograms Convention" (2003), in WIPO publication No. 891
19. Agreement on Trade-Related Aspects of Intellectual Property Rights, in WIPO publication No. 223
20. "Implications of the TRIPS Agreement on Treaties Administered by WIPO," WIPO publication No. 464
21. "Records of the Diplomatic Conference on Certain Copyright and Neighboring Rights Questions – Geneva 1996," WIPO publication No. 348
22. WIPO Copyright Treaty (WCT), WIPO publication No. 226
23. Mihály Ficsor: "Guide to the Substantive Provisions of the WCT," in WIPO publication No. 891
24. WIPO Performances and Phonograms Treaty (WPPT), WIPO publication No. 227
25. Mihály Ficsor: "Guide to the Substantive Provisions of the WPPT," in WIPO publication No. 891

Major international symposiums and forums

26. "WIPO Worldwide Symposium on the Intellectual Property Aspects of Artificial Intelligence" (Stanford University, 1991), WIPO publication No. 698
27. "WIPO Worldwide Symposium on the Impact of Digital Technology on Copyright and Related Rights" (Harvard University, 1993), WIPO publication No. 723
28. "WIPO Worldwide Symposium on the Future of Copyright and Neighboring Rights" (Paris, 1994), WIPO publication No. 731
29. "WIPO Worldwide Symposium on Copyright in the Global Information Infrastructure" (Mexico City, 1994), WIPO publication No. 764
30. "WIPO World Forum on the Protection of Intellectual Creations in the Information Society" (Naples, 1995), WIPO publication No. 751
31. "WIPO World Symposium on Broadcasting, New Communication Technologies and Intellectual Property" (Manila, 1997), WIPO publication No. 757
32. "WIPO International Forum on the Exercise and Management of Copyright and Neighboring Rights in the Face of the Challenges of Digital Technology" (Seville, 1997), WIPO publication No. 756
33. WIPO CD-ROMs of the First and Second International Conference on Electronic Commerce and Intellectual Property (Geneva, 1999 and 2001), WIPO publication No. CD772

Folklore/traditional cultural expressions

34. "UNESCO-WIPO World Forum on the Protection of Folklore" (Phuket, 1997), WIPO publication No. 758
35. "Intellectual Property Needs and Expectations of Traditional Knowledge Holders," WIPO publication No. 768
36. "Consolidated Analysis of the Legal Protection of Traditional Cultural Expressions/Expression of Folklore," WIPO publication No. 758

Exercise, management and enforcement of rights

37. I. Fred Koenigsberg, Lois F. Wasoff, Bert Sugayan, Howard M. Frumes, Tomohiro Tohyama, Pravin Anand, Mihály Ficsor and Nils Bortloff: "WIPO Guide on the Licensing of Copyright and Related Rights," WIPO publication No. 897
38. Mihály Ficsor: "Collective Management of Copyright and Related Rights," WIPO publication No. 855
39. David Vaver, Pierre Sirinelli and Hossam Loutfi: "Principles of Copyright: Cases and Materials," WIPO publication No. 844
40. Louis T. Harms: "The Enforcement of Intellectual Property Rights: a Case Book," WIPO publication No. 791

4

Teaching trademark law

JEREMY PHILLIPS

Introduction

A personal note

In common with most teachers of trademark law who belong to my generation, I did not have the benefit of formal instruction in the subject. I was, however, fortunate to experience trademarks in many different ways. As a consumer, I have relied on the information conveyed by trademarks when making my purchase decisions. I have published *Trademark World* magazine and have been threatened with legal proceedings for trademark infringement. I have edited the *European Trademark Reports* and written *Trademark Law: a Practical Anatomy*. During brief spells out of academe, I was responsible for protecting and enforcing a trademark for food preparations and also gained first-hand experience of trademark creation when I worked for a branding consultancy. As a law teacher, I have studied both the theory and practice of trademark law, noting the points at which it borders other legal subjects (e.g. unfair competition, copyright, competition law) and non-legal subjects (e.g. economics, psychology, management studies).

It may be helpful to list here the range of trademark law teaching that I have carried out. My target audiences have included fully qualified, part-qualified and trainee lawyers and trademark attorneys; OHIM[1] staff; groups of trademark owners and groups of employees drawn from a single trademark owner; newspaper publishers; and postgraduate and undergraduate students. Topics taught range from the mundane (registrability, infringement, opposition) through the speculative (need for law reform, the predicted consequences of new laws) to the relatively exotic (trademarks and freedom of speech, securitization and brand valuation). The

---

[1] Office for Harmonization in the Internal Market (the European Community's trademark and design-granting office based in Alicante, Spain).

takeaway message from this is that it can never be assumed that "one size fits all." The law may remain the same, whoever you teach it to, but the way you get it across will depend on the intellectual capacity, the level of interest, the linguistic skills and the functional needs of each member of your class.

My trademark teaching and training activities in the past three decades are no guarantee that my observations in this chapter are going to be applicable for all readers in the future. But I can say that they form a corpus of experience that has enabled me to draw distinctions between different issues in trademark law teaching that might not have occurred to me, had I contemplated the subject only in the abstract. My track record has equally qualified me to recognize errors of judgment that might have been avoided, if my attention had only been directed to the advice that this chapter contains.

I am grateful for the broad perspective that these experiences have given me and for the opportunity that WIPO has given me to distil my thoughts on trademark teaching into a chapter of this book.

What is your aim as a teacher?

A teacher may think he is teaching trademark law, but that is wrong. He is teaching people. The relationship of teacher to pupil is one in which the teacher opens up a subject so that the pupil can understand it, by sharing his expertise in the subject and by holding nothing back; the pupil in turn gives the teacher his attention, his trust and his respect. The teacher imparts a set of values, skills and perspectives, regardless of whether the subject of study is trademark law or anything else. If the teacher is successful, the pupil will be able to stand in the teacher's place; he will be empowered in the subject of study; and he will reflect the values which, through the refracting prism of the syllabus, the teacher imparts.

The fact that teaching is becoming a commodity rather than a face-to-face exercise, with distance learning and internet-driven classes a reality, does not lessen the obligation of the teacher, any more than it diminishes the desire of the pupil to learn. It just makes successful teaching more difficult to achieve. In the light of these obligations, the methodology of teaching trademark law is a subject whose time has come.

Not a solitary pursuit

Trained specialist trademark law teachers are few in number. Whatever be the reasons for this, it is a fact that in many jurisdictions it is unusual for a teacher of trademark law to have the benefit of advice from a colleague who teaches the same subject. Indeed, even within some countries in which there is an active trademark law culture, teachers of the subject may be isolated by factors such as local geography, lack of necessary research materials and pressures imposed by other commitments. Many trademark law teachers are full-time legal practitioners who take time out from practice in order to explain their subject to students; they may never have had the opportunity of discussing how best this teaching is done, particularly if their teaching is done outside normal office hours and they do not encounter teaching colleagues at all.

There is, however, some scope for trademark law teachers to come together and share their experiences. The International Association for the Advancement of Teaching and Research in Intellectual Property Law[2] (ATRIP) holds an annual conference at which people with an active interest in intellectual property teaching can discuss topics of mutual interest. Although the content of the conference sessions reflects issues in substantive intellectual property law and theory, the meeting provides a forum for informal networking between colleagues. The International Trademark Association (INTA)[3], a far larger organization and one which is more driven by commercial and professional imperatives, has also recently formed groupings for academics who participate in trademark law teaching; these groupings supplement that organization's long-standing involvement in training and education for trademark professionals, including both practicing lawyers and paralegals. While it is too early to predict how much advantage trademark law teachers will be able to derive from INTA involvement, that organization's efforts and enthusiasm to integrate academic trademark law professors within its community are manifest.

Some golden rules for teaching

The most important rule in teaching trademarks (or anything else, for that matter) is this: do not start off by calculating what you can put into your classes. Rather, begin by calculating what your class can absorb, then

---

[2] The activities of this organisation are listed on the ATRIP website: www.atrip.org/default.htm.

[3] Details of this organisation, originally founded as the United States Trademark Association (USTA) as long ago as 1878, can be found in its website at www.inta.org/. INTA retains a predominantly United States-based membership but is increasingly reaching out to other jurisdictions.

work back from there and decide what you can select for your instructional material. You can construct the most intellectually cogent, conceptually succinct, dramatically stimulating and witty trademark training program in the world – but every word of it that your students do not understand is lost forever, a waste of your effort in preparing it and a waste of their effort in trying to absorb it.

Because trademarks are, in any consumer-led society, so much a part of everyday life, it is easy to assume a greater degree of knowledge of trademark law on the part of one's audience than they possess. The opposite is, however, more likely to be true: even people who work within a trademark environment often have what they recognize as alarming gaps in their knowledge, but they are often slow to ask for help or explanation, fearing that any confession of ignorance or lack of understanding will be met with exclamations of ridicule or surprise. The teaching of trademark law should, therefore, make the audience comfortable with the notions of asking questions, seeking elucidation and obtaining guidance. In this respect, distance learning confers advantages over classroom teaching: the element of personal embarrassment or reticence is eliminated where the student can repeatedly access the same materials and take as long in perusing them as is necessary for their absorption and comprehension.

In classroom teaching, however, once the audience is able to ask questions and respond to answers, the teaching has become an interactive process that places a heavy burden upon the teacher. He can no longer take refuge behind the lectern, hide behind his slides or refuse to budge from the text he has prepared. No teacher can expect to prepare for every unexpected question or enquiry that comes his way. He can, however, feel confident that the very fact that he has provoked a response from his audience means that he has established some sort of relationship with them.

Challenges posed by the subject

Over-familiarity with the subject matter

Every subject poses its own problems and trademark law is no exception. Many subjects, in intellectual property law as anywhere else, are difficult to comprehend because of their remoteness. Any lawyer who has ever struggled to read materials concerning patent disputes in the bio-sciences or the details of computer circuitry and software code will know this from painful experience of trying to apply the law – which he knows and understands – to facts that are as unfamiliar to him as the dark side of the moon and which are couched in terms too recent to be included in his dictionary.

Trademark law poses the opposite problem: its subject-matter is almost too familiar. This is because, in consumer economies, almost the entire population consists of consumers who rely on trademarks daily, who favor some over others in making apparently illogical decisions (such as purchasing a more expensive branded product in preference to its identical unbranded competitor). In economies that are not driven by consumer choice, the rationale for trademark law may, however, seem esoteric and incomprehensible.[4]

The problem of familiarity is acute in trademark infringement and opposition proceedings, in which the arbiter may be called upon to exercise a degree of self-discipline when applying the law, so as not to substitute his intuitive response as a consumer for his technically more sophisticated response as a legal expert. There is no guaranteed solution to this problem, although the trademark lawyer who is reminded of it often enough will be sensitized to its existence and thus better equipped to deal with it.

Conceptualization and complexity of the law

At its simplest level, trademark law is a subject that is accessible to everyone. To understand why goods are marked with signs, why two or more businesses cannot use the same sign for the same goods or services, why it is not a good idea for those signs to be very similar to one another, why you should not be able to stop someone using a sign if you have it but do not use it yourself, and so on – these are topics that are quite amenable to human understanding.

At the other end of the extreme, doctrines developed by case law, often in response to the interpretational challenges posed by legislative drafting, may not be self-evident: they may be difficult to grasp and even more difficult to apply. Anyone who, having considered the extremely simple factual situations that form the basis for typical trademark

---

[4] Attending a conference on trademark law in Moscow during the late Communist era, the author remembers the bemused response of many Russian participants to the proposition that it was either necessary or desirable to mark biscuits with different trademarks to indicate their origin if they were effectively the same product in the first place.

litigation, is faced with what might be upwards of a hundred paragraphs of dense textual reasoning, might well consider that trademark law is too conceptually complex a topic to be opened up for all. The significance of this point is that, since conceptually complex issues can be so difficult to comprehend in the abstract, a teacher must be prepared to make repeated reference to simple factual examples that support or illustrate his arguments.

Striking the balance between teaching and training

There are two poles between which education in trademark law extends. One represents teaching – the process of imparting a degree of understanding of the way trademark law operates, its conceptual parameters and its corpus of legislative and jurisprudential data. The other represents training – the process of imparting a specific skill or set of skills that can be replicated by the person exposed to the necessary techniques. When determining how to communicate trademark law, it is thus necessary to ask first (i) where the balance should lie between these two poles and (ii) how one can attain it.

It should not be thought that teaching and training are mutually exclusive categories. The one is often best consolidated and reinforced by the other. Thus, an academic study in the exclusion of descriptive terms from registrability in the absence of proof of distinctiveness acquired through use may be successfully reinforced by dividing the audience into opposing groups which are given lists of words, shapes or devices: half the groups are "applicants," who must articulate the grounds upon which they consider their mark to be inherently distinctive, while the other half are "examiners," who determine the validity of the grounds made out by the "applicants". This approach, combining the imparting of knowledge with an element of practical application, may be brought to bear on most areas of trademark law, in particular that of trademark licensing in which both the negotiation and drafting of a contract and its legality and parameters can be subjected to scrutiny and examination.

Identification of target audience

The correct identification of the target audience for trademark law teaching is vital. This is because there exist so many clearly identifiable interest groups and stakeholders within the field of trademarks. These include trademark practitioners, trademark owners, trademark administrators and trademark ancillary service providers, as well as students and even school children.

Trademark legal practitioners

Trademark legal practitioners may themselves be divided between fully qualified lawyers and those who practice within the field of trademark law with specialist trademark qualifications or as paralegals. While there are substantial areas of overlap between their respective roles, their perspectives and professional ethos may make quite different demands in terms of teaching requirements. Fully qualified lawyers, for example, are expected to give advice and exercise both professional and commercial judgment in areas that are peripheral to the "core" of trademark work, such as the restructuring of a corporation's intellectual property holdings and licensing schemes that will make it less vulnerable to double taxation or withholding tax, while paralegals often need to take swift and sound decisions on matters such as how to respond to an official action in an ongoing dispute before the local trademark registry.

Essentially, the skills of trademark legal practitioners can be divided as follows:

Trademark prosecution work. Into this category fall such topics as filing trademark applications, oppositions, applications for amendment, revocation or cancellation of a trademark, applications for extensions to official deadlines and the like. Collectively, activities such as these may be regarded as "office actions," since the practitioner provides the link between a client and the mechanisms of the trademark registry or granting office. Practitioners in this category may typically have many actions ongoing at the same time, each of which frequently needs attention, often to matters of procedural detail.

The training of people working in this field will frequently be focused as much on the daily practices of the national or regional trademark office as on the black letter of the law as laid down in primary or secondary legislation. There is much justification for this. A statute might say that a trademark may not be registered if it is a term in common use within trade circles, but it is crucially what a trademark examiner is trained to say is "common use within trade circles" that will determine whether the vast majority of unchallenged decisions of trademark examiners lead to registration or rejection of any given application. A further area of training lies in the field of file management, a subject that is best not undertaken by anyone who has not been exposed to the flow of work that has to be managed.

Trademark litigation. This category is not entirely separate from that under the previous heading, since contested office actions that are not resolved at the level of the national or regional registry may be appealed to the highest judicial or administrative courts, at which point the specialist skills of a litigation lawyer may be joined to those of the prosecution lawyer, or may replace them entirely. The work of the trademark litigator will include trademark infringement actions, proceedings to enforce a trademark license or to challenge its validity, as well as applications for the discovery of evidence, for the preservation of evidence pending a trial, for the stay of one set of proceedings until another has been dealt with, as well as actions involving the suspensive detention of suspected counterfeit or infringing goods, and the establishment of criminal liability in respect of many types of commercial infringement. Unlike those involved in prosecution, litigation lawyers rarely need an intimate knowledge of office (i.e. registry) practice unless they are challenging its validity.

Even in sophisticated jurisdictions that provide fertile ground for specialization, litigation lawyers do not tend to specialize in trademark litigation alone. Most will deal with other areas of intellectual property and often areas of commercial or regulatory law that are quite separate from it. Teaching and training for this audience will often, therefore, require the teacher to possess wide peripheral knowledge of litigation procedures and strategies in general.

Trademark exploitation. This category of practice includes the negotiation and drafting of trademark licenses, distribution agreements and merchandising contracts. Other forms of trademark exploitation that have developed their own expertise, terminology and templates include event and activity sponsorships, business format franchising, product placements, celebrity endorsements and television program format licenses. Further, still developing additions to this list include the outsourcing (or offshoring) of the manufacture of goods and the provision of financial services.

Specialists in this category often term their work "non-contentious," since it is not viewed as being directly related to "contentious" issues such as trademark infringement or the challenge to another mark's validity. This terminology is misleading, since the work of such practitioners often embraces the negotiation of terms that settle an ongoing dispute or seek to prevent the resurrection of a dispute which has been previously settled, not to mention the renegotiation of licenses so as to prevent one or both parties being in breach of them. In other words, this work includes the consensual resolution of contentious issues.

The teaching and training of trademark exploitation practitioners is often most effective when it is tackled by reference to the particular industrial sector rather than in terms of its legal content. Thus, fast-food business format franchise contracts provide the most vivid training materials for those who deal in that sector, while they may be difficult to cope with for those working in sectors such as windshield replacement or domestic drain unblocking services – even though the law is the same in each instance.

Trademark housekeeping. Often regarded as menial work, fit only for trainee lawyers or paralegals, trademark housekeeping is vitally important. It involves keeping track, within the context of any commercial enterprise, of (i) the number of trademarks registered; (ii) the classes of goods or services for which they are registered; (iii) the nature of the use, if any, that has been made of each registered trademark; (iv) the date(s) of such use; (v) any variations between the trademark as registered and as used, in terms of the mark itself and between the classes for which it has been registered and those for which it has been used; (vi) any licenses granted in trademarks, and to whom; and (vii) any tolerated unlicensed use.

The skills of good housekeeping become extremely important where, for example, a business is acquiring the assets of another, including its trademark portfolio, and needs to know if it can expect to receive what it has offered to pay for. Training in due diligence is therefore required if these tasks are to be performed properly.

Trademark strategists. There remain a number of high level roles that may be fulfilled by trademark lawyers, sometimes acting as independent lawyers but often serving as senior directors of a trading corporation. These roles include determining whether to deploy intellectual property, including trademarks, in the securitization of assets; the decision whether to extend a successful brand from one product or service to another; where to locate a parent company or intellectual property holding company within a tax-efficient jurisdiction, and so on. At present, it is probably fair to say that most of these roles are not viewed as part of the normal portfolio of skills that a trademark practitioner would be expected to display. They would thus fall outside the scope of his regular teaching or training.

In small and less economically active jurisdictions, the same person may be regularly called upon to demonstrate skill and expertise in many or all of the areas listed above, while in the more advanced, complex economies of the most highly developed countries, each of these areas is likely to be an area of specialization in its own right.

Trademark owners

The educational needs of trademark owners (and, more importantly, their employees) are often neglected, for a variety of reasons. Many businesses with well-established trademark portfolios have developed their own in-house systems for processing and dealing with trademarks; operative knowledge of these systems may be transmitted to employees as part of their corporate culture. In such an environment, a person may become skilled in the performance of his employment duties without ever obtaining a more rounded comprehension of the operation and the potential of the system of which he is part.

A second reason why the education of trademark owners is neglected is that it is difficult to generalize a teaching or training approach to a subject in which there may be wide practical or commercial differences between economic sectors. Thus, the role of trademarks in the pharmaceutical industry (where the use of trademarks is heavily regulated and they must coexist with generic terms and international non-proprietary names) is quite different from that of trademarks in fields such as wines and spirits (where issues involving geographical indications and appellations arise) and the fashion, leisure or tobacco industries.

Trademark system administrators

Administrators of the trademark system also require instruction, but of a very different order from that needed by private practitioners or trademark owners. Given that the performance of their functions will of necessity be at an operational level that takes events forward within a national or supranational trademark-granting authority, administrators demand a familiarity with subordinate legislation that implements and fleshes out the details of statutory trademark law that goes above and beyond that of regular practitioners.

Two things can be said of this target audience. First, it is unusual to find a teacher from outside the trademark administration who possesses the degree of knowledge and familiarity with those elements that fall within the special duties which administrators perform. Secondly, in the case of trademark examiners, there exists an extra level of functionality to be attained: teaching of basic principles and training in how to apply them must result in the largest number of examiners reaching the same conclusion in the application of any set of facts to the law on the largest number of occasions. If that functionality is not achieved, the fate of a trademark application, an opposition or an application for cancellation will appear to depend on the personal whim of the administrator who is processing the matter.

Trademark ancillary service providers

When attending large gatherings of the trademark fraternity, such as the annual meeting of the International Trademark Association, it is difficult not to be struck by the very large number of people in attendance who neither own trademarks nor practice trademark law. These include providers of brand creation services, trademark search services for newly created marks, watch (monitoring) services for detecting potentially conflicting later marks, infringement insurance agencies and underwriters, trademark management software, trademark renewal services, licensing and marketing consultancy advice, and online and paper-based trademark law.

The common factor shared by all of these disparate services is not solely their dependence on the trademark-based industries and professions for their work, but also their knowledge of trademark law. Yet they are generally not trademark lawyers and have no training or education as such. Curiously, while they require training in order to discharge their own functions, they are frequently of great use in enhancing the training of others. Thus, the interaction of trademark watch experts with trademark lawyers may enable the latter to gain a large degree of understanding as to how and why the proprietor of an earlier mark is prompted into challenging an attempt to register a later mark that may on its face seem to pose little threat to it.

The judiciary

Judges also need to know how to deal with trademark law, if they are to provide an acceptable outcome for disputes that they are required to resolve. On this basis, special courses in trademark law have been organized for members of the judiciary in a number of new entrants and candidate countries seeking admission to the European Union. These countries include Bulgaria, Latvia and Turkey.

While there is no doubt that judges need to know the law and to understand it before they can give rulings in a specific instance, it may be asked whether the training of judges, in the abstract, will be of any direct benefit when, at a later stage, they have a dispute to resolve. The fact that judges are selected for training in this field suggests that there is little skill, expertise or knowledge in intellectual property in the jurisdiction concerned. That being so, teaching and training are unlikely to be sourced from that country and thus contain mainly elements of generalized trademark law that is not country-specific, or the details of the trademark law of foreign countries whose laws they will not be able to apply. In situations such as this, it may be that the training of judges in trademark law is not intended to boost the legal ability of the judiciary but to give foreign investors confidence that trademark-based investments will be well protected.

The police and other criminal enforcement agencies

It is frequently forgotten by intellectual property teachers at all levels that a significant proportion of trademark law consists of criminal provisions that are aimed against those who perpetrate commercial infringements and those who abet them. In most jurisdictions, crimes relating to intellectual property are accorded very low priority by enforcement agencies which, perennially under-resourced, must tackle homicide, terrorism, organized theft and robbery with violence before they deal with counterfeits and unauthorized replication of trademarks. A further handicap to the enforcement of criminal provisions relating to intellectual property lies in the perception by police agencies that infringements of these rights are more properly matters to be brought before the civil courts.

It is apparent from the foregoing that the education of the police, together with the training of civil servants and local government employees who are responsible for enforcing trading standards and market regulations, is an aspect of trademark law teaching for which a need has not been fully perceived.

Students

Since most university students come into contact with trademark law as an academic discipline, it is unsurprising that their view of the subject is conditioned by such arbitrary and unrealistic items as the contents of the examinable syllabus, the suitability of topics for essays or to be answered in examinations, and the pressure of time under which their study is undertaken. For this reason, most law students who are exposed to trademark law will know a great deal about the criteria of distinctiveness, this being a subject that has generated clearly articulated principles, easily memorable case law and a lively, accessible literature. In contrast, very few law students will come away from their studies with more than a distant acquaintance with topics such as trademark licensing which, despite their great commercial importance, appear as little more than adjuncts to regular contract law and which have spawned little literature that appeals to students. Other topics are generally viewed as being quite outside the scope of study: brand valuation and the securitization of intellectual property rights, for example.

Not all university students who encounter trademarks do so as law students. Over the past two decades, there has been a slow but gradual trend towards introducing trademarks to non-law students who are engaged in degree studies in subjects such as Business Studies, Management Studies, Marketing, Leisure and Entertainment Studies. Trademark law may even feature in rudimentary form as a component of an intellectual property module for students in subjects such as Engineering or Computer Science. In such circumstances, exposure to principles of trademark law will be brief and superficial: their purpose is not to empower the student to resolve problems but rather to let him know if he has a problem so that he can seek professional assistance in resolving it.

School children

Trademark law is probably the component of intellectual property law that is most easily capable of being grasped by children in brand-conscious societies. At present, there is little attempt to introduce trademark law into the school syllabus and this is likely to remain the case for as long as priorities such as the acquisition of literacy, numeracy and social skills continue to prove so troublesome.

The general public

The popularization of intellectual property, together with institutions such as World Intellectual Property Day, has served not so much as an education device in itself as a peg upon which to hang educational devices and events. The potential for exploitation of this day is beyond the scope of this chapter, but it should not be ignored.

Subject matter of the curriculum

I have listed below a loose and approximate ranking of trademark law topics, in which the categories might be described as reflecting a descending order of importance. This ranking is to be regarded as a general statement of probability that an acquired skill or piece of knowledge within the field of trademark law will be valuable; it should not be taken as governing any specific situation or teaching/training requirement. Thus, knowledge of the criteria of registrability is not a priority for someone who needs to acquire the skills of due diligence; likewise, a deep understanding of the mechanics of licensing law will be of little concern to a scholar or practitioner whose main interest is the trademark common and the protection of publicly available words against the encroachment of private rights.

Matters of core significance

- Sources of trademark law at international, regional and domestic levels;
- Definition of a trademark;
- Concept of registrability; criteria of registration; grounds for opposing registration and for cancellation of marks registered;
- Frameworks for the registration of trademarks (national, regional and international processes);
- Infringement and relief against infringement;
- The use of trademarks in comparative advertising;
- The significance of a trademark being unused, little used, well-used or famous;
- Trademark dispute resolution mechanisms (office proceedings; court litigation; arbitration; mediation);
- Transactions involving trademarks: assignment, licensing, mortgages etc.;
- Specific types of trademark transactions [in outline only]: franchising, character and event merchandising, event and activity sponsorship, product endorsement;
- Systems for the registration and protection of domain names;
- Protection of trademarks other than through the trademark system: the relevance of copyright, design right, unfair competition, passing-

off, slavish imitation, unfair market practices, privacy and publicity rights etc.;
- Trends in domestic and international trademark law reform.

Matters of secondary significance

- Registration and protection of company names (as distinct from either trademarks or names under which companies actually trade);
- Protection of geographical indications and of appellations relating to a product's qualities rather than its origins;
- Specific types of trademark transactions [in detail]: franchising, character and event merchandising, event and activity sponsorship, product endorsement, product placement;
- The interface between trademark law and competition law;
- Trademark record-keeping;
- Due diligence;
- Trademark search and monitoring of new applications;
- The legal and cultural history of trademark protection.

Matters of peripheral significance to trademark practitioners in that they fall more properly within the expertise of other professions

- Brand management issues such as disaster management following a product recall;
- Management of international trademark disputes;
- The use of product security technologies such as holograms, lasers and DNA as a means of detecting whether products are genuine or counterfeit;
- Marketing techniques such as brand extension;
- Taxation issues arising from transactions involving the assignment or licensing of a trademark by itself or with other accompanying intellectual property rights;
- Extraction of commercially significant information from the trademark register and from official publications;
- Creating a brand and imbuing it with a particular ethos; brand psychology.

My preference would be for the use of this list as a convenient checklist against which trademark law teachers can measure (i) the content of their courses and (ii) the relative weighting of different topics.

Approaches and methods to teaching in this area

There are probably as many valid ways of teaching trademark law as there are people who are committed to teaching it; and there are as many reasons for demanding the study and evaluation of how trademark law is taught as there are people who seek to study it.

At all levels, I have favored the employment of an empirical approach, not as a substitute for classroom teaching or written exercises but as a supplement to it. Later in this chapter, I describe some of my experiences with field trips, a teaching method that is labor-intensive and effective only for small groups but which yields rich returns in terms of stimulating student interest and fixing in the mind of participants the lessons that are learned through them. The field trip is not, however, the only form of empirical instruction. I also discuss the use of random collections of items with trademark significance: these can be potent in the acting out of role-playing exercises in which one student is the "lawyer" while the others are clients, each bearing an object and asking questions regarding problems in its exploitability.

Materials, references, cases and other sources of assistance

While all trademark law teachers are agreed that it is necessary for their audience to gain exposure to teaching materials, there is less consensus as to what those materials should be. Most practitioners' reference works and student texts are specific to the jurisdiction for which they have been prepared, while books that focus on international or generalized propositions of trademark law can be unhelpful for the teacher who wishes to identify a pedagogic aid that is country-specific.

This chapter will not discuss text books in the field of intellectual property in general, or trademark law in particular. The list of books is large; their tendency to grow out of date quickly is not a slight to the slow rate at which they are prepared for publication but a compliment to the speed with which the courts, legislators and litigants respond to new issues, leaving a trail of fresh case law and innovative concepts in their wake. Suffice it to say that every trademark law teacher, including this author, will have his preferred texts and will be unlikely to amend those preferences after reading anything written here.

The comments that follow can only be of a general nature. Readers will be sure to supplement them with their own preferences, based on their own experiences.

Official materials

Many trademark granting authorities now operate websites that provide access to basic law, the answers to so-called Frequently Asked Questions (FAQs),[5] the full text of official decisions concerning trademark applications, oppositions and cancellations, links to other useful information sources and so on. International organizations such as the World Intellectual Property Organization and the World Trade Organization, together with arbitral bodies such as the Internet Corporation for Assigned Names and Numbers (ICANN) do likewise. Much of the information available is prepared on the basis that it must be accessible to the population at large rather than specialist lawyers; where this is the case, it will be generally readable if somewhat simplistic.

Other extremely useful material provided at official level includes the guidance issued by trademark granting bodies for the benefit of their examiners. The function of examiners' manuals may be to ensure that all examiners within the same office adopt a consistent approach when considering issues such as the distinctive character of slogans, colors or common surnames, but the great value of these documents is in demonstrating to students the gap that may exist between how the courts apply the law – in the relatively rare circumstance that a case is litigated – and the way the same law is applied in applications and in opposition hearings before administrative officials.

Materials of this nature are not made available for the specific purpose of teaching. The trademark law teacher cannot therefore use them without providing adequate guidance as to how to use them and what, if any, is their degree of interface with other materials.

Non-official materials

The main sources in this category are weblogs, often highly idiosyncratic chronological postings on easy-to-use websites of case law, comments, criticisms and the like. On the positive side, material posted on weblogs can refresh and update the content of text books, lecturers' notes and slow-moving official websites; some material is hyperlinked to sources that verify the material posted on the weblog. On the negative side, the material is generally unreferenced and sometimes unreliable, often

---

[5] In my experience FAQs as a genre frequently reflect the information that an institution would like to be asked, rather than the questions it actually receives.

opinionated and may be unbalanced. Trademark law teachers will familiarize themselves with weblogs that they feel confident with as teaching aids.[6] Some university law schools have created their own intellectual property weblogs,[7] the content of which is often of good quality.

Field trips

My experiences in regard to field trips have demonstrated that they can highlight points that are sometimes difficult to appreciate when encountered only in print, on screen or across a lectern.

There is no typical format for a field trip, but I have found that the following points suggest how best they can be deployed:

Select a suitable site to visit. I have taken students of trademark law to venues varying in size from a small store selling basic foodstuffs, stationery and general provisions on-campus for the benefit of a residential community of university staff and students, to a major department store with several thousand meters of shopping floor-space spread across many storeys. In each case, it is necessary to check out the site prior to the field trip and note the range and nature of its stock.

Prepare relevant questions in advance. In my experience, field trips have enabled trademark students to appreciate the similarities between leading brands and me-too products (particularly where the packaging and style of market leaders are reflected in the own-brand goods bearing the retail outlet's own trademark). Other points that can be illustrated are how features of shape and color that are apparently distinctive, when a branded product is viewed in isolation, are recognized as being common within a particular sector.

Allow the students to work in small groups. By giving out sheets of questions and letting them work on them together, field trips encourage students to articulate their own answers among their peers, thus gaining confidence in their ability to express their reasoning. If possible, instances which have resulted in different groups coming up with different answers

---

[6] Within the field of trademarks, mention may be made of the following US-based weblogs, the Trademark Blog (www.schwimmerlegal.com/), Likelihood of Confusion (www.likelihoodofconfusion.com/), IP Watchdog (www.ipwatchdog.com/), the Shape Blog (www.shapeblog.com/) and the TTABlog (http://thettablog.blogspot.com/). Other sites that currently contain information regarding trademarks and names include the IPKat (http://ipkitten.blogspot.com), Markenbusinessnews (www.markenbusiness.com/) and Domain Name/Nom de Domaine! (http://domaine.blogspot.com/).

[7] Law School-based IP weblogs include the Berkeley Intellectual Property Weblog (www.biplog.com/) and the Pierce IP Law Center Blog (http://ipnewsblog.com/).

to the same questions can be "saved" and used for class discussion on a later occasion.

Encourage the students to ask questions of the staff. Gentle questioning by students has elicited some information which came to them as a great surprise. For example, in one visit to the luxury goods department of a major department store, my group of student lawyers discovered that sales staff, while wearing badges that identified them as store employees, were actually employed by the brand owners of the displayed goods, rather than the store.

Randomly selected materials

Many trademark teachers have assembled their own private collections of useful teaching objects. These objects need not be fancy. My own collection includes a packet of Wrigley's ORBIT chewing gum, a small mirror with a frame that has been overlaid with crushed COLA-COLA cans, and various (empty) bottles and cartons that have been rescued from the refuse collector. These objects can be passed round class for discussion; an alternative approach is to get participants to open up their purses or empty their pockets for a "show and tell" session. As a matter of principle, I do not use any products that are actual infringements.

The use of such teaching aids is in my opinion most effective towards the end of a course, by which time the audience will know what to look for in terms of trademark protectability, use, infringement and so on.

The cinema

Because of the status of brands (and, by association, trademarks) as cultural icons, vehicles for popular culture may themselves be searched for materials that work well for trademark teaching purposes. A good way of introducing discussion of product placement issues is by watching movies together and spotting the brands. Some movies by their very nature raise intellectual property exploitation issues that should interest the trademark fraternity. Examples include, among fiction works, 'Jerry Maguire' (story of an employee of a sports agency who becomes stricken by his conscience over the commercial exploitation of sports stars)[8] and 'The Truman Show' (an abandoned baby grows up as the unwitting star of a TV program that is dedicated to

---

[8] Details available at www.imdb.com/title/tt0116695/.

product placement and brand advertising).[9] Documentary works include 'Super Size Me' (the exploits of a person whose diet for a period of time consists exclusively of foods prepared by a leading brand of fast-food restaurant that had been criticized for its attitude towards health considerations)[10] and 'The Corporation' (analogizing corporate behavior in, among other respects, the promotion of brands, to psychotic behavior in a human being).[11]

Future Trends

Even without the benefit of a crystal ball or prophetic talent, it is not hard to see that distance-based learning will continue to attract more adherents. For many prospective trademark law students, there is no viable option: the expense and inconvenience of study at one of a small number of centers of academic excellence is an obstacle that cannot be easily surmounted. However, care must be taken to ensure that distance learning is made to act only as a means of enabling the student to understand and appreciate trademark law with all its faults and problems: there is not necessarily one correct answer to every problem, nor indeed one correct position to be taken on any given issue.

It seems inevitable too that trademark- and brand-based professions will continue to provide their own, highly specialized training, focusing less on general principles of law and more upon the acquisition of specific skills. It is hoped that the theory and the practice of trademark law will continue to be able to enrich each other. This will continue to be one of the main challenges faced by trademark law teachers in the coming decades.

Conclusions

There has never been a greater availability of teaching facilities for trademark law, nor a greater supply of teachers and trainers in this field. The availability of the electronic media, the increased flexibility of educational institutions, the need for continued professional training for practitioners and the better education of consumers have combined to raise the general level of consciousness of what a trademark is, as well as

---

[9] Details available at http://en.wikipedia.org/wiki/The_Truman_Show.
[10] Details available at www.supersizeme.com/.
[11] Details available at www.thecorporation.com/.

administrative, commercial and professional competencies in addressing trademark law-related issues.

This chapter is not the last word on the subject. It seeks to open a debate as well as to provide ideas and possible solutions. I very much look forward to that debate being continued as the next generation of trademark law students, and their teachers, comes forward to face the future.

5

Teaching industrial design law

WILLIAM T. FRYER III

I. Introduction to teaching industrial design registration law

Industrial design registration law, also known as design patent law, are important parts of intellectual property (IP) protection. An IP law survey course usually teaches industrial design registration law after the patent law topic, since there is a close relation between these areas of law. In addition, trademark, copyright and unfair competition law may included some industrial design protection law. Several industry specific laws fit into the broad industrial design law category.

An alternative and sound approach to introducing IP law is to start with teaching industrial design law. Many of the basic IP law concepts and principles can be introduced in a coordinated and focused manner this way. The products used in these explanations will be familiar to persons who are not skilled in science and engineering. Those who have a science or engineering background will develop a broader understanding of IP law from this approach. This chapter will illustrate how industrial design law fits into each of the main areas of IP law. It will provide an outline for teaching industrial design law to introduce the main forms of IP law, as well as an introduction to teaching industrial design law in an IP survey course.

A unique feature of this chapter is that it starts with an international view, to study industrial design registration law. Teachers can develop their teaching outlines tailored to their country's international agreements obligations to protect industrial designs. These international requirements set the minimum standards a country has to follow. This international view also brings into focus the recommended international standards that may not be required, but which are widely followed. Often, these standards are suggested in international agreements. These optional international standards facilitate international harmonization.

The international view of industrial design registration protection has another advantage. It allows use of an international comparative law teaching approach. The selected national laws can be studied, to make clearer the advantages and limitations of the national system in a teacher's country.

Extensive resources for teachers are available on the Internet. This chapter includes citations to and explanations of how to use key Internet resources. With this support, teachers will be able to access current, essential materials to teach industrial design law.

Teaching suggestions are included throughout the chapter. These ideas are drawn from the author's experience. There are many ways to incorporate examples from local and national products and businesses to demonstrate how industrial design law is important to the economy.

The recommended outline for teaching industrial design law begins in the next section, with the introduction of "What industrial design is".

II. What industrial design is

A. *The industrial design aspects of a basket*

In general terms, a product has two primary roles. The function of a basket, for example, is to hold fruit while the basket is carried by a person on a ladder picking fruit, or while walking. Certain features make the basket capable of serving this function. At the same time, baskets have many shapes and there are patterns on baskets, making the baskets more visually attractive. It is a fact that the better the product appearance, the more likely that the basket will be purchased. People like to have products that are pleasant to see as well as effective to use.

The fact that product function and appearance features are interrelated is a key concept of industrial design registration law. It is said that in industrial design form follows function. This statement means that there may be functional parts that create the industrial design appearance. Many product shapes can be used to carry out the same utilitarian function, such as for the basket discussed above. The functions that are necessary for a product to work effectively are generally identified as "primarily functional," or "solely functional". In some legal opinions the phrase is shortened to functional, but the intended meaning is to isolate those features in the appearance that are necessary for a product to perform its utilitarian function. It is a major step in understanding industrial design registration law to be able to separate what features are primarily functional, and the features that serve to improve the product appearance and that are not primary utilitarian functional. A few examples will help illustrate these basic concepts.

The basket discussed above needs a side or rim to prevent fruit from rolling out of the basket. The basket rim and bottom combination in a general form is a primarily functional design, and it cannot be protected by industrial design law. It is the purpose of patents or utility models to protect this primarily functional combination. The use of the term "patent" is in the generally accepted international meaning, which is limited to technology inventions. In some countries, the term "patent" has other names, such as in the US, where technology type patents are called utility patents.

When a handle is added to carry a basket, this feature, in combination with the bottom and side, is another example of a patent or utility model protected product, in general form. Industrial design registration protection may occur when there is a pattern or shape that makes the basket attractive, and the product's functional effectiveness is not improved significantly by these features. This example helps illustrate what industrial design registration law can protect and its relation with patent and utility model laws.

B. The industrial design aspects of a chair

Another example is a chair. A patent or utility model could have been obtained for the first development of a chair, and it would have protected the functional combination of a seat of any type and legs attached to the seat, so that a person could sit comfortably above the floor. This combination is primarily functional. Of course, chairs can have many types of legs, like spiral ones, to create an attractive appearance. Seats can be in many shapes or surface appearances, like heart shaped or with a picture on the surface. This chair appearance may be protected by industrial design registration law. While these product features perform the function that may be protected by a patent, they contribute to the appearance of the product and do not contribute significantly to how the chair is used. Industrial design law protection may be given to a product appearance, or the appearance of a product part.

Historically, some industrial design registration systems have allowed overlap between what patents and utility models protect and what industrial design registrations protect. This overlap has not been large, and the trend now is to respect the traditional separation described above, leaving the industrial design registration to protect appearance features that do not contribute significant commercial effect to a product's competitive usefulness. Each national IP law system has to be reviewed to see what the approach is concerning this possible overlap. As the use of utility model

IP protection systems becomes more widely accepted in national systems, the perceived need for overlap will likely disappear.

It is a good time to pose a question to the class about what would be the result if each leg of a chair had a coil-shaped leg. Would that appearance be protected by a patent, or utility model, or under industrial design registration law? The answer is that it depends on the springs. If the coils are flexible, like a shock absorber, to make it more comfortable to sit in the chair, the general use of springs as chair legs in combination with other parts of a basic chair may not be protected by industrial design registration law. A patent or utility model will be used to protect this combination of parts. However, if the coil-shaped chair legs do not flex, then their purpose is primarily for appearance. An industrial design registration could be used to protect this product's appearance.

C. Industrial design aspects of scissors

Paper cutting scissors are a product that has both primarily functional and non-primarily functional visual features, the non-functional features may be protected by industrial design registration, and the primarily functional features may be protected by patents or utility models. The scissor blades must have a crossed shape to perform the cutting action. That shape is primarily functional. As features are added to the scissors to make their appearances attractive, an industrial design registration may protect the product's appearance.

D. Industrial design aspects of textile designs

Two-dimensional designs, like textile designs, may be used to enhance a product's appearance and value, and these designs may be protected by industrial design registration. Some two-dimensional industrial designs may be useful on many different products. Separate industrial design registrations may be needed for each product application of these designs.

E. Industrial design registration examples

Several examples are given below, with explanations, of recent industrial design registrations that show products with protectable industrial design features. These design registrations will start the introduction of many principles and procedures that will be explained in more detail in other sections.

Dépôts publiés selon l'Acte de 1960 /
Deposits published under the 1960 Act

(11) DM/062739 (15) 29.11.2002
(73) INTERIOR'S S.A.S., 68, Bd Jules Durand, F-76071 LE HAVRE CEDEX (FR)
(86)(87)(88) FR (74) LESUEUR EVELYNE 68, Bd Jules Durand, F-76071 LE HAVRE CEDEX (FR) (72) JEAN MICHEL LE BROUSSOIS (28) 1 (54) Corbeille décorative avec anse / Decorative basket with handle (51) Cl. 11-02 (81) I. AN, EG, ES, ID, TN, VA. II. BG, BX, CH, DE, FR, GR, HU, IT, LI, MD, MK, MN, RO, SI, YU (45) 31.03.2003

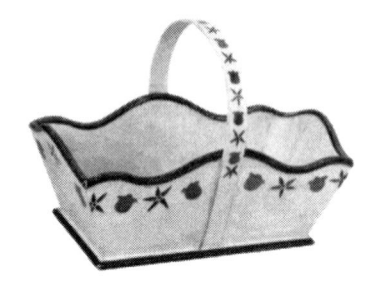

Figure 1: International registration DM/062739 for a basket

Figure 1 shows international registration DM/062739 for a basket. It has a unique container shape and decorations on the container and the handle. Under some national laws, the container shape might be protected alone as the primary impression, as discussed in section VI, below, on infringement. An international registration is approved by the World Intellectual Property Organization (WIPO) as part of the Geneva Act of the Hague Agreement Concerning the international registration of Industrial Designs, a centralized protection system for industrial designs. An international registration is forwarded for processing to the national offices designated for protection. When the international registration is approved by the national office it will be the basis for protection. More details on the Hague Agreement are given in section III(D).

In Figure 2, the chair has a very distinctive back, in combination with a unique cushion. The combination of the legs, seat cushion and back may be protected by industrial design registration. In the international registration Figure 2, the back is shown alone. Since an international registration may be allowed to have several designs in one registration, the back is separately protected.

Figure 3 shows a unique shaped scissor. The mechanical features that form the blade may not be protected by industrial design registration, as

TEACHING INDUSTRIAL DESIGN LAW 89

Dépôts publiés selon l'Acte de 1960 /
Deposits published under the 1960 Act

(11) DM/053603 (15) 19.09.2000
(73) ID EXPORT SRL, Via Nazionale, 65, I-33048 S. GIOVANNI AL NATISONE (UD) (IT) (86)(87)(88) IT (74) GLP Srl Piazzale Cavedalis, 6/2, I-33100 UDINE (IT) (28) 2 (54) Chair and back element of a chair / Chaise et dossier de chaise (51) Cl. 06-01, 06 (81) BX, CH, DE, FR, IT (45) 31.12.2000

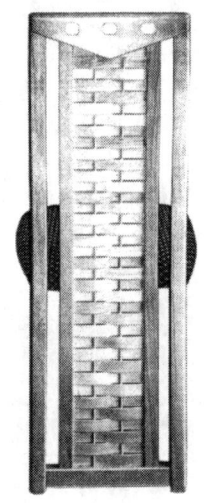

Figure 2: International registration DM/053603 for a chair

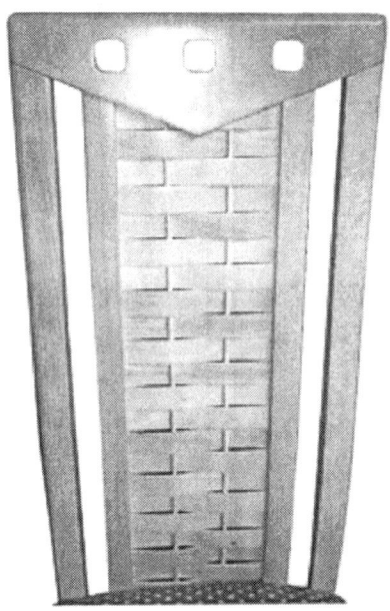

Figure 2: (*cont.*)

Enregistrements internationaux issus de demandes internationales régies exclusivement ou partiellement par l'Acte de 1999 et/ou l'Acte de 1960 /
International registrations resulting from international applications governed exclusively or partly by the 1999 Act and/or the 1960 Act

(11) DM/067454 (15) 06.02.2006
(22) 06.02.2006 (73) MAPED, 530, route de Pringy, F-74370 ARGONAY (FR) (86)(87)(88) FR (74) CABINET GERMAIN & MAUREAU 12, rue Boileau, F-69006 LYON (FR) (72) Daniel RACAMIER, No. 4 – Lotissement "Le Vert Village", F-74330 LA BALME DE SILLINGY; Jérôme CARRIER, 10, route de la Paix, F-74000 ANNECY (28) 1 (51) Cl. 08-03 (54) 1. Ciseaux / 1. Scissors (57)(55) Les ciseaux possèdent à l'avant deux crantée avec un profil en dents de scie; à l'arrière ils présentent deux poignées symétriques l'une de l'autre avec des oeillets en forme de haricot; dans la partie centrale au niveau de l'articulation, une pièce de forme oblongue comporte des motifs décoratifs à chevrons; les faces extérieures de chacune des lames comportent en surépaisseur une pièce rapportée dont l'un des côtés à une forme en dents de scie / The scissors have two pinked sections to the front with a saw teeth profile; to the rear there are two symmetrical handles both with bean-shaped eyelets; in the central part near the hinge, an oblong-shaped part has decorative chevron motifs; the outer sides of each blade have in increased thickness an added part with one of the sides in the shape of teeth of a saw (81) I. AN, EG, ES, ID, TN, VA. II. CH, HU, MA, RO, UA. (30) No 1: 26.12.2005; 000 459 748; EM (45) 31.03.2006

Figure 3: International registration DM/067464 for scissors

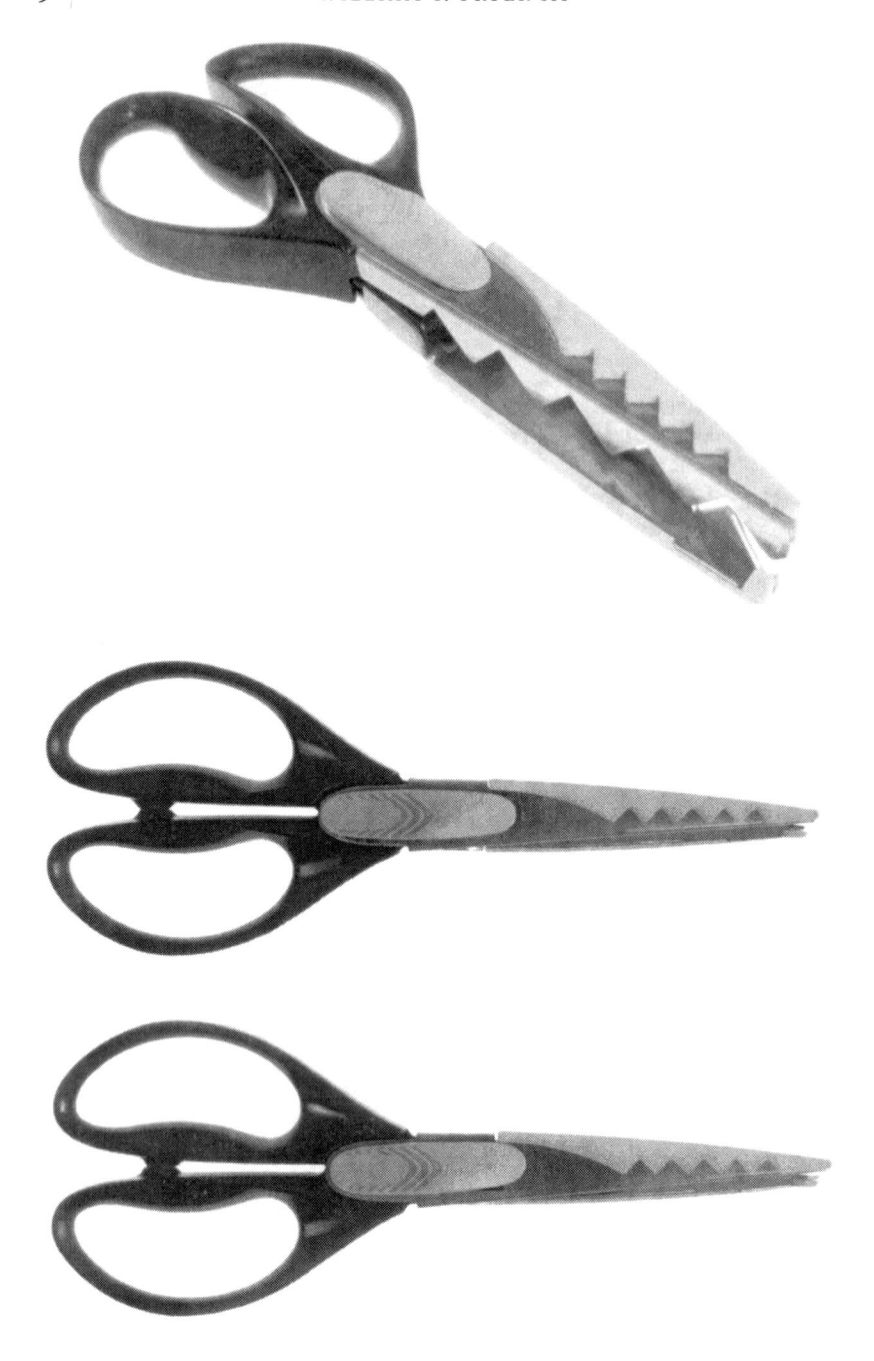

Figure 3: (*cont.*)

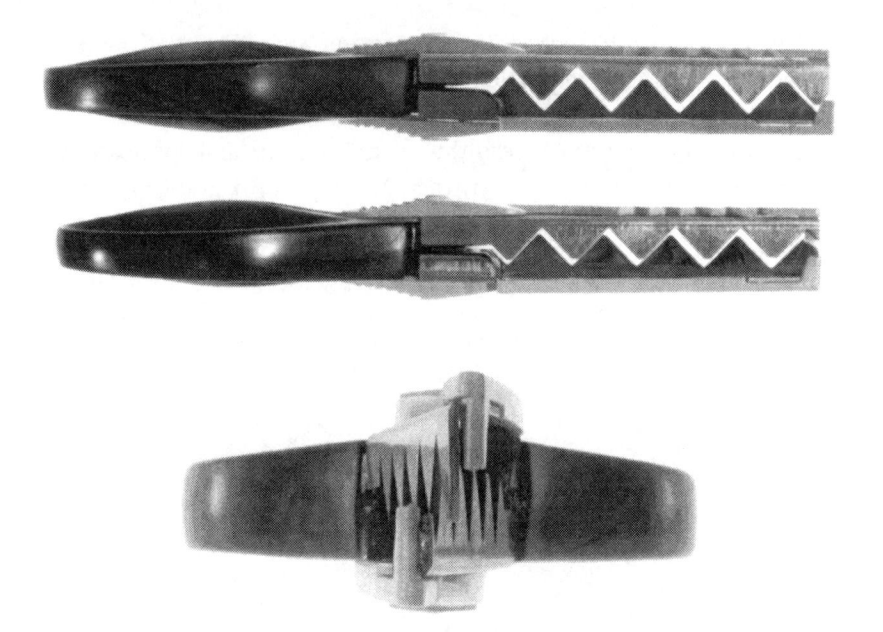

Figure 3: (*cont.*)

they may be primarily functional and the subject only for patent or utility model protection.

Figure 4 shows an overall distinctive shape for a motorcycle from the side and front, with decorative features painted on the sides. This combination may be protected by industrial design registration.

Figure 5 shows a camera with a distinctive shape. Since there are many ways to arrange a camera's controls, and some features are added to create a pleasing appearance, this arrangement may be protected by industrial design registration.

F. *Concept introduction*

A teacher can take advantage of the opportunity to use the above introduction of industrial design law to highlight topics that will be presented later. These topics can include how a typical industrial design registration system works. Students will start asking questions about industrial design registration. They will have seen several industrial design registrations in the above examples. A beginning list of topics that may be introduced is given below.

Enregistrements internationaux issus de demandes internationales régies exclusivement ou partiellement par l'Acte de 1999 et/ou l'Acte de 1960 /
International registrations resulting from international applications governed exclusively or partly by the 1999 Act and/or the 1960 Act

(11) DM/066970 (15) 17.05.2005
(22) 17.05.2005 (73) KEEWAY NEMZETKÖZI FEJLESZTÉSI KFT, Brassói u. 15, H-3519 Miskolc (HU) (86)(87)(88) HU (74) S.B.G. & K. Patent and Law Offices Andrássy út 113, H-1062 Budapest (HU) (72) Peter Neumann, Hohenbrunner Str. 44, 81825 Munich, Germany (28) 1 (51) Cl. 12-11 (54) Motorcycle / Motocycle (81) II. BG, MC, MK, YU (45) 30.09.2005

Figure 4: International registration DM/066970 for a motorcycle

Figure 4: (*cont.*)

Dépôts publiés selon l'Acte de 1960 /
Deposits published under the 1960 Act

(11) DM/052645 (15) 26.07.2000
(73) SONY OVERSEAS SA, Rütistrasse 12, CH-8952 Schlieren (CH) (86)(87)(88) CH
(74) William Blanc & Cie Conseils en Propriété Industrielle SA 9, rue du Valais, CH-1202 Genève (CH) (72) Kubota, Yuki (28) 1 (54) Electronic still camera incorporating a monitor display / Appareil photographique électronique avec moniteur de visualisation incorporé. (51) Cl. 16-01 (81) I. AN, EG, ES, ID, TN, VA. II. BG, BJ, BX, CH, CI, DE, FR, GR, HU, IT, KP, LI, MA, MC, MD, MK, MN, RO, SI, SN, SR, YU. (30) 31.01.2000; 2000-4638; JP (45) 31.10.2000

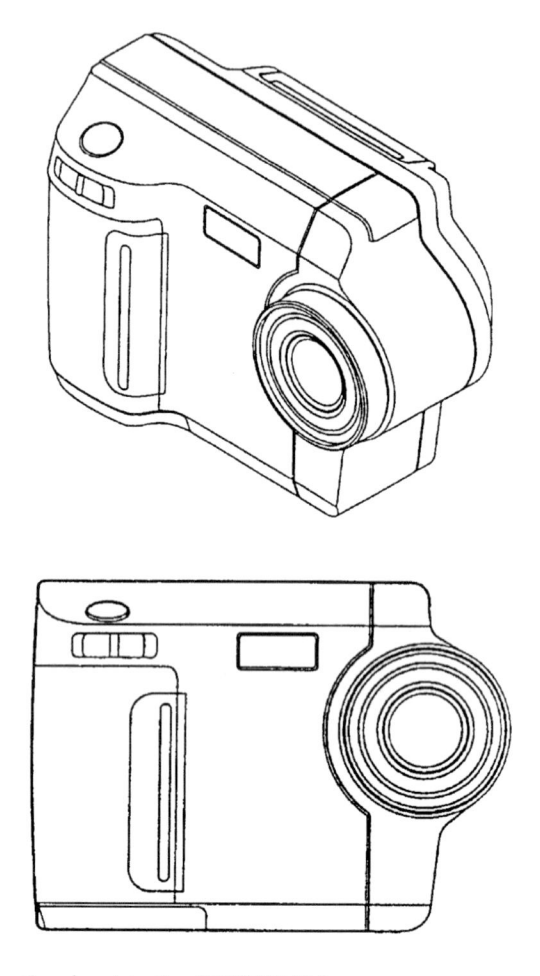

Figure 5: International registration DM/052645 for a camera

TEACHING INDUSTRIAL DESIGN LAW 97

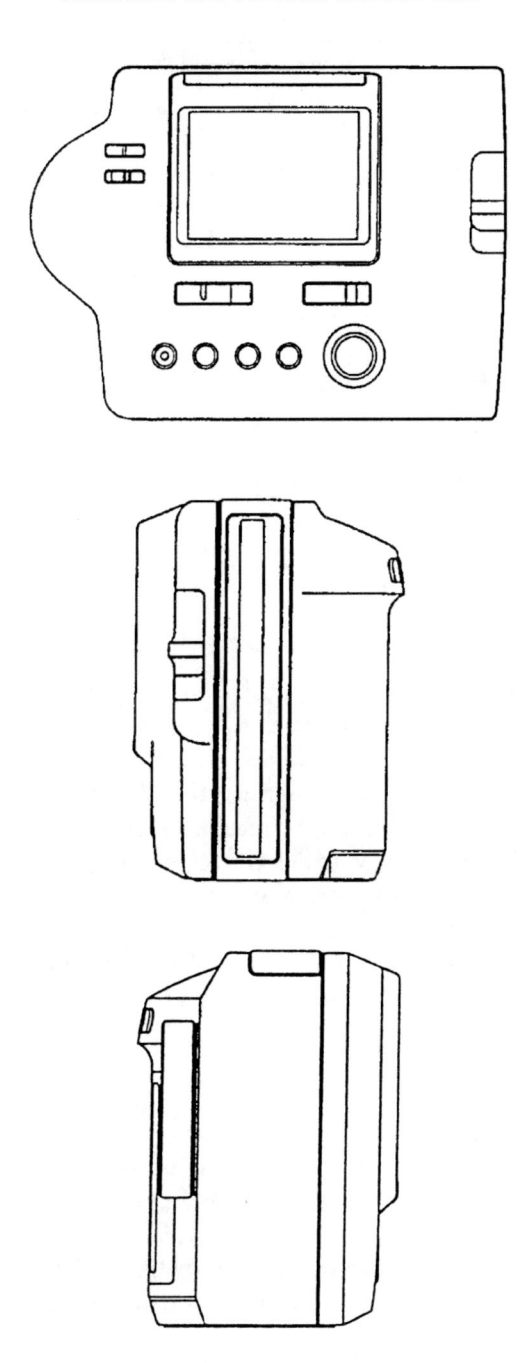

Figure 5: (*cont.*)

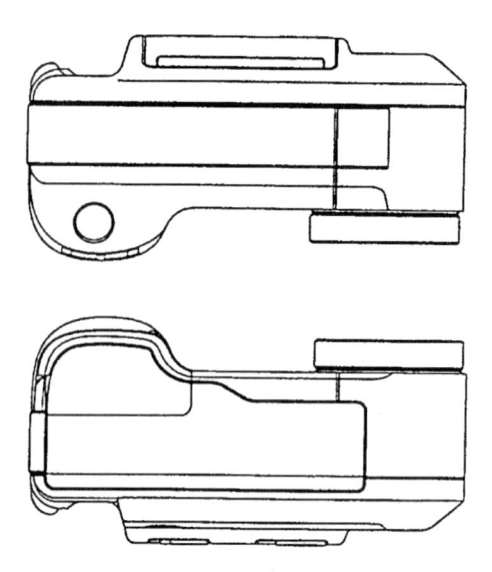

Figure 5: (*cont.*)

1. An industrial design registration will show the product, or part of the product that has the protected design features.
2. Infringement of an industrial design registration right will require a comparison of the protected design and the alleged infringing product.
3. The determination of who should receive an industrial design registration right will depend on who files the registration application first for a specific design, in most national systems.
4. Both a patent and an industrial design registration may protect their respective features on the same product. This fact was demonstrated in the discussion of the above industrial design registration figures.

G. Resources on the industrial designer and architect professions

There are professional organizations set up for persons who specialize in product industrial design development and architecture. These individuals are skilled in making products and buildings more useful and look better, and consequently more marketable. A leading international organization of industrial designers is The International Council of Societies of Industrial Design, a partner of the International Design Alliance, whose website is at www.icsid.org. This website has locator information for websites of national industrial designer organizations. Many countries have related chapters of this organization that hold national conferences and meet regularly on an international level. There is an extensive amount of useful information about industrial design on these national websites. For example, in the US, the Industrial Designer Society of American website, at www.idsa.org, has basic information explaining what an industrial designer does, and illustrating award winning products. Since buildings can be protected by industrial design registrations and other industrial design laws, the websites of architect organizations provide helpful background information. For example, the International Union of Architects (UTA) unites architects of all countries. It has a comprehensive website at www.uia-architectes.org. The US related architects organization is the American Institute of Architects, whose website is at www.aia.org.

III. International agreements on industrial design registration and other industrial design international requirements and options

A. Introduction

Each country and regional group of countries may have obligations under one or more treaties or other agreements concerning industrial design registration and other industrial design protection. These international commitments of a country or regional organizations are a logical place to start teaching industrial design registration law and other design protection laws. A teacher can review the treaties and other international agreements that their country's legal system adopted, and present these treaties and agreements as a framework for discussion of the national industrial design registration laws and the other industrial design laws.

There may be important bilateral agreements between countries and regional groups of countries on intellectual property law. The bilateral agreements may supplement the treaty obligations, or address specific new concerns in industrial design protection. The regional agreements may set up industrial design regional registration systems, such as the European Union Community Design Regulation.

There are three main treaties related to industrial design protection: the Paris Convention for the Protection of Industrial Property (Paris Convention), first adopted in 1883; the Agreement on Trade Related Aspects on Intellectual Property rights (TRIPS), approved in 1994; and the Geneva Act of the Hague Agreement for the International Registration of Industrial Designs, approved in 1999 (Geneva Act) (See section III(E), below, for Internet access to full text copies of these treaties).

The development history and basic features of industrial design registration and other design protection laws can be introduced by reviewing these treaties. Most countries have joined the Paris Convention and TRIPS, making the requirements in these treaties a common source of national laws, as well as a strong political influence to adopt the optional provisions.

B. Paris Convention

The Paris Convention was the first main treaty addressing industrial property, which included industrial design, patent, unity model, trademark, and unfair competition laws. Article 5*quinquies* stated: "Industrial designs shall be protected in all the countries of the Union." In the context of this treaty at that time, it was industrial design registration that was suggested as the way to protect an industrial design. The treaty did not define what was an "industrial design." It was up to each country in their national laws to set up the protection system. Many countries had industrial design registration systems at that time, and for countries without such systems, the Paris Convention encouraged them to adopt an industrial design registration system. Later, TRIPS recognized that industrial designs could be protected by several forms of intellectual property laws.

The Paris Convention required that an industrial design registration system have an application filed that presented the design for which protection was desired. Usually, the design was shown in a drawing. Design registration systems existed in France and England in the 1840s, as discussed below in section IV(A) on national industrial design registration law.

The Paris Convention addressed several common procedural problems involved in national registration systems. The treaty did not include procedures that strongly affected the rights obtained under national registration systems. In particular, the Paris Convention. Article 4, addressed the problem of filing design applications in a foreign country without the loss of rights, by creating what was called the right of priority. The gist of the problem was that an application filing in many countries had to be made before any public knowledge of the design occurred in the country where filing was made. The solution used in the Paris Convention was to allow a fixed maximum period to file in another country that was a member of the treaty, six months in the case of industrial design registrations. During that time, the application in the foreign country office, for a corresponding design application filed in the home country office, would be treated as if it was filed on the same date as the home country application. This provision gave the foreign application the priority date of the home application, and no publication disclosures after that date could affect the validity of the foreign filed application. The delay and inconvenience of filing foreign applications was removed, to a great extent. This feature of the Paris Convention has proven to be a valuable arrangement for all parties to the Convention. Patents, utility models and trademarks had the same type of arrangement.

An interesting fact was that the time allowed for trademarks and industrial designs was the same. Patents and utility models were allowed one year to complete the filing. Apparently, the treaty participants thought that designs were more like marks in their procedures, and more easily processed in a filing system, and should be protected promptly, points to remember for future discussions. It is a clue that the procedure for design registration should be simple and less expensive than for patents, and more similar to trademark protection. In many countries, this simplicity did exist, but in some national laws, patent procedures became more closely associated with industrial design registration. This fact created the major differences in the types of industrial design registration system now in use.

Another principle adopted in the Paris Convention, applying to industrial designs and other industrial property, was national treatment, Article 2. It gave design owners in one member country the same right to protection as nationals in a member country. If a foreigner filed in a country, for the same design as a national, each would be treated the same. Discrimination against foreigners was a problem, and this provision solved the problem, to a degree. This provision is another one that has proved to be quite valuable.

In addition, the Paris Convention dealt with a problem that faced patents, utility models and design registration due to the effect of exhibitions of new products at a trade show in another country. Since public disclosure might end the right to file an application, due to the novelty requirement usually found in industrial design registration systems, the Paris Convention Article 11 mandated protection for a short time after the exhibition, allowing the product owner to file the application in member countries after the exhibit occurred. It was a very limited, special arrangement. The purpose was important, as this agreement was created to encourage international trade, through exhibitions at trade shows. The discussion how to improve international cooperation for this purpose concerning intellectual property continues today.

A unique advantage was given to industrial design registrations in terms of the Paris Convention special procedures concerning compulsory licensing in a member country, where the protected product was not manufactured by the registration owner in that country. Patent owners were given strict rules to follow concerning when a third party could be prevented from obtaining a government license under their patents. In Paris Convention Article 5(B), it was provided that these compulsory licensing provisions did not apply to industrial designs. Therefore, industrial design registrations had more flexibility as to where the protected product was made and less likelihood that there would be government interference through compulsory licensing. This greater flexibility in industrial design registration rights was a recognition that the economic impact of industrial design registrations was different from patents. The separate roles of patents and industrial design registrations were discussed in section II on "What industrial design is." This background makes the Paris Convention provision on industrial designs and compulsory licensing clearer.

As demonstrated by the above discussion of the Paris Convention provisions related to industrial design registration, international treaty analysis is an effective way to start the presentation of industrial design registration law. At the same time, national laws that were adopted based on the Paris Convention can be discussed, in their unique form. This teaching approach also helps to introduce the importance of international agreements in the development of national laws. International agreements are one of the driving forces now for procedural and substantive law harmonization. The main example of this development is in the recent revision of the Hague Agreement Concerning the International Registration of Industrial Designs by the Geneva Act (1999), a topic discussed in section III(D) below.

TRIPS, the next treaty discussed below, represented a major agreement on procedural and substantive intellectual property law, both mandating and urging changes in national industrial design laws.

C. TRIPS

1. Introduction

TRIPS offers another opportunity to teach several fundamental features of industrial design law. In perspective, TRIPS is part of a broad economic treaty called the General Agreement on Tariffs and Trade (GATT), separately administered by the World Trade Organization (WTO) (see section III(E), below, for full text and other WTO information, Internet and related references). The addition of TRIPS was the first time that IP topics were in GATT and industrial design law was a part of the negotiations. The key provisions adopted were:

SECTION 4: INDUSTRIAL DESIGNS

Article 25

Requirements for Protection

1. Members shall provide for the protection of independently created industrial designs that are new or original. Members may provide that designs are not new or original if they do not significantly differ from known designs or combinations of known design features. Members may provide that such protection shall not extend to designs dictated essentially by technical or functional considerations.
2. Each Member shall ensure that requirements for securing protection for textile designs, in particular in regard to any cost, examination or publication, do not unreasonably impair the opportunity to seek and obtain such protection. Members shall be free to meet this obligation through industrial design law or through copyright law.

Article 26

(a) Protection

1. The owner of a protected industrial design shall have the right to prevent third parties not having the owner's consent from making, selling or importing articles bearing or embodying a design which is a copy, or substantially a copy, of the protected design, when such acts are undertaken for commercial purposes.
2. Members may provide limited exceptions to the protection of industrial designs, provided that such exceptions do not unreasonably conflict with the normal exploitation of protected industrial designs and do not unreasonably prejudice the legitimate interests of the owner of the protected design, taking account of the legitimate interests of third parties.
3. The duration of protection available shall amount to at least 10 years.

2. Relation to the Paris Convention

As an overview, TRIPS section 4 was not the only part related to industrial designs. TRIPS also incorporated by reference the Paris Convention industrial design provisions discussed above in section III(B). Members of TRIPS had to comply with these provisions even if they were not members of the Paris Convention (TRIPS Article 2(1)). This requirement provided for the first time an enforcement process for these Paris Convention provisions, based on the WTO dispute resolution provisions.

3. Relation to other forms of IP protection

Another general comment is that TRIPS was not limited to industrial design registration law improvement in design protection laws. TRIPS addressed industrial design protection in a broad context, recognizing that several different IP forms could protect industrial designs.

More specifically, an international requirement was stated in TRIPS that each member shall protect "new or original" industrial designs, Article 25(1). The fundamental principle of novelty as a requirement for protection of an industrial design was part of most industrial design registration systems. The reference to "originality" recognized that copyright law could protect industrial design if the basic requirement of originality was present. Each country had the right to define what was novel, and when a work was original. National industrial design registration systems generally required that an industrial design had to be novel for protection. This meant that an industrial design had not been made public, through publication or use, prior to the filing of the industrial design registration application. Copyright law generally used the principle of originality to identify that the designer had contributed their own, independently developed creative content in the design. The level of artistic content required was a subject of different approaches in various national laws. At least there was agreement under TRIPS that industrial designs should be protected either by industrial design registration or copyright, or perhaps both industrial design registration and copyright under certain circumstances.

4. Relation to the primarily functional exclusion

TRIPS did allow the national laws of members the option to exclude from industrial design protection those designs that were exclusively functional (Article 25(1)). This topic goes back to the discussion in section II, above, on "What industrial design is."

5. Review of industrial design law basics

TRIPS Article 25(1) offers an opportunity to use the industrial design registrations presented in section II, above, as a review of the novelty and primarily functional principles. These and other principles can be more easily taught by using visual examples.

A good question to ask at this point is why TRIPS did not spell out exactly what the novelty requirements should be, or why TRIPS did not select the IP form that would be used to protect industrial designs, or mandate that national systems exclude primarily functional design features. At a given time, treaty negotiations can bring issues only into better focus and concentrate on where there is agreement. They cannot come to an agreement on some issues. TRIPS Article 25(1) discussions did have an impact, as national laws were reviewed for improvement, even if TRIPS did not mandate changes. Members were encouraged to adopt the suggested principles.

6. Protection right

After setting a minimum requirement for the sort of industrial designs that must be protected, TRIPS mandated that there shall be a right to prevent copying and substantial copying of protected industrial designs (Article 26(1)). TRIPS left a lot of flexibility for national laws to implement this requirement. Copying, in one sense, is an act of seeing or learning about another's design and duplicating it. This right can be very valuable, but it does not prevent independent development of the same design, which is a right given by most industrial design registration systems. A question is what did TRIPS mandate: a more limited right that required knowledge of another persons design, or one that just required that the designs were essentially the same in appearance, no matter what the reason?

It was apparent that the TRIPS negotiations did not reach an answer on whether design protection should have an exclusive right, independent of whether there was knowledge and copying of a protected design. It did reach a very important conclusion, that when a protected industrial design was copied, the design owner must have the right to stop the copying. Industrial design registration law or copyright law, or both of them, must provide that right. TRIPS did provide a very good start in addressing the requirements for industrial design protection that national laws of member countries would have to follow.

7. Local products and comparison of industrial design registration and copyright protection

There are many examples of design piracy with which students will be familiar in their own country, on products they see and use. It would be an effective step to integrate these products into the discussions.

At this point in the TRIP topic, it may be useful to have a class discussion on whether industrial design registration or copyright would be the most effective means of protecting industrial design. As discussed in section III(C)(6), above, copyright laws generally provide the more limited right, requiring knowledge and use of the design owner's work. This discussion can include whether overlapping industrial design registration and copyright protection should be given under national law, a topic discussed in more detail in section VII(C). These issues will help the students see the full dimensions of the issues that make industrial design law so interesting and at the center of many IP law developments.

8. Textile Industrial designs

At the TRIPS negotiations, the textile industries, such as creators and manufacturers of fabric design and fashion designs, were very influential, as evidenced by the inclusion of Article 25(2). This general mandate to improve textile design protection made it clear that these industrial design industries were not satisfied with current industrial design law protection procedures and rights. The TRIPS answer was to encourage change, not mandate what was needed, in most cases, to help the textile industries obtain cost effective protection. The enhanced protection was not long in coming, as the Geneva Act of the Hague Agreement, discussed in section III(D), below, provided specific and substantial benefits.

9. Integrated circuit designs

TRIPS helped the integrated circuit industry to protect semi-conductor chip layout designs. In the economic world of GATT negotiations, many trade issues were considered. Industries worked hard to gain benefits from the negotiations, such as for textile designs, discussed in section III(D)(8). TRIPS (Articles 35–38) included a mandate that members shall be obligated to adopt certain provisions of the Treaty on Intellectual Property in Respect of Integrated Circuits (Integrated Circuit Treaty) (see section III(E), below, for Internet and related references to this treaty; it is identified in short form as the Washington Treaty).

The Integrated Circuit Treaty was an industry specific treaty, based on a similar US law (17 U.S.C. sections 901–914, The Semi-Conductor Chip Protection Act 1984). The manufacture of a semi-conductor chip involved the layout of design patterns. A protection system to prevent copying of these design layouts was selected that had been considered in the US for general improvement of design protection. The general corresponding legislation was not enacted in the US, but the integrated circuit-focused legislation was enacted promptly to meet the industry need (see section VII(E). for more information on this topic).

10. National perspective

The Integrated Circuit Treaty history and its inclusion into TRIPS gives an opportunity at this point in the course to look at local national laws to see what industries have received special attention in protecting industrial designs. This topic could be implemented by a short research project for class reports. In the alternative, the teacher could prepare a list of national, industry-specific industrial design protection legislation. A discussion could be initiated on national industries that need more protection and the content of the legislation that might be used. This discussion would help students see how national industries benefit from industrial design protection. In the US, for example, the Vessel Hull Design Protection Act 1998, 17 U.S.C. §§1301–1332, was enacted with significant industry support, to prevent the copying of boat industrial designs. This Vessel Hull Design Protection legislation used a similar approach to the Semi-Conductor Chip Protection Act. More recently, the fashion design industry has proposed legislation using essentially the same legal structure as the Vessel Hull Protection Act, to protect several fashion products (legislation H.R. 5055, 109th Congress, Second session).

The next and final treaty presented, the Geneva Act of the Hague Agreement Concerning the International Registration of Industrial Designs, is the most recent industrial design related treaty, enacted in 1999. Its focus was primarily to improve procedures for obtaining industrial design registration protection around the world.

D. The Geneva Act of the Hague Agreement Concerning the International Registration of Industrial Designs

1. Introduction

National design registration protection extends only to that country, and regional registration applies to the region. What if a business wants to protect the same design in other countries or in a regional system? For many years, the only way to proceed was to file individual national or regional applications. Usually this step required preparing the application in the national language, or selection from a few languages, under the guidance of an attorney in that country or region, completing the unique application forms and paying the fees in national or regional currency.

It would be a tremendous advantage to have a centralized filing system for industrial design registration applications, where the design owner could file directly, without the need for a local representative, on one form for selected countries, and pay the fees in one currency. The Geneva Act of the Hague Agreement Concerning the International Registration of Industrial Designs (Geneva Act) has these features in a centralized filing system for industrial design registrations.

The industrial design registrations shown in Figures 1 to 5 of section II are all Geneva Act international registrations. These Figures show the registration format, for stating the owner, an indication of the product on which the design is applied, and the countries for which protection was sought.

2. History and purpose

The Hague Agreement Concerning the International Deposit of Industrial Designs originated in 1925, to facilitate the filing of an international registration industrial design application through a centralized filing system now administered by the World Intellectual Property Organization (WIPO). This treaty included procedures to obtain protection in the member countries and regional organizations designated in the application. The most recent version, the Geneva Act of the Hague Agreement, with a slight name change was the Hague Agreement Concerning the International Registration of Industrial Designs. The Geneva Act was adopted in 1999, and it became operational on April 1, 2004. There were 19 members of the Geneva Act as of April 15, 2006. Under the Geneva Act, a single application could be prepared, in French or English, to obtain protection in members of the 1999 Act. In general concept, the Geneva Act had the same purpose as the Patent Cooperation Treaty had for patents, and the Madrid Protocol had for marks.

The prior Hague Agreement versions did not have global acceptance, for several reasons. Primarily, there were two types of industrial design registration systems, and these earlier Hague Agreement versions worked effectively with only one of these systems. One type of registration system, the most widely used, had no novelty examination before registration (non-novelty examination). Applications were filed and rights obtained with only formal review of the file to see that it was complete. Rights were usually obtained promptly. The registration scope and validity were determined after registration in administrative proceedings, and in the courts, when these rights were challenged by competitors. Courts handled the issue of whether there was infringement of the registration rights. The other main type of industrial design registration system did require novelty examination before registration (novelty examination system). A significant delay occurred in granting the registration rights, and the novelty examination system added to registration costs.

The pros and cons of these different registration systems could have been debated in the development of a revised Hague Agreement treaty, to come up with one common system for filing and determining rights. Instead, the Geneva Act of the Hague Agreement set up only an International Registration system to work with both types of national filing and rights systems in a reasonably effective manner. A number of compromises were made. The goal was to have a more effective international industrial design filing system. The Geneva Act did not attempt significantly to harmonize substantive law provisions in the national industrial design registration systems. It improved the national filing system efficiency, so that rights could be obtained earlier. The administrative convenience of the Geneva Act was a valuable feature, with centralized records and direct contact by the design owners with WIPO staff to facilitate filing the international registration application.

An international registration application under the Geneva Act may be filed in a national office of a member country and the national office will mail the application to WIPO. Figure 6 below shows a general diagram of how the Geneva Act system operates, and a list of main features follows the diagram.

Geneva Act of The Hague Agreement Concerning the International Registration of Industrial Designs

International registration (IR) date WIPO	Formality Review only	IR transmitted to designated members' National Office for processing	Process same as national application; same rights as national application
		International registration published or may be deferred (kept secret) for limited time	End of registration right

National Office International registration application filed

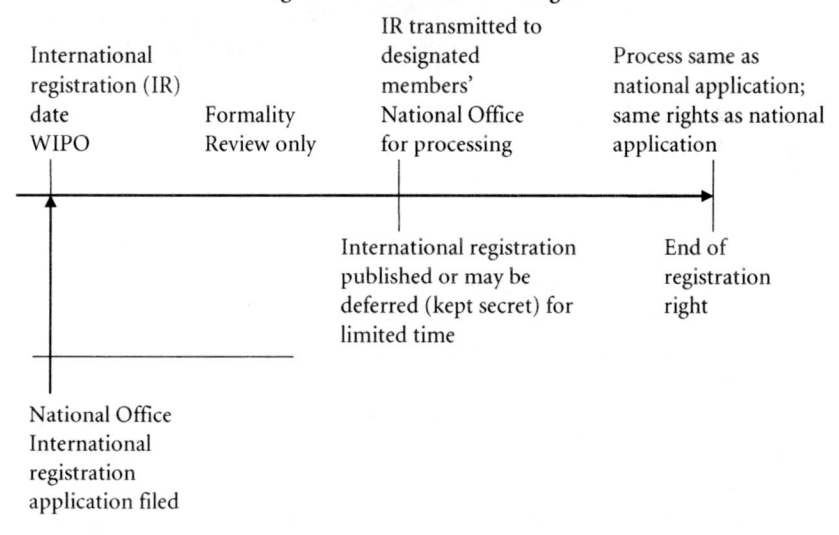

Figure 6: Geneva Act of the Hague Agreement Operation

3. Geneva Act main features

(a) An international registration can be filed directly with WIPO or through a national office. The effective date of an international registration is the date the application is filed at WIPO, or at the national office, within limits. The international registration application is processed according to the national office procedures. Almost all fees are paid in Swiss currency to WIPO.

(b) Up to 100 designs in the same Locarno Agreement class can be in the international registration application. Background information on the Locarno agreement can be found on the WIPO website at www.wipo.int/hague/en/general/classification.html.

(c) If secrecy is needed, publication of an international registration design can be deferred, for up to 30 months, depending on the national laws of designated offices.

(d) National laws determine the term of protection. Rights must not end earlier than 15 years from the WIPO international registration application filing date.

(e) Deferred two-dimensional design international registration applications can be filed with samples of the textile material, for example. The application can be completed later, adding the drawing, and allowing time to determine which designs warrant protection. These steps save significant costs.

(f) The international registration has the same national effect as a national registration application filed in the designated member office, for most purposes.

(g) The overall effect of the Geneva Act was to create by international agreement an international registration with rights determined on most features by the national law of the member designated for protection.

4. Other topics for Geneva Act class discussions

(a) The Geneva Act diagram, Figure 6, is a simplified diagram of the way a design owner may use the treaty. There is still the option to file applications for registration directly with each national office, using a national representative, completing a national form in the national language, and paying fees in local currency. A useful class discussion topic would be to ask students to compare the procedures for direct filing in a national office under national laws with the Geneva Act approach. This exercise would be a good way to introduce the Geneva Act operation and benefits. Students could obtain their information on the national systems from the national offices websites, and more information on the Geneva Act of the Hague Agreement from the WIPO website on the Hague Agreement System (See section III(E), below, on Internet resources). The class discussion could start with reports from students on their research, or written reports could be turned in for review by the teacher.

(b) Another class demonstration could be to show the international registration application form available on the WIPO Hague Agreement System website. Students could be asked to help fill it out in class. The teacher could select the industrial design owner's member country and the countries designated for protection. Selection of Hague Agreement countries that are not members of the Geneva Act is not recommended, as this relationship adds unnecessary complications to the exercise.

(c) The Geneva Act special treatment for textile international registration applications is a good point to emphasize, as it followed the general mandate in TRIPS Article 25(2), discussed in section III(C) above.

(d) The preceding introduction to the main treaties on industrial design protection should give the students an understanding of the international origin of key industrial design law features in their national design protection system.

E. Resources on intellectual property treaties and other agreements

The WIPO and WTO websites have full texts of the cited treaties. The WIPO website main page for accessing all the treaties it administers is at www.wipo.int/treaties/en. The full text of the GATT with the TRIPS Annex 1C can be found on the WTO legal documents page at www.wto.org/english/docs_e/legal_elegal_e.htm. There are several ways to access these treaties on the WIPO and WTO websites. Even if these websites have been rearranged, access to the WIPO website home page at www.wipo.int. and to the WTO website home page at www.wto.org should locate the desired documents. In addition to treaties, the WIPO website has a comprehensive set of instructional documents on how to use the Geneva Act. These documents are collected under the heading of the Hague Agreement System and found at www.wipo.int/hague/en.

Comprehensive historical reviews and analysis of several of these treaties have been published: G. H. C. Bodenhausen, *Guide to the Application of the Paris Convention for the Protection of Industrial Property*, as revised at Stockholm in 1967, published by BIRPI (1968) (ISBN 92-805-0368-5); Daniel Gervais, *Trips Agreement: Drafting History and Analysis*, 2nd edn (2003), published by Sweet & Maxwell; William T. Fryer III, *The Geneva Act (1999) of the Hague Agreement Concerning the International Registration of Industrial Designs: Drafting History and Analysis* (2005), published by Kluwer Law International (ISBN 90-411-2117-x).

A very useful step is for the teacher to download a copy of the treaties discussed in this chapter for easy access. The WIPO and WTO files open using Microsoft Word.

IV. National industrial design registration systems

A. Introduction

In teaching the features of current national industrial design registration systems, it is very important to review the international treaty history that affected each national system, discussed in section III, above.

The Geneva Act of the Hague Agreement development, discussed in section III(D) above, explained the sharp differences between the two main types of current industrial design registration systems. These systems are the one without pre-registration novelty examination (non-novelty examination) that has relatively prompt registration and rights, and the one with pre-registration novelty examination system (novelty examination) that may have significant delay before rights are obtained.

The origin of these systems is explained by their history. One of the first industrial design registration systems was established in Lyon, France, in 1711, to protect textile designs (see History of Industrial Designs, Japanese Patent Office website, at www.jpo.go.jp/seido_e/ index.htm). A design representation of the design was placed in an envelope and sealed. If a conflict occurred, the secret file was opened to challenge the alleged infringer. This approach stressed the importance of secrecy, so the registration system was not a source for copiers. A secrecy option feature remains in many national industrial design registration laws, for limited time periods.

Registration of industrial designs in England was introduced starting in 1839, although laws existed earlier to protect some textile goods (see History of Designs, UK Patent Office, at www.patent.gov.uk/design/ deshistory.htm, last viewed July 13, 2006; no longer on the Internet; copy available from author on request). Registration was required before the design was published, or the right to protect the design was lost. The office did not determine whether a registration was novel. This determination was made after registration when a conflict arose, or a registration was challenged.

The English Industrial Designs Registration Office records were open to the public at first. However, concern over copiers using the office records forced the office to change its procedures and to keep its records secret. It was required that the registered design be novel prior to registration. An applicant had to identify the features that were not novel. The law was expanded to other products, including ones with functional features. At first, there were no limits on whether primarily functional features could be protected, and later it was a requirement.

The influence of the English registration system encouraged the US, in 1842, to adopt a design patent system. It evolved as part of the US patent law and remains in that form today (35 U.S.C. 170–172). This design patent system required examination for novelty, within limits, and a level of invention, and rights were obtained at the time of approval of the registration. Since there could be considerable delay in approval of a design patent, a product could be without protection at the initial marketing stage.

US patent law (utility patents) protected primarily functional features, and design patents protected only non-primarily functional features, as discussed in section II, above. Initially, the US design patent law did not restrict protection to non-primarily functional features. The principle of ornamentality was added to the statute to identify the fact that features other than primarily functional ones had to be present in the design for there to be a protectable design.

B. *Types of national industrial design registration systems*

This historical evolution of industrial design registration systems into two main types is important background. A way to teach how these systems work is to construct representative types of systems that show the basic features and discuss them in class. Figures 7 and 8, below, are non-novelty examination and novelty examination systems, respectively. They are not the industrial design systems of a country, but they are very similar to the systems found in many countries. A comparative review of these systems from a design owner's point of view is given below. Included in this analysis is use of the Geneva Act of the Hague Agreement with each of these systems.

1. Operation of a design registration system without novelty examination

Non-novelty examination system

```
                    Formality              Infringement
                    review only            decided in court
                                           Can challenge
                                           Validity
├────────────────────────────────┼────────────────────────────────►
│                                │                                │
Registration application                                    Limited term
filed in national office         Registration grant         of protection
                                                            ends
Registration may be kept         Rights may start from
secret after registration        filing date
```

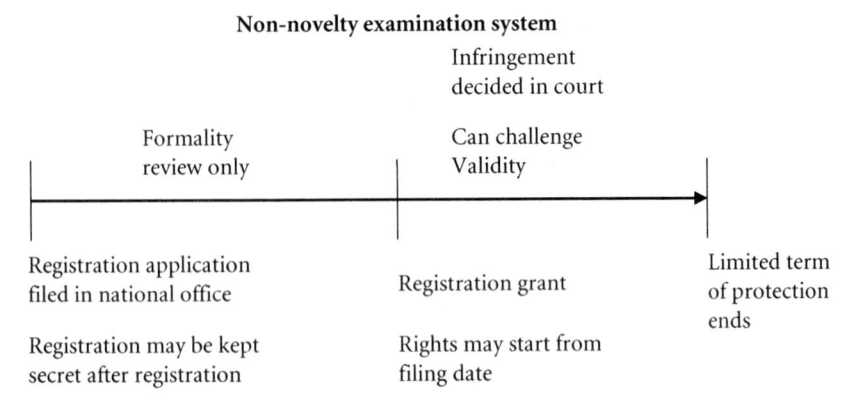

Figure 7: Operation of an industrial design registration, non-novelty examination system

2. Main features of a typical design registration system without pre-registration novelty examination (Figure 7):

(a) Application is filed for protection.
(b) Essentially only formality review occurs, to determine if the application papers are complete before registration is completed, and registration usually occurs in less than one year.
(c) Registration can be kept secret, while rights have been granted, at the option of the applicant, for a limited time, to prevent copying of the design.
(d) Rights under registration may start from filing date once the registration is approved, and protection may be renewed at intervals up to 25 years from the filing date with payment of additional fees.
(e) Application has a drawing of the design and protection is based on what is shown in the drawing, as well as any description of the design in the application.
(f) The registered design must be novel, e. g., not substantially identical to an industrial design made public before the registration filing date.
(g) After grant of the registration, anyone who uses a substantially identical design infringes the industrial design registration right.
(h) The right granted is exclusive, whether the design is copied from the registration owner's design or independently created.

(i) The challenge to the design registration validity, due to lack of novelty or other reasons, occurs after the registration in the national office, usually, or in the courts.

Novelty examination system

```
                    Formality,              Infringement
                    novelty, and            court action
                    ornamentality
                    review                  Challenge to
                                            registration
                                            validity
────┼───────────────────┼───────────────────┼──────────▶
    │                   │                   │
Registration        Registration with    End of
application filed   right beginning at   registration
                    this time            right
Application is kept
secret until
registration
```

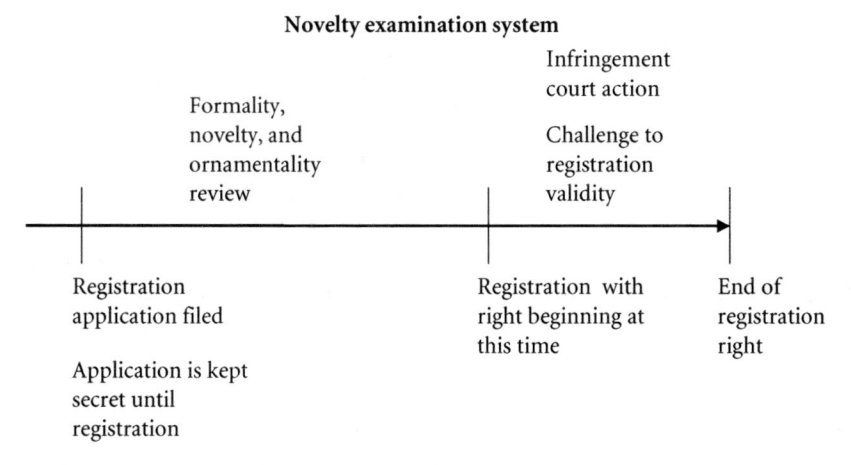

Figure 8: Basic operation of a design registration novelty examination system

3. Main features of a design registration system with pre-registration novelty examination (Figure 8):
(a) Application is filed for protection.
(b) There is a formality review, to determine if the application papers are complete and an examination to determine novelty, level of invention and ornamentality before registration. This process may take up to two years or more.
(c) Registration cannot be kept secret after rights have been granted.
(d) Rights start upon registration; there are no rights until that date. Protection may be renewed at intervals up to 25 years from the registration filing date.
(e) Application has a drawing of the design; protection is based on what is shown in the drawing, as well as any description of the design in the application.
(f) The registered design must be novel, e. g. not substantially identical to a design made public before the registration filing date.
(g) After grant of the registration, anyone who uses a substantially identical design infringes the design registration right.
(h) The right granted is exclusive, whether the design is copied from the registration owner's design or independently created.

(i) In addition to the pre-registration novelty and level of invention examination, a challenge to the design registration validity, due to lack of novelty or other reasons, can occur after the registration, in the national office, on a limited basis, or in the courts on all issues.

4. Design owner perspective in comparing the non-novelty examination system of Figure 7 and the novelty examination system of Figure 8.

(a) A non-novelty examination system results in more prompt registration and grant of rights. The novelty examination system delay in granting rights is due to administrative review. Often, the rights obtained in the non-novelty examination system are from the date of the application filing, discouraging attempts to copy the design.

(b) The non-novelty examination system is cheaper initially. It may be more expensive in the long run, after challenges to invalidate the registration. The cost to businesses to determine what designs can be used is another expense. The novelty examination system has a major cost in the provision of the staff needed to review the registration applications.

C. Geneva Act interactions with national law systems

1. After review of the types of industrial design registration systems, it is a good time to apply the Geneva Act of the Hague Agreement to these systems. Figure 6, in section III(D)(2), above, showed the Geneva Act operation, and Figures 7 and 8 showed the national systems to use in the discussion.

2. The history of the Hague Agreement Concerning the International Registration of Industrial Designs, discussed in section III(D)(2), above, is very important in making this comparative analysis. In summary, before use of the Hague Agreement treaty was available, protection in another country required filing an application in the national system. Each national system had its unique requirements for a local attorney to complete and file the application. A major contribution to foreign filing of industrial design registration was the 1999 revision of the Geneva Act of the Hague Agreement. This treaty provided International Registration protection in designated Geneva Act members.

3. The diplomatic conference on the Geneva Act was made more difficult by the differences in the two main types of national industrial design protection systems, the non-novelty examination system and the novelty examination system. Each group of countries favored their system

benefits. The short time to obtain rights and the lower initial costs to obtain protection were favored by the countries with non-novelty examination systems. The novelty examination system group considered their registration more valuable, after novelty examination, and the business cost in determining what design registrations could be used may have been less.

4. The goal of establishing more widely acceptable international design protection systems was shared by each of the groups. A compromise was reached. The novelty examination system countries committed to make their procedures more efficient, by providing the first office actions within 12 months from the filing date of the WIPO application. The non-novelty examination countries agreed to provide a flexible approach to when secrecy was available after registration. Special procedures were included, as encouraged by TRIPS Article 26(2), for textile design registration. The result was that one application in a standard format could be prepared in French or English, and payments made in one currency. The international registration application would be filed with WIPO and sent to the selected member offices. The international registration application would be processed under the national procedures and national laws, with some limits to ensure there was flexibility to accommodate special national system features.

5. A design owner could file national applications in countries or regional offices where that step appeared to be the best practice, or the Geneva Act could be used to file centrally an international registration application, with several advantages resulting from the international registration common procedures.

V. EU Community Design registration system

A. Introduction

1. If there is time in the course, it is suggested that the European Union (EU) regional industrial design registration system and other regional design protection systems be studied. The teacher has one of the best opportunities at this point to review the basic principles of industrial design registration as applied in the recently adopted EU Community Design system.

2. Work on the EU Community Design began at the Max Planck Institute for Patent, Copyright and Competition (now the Max Planck Institute for Intellectual Property) in Munich, Germany. After extensive discussions the EU issued a Directive (98/71/EC of the European

Parliament and of the Council of 13 October 1998 on the legal protection of designs), to require member countries to adjust their industrial design laws to several common standards. A Community Design Regulation established the Community Design system (Council Regulation (EC) No. 6/2002 of 12 December 2001 on Community Designs (Consolidated Version)). It became operational, in part, during 2002, and fully available in January 2003. Use of the Community Design is increasing. This system is a bold, new approach for industrial design protection, combining unregistered initial protection followed by registration.

3. The EU Community Design unregistered right prevented copying for three years maximum from the time when a product was introduced to the market. If longer protection was needed, an application for registration was required that had to be filed within one year of the product's market entry, and preferably as soon a possible.

4. The registration application was processed by the EU Community Design Office and registration occurred relatively soon, without novelty examination. The right from registration was effective from the date of the application filing. Periodic renewal of the registration could be made for up to a maximum total of 25 years from the application filing date. After registration, the Community Design could be challenged administratively for lack of novelty, or for being solely functional, for example. Enforcement of an EU Community Design right was by the courts designated to review infringement issues, while validity determinations were made initially by the Examination Office. The basic operation of the EU Community Design system is shown in Figure 9 below:

5. In these respects, the EU industrial design registration system was essentially the non-novelty examination system discussed in reference to Figure 7, in section IV(B), above.

B. Additional Features of the EU Community Design system

1. Novelty is one of the requirements, as of the filing date, to obtain a registration. The prior art that is considered in the novelty review is accessible within the European Community.

2. The registered Community Design right is exclusive, preventing copying or independent creation of a substantially identical design.

3. Multiple designs can be included in a Community Design registration, with some limitations, and the Locarno Agreement international design classification is used to determine what designs can be in a registration.

EU Community Design System

Unregistered protection against copying	Application for EU Community design registration		Cancellation action; court infringed action; novelty required	
		Formality review only		
Product with design enters market	Unregistered protection; ends 3 years from market entry: rights under registration begin here, upon registration, back to filing date		Registration, and design publication or deferral for limited time	25 years maximum protection

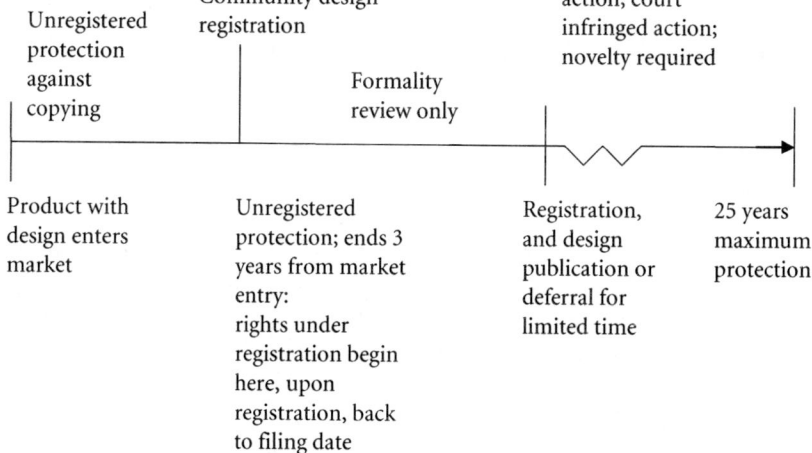

Figure 9: Basic operation of the EU Community Design system

4. Product parts of complex products are not protected when used for repair purposes. The Commission has proposed a change to the Directive 1998/71/EC to deny protection of replacement parts in national laws. The debate has been intense and it appears to be coming to a conclusion (see report by Alan Davis, July 7, 2006, at http://lawzone.thelawyer.com/cgi-bin/item.cgi?id=112452&d=204&h+24&F=259, last viewed on July 13, 2006, no longer on the Internet; copy available from author on request).

5. Design features that are required to connect a product functionally with other products are not protected.

6. In discussing the Community Design system, a point to review as an introduction to the next main section is the Community Design unregistered initial protection. It is evidence that other forms of design protection can be combined with registration protection for an effective system.

C. Resources on the EU Community Design system

1. There are comprehensive Internet resources on the EU Office of Harmonization in the Internal Market website at http://oami.europa.eu. The Community Design page is at http://oami.europa.eu/en/design/default.htm. The published registrations, administrative and court decisions, and legal texts can be reviewed from the website designs page.

D. Other regional design registration systems

There are other regional design registration systems, where countries have utilized a central office to issue design registrations that are effective, or subject to acceptance by member countries under a common set of laws. The Benelux regional system has a common law for the Netherlands, Luxembourg and Belgium, and single design registration office that issues one industrial design registration after only a formal examination, effective in each country (see Benelux Designs Office website at www.bmb-bbm.org/modellen/en/index.php).

In Africa, there are two main regional industrial design registration offices. The English speaking countries formed the African Regional Intellectual Property Organization (ARIPO). The office provides centralized filing and it registers an industrial design with only formal examination. A member accepts the registration, subject to later invalidity challenges. The ARIPO website is at www.aripo.org. The French-speaking countries formed the African Intellectual Property Organization (OAPI) which included a common industrial design registration. The OAPI website is at www.oapi.wipo.net.

VI. Industrial design registration infringement

A. Introduction

In general, national industrial design registration laws have essentially a common approach to determining if a registration right is infringed. The tests are expressed in different ways. The visual impression of the alleged infringing product and the design shown in the registration are compared. If the comparison gives the same overall impression, there is likely to be infringement. The standard is whether there is a likelihood of confusion by purchasers that the products are the same. An exact copy of a registered design that is not primarily functional or not in the prior art is an easy case in which to find infringement. However, most situations are not that simple to resolve.

B. Infringement analysis of primarily functional features

The more difficult analysis occurs when the common appearance is due to primarily functional features, a topic discussed in section II, above, and the non-primarily functional features are different. The analysis in this situation may result in a conclusion of non-infringement. If a national law allows a wider protection scope for primarily functional features, the result may be a finding of infringement.

C. Infringement analysis of substantially identical industrial designs

In the US, for example, a leading US Supreme Court decision, *Gorham Company* v. *White*, 81 U.S. 511 (1871), applied the design patent infringement test. The *Gorham* design patent drawing is shown in Figure 10, below.

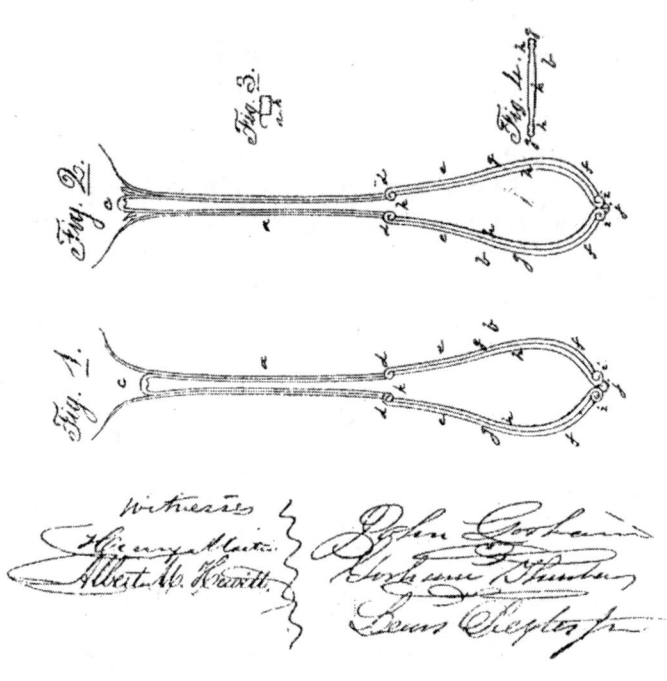

Figure 10: US Design Patent 1440 (page 1 of 3 pages), patented July 16, 1861, inventors: J. Gorman, G. Thurber & L. Dexter, Jr.

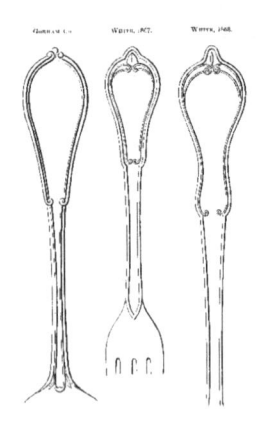

Figure 11: Illustration diagram from *Gorman* design patent US Supreme Court Opinion, 81 U.S. 511 (1871)

Infringement was held, even though there were differences between the alleged infringing products' appearances and the design patent drawing. This opinion has very helpful documents for class use. The Court provided a diagram with a comparison, shown in Figure 11 below, of the design patent claim (drawing) and the alleged infringing products. Students can make their own visual analysis. The alleged infringer was identified as White in Figure 11.

The primary impressions of the design patent drawing and the White products were the same, and the other features did not change the overall visual impression. This analysis approach gave the industrial design registration some analysis flexibility and fairness, acting as a general test for visual equivalency.

In some national systems, infringement standards may be more precisely defined.

For example, in the US, after the *Gorman* case decision, it was clear from the case law on design patents that at least some novel features of the design patent must be present in the alleged infringing product for there to be infringement. A leading case on this requirement is *Litton Systems Inc. v. Whirlpool Corp.*, 728 F. 2d 1423 (Fed. Dir. 1984), with the relevant text on page 1444. The standard known as the "points of novelty test" assured that infringement was not due to only common features found in the prior art or primarily functional features.

In the final analysis, infringement occurs when the overall impression between the design shown in the design patent, and the alleged infringing product, creates a likelihood of confusion. This analysis must be adjusted to assure that the protected design is new and the common features are not primarily functional.

As a matter of policy in the US, a design patent cannot provide protection that is the same as a utility patent. There must be added ornamental features to the technical functional features for design patent protection.

A question for class discussion would be how to change the White products, in Figure 11, to make the altered design non-infringing. In this analysis, the focus should be on whether the primary visual appearance of the altered design is the same as that in the design patent.

D. Broken line drawing practice infringement analysis

In a growing number of countries, the practice is used of showing some features in an industrial design registration drawing in broken lines for broader infringement scope, often called "partial product design protection." It is a practice followed in the US and recently adopted in Japan. The product features that are the primary focus of the customer's attention are in the industrial design registration drawing solid lines, while the other features that indicate incidental features of the product are in broken lines. A statement in the registration makes clear that the broken lines are not part of the protected designs. As an example, this approach may be used for the unique design of a basketball shoe toe.

The result of using broken lines in an industrial design registration drawing is to define more clearly the protected primary design features. An attorney must make this determination in preparing the industrial registration application. It sets the stage for the infringement analysis, to determine if a likelihood of confusion exists with the more focused features. The question is whether a different appearance is shown in the alleged infringing product.

In infringement cases with industrial design registrations that do not use broken line features in their drawings, the analysis is to find the primary features, even though other features are shown. As mentioned in section VI(C), above, there is some flexibility and fairness in that analysis. The broken line practice aims the analysis at the primary features, and the question is whether that design is the visual image that a customer sees in the alleged infringing product. Each of these drawing format approaches has advantages and disadvantages. For some designs that stand out and cannot be easily altered, the broken line practice should be most effective. On the other hand, a drawing that shows more details than appears in the alleged infringing product may still infringe. Courts have used a flexible approach to infringement analysis for drawings with more details than needed, relying on the primary impression concept. The risk of a holding of non-infringement suggests that both approaches should be available for a design owner to obtain adequate protection scope.

E. Resources on industrial design registration infringement

For more information on the US court cases cited in this section, the teacher and students may want to review the court opinions. Several private databases have a copy of these opinions at the citations indicated. In addition, on the Internet, US Supreme Court opinions are available under the case name and date from the US Supreme Court website for recent opinions at www.supremecourtus.gov/. The *Gorman* case is an old opinion, and it must be obtained from a private database or a published legal reporter. The recent Federal Circuit opinions are available on the Court of Appeals of the Federal Circuit website at www.fedcir.gov/daily-log.html, and all Federal Circuit cases are on the Georgetown University Law School website for earlier cases at www.ll.georgetown.edu/federal/judicial/cafed.cfm.

VII. Other intellectual property laws protecting industrial designs

A. Introduction

What makes industrial design law such a fascinating topic is the wide range of IP laws that can be used to protect industrial designs. Trademark law, copyright law, unfair competition law and several special industry type laws may be available in a country or regional organization. The Integrated Circuit Treaty introduced in section III(C)(9) is one of the industry laws that reached wide international acceptance. These industrial design protection laws have unique requirements. Only an introduction will be given here of the principles and special features of these other forms of industrial design protection.

B. Trademark law

A basic principle of trademark law is that a word, packaging or product configuration must identify to the purchaser the product source. The term "trade dress" has been used to identify packaging and product configuration designs that have become marks. TRIPS, discussed in section III(C), mandated in Article 15(1) a broad scope of what subject matter can be a mark when the source identification is present. The shape of the famous Coca Cola bottle is widely accepted around the world as a mark. It also may be protected by industrial design registration. Most countries permit trademark protection to continue after expiration of the industrial design registration on the same design, if trademark requirements are met. The reasoning may be that these IP laws differ in public policy purpose, economic impact and requirements. There are other laws that protect the public against abuse of trademark law.

C. Copyright Law

The international community was divided on whether copyright law could be used to protect industrial designs. Section III(C)(3) and (6), above, introduce the Berne Convention on copyrights. France approached copyright law as capable of broad protection for industrial designs. Other countries required separability from the product function to identify the copyright protected industrial design. The Berne Convention left it to national law to decide what subject matter could be protected by copyright. Architectural design protection was required by the Berne Convention. In many countries, significant industrial design protection could be provided under copyright law. For example, in the US, toys are protected by copyright law. In the age of piracy and counterfeiting, these rights are quite valuable. There is general acceptance in most situations that when protection of a design is obtained on a work by copyright, the same design can be protected by other industrial design law, including after the expiration of the industrial design registration. Each of these laws relies on different policies and requirements. Some national laws restrict what industrial designs can be protected by copyright law.

D. Unfair competition law

Industrial design protection may be possible under unfair competition law. The general international provision on unfair competition is in the Paris Convention, discussed in section III(B). Unfair competition laws restore a degree of fairness in business practices, under broad principles. These laws are not used as a substitute for industrial design registration, trademark or copyright rights. In Japan, unfair competition law prevents copying of certain product industrial designs for a limited time.

E. Industry related industrial design laws

The evolution of industry-focused industrial design laws was due to special needs for protection. In the UK, the design right met the need for protection at the time a product was introduced to a market. It allowed protection of functional as well as non-functional features for a short time and made the product design available for general licensing there after a limited period of time. No registration was required. The UK design right system met a need for start up protection. It provided a manageable system against copying, less valuable than an industrial design registration with its exclusive right against independent creation, but it was important when a product entered a market. The concept of market entry protection against copying carried forward into the unregistered protection part of the EU Community Design system.

Integrated circuits were the latest high technology when the US adopted the national Semi-Conductor Chip Act in 1984 to prevent copying of integrated circuit designs (17 U.S.C. 901–914). Chip technology was based on the layout (visual appearance) of electronic circuit layers. Later, at the urging of the US, it became a part of the Integrated Circuit Treaty (see section III(C)(9), above). TRIPS mandated certain parts of the adoption of the Integrated Circuit Treaty for all members. Another example followed in the US for the boat manufacturing industry that successfully sponsored the Vessel Hull Design Protection Act 1998 (17 U.S. 1301–1332; on the Copyright Office website), to prevent copying of boat appearances. The Chip Act and Vessel Hull Act had extensive limitations to protect the innocent user. In 2006, the US Congress was considering a bill (H.R. 5055, 109th Congress, second session) that provided protection for some fashion design products, using essentially the same legal structure found in the Vessel Hull Design Protection Act.

F. Resources for industry-related industrial design laws

The primary source of information on the Semi-Conductor Chip Act and the Vessel Hull Design Protection Act is the US Copyright Office website at www.copyright.gov. This office administers registrations under these statutes. The website has the laws, regulations and registration forms for the Vessel Hull Design Protection Act, and the registrations can be viewed. In addition, the Fryer Institute website at www.fryer.com has links to government documents on these industrial design laws, as well as other information on industrial design protection laws.

VIII. Future industrial design law development trends

It is always difficult to predict what laws national governments will enact. Many political factors influence these developments. On the other hand, there are helpful indications, based on trends observed, particularly from an international perspective. It is another reason that starting teaching of industrial design registration law with an international treaty view is an effective approach.

The following trend observations can be used for class discussions:

1. International developments will have a continued, major impact on industrial design changes. The Geneva Act of the Hague Agreement Concerning the International Registration of Industrial Designs should become accepted around the world. It will offer a common platform for filing industrial design registration applications, as well as providing the forum for discussions towards greater harmonization of national procedures and laws. The Geneva Act will give national design owners an important option for obtaining efficient foreign industrial protection.

2. There has been a significant increase in the extent of international and national design protection due to product piracy and counterfeiting.

3. The EU Community Design system will help shape changes in national design law around the world.

4. Unregistered design protection, such as in the UK design right system, the EU regional community design system unregistered right, and industry sponsored industrial design laws, will be most effective against piracy. A combination of the unregistered design protection with an industrial design registration system, such as in the EU Community Design system, is a logical and effective approach. The unregistered design protection against copying helps establish a more level playing field for business. The lack of extensive litigation over the unregistered industrial laws may suggest that industries can adjust to this level of protection, to stop outright copying of new designs, where the designs are relatively novel.

5. The debate over whether part or only all of a product can be protected in an industrial design registration should be resolved through international negotiations, hopefully, to allow the option to use both formats.

6. The revision of international copyright industrial design protection under the Berne Convention would be a major step forward. There is room to expand copyright law industrial design protection. The reciprocity limitations in the Berne Convention for copyright on industrial

designs is an unnecessary limitation on the opportunity for national design owners to obtain useful protection in other countries. It is an incentive for expanding copyright industrial design protection.

7. One useful addition to the Geneva Act of the Hague Agreement would be a procedure and related law for initial, short-term unregistered protection, similar to the EU Community Design Registration procedure. The experience to date using similar procedures has been relatively successful.

8. A need exists to review the interfaces between industrial design registration laws and other types of design protection laws. This review should examine whether industrial design registration can exist at the same time as protection under other industrial design protection laws, and whether the expiration of the industrial design registration protection precludes continued protection of the design under other industrial design protection laws. The prevailing view in most countries is that each protection form can stand separately and continue on its own fundamental principles and merits, unless there is a specific exclusion stated in a statute. One example of an exclusion is in the US Vessel Hull Design Protection Act transition from unregistered design protection to registered design protection, where the unregistered right is ended when a design patent is obtained for the same design. Discussion of these interfaces between industrial design registration protection and other forms of design protection is an excellent way to review the legal principles, public policies and economic basic for each type of intellectual property protection of industrial designs.

IX. Review of main suggestions for teaching industrial design law

A. This chapter was developed with the plan that its main topics could be an outline for teaching industrial design law. The primary headings are:

1. What industrial design is
2. International industrial design registration and other industrial design international requirements and options
3. National industrial design registration systems
4. EU Community Design registration system
5. Other intellectual property laws protecting industrial designs
6. Future industrial design law development trends.

B. Internet resources are given in this chapter whenever possible, as students around the world have greater access to these sources. These resources can provide depth to chapter topics.

C. Other ideas for teaching techniques that may work very well for industrial design law topics are listed below:

1. The teacher may show products that are being protected, or on which there should be protection under national design laws, due to the economic value of the designs and the unauthorized copying of them by competitors. A trip to local stores usually finds these product examples.

2. The use of diagrams to illustrate the operation of a design protection system has proven very effective to explain the operation of a protection system and stimulate class discussion. In this chapter, several diagrams have been provided that may be useful.

3. A useful question to ask, when comparing the system diagram of non-novelty and novelty examination systems, Figures 7 and 8 respectively, is which national system is most effective and why?

4. Another question to ask students, when studying national design registration systems, is: what changes or additions should be made to improve their national industrial design registration system? Students should be asked what public policies and economic benefits for the country or region support their proposals.

5. After reviewing the national industrial registration law topics, and the Geneva Act Agreement, a stimulating discussion may be started by asking students if they recommend that their country or regional organization join that Geneva Act; ask them to explain why.

6

Teaching intellectual property, unfair competition and anti-trust law

THOMAS COTTIER AND CHRISTOPHE GERMANN

Introduction

Market economies ideally operate under conditions of competition between producers, traders and consumers. The legal order, both national and international, and economic law in particular, provide the framework for competition. That legal order is composed of many ingredients, ranging from company law to contracts for the purposes of business transactions, to regulating international trade and government intervention and to competition law and policy, properly speaking. The latter entails a number of regulatory areas. In a narrow sense, it comprises the field of competition law or anti-trust law, and rules against unfair competition. In a broader sense, it also entails intellectual property protection, disciplines on state monopolies, on subsidies and on government procurement. All these areas define conditions of competition, and they mutually interact and cannot be read in isolation. Partly, they are regulated by international law and are part of what we call international trade regulation.[1]

This chapter addresses the relationship of intellectual property, unfair competition and anti-trust rules. After briefly recalling the functions of intellectual property rights and their role for competition, we will turn to unfair competition and anti-trust rules. The three areas find themselves in a close and complex relationship. All are essential in creating fair conditions of competition. In particular, intellectual property laws need to be shaped and interpreted in accordance with related rules, as much as other rules need to consider the functions of intellectual property. The three areas may briefly be characterized as follows.

---

[1] See generally Thomas Cottier and Matthias Oesch, *International Trade Regulation: Law and Policy in the WTO, the European Union and Switzerland*, Berne/London 2005.

The main function of intellectual property laws is to provide incentives for innovation and creation in the form of exclusive rights that can be considered as private monopolies, either limited in time (patents, copyright, related rights etc.), or for potentially unlimited duration (indefinitely renewable trademark registrations, trade names etc.). Intellectual property law works as an instrument to appropriate knowledge that is understood in a broad sense as encompassing, in particular, scientific and artistic content as well as market relevant information. The forms of protection provided by intellectual property laws range from patents for inventions over exclusive rights on industrial models, plant varieties, layout-designs or integrated circuits, industrial design, to copyright and related rights. The protection of undisclosed information functions as a supplement to the patent system. Trademarks, geographical indications and, to some extent, protection of industrial designs, on the other hand, are intended to serve as identifiers and as incentives for investments in reputation (goodwill, quality). In this light, the individual user's primary interest lies in obtaining access to protected goods and services under affordable conditions, and to not be misled with respect to identifiers. The classical approach is based on a duality of paradigms where the patent paradigm typically protects functional or utilitarian achievements, whereas the copyright paradigm protects creative results that do not need to show practical applications such as artistic works. This duality has, however, been gradually eroded, for example in the area of information technology where copyright is used to protect software.[2] A further category of intellectual property rights to be labeled as "identifiers" protects distinctive signs such as trademarks, trade names or geographical indications. Eventually, intellectual property law traditionally also includes rules prohibiting unfair competition although these rules do not provide exclusive rights.

Unfair competition law commonly protects fair competition with a particular focus on good faith in business dealings and fair business practices. Like intellectual property rights, unfair competition law essentially

---

[2] The Paris Convention of 1883 on industrial property and the Berne Convention of 1886 on copyright as well as the other WIPO administered conventions enshrined the regulatory dualism between "industrial" (patents, trademarks) and "intellectual" (copyright) property. On this dualism and its challenge see, inter alia, J. Wiley, "Copyright at the School of Patent", *Univ. Chicago L. Rev.* 1991, 119; J. C. Ginsburg and R. P. Merges, *Foundations of Intellectual Property*, New York 2004; W. Cornish, *Intellectual Property: Patents, Copyright, Trademarks and Allied Rights*, London 2003; J. H Reichman, "Charting the Collapse of the Patent-Copyright Dichotomy: Premises for a Restructured International Intellectual Property System", *Cardozo Arts & Entertainment Law Journal* 1995, 475.

aims at protecting physical and legal persons (individuals and companies) against "free riding" on investment in knowledge and the fruits of labors created by others.

Competition (anti-trust) legislation typically aims at protecting the market, and more precisely at preserving an effective competitive framework that shall promote the best quality of goods and services at the lowest costs for consumers, as well as ensure the suppliers' freedom of access to the market and the demands associated with freedom of choice.[3] Competition rules, or anti-trust rules, essentially operate as legal restrictions on the freedom of contract between economic operators who are mutually placed in a competitive relationship. The law intervenes to avoid collusion and concertation which diminishes workable competition to the detriment of consumers. Also, competition law disciplines the conduct of dominant operators who otherwise need not consider other market participants. Anti-trust thus operates as a limitation on freedom of conduct to the benefit of markets and consumers.

Often, intellectual property rights are considered anathema to competition as they offer exclusive rights and thus exclude competition. However, they form an essential basis for competition. Without proper protection, investment will not be encouraged and third parties cannot be prevented from free-riding and unfairly using the fruits of investment without compensation. In operational terms, intellectual property protection and protection against unfair competition are complementary, as they essentially pursue comparable goals. Anti-trust rules, on the other hand, provide a counterbalance to the granting of exclusive rights. They assist in combating abuses of such rights detrimental to competition on markets.

By analyzing the various aspects of the regulatory framework on intellectual property protection, one can perceive a dialectic relationship between "property" in terms of exclusive rights on one hand, and "freedom" of economic players to access the market and to operate there on a level playing field as promoted by competition law, that indirectly furthers the freedom of choice of consumers, on the other hand.[4] As Ghidini postulates, one should recognize a dialectical exchange between

---

[3] For example, Article 6 of the Swiss federal law on cartels and other restraints of October 6, 1995 provides that its purpose is to prevent harmful economic or social effects of cartels and other restraints of competition and, by so doing, to promote competition in the interests of a market economy based on liberal principles.

[4] Gustavo Ghidini, *Intellectual Property and Competition Law. The Innovation Nexus*, Cheltenham, Northampton 2006 (Edward Elgar), p. 1.

the two disciplines which aim at different but often synergic objectives. According to that author, both categories of law often interact to eliminate situations that would obstruct innovation, creation and competitive dynamics. Thus, through "this dialectical exchange, each discipline, by fulfilling its function, can also *indirectly* serve the aim of the other."[5]

In mature legal orders, the disciplines of intellectual property, competition law (anti-trust) and unfair competition rules develop in tandem and provide an appropriate balance. In many quarters of the world, such a basis does not yet exist. While international law prescribes advanced standards of intellectual property and rudimentary rules on unfair competition by means of international treaty obligations, in particular the Agreement on Trade-Related Aspects of Intellectual Property Rights (TRIPS Agreement) of the World Trade Organization (WTO), anti-trust rules have largely remained a matter of domestic law, still lacking in many countries. Vice-versa, competition law may be developed while common standards of intellectual property protection remain deficient, as has been the case in European Community law. Overall, this results in constellations of imbalance which future efforts on the national, international and regional levels need to remedy. We return to this point in the conclusions offered at the end of the chapter.

Rationales underlying the grant of intellectual property rights

Before turning to the relationship of intellectual property, unfair competition and anti-trust rules, it is useful to recall the rationale underlying the grant of intellectual property rights. They essentially respond to market failures which are inherent in the nature of knowledge. Knowledge has two characteristics: it is a "non-rival public good"; and it can be easily copied. The former feature means that one person's knowledge does not diminish that of another. The creation of knowledge inherently benefits the public at large. This per se is beneficial. At the same time, its very nature discourages investment and efforts; it is per se not suitable for marketing. The latter aspect refers to the issue of market failure due to the fact that inventive or creative efforts may be substantial, whereas the copying of the results of these efforts may only cost a fraction thereof. In other words, if a good or service embodying knowledge requires considerable creativity, ingenuity and research, there are normally insufficient financial incentives to devote resources to these efforts, if the good or

[5] Ibid., p. 115.

service can be copied with lower efforts.[6] In order to offset such effects, exclusive rights to use and dispose of knowledge were created.

Intellectual property protection shall provide an incentive for innovation and creation by granting a competitive advantage to the right holders. This rationale requires a careful balance which is difficult to achieve. Levels of protection that are too low may lead to a situation where intangible assets risk being excessively utilized (so-called "tragedy of commons").[7] On the other side, levels of protection that are too high may deter creators, innovators and users, because too many owners can block each other (so-called "tragedy of anti-commons").[8]

Different rationales are commonly invoked to justify intellectual property protection. According to the "natural-rights" approach, the creator or inventor has a "natural" property right in his intellectual achievements, and society is morally obligated to recognize and implement this property right. Article 27 of the Universal Declaration of Human Rights refers to a natural property right concept when it states that everyone "has the right to the protection of the moral and material interests resulting from any scientific, literary or artistic production of which he is the author." Article 15, sec. 1 let. (c) of the International Covenant on Economic, Social and Cultural Rights expresses the same approach by a similar wording. According to the "reward-by-monopoly" theory, a creator or inventor should receive reward for his or her services in proportion to their usefulness to society. The reward takes the form of temporary exclusive rights pertaining to the creation or invention. Based on the "monopoly-profit-incentive" thesis, intellectual property protection is supposed to grant an incentive for creators, inventors and their financial investors to make intellectual efforts and take entrepreneurial and financial risks reasonably worthwhile by increasing their profit expectations through the exclusive rights limited in time which they are granted in return. Eventually, in the field of patents, the "exchange-for-secrets" rationale will provide an incentive for inventors to disclose their achievements to society in exchange for exclusivity that will grant them a competitive advantage for a limited period of time. These latter three

---

[6] See Commission on Intellectual Property Rights, *Integrating Intellectual Property Rights and Development Policy*, London 2002, p. 14, with further references.

[7] See Garrett James Hardin, "The Tragedy of the Commons" *Science* 162, 1968, 1243–1248, and Achim Lerch, Property Rights and Biodiversity: *European Journal of Law and Economics* 6, 1998, p. 285–304.

[8] See Michael A. Heller and Rebecca S. Eisenberg, "Can Patents Deter Innovation? The Anticommons in Biomedical Research", *Science* 280, May 1998, 698–701.

concepts are intended to justify patent protection; and except for the "exchange-for-secrets" rationale, the same applies to copyright, performers' rights and industrial design protection.

On the international level, in particular with respect to the TRIPS Agreement binding upon the members of the World Trade Organization (WTO), one can add to the list of these rationales the aim of promoting sustainable development, in particular with respect to the "transfer and dissemination of technology" from industrialized to developing countries and least developed countries, to the benefit of local producers and users. These rationales are invoked to justify the protection by patents, copyright, related rights and layout-design (topographies) of integrated circuits. The integration of intellectual property law into the world trading system via the TRIPS Agreement was based on the rationale of the comparative advantage theory that underlies progressive trade liberalization.

It is submitted that current laws on intellectual property are mainly based upon this utilitarian concept. While the "natural-rights" approach is suitable to explain protection closely relating to personality, such as moral rights, utilitarian concepts are much better placed to fine-tune the scope of rights and to explain their limitations in substance and time. Moreover, it will be seen that a utilitarian rationale alone is capable of bringing about appropriate coordination with laws on unfair competition and anti-trust rules.

Protection against unfair competition

Principles and objectives of unfair competition legislation

Fairness in business operations, as much as in human relations in general, is an ethical concept underlying law. Closely relating to good faith and the protection of legitimate expectations, it seeks to discourage and to sanction conduct inconsistent with honesty. Competition should take place in the spirit of a sports person: rule-based, open, frank, and respecting the efforts and achievements of others. Fairness, at the same time, is an elusive concept. It is required to find more specific expressions in law in order to operate and to offer predictability and legal security. Fairness has thus found expression in many provisions of the legal order. It is inherent in constitutional rights, procedural guarantees and norms of substantive law which seek to implement ethics. The same is true for laws protecting specifically against unfair competition and conduct in business relations. The law developed different responses to the problem in different national and regional jurisdictions.[9] It is interesting to observe that harmonization of unfair competition rules is limited to consumer protection, while business-to-business relations have remained in the exclusive competence of the Member States of the European Union/Community.[10] Moreover, that harmonization is relatively recent, and occurred much later than in the fields of intellectual property protection and anti-trust law. From a perspective of global law, it is far from showing harmonized and uniform standards.

On the national level, the legal basis for the repression of unfair competition can range from a tort provision phrased in general terms to detailed articles of law, and a mixture of these two legislative approaches.[11] The standards of fairness or honesty in competition commonly reflect the sociological, economic, moral and ethical concepts of a given society, and may therefore differ from one country to the other and vary over time.

Unfair competition law grants protection to the market players from unfair business practices. One can distinguish between unfair business-to-business practices (relationship between competitors) and unfair business-to-consumer practices (relationship between supply and demand). Pursuant to European law, a business-to-consumer practice is considered as unfair if it is contrary to the requirement of professional diligence and if it materially distorts the economic behavior with regard to the product or service of the average consumer to whom it is addressed. In particular, commercial practices are deemed unfair if they are misleading or aggressive.[12] Unfair business practices between competitors essentially focus on

---

[9] For national legislations see WIPO's Collection of Laws for Electronic Access (CLEA) database at: www.wipo.int/clea/en/index.jsp (visited June 2006).

[10] Directive 2005/29/EC of the European Parliament and of the Council of 11 May 2005 concerning unfair business-to-consumer commercial practices in the internal market and amending Council Directive 84/450/EEC, Directives 97/7/EC, 98/27/EC and 2002/65/EC of the European Parliament and of the Council and Regulation (EC) No 2006/2004 of the European Parliament and of the Council, L 149/22, 11.6.2005.

[11] The Swiss Unfair Competition Act of 1986, for example, contains both a general provision and detailed provisions addressing specific types of dishonest business practices. Within this law, the special provisions prevail over the general one according to the principle *lex specialis derogatlegi generalis* whereas the former rule is applied when the latter ones fail to cover an unfair practice that is contemplated by the overall purpose of the law.

[12] See Articles 5 to 9 of the EC Unfair Commercial Practices Directive. According to these provisions, "misleading" means that a commercial practice if it contains false information and is therefore untruthful or in any way, including overall presentation, deceives or is likely to deceive the average consumer, even if the information is factually correct, in relation inter alia to the nature of the product, its main characteristics, its price, the need for a service, replacement or repair. A commercial practice is regarded as "aggressive" if, in its factual context, taking account of all its features and circumstances, by harassment, coercion,

use and appropriation of efforts, work and achievements of competitors ("free riding"). Beyond the narrow relationship between businesses and consumers, many national unfair competition laws also protect society at large with respect to its interest in free competition as a public good and its impact on the economy. This broader objective brings unfair competition law close to competition (anti-trust) law. Exceptionally, unfair competition laws not only offer protection against unfair conduct by competitors, but also defend businesses from allegedly unfounded criticism of products by private consumer protection organizations and the press at large. Such laws inherently create tensions with freedom of information and of expression, and often exert an unduly protectionist effect.[13]

Ever since, protection against unfair competition has been closely related to the evolution of intellectual property rights, supplementing as general principles more specialized rules of intellectual property protection. There is an obvious link between patents, copyright, trademarks and trade names on one side, and unfair competition legislation on the other side with respect to the prohibition of acts contrary to honest business practices such as "free riding" in general and "passing off" in particular.[14] Specific forms of intellectual property protection emerged as an emanation of the ethics underlying the laws of unfair competition. New issues often appear first under the heading of unfair competition and eventually find their way into specific forms of intellectual property protection.

Close links also exist with competition (anti-trust) law and policy, since both sets of legal norms aim at ensuring the efficient functioning of the market economy. Competition law equally embodies principles of fairness with its functions of combating restraints on trade and abuses of market power, the most obvious case of unfairness being boycotting potential

including the use of physical force, or undue influence, it significantly impairs or is likely to significantly impair the average consumer's freedom of choice or conduct with regard to the product and thereby causes him or is likely to cause him to take a transactional decision that he would not have taken otherwise.

[13] See for example the case *Hertel v. Switzerland*, Judgment of the European Court of Human Rights of August 25, 1998(59/1997/843/1049). This case concerned a ruling by the Swiss Federal Court based on unfair competition law against a scientist who published his study on the effects on human beings of the consumption of food prepared in microwave ovens. For a discussion of this case, see Thomas Cottier and Sangeeta Khorana, "Linkage between Freedom of Expression and Unfair Competition Rules in International Trade: The Hertel Case and Beyond", in: Thomas Cottier, Joost Pauwelyn and Elisabeth Burgi (eds), *Human Rights and International Trade*, Oxford 2005, p. 245.

[14] In certain jurisdictions, "passing off," meaning unauthorized use of a trademark that has not been registered, is considered under certain conditions as illegal.

competitors. Again, different cultures have developed differently, and it is impossible to deal with the subject matter in a comprehensive manner as domestic legislations may vary largely.

Relationship to intellectual property protection

Since unfair competition law and the protection of intellectual property pursue partly overlapping goals and objectives, the two areas have developed a rather complex relationship which may vary, again, from country to country. A few general observations can be made on the basis of selected case law.

Independent application

In many instances, unfair competition rules serve to supplement what intellectual property laws do not or cannot provide in particular circumstances. For example, according to the Swiss Federal Court, trademark legislation constitutes no special law vis-à-vis unfair competition legislation that would allow the former to prevail as *lex specialis* over the latter.[15] This case law concludes that trademark and unfair competition laws obey different rationales.[16] Unfair competition law aims at promoting fair and undistorted competition. As a consequence, a trademark owner may not use her exclusive rights in a way that qualifies as unfair competition. Article 3 lit. d of the Swiss Unfair Competition Act prohibits an indication or make-up and presentation of a product (*Aufmachung*) that leads to confusion in respect of older goods or services. The Court recalled that any behavior that is misleading or that otherwise infringes the principle of good faith and that influences the relationship between competitors or between supply and demand is deemed to be unfair and illicit.[17]

Unfair competition law may substitute for protection where such protection is not available under intellectual property laws. A good example is the protection equivalent to moral rights in US law. In the case *Monty Python v. American Broadcasting Companies, Inc. (ABC)*, the appellants

---

[15] Judgement of the Swiss Federal Court 129 III 358, 4C.343/2002, of March 17, 2003.
[16] In *Puls Media AG Swiss Radio and Television Corporation SRG*, the litigating parties that used to cooperated with each other eventually split while Puls Media AG registered "PULS-Tip" as a trademark for the services provided under the former partnership (broadcast and printed information on health questions), and kept using the sign as a trade name and Internet domain name. In this case, the defendant as the trademark right holder eventually had to stop using its trademark since this use caused a risk of confusion between the claimant's television broadcast and the defendant's printed product and the respective trade names.   [17] Judgment of the Swiss Federal Court 129 III 352.

invoked the theory that the editing cuts made by the broadcaster without their consent constituted an actionable mutilation of their work.[18] This cause of action, which seeks redress for the deformation of an artist's work, finds its roots in the continental concept of *droit moral*, or moral rights, as set forth in Article 6*bis* of the Berne Convention. US copyright law does not recognize moral rights since this law seeks to vindicate the economic, rather than the personal, rights of authors. However, the economic incentives for artistic and intellectual creation that serves as the foundation of the American Copyright Act, cannot be reconciled with the inability of artists to obtain relief for mutilation or misrepresentation of their work to the public on which the artists are financially dependent. American courts have long granted relief for misrepresentation of an artist's work by relying on theories outside the statutory law of copyright, such as contract law, or the tort of unfair competition. In the case at stake, Monty Python's members claimed that the editing done for ABC on their television programs violated the Lanham Act § 43(a), 15 U.S.C § 1125(a), the federal unfair competition act. This statute provides in particular that any person affixing, applying, annexing, or using in connection with any goods or services a false designation of origin, or any false description or representation, and causing such goods or services to enter into commerce, shall be liable to a civil action by any person who believes that he is or is likely to be damaged by the use of any such false description or representation.

Pre-emption of unfair competition rules

Protection under unfair competition law should generally not be considered as an alternative to intellectual property protection. Pursuant to the principle of pre-emption, protection under unfair competition law will be generally denied – except in certain cases of confusion – if protection under specific intellectual property rights were available, at least for a certain period of time, and expired thereafter. For example, in *Schweizerische Interpreten-Gesellschaft*,[19] the Swiss Federal Court stated that gaps in a particular law relating to intangible property rights cannot be closed by means of the general clause of the Swiss Unfair Competition Act. In principle, the results of efforts and labor which, according to the

---

[18] United States Court of Appeals for the Second Circuit 538 F. 2d; 1976 U.S. LEXIS 8225, June 30, 1976; see excerpts in: Frederick Abbott, Thomas Cottier and Francis Gurry, *The International Intellectual Property System: Commentary and Materials*, Kluwer Law International, The Hague, London, Boston 1999, p. 1096 ff.

[19] BGE 110 II 411 (2 October 1984).

special law, are no longer protected or cannot be protected at all, may be used by anyone, even competitors. An interpretation to the contrary would amount to a monopolization of non-copyrighted content. The Court further recalled that the only exception allowed by case law relates to special circumstances under which a particular conduct or measures are genuinely unfair and therefore justify the application of the general clause of the Unfair Competition Law.[20]

The principle of pre-emption, emanating from the principles of *lex specialis derogat legi generali*, takes its substantive legitimacy from the assumption that intellectual property law is supposed to materialize a specific balance of the various stakeholders' interests (creators, innovators, users and society) by featuring built-in "competitive antibodies" that promotes innovation and creation within the paradigm of monopoly-like exclusive rights.[21] Applying unfair competition rules would therefore, in general, undermine the balance between appropriation and public domain.

Basis for codification of intellectual property

Unfair competition law often serves as a basis for intellectual property legislation. In various jurisdictions, legislators have the tendency to codify consolidated case law on unfair competition caused by confusion and misappropriation within their intellectual property legislation, in particular within laws on trademarks, trade names and geographical indications. In this way, intellectual property laws dealing with these issues are eroding the proper scope of application of unfair competition laws. This tendency is reinforced by international instruments such as the TRIPS Agreement harmonizing the approaches that deal with the prohibition of confusion and misappropriation, discussed below.

Protection in international law

Foundations

National legislation, divergent as it may be, has to be consistent with applicable international instruments, such as the TRIPS Agreement and the Paris Convention. We therefore focus on common rules available in international law and thus binding on many countries being part of global law. Protection was recognized as forming part of intellectual

---

[20] BGE 108 II 332–333 (July 13, 1982).   [21] Ghidini (note 4 above), p. 7.

property for more than a century. In 1900, the Brussels Diplomatic Conference for the Revision of the Paris Convention for the Protection of Industrial Property introduced Article 10*bis* that specifically addresses unfair competition. It was eventually revised in the Stockholm Act of 1967 of the Paris Convention. The provision reads as follows:

Article 10*bis*

Unfair Competition

(1) The countries of the Union are bound to assure to nationals of such countries effective protection against unfair competition.
(2) Any act of competition contrary to honest practices in industrial or commercial matters constitutes an act of unfair competition.
(3) The following in particular shall be prohibited:

  (i) all acts of such a nature as to create confusion by any means whatever with the establishment, the goods, or the industrial or commercial activities, of a competitor;
  (ii) false allegations in the course of trade of such a nature as to discredit the establishment, the goods, or the industrial or commercial activities, of a competitor;
  (iii) indications or allegations the use of which in the course of trade is liable to mislead the public as to the nature, the manufacturing process, the characteristics, the suitability for their purpose, or the quantity, of the goods.

Article 10*ter* of the Paris Convention requires providing "appropriate legal remedies" against the violation of unfair competition law as contemplated by Article 10*bis*. Pursuant to the second paragraph of this provision, member states must grant the right to be a party in judicial or administrative procedures to federations and associations representing interested industrialists, producers, or merchants who otherwise could not invoke any particular form of intellectual property protection, provided, however, that the law of the country in which protection is claimed allows such action by federations and associations of that country.

The TRIPS Agreement explicitly refers to Article 10*bis* and 10*ter* of the Paris Convention and it incorporates those provisions on the basis of its Article 2. In addition, special reference to Article 10*bis* of the Paris Convention offers the basis for particular regulation of geographical indications in Article 22, and for the protection of undisclosed information in Article 39 of the TRIPS Agreement.

With the inclusion of Article 10*bis* of the Paris Convention into the TRIPS Agreement, unfair competition law finally is made subject to effective international dispute settlement under the Dispute Settlement Understanding of the WTO. This is of particular importance as the law of unfair competition inherently builds upon case law. At this point in time, Article 10*bis* of the Paris Convention has not been subject to panel or Appellate Body decisions, and little guidance exists as to how the broad principles should be interpreted on the level of international law.[22] The field is far from settled and mature.

The provisions on unfair competition in Article 10*bis* of the Paris Convention is broadly termed and refers to elusive concepts, requiring careful interpretation. The norm obliges WTO Members (and other Member States party to the Paris Convention) to provide appropriate protection in domestic jurisdictions, and to enact, if necessary, appropriate legislation. The terms primarily leave the determination of the notion of honesty in industrial and commercial matters to the national courts and administrative authorities. They are not strictly limited to producer and consumer relations. Member States of the Paris Union are free to grant protection against certain acts even if the parties involved are not competing against each other.[23]

---

[22] Unfair competition has largely remained an untouched area in WTO disputes settlement. A violation of Article 10*bis* and 10*ter* of the Paris Convention was claimed in European Communities – Trademarks and Geographical Indications. Australia argued that the European Council Regulation of July 14, 1992 on the protection of geographical indications and designations of origin for agricultural products and foodstuffs, including its amendments and related implementing and enforcement measures, provides a Community-wide system of registration of GIs that grants "effective protection from acts of unfair competition, including in relation to later trademark applications, within the Community, but not a Community-wide system of effective protection of trademarks from acts of unfair competition arising from the later registration of GIs under the Regulation." (para. 7.719). The Panel left this question open by concluding that Australia did not make a prima facie case in support of its claims under Articles 10*bis* and 10*ter* of the Paris Convention as incorporated in the TRIPS Agreement since Australia has not clearly explained the premise of its claims according to which the EC must provide at Community-level protection for trademarks against unfair competition arising from GIs. However, the Panel pointed out that unfair competition laws might be adequate to implement GI protection under Article 22.2 of the TRIPS Agreement (para. 7.503); European Communities-Protection of Trademarks and Geographical Indications for Agricultural Products and Foodstuffs, WT/DS290R (complaint by Australia initiated by a Panel request of August 18, 2003; the simultaneously initiated dispute by the United States against the European Communities, WT/DS174/R, presented substantial overlap with respect to the claims and the Panel's findings).   [23] See note 13 above.

While leaving ample room to domestic jurisdiction, international law nevertheless provides guidance as to the scope and interpretation of these broad precepts and principles. Firstly, Members need to respect requirements emanating from other applicable regional and international treaties, in particular international instruments on human rights. Secondly, the notions of honest business practices, and the constellations addressed in the non-exhaustive list, are notions of international law. They are subject to specification in dispute settlement and fully operational in international disputes brought before the WTO. It is submitted that these specifications, amount to minimal standards which Members will need to respect, irrespective of domestic definitions adopted in legislation and case law. Also, it is submitted that these minimal standards are suitable for direct effect before domestic courts and administrative authorities, where constitutional law so permits. The provision of Article 10*bis*, paragraph 1, does not imply a dualistic concept. At any rate, and once a substantial body of case law exists on the subject in WTO law, national courts should take it into account under the doctrine of consistent interpretation. Domestic terms of unfair competition should be construed in the light of minimal standards emanating from Article 10*bis* of the Paris Convention.

Protection against dishonest practices, confusion and false allegations

Pursuant to Article 10*bis*, paragraph 2 of the Paris Convention, any act of competition contrary to honest practices in industrial or commercial matters constitutes an act of unfair competition. Unfair competition in the relationship between competitors may take various forms. Article 10*bis*, paragraph 3 of the Paris Convention mentions in particular all acts of such a nature as to create confusion by any means whatever with the establishment, the goods, or the industrial or commercial activities, of a competitor (sub-para. 1), as well as false allegations in the course of trade of such a nature as to discredit the establishment, the goods, or the industrial or commercial activities, of a competitor (sub-para. 2).

Article 10*bis*, paragraph 3 provides for a non-exhaustive list of dishonest practices that shall be prohibited including acts creating confusion by any means whatever with the establishment, the goods, or the industrial or commercial activities, of a competitor, false and discrediting or misleading indications and allegations. It aims at protecting competitors against a risk of confusion and false allegations having a discrediting effect, as well as the public against misleading information as to the nature, the manufacturing process, the characteristics, and the suitability for their purpose, or the quantity, of the goods.[24]

Article 10*bis*, paragraph 3(1) of the Paris Convention does not make the prohibition of confusion conditional to intent or negligence in acting, or omitting to act. Bad faith, however, may be taken into account in respect of the sanction for an infringement. Likelihood of confusion is sufficient. It is therefore not necessary that the confusion actually has taken place. Confusion mainly occurs in relation to indications of origin of goods and services (confusion as to affiliation or as to sponsorship) and to their appearance (confusion as to product shape). Accordingly, for generic and commonplace goods and services, the likelihood of confusion can normally be denied since they no longer have an original or distinctive character. Specific trademark and trade name legislation provides protection against confusion, and often makes recourse to unfair competition redundant. However, intellectual property protection may not always be appropriate and adequate, for example in the case of protection of well-known trademarks as addressed by Article 6*bis* of the Paris Convention and Article 16 of the TRIPS Agreement.[25] Member States may implement the prohibition to use a well-known trademark pursuant to Article 6*bis* of the Paris Convention on the national level via their unfair competition legislation, in the absence of corresponding restrictions in their trademark legislation.

---

[24] Apart from Articles 10*bis* and 10*ter*, the Paris Convention contains several provisions relevant to protection against acts of unfair competition in a broader sense, especially those concerning trademarks and trade names. For example, Articles 6*sexies* and 8 provide for the protection of service marks and trade names, respectively. The protection of indications of geographical origin, to the extent that it is not provided by Article 10*bis*(3), results from Article 10 and Article 9, to which Article 10 refers. Special agreements concluded within the Paris Convention, namely, the Madrid Agreement for the Repression of False or Deceptive Indications of Source on Goods and the Lisbon Agreement for the Protection of Appellations of Origin and their International Registration, along with the TRIPS Agreement and bilateral treaties, specifically provide for the international protection of geographical indications.

[25] Article 16.2 of the TRIPS Agreement extends the scope of Article 6*bis* of the Paris Convention to service trademarks. Furthermore, Article 16.3 of the TRIPS Agreement requires the WTO Members to apply Article 6*bis* of the Paris Convention, *mutatis mutandis*, to goods or services which are not similar to those in respect of which a trademark is registered, provided that use of that trademark in relation to those goods or services would indicate a connection between those goods or services and the owner of the registered trademark and provided that the interests of the owner of the registered trademark are likely to be damaged by such use.

Protection against free riding

Undue advantage of efforts and achievement by others and recognized by consumers and other market participants may be taken by imitating products and services or their identifiers, including trade marks, trade names and other forms of commercially relevant indications. Article 10*bis* of the Paris Convention encapsulates this under the doctrine of competition contrary to honest practices in paragraph 2, while leaving it, astonishingly, without mention in the non-exclusive list of paragraph 3. Preventing and combating free riding on work and products of others is an essential and core function of unfair competition rules and of intellectual property protection alike. Whereas free riding is considered as a dishonest business practice under unfair competition law, it is deemed to hinder innovation, creativity and the supply of reliable market information under intellectual property law.

Protection against free riding amounts to one of the major functions of intellectual property and its different forms. Unfair competition rules take place where such protection is not sufficiently available or existent. They provide complementary protection. For example, a school may offer a particular curriculum or training program, composed in a particular manner. It is neither protected by trademark or copyright. Competitors nevertheless are not allowed to imitate the structure of the program without the consent of the school. As a prerequisite of the protection against free riding on a firm's identity and reputation, the indication, the good or service must have some distinctiveness. In other words, unfair competition does not protect against the imitation of mere banality. However, the degree of distinctiveness may be lower than what is required under intellectual property legislation.

The TRIPS Agreement further elaborates protection against free riding in relation to geographical indications, to undisclosed information and to test data. Today, and due to WTO law, these areas clearly pertain to the protection of intellectual property, but remain essentially informed in terms of foundations and scope to the protection of unfair competition. The respective provisions refer to Article 10*bis* of the Paris Convention.

Article 22, paragraph 2(a) of the TRIPS Agreement protects geographical indications to the extent that the designation or presentation of a product suggests that the product originates in a geographical area different from the true place of origin in a manner which misleads the public as to the geographical origin of the good. Except for wines and spirits in accordance with Articles 22 and 23 of the TRIPS Agreement, the indication of the true origin of the product protects from violating the obligation. For example, it is possible to label "Gruyère Cheese made in the US" since consumers are thus informed about the true origin of the product despite the fact that the product is based upon qualities relating to a Swiss region. Protection therefore is limited. This explains why enhanced protection applicable to wines and spirits is thought to be extended to all agricultural products in the Doha Round negotiations. The question arises as to whether such use may otherwise constitute an act of unfair competition in accordance with paragraph 2(b) of the provision, which generally refers to Article 10*bis* of the Paris Convention. To the extent that – despite the absence of confusion as to the true origin – the product is essentially based upon free riding in terms of traditional know-how and experience and thus traditional knowledge, a case can be made under Article 10*bis* of the Paris Convention.

The same relationship is contemplated by the protection of undisclosed information (trade secrets) pursuant to Article 39 of the TRIPS Agreement. Provided that the conditions under Article 39.2 of the TRIPS Agreement regarding the secrecy and commercial value of the information are met, natural and legal persons shall have the possibility of preventing information lawfully within their control from being disclosed to, acquired by, or used by others without their consent in a manner contrary to honest commercial practices.[26] Such practices have in common a business's attempt vis-à-vis other businesses to succeed in competition without relying on its own achievements in terms of quality and price of its products and services, but rather by taking undue advantage of the work of another (free riding) or by influencing consumer demand with false or misleading statements.

Article 39.3 of the TRIPS Agreement provides that WTO Members must protect undisclosed test or other data that took considerable effort to be generated, against unfair commercial use when they require that such data must be submitted to their agencies for the purpose of marketing approval for pharmaceutical or agricultural chemical products utilizing new chemical entities. Furthermore, WTO Members must protect such data against disclosure, except where necessary to protect the public

---

[26] In comparison, Article 1721(2) of NAFTA reads as follows: "... 'a manner contrary to honest commercial practices' shall mean at least practices such as breach of contract, breach of confidence and inducement to breach, and includes the acquisition of undisclosed information by third parties who knew, or were grossly negligent in failing to know, that such practices were involved in the acquisition."

or unless steps are taken to ensure that the data are protected against unfair commercial use.

Legally, the provision can be seen as an enlargement of the list of acts that are prohibited under Article 10*bis*, para. 3 of the Paris Convention.[27] In other words, Article 39.3 of the TRIPS Agreement addresses the unfair use of undisclosed data submitted to authorities by private competitors. The prohibition of such use pursuant to this provision aims at protecting applicants for marketing approval of a pharmaceutical or an agricultural chemical product from misappropriation and free riding by others of their test data produced at high costs. This provision prohibits subsequent applicants from relying on test data submitted by a first applicant without her consent. The authorities in charge of the approval procedure are therefore not allowed to take into account the data of the first applicant when examining the file of a competitor, e.g. in the case of a generic drug, because this would lead to a commercially unfair imbalance between the competitors. As an alternative, WTO Members may require the second applicant to compensate the first applicant for its reliance on the test data. This approach allows saving efforts on the tests by obliging applicants to share their test data and the costs of generating that data.[28]

A recent example of linking new forms of protection to unfair competition and eventually intellectual property rights can be observed with the emerging protection of Traditional Knowledge. While currently left in the public domain, Traditional Knowledge can be freely used in the context of biotechnology as an important source of information and a

---

[27] This solution was found by the negotiating parties in order to overcome the obstacle that protection of undisclosed information, including test data, did not form part of the traditional body and the *numerus clausus* of intellectual property rights of many jurisdictions; see Ingo Meitinger, "Commentary on Article 39 of the TRIPS Agreement", in: Thomas Cottier and Pierre Véron (eds.), *Concise International and European IP law*, Kluwer law International 2007 (forthcoming). The decision of the European Commission of March 24, 2004 in the *Microsoft* case provides an example of the interaction between the protection of undisclosed data and competition law where the refusal to supply the relevant information to competitors was considered as an abuse of dominant position, see infra note 44.

[28] Ingo Meitinger, note 27 above. This solution has been chosen by the EC and Switzerland in the area of agricultural chemical products, as far as animal testing is involved (see, e.g. Article 13 of the Biocidal Directive of the EC and Articles 28 and 29 of the Swiss Regulation on Plant Protection Products). The USA took a similar approach in their pesticides legislation. The FIFRA foresees in § 136a(c)(1)(F)(iii) an obligation to compensate for reliance on test data during a period of five years following a ten-years period of exclusivity. If a WTO Member provides for a compensation system, it must ensure that the compensation is adequate and fair in order to meet the requirements of Article 39 para. 3 of the TRIPS Agreement.

basis for new products which are eligible for patent protection. Current efforts at WIPO to protect Traditional Knowledge are essentially based upon the concept of unfair competition[29] in combination with requirements to disclose the source of information in subsequent patent applications; these efforts may eventually be developed into protection under other forms of intellectual property rights which would offer a clear basis for protecting or licensing such information, with a view to extracting appropriate benefit sharing beyond contractual models enshrined in the Convention on Biological Diversity.[30]

Finally, a potential field of application of unfair competition rules in international law relates to the protection of Internet domain names involving more than one jurisdiction, which are dealt with by the Mediation and Arbitration Center of the WIPO.[31] For the time being, the substantive rules only provide rules for the conflict between a domain name and a trademark, where the domain name registered by the domain name registrant is identical or confusingly similar to a trademark in which the complainant has rights (para. 4(a) UDRP).[32] In this case, the rights of the registered trademark owner prevail over the interests of the domain name registrant unless the latter is in good faith. However, there is no similar dispute settlement mechanism available with respect to conflicts between domain names that are not registered as trademarks, or between domain names and trade names. These cases are essentially dealt with under the unfair competition law of national or regional jurisdictions. Corresponding judgments may be substantially more difficult and costly to enforce in foreign jurisdictions as arbitration awards under the

---

[29] See, in particular, WIPO document WIPO/GRTKF//IC/10/5 "The Protection of Traditional Knowledge: Draft Objectives and Principles, Document" prepared by the Secretariat for WIPO Intergovernmental Committee on Intellectual Property and Genetic Resources, Traditional Knowledge and Folklore" (October 2, 2006).

[30] See Thomas Cottier and Marion Panizzon, "Legal Perspectives on Traditional Knowledge: The Case for Intellectual Property Protection," in: Keith E. Maskus and Jerome H. Reichman (eds), *International Public Goods and Transfer of Technology under a Globalized Intellectual Property Regime*, Cambridge 2005, p. 565; Susette Biber-Klemm and Thomas Cottier (eds.), *Rights to Plant Genetic Resources and Traditional Knowledge*, CABI 2006.

[31] www.arbiter.wipo.int/

[32] In addition, the defendant to the mandatory administrative proceeding must have no rights or legitimate interests in respect of the domain name at stake and must have registered this domain name and used it in bad faith. In the administrative proceeding, the complainant must prove that each of these three elements are present; see UDRP at: www.icann.org/udrp/udrp-policy-24oct99.htm and WIPO Guide to the Uniform Domain Name Dispute Resolution Policy (UDRP) at: http://arbiter.wipo.int/domains/guide/index.html.

UDRP. It would therefore be suitable to extend protection to such signs by taking recourse to Article 10*bis* of the Paris Convention, or to create appropriate additional rules under the UDRP. Again, it is a matter of refining intellectual property protection on the basis of experiences made under the case law approach of unfair competition protection.

Competition (anti-trust) law

Principles and objectives of competition law

The purpose of competition policy and competition law is to encourage economic efficiency by creating a business environment that favors innovation and creativity while keeping costs down. A market economy without competition policy is at risk over time to be captured by monopolists who drive supply against the demand's interests. Anti-competitive agreements among economic players in the form of restrictive contractual arrangements and concerted practices, as well as undertakings improperly exploiting their economic power over weaker competitors (abuse of a dominant position on the market), generally result in high pricing of products, often curb innovation, and are deemed to be detrimental to the general welfare. Furthermore, the objective of national and regional competition policies is to function as an incentive to ensure that local undertakings, goods and services are competitive on world markets. In the context of customs unions and free trade agreements, competition policies further assure that the dismantlement of trade barriers is not offset by privately induced restrictions; in the European Union, the creation of a common market is an essential goal of competition law which cannot be explicitly found in nation states.

Prohibition of certain agreements or practices restraining competition

An agreement or practice between undertakings that prevents, restricts or distorts competition is an arrangement whose objective is to limit or eliminate competition between its parties. Such concerted behavior based on formal contracts or collusive behavior usually addresses price-fixing, production quotas, sharing markets, customers or geographical areas, bid-rigging or a combination of such practices. One usually distinguishes between "restrictive agreements" and "concerted practices" or "parallel conduct." The latter arrangements commonly involve coordination or collusive action or inaction between firms which fall short of a formal agreement, i.e. an agreement that is not legally enforceable while usually remaining to a variable extent de facto enforceable. If these agreements and concerted practices aim at increasing prices and profits of the parties concerned without producing any objective counterbalancing advantages, they damage consumers and society as a whole. The state is called to regulate against these effects to reinstall conditions of free competition. One can further distinguish between "horizontal agreements" which are agreements between actual or potential competitors, i.e. between undertakings at the same stage in the production or distribution chain (e.g., research and development, production, purchases or marketing). In other words, the term "agreements affecting competition" means binding or non-binding agreements and concerted practices between enterprises operating at the same (horizontal) or at different (vertical) levels of the market, the purpose or effect of which is to restrain competition.

Horizontal agreements can have positive and negative effects. They are considered as beneficial as instruments of sharing risks, cutting costs and pooling know-how in order to launch innovation on the market more rapidly and efficiently. On the other hand, market power based on such cooperation can have negative impacts on innovation, production, prices, diversity and quality of the products.

Vertical agreements are contractual arrangements or concerted practices between parties operating at different levels of the production or distribution chain. These agreements affect the conditions under which the parties can buy and sell goods and services. Most often, they are considered as anti-competitive. In certain cases, they can be justified to preserve legitimate interests, e.g. book price fixing schemes to promote cultural policies.

Prohibition of abuse of dominant positions and merger control

An undertaking having a dominant position in terms of market shares can abuse this situation by influencing the structure of the relevant market or the degree of competition.[33] There is a dominant position if one or more undertakings are able, as regards supply or demand, to behave in a substantially independent manner with regard to the other participants (competitors, suppliers or customers) in the market. An

---

[33] A dominant position in the market can also be collective, see for example the judgment of the European Court of first instance of July 13, 2006 in case T-464/04, *Independent Music Publishers and Labels Association (Impala)* v. *Commission of the European Communities*, with further references.

abuse of such a dominant position may consist in directly or indirectly imposing unfair prices or other unfair trading conditions, limiting production, markets or technical development to the detriment of consumers, applying dissimilar conditions to equivalent transactions with other trading parties, and making the conclusion of contracts subject to acceptance by the other parties of supplementary obligations which have no connection with the subject matter of such contracts. Certain jurisdictions, such as the European Union, proceed to an *ex ante* control of corporate transactions that lead to concentration (mergers and acquisitions).[34] These procedures are aimed at preventing concentrations which create or strengthen a dominant position as a result of which effective competition in the market is significantly impeded.[35] There is a merger or acquisition when a firm acquires exclusive control of another firm, or of a firm it previously controlled jointly with another firm, or where several firms take control of a firm or create a new one.[36]

Relationship to intellectual property protection

Coexistence, tensions and balance

Competition law and intellectual property protection are both essential ingredients of a market economy; both are preconditions for innovation, creativity and efficiency for reasons stated above. Intellectual property and competition law are necessary, but not sufficient, conditions of a competitive environment. Operationally, they create a dialectical tension and require mutual balancing. On the one hand, exclusive rights granted under intellectual property by definition exclude competition in a particular setting and allow excluding third parties from directly competing with the right holder. On the other hand, competition law seeks to facilitate direct competition and tends to limit the use of exclusive rights. A balance between the two needs to be struck in legislation and adjudication: in

---

[34] See Regulation No 1/2003.
[35] In the *Continental Can* judgment of 1973, the European Court of Justice ruled that there is an abuse of a dominant position if an undertaking already holding such a position strengthens it by acquiring a competitor. In 1987, in the *BAT/Philip Morris* case, this Court further developed this approach by accepting that in the absence of a dominant position, such an acquisition could qualify as an anti-competitive agreement (Article 81 of the EC Treaty).
[36] For example, Article 4 para. 3 of the Swiss Cartel Act of October 6, 1995 defines the term "concentration of enterprises" as (a) the merger of two or more enterprises hitherto independent of each other, or (b) any transaction whereby one or more enterprises acquire, in particular by the acquisition of an equity interest or conclusion of an agreement, direct or indirect control of one or more hitherto independent enterprises or of a part thereof.

defining the scope of intellectual property rights, in defining appropriate concepts of exhaustion of rights, in defining exceptions, such as fair use and legal exceptions, and in defining limitations to terms of licensing agreements and in providing *ultima ratio* compulsory licensing. On a case-by-case basis, competition law essentially rebalances intellectual property by means of lifting and restricting the principle of exclusive use and the power of right holders to prevent third parties from using rights without their consent.

Vice-versa, intellectual property rights tends to limit the rigors of competition law, in particular the limitations on cooperation and concertation among competitors. In the field of research and development, such agreements, often based upon intellectual property, may be useful to foster technological advances. Competition law therefore defines terms and conditions for exceptional concertations.

The proper balance of competition law and intellectual property is a constant and never ending theme, even in mature legal orders. Intellectual property anti-trust law is of utmost complexity.[37] Emerging technologies require new balancing and fine-tuning. Similar to the protection of unfair competition, national jurisdictions do not provide identical answers. Competition law has been strongly shaped by the United States (Sherman Act) and, more recently, the European Union. Competition law is based upon Articles 81 and 82 of the European Community Treaty. Until recently, EU Member States pursued their own policies and harmonization in the EU has only started recently to take place with new regulations extending the jurisdictions to Member States to apply EC competition law.[38]

In the United States, the two fields were originally conceived as separate and mutually exclusive (inherency doctrine). The exercise of intellectual property rights, and thus monopolies, was not held subject to competition law. At the same time, terms of licensing intellectual property exceed the monopoly rights strictly speaking, and were fully subject to competition rules and often per se prohibited. Subsequently, detrimental effects of per se prohibitions were removed under the influence of

---

[37] For an excellent and comprehensive analysis, see Andreas Heinemann, *Immaterialgüterschutz in der Wettbewerbsordnung*, Tübingen 2002.

[38] Council Regulation (EC) No 1/2003 of 16 December 2002 on the implementation of the rules on competition laid down in Articles 81 and 82 of the Treaty, OJL 1/1 (4.1.2003). See, for example, the rules applicable to firms compiled at http://europa.eu/scadplus/leg/en/s12001.htm and those applicable to postal services, telecommunications, agriculture and transport at http://europa.eu/scadplus/leg/een/s12003.htm.

the Chicago School, and eventually gave way to a case-by-case analysis, based on the rule of reason. All pertinent factors are taken into account, and licensing agreements are examined under what is called the "post-Chicago approach." A comparable, albeit not similar, development can be observed in European Community law. As a result, competition law and intellectual property interact in a most complex manner, strongly dependent upon the case law of the courts.

Anti-trust guidelines and block exemptions for licensing of intellectual property

Defining the relationship of competition law and intellectual property on a case-by-case basis responds to the needs of reality, but offers little legal security for business transactions. Authorities have, therefore, made attempts to codify pertinent principles and rules applicable to licensing of intellectual property rights. In the United States, the Justice Department and the Federal Trade Commission enacted Anti-trust Guidelines for Licensing of Intellectual Property in 1995.[39] Building upon case law, these guidelines define allowable terms for intellectual property licensing agreements. Similarly, the European Commission enacted Technology Transfer Block Exemptions in 1996.[40] They were subsequently revised in 2004.[41] These regulations define transfer agreements which are automatically exempt from the application of Article 81 of the EC Treaty where market shares do not exceed 20 per cent.

Intellectual property rights and the "essential facilities" doctrine

Dominant positions may be based upon intellectual property rights, such as patents. Competition law breaks them by imposing compulsory licensing, i.e. the obligation to allow third parties to use such rights against compensation. Prominently, the "essential facility doctrine" serves as a legal concept, initially developed by US case law, to address such constellations. This doctrine – which is not restricted to intellectual property – may impose restrictions on companies exclusively controlling an essential facility (such as a port, a railway station, a utility, a network). In the absence of voluntarily granting reasonable access to competitors on a contractual basis, competition authorities and courts may order such access. The US Supreme Court first articulated this doctrine in *United States* v. *Terminal Railroad Ass'n*, 224 U.S. 383 (1912). In this case, a group of railroads

---

[39] www.usdoj.gov/atr/public/guidelines/0558.htm (visited October 2006).
[40] Regulation (EC) No. 240/96, 31.1.1996, OJ L 31/2.   [41] Regulation 772/2004.

controlling all railway bridges and switching yards into and out of St. Louis prevented competing railroad services from offering transportation to and through that destination. This, the court held, constituted both an illegal restraint of trade and an attempt to monopolize. Because the essential facilities doctrine represents a divergence from the general rule that even a monopolist may choose with whom to deal, courts have established widely adopted tests that parties must meet before a court will require a monopolist to grant access to an essential asset to its competitors. Specifically, to establish anti-trust liability under the essential facilities doctrine, a party must prove four factors: (1) control of the essential facility by a monopolist; (2) competitor's inability practically or reasonably to duplicate the essential facility; (3) the denial of the use of the facility to a competitor; and (4) the feasibility of providing the facility to competitors.

This test for anti-trust liability has been adopted by virtually every United States court to consider an "essential facilities" claim.[42] Rulings of these courts also suggest that anti-trust liability under the essential facilities doctrine is particularly appropriate when denial of access is motivated by an anti-competitive animus – usually demonstrated by a change in existing business practices with the apparent intent of harming rivals. In view of the various contexts in which the essential facilities doctrine has been applied, courts have declined to impose any artificial limit on the kinds of products, services, or other assets to which the doctrine may appropriately be applied. The essential facilities doctrine is not limited to major works of infrastructure. Nor is the doctrine specifically inapplicable to tangibles, such as a manufacturer's spare parts. The term "facility" can apply to tangibles such as sports or entertainment venues, means of transportation, the transmission of energy or the transmission of information and to intangibles such as information itself.[43] In the context of the relationship between intellectual property law and competition law, one should therefore note that the dominant positions that are contemplated by the essential facilities doctrine can also be based on, or reinforced by, intellectual property rights.[44] The European Court of

---

[42] The European Court of Justice added a fifth criterion requiring the absence of legitimate business reasons to refuse the access to the facility.

[43] Christophe Germann, "Towards a Cultural Contract to Counter Trade-Related Cultural Discrimination", in Nina Obuljen and Joost Smiers (eds.), *UNESCO Convention on the Protection and Promotion of the Diversity of Cultural Expressions – Making it Work*, Zagreb 2006, with further references.

[44] In its decision of 24 March 2004 relating to a proceeding under Article 82 of the EC Treaty in the *Microsoft* case (COMP/C-3/37.792), the European Commission established that

Justice, albeit refraining from adopting the terminology of essential facilities, adopted an essentially similar approach. It is summarized in the Advocate General's opinion of May 28, 1998 in the *Oscar Bronner* case.[45]

In the recent *IMS* case concerning a statistical device ("brick structure") aimed at presenting sales data of pharmaceutical product and protected by copyright, the European Court of Justice recalled that, according to settled case law, refusal to grant a license, even if it is the act of an undertaking holding a dominant position, does not per se constitute an abuse of such a position. It is a legitimate exercise of intellectual property rights.[46] However, pursuant to this case law, the exercise of an exclusive right by the owner may, in exceptional circumstances, involve abusive conduct. The Court held that such exceptional circumstances were present in a previous case dealing with intellectual property rights, namely the *Magill* case. Several television channels in a dominant position relied on the copyright conferred by national legislation on the weekly listings of their programs in order to prevent another undertaking from publishing joint information on those programs together with commentaries, on a weekly basis.[47] In this case, the exceptional circumstances resulted from three sets of considerations. Firstly, from the fact that the refusal in question concerned a product (information on the weekly schedules of certain television channels), the supply of which was indispensable for carrying on the business in question (the publishing of

---

Microsoft is abusing its dominant position by refusing to supply Sun and other undertakings with the specifications for the protocols used by Windows work group servers in order to provide file, print and group and user administration services to Windows work group networks, and allow these undertakings to implement such specifications for the purpose of developing and distributing interoperable work group server operating system products. In this context, the Commission outlined that it could not be excluded that ordering Microsoft to disclose such specifications and allow such use of them by third parties restricts the exercise of Microsoft's intellectual property rights (recitals 547 to 791); see: http://ec.europa.eu/comm/competition/antitrust/cases/decisions/37792/en.pdf.

[45] For an overview on the "essential facilities" doctrine with further references, see the opinion of the Advocate General Jacobs of 28 May 1998 in the case *Oscar Bronner GmbH & Co. KG v. Mediaprint Zeitungs- und Zeitschriftenverlag GmbH & Co. KG, Mediaprint Zeitungsvertriebsgesellschaft mbH & Co. KG and Mediaprint Anzeigengesellschaft mbH & Co. KG*, Case C-7/97, ECR 1998 I-07791. The Court came to the conclusion that there was no essential facility in the case at stake. See also Temple Lang, *The Principle of Essential Facilities and its Consequences in European Community Competition Law*, Oxford 1996.

[46] *IMS Health GmbH & Co. OHG v. NDC Health GmbH & Co. KG*, Case C-418/01, para. 34 ff., with references to the judgments in Case 238/87 *Volvo* [1988] ECR 6211, para. 8.

[47] Joined cases C-241/91 P and C-242/91 P, *RTE and ITP v. Commission* ("Magill"), (1995) ECR I-743.

a general television guide). Secondly, from the consideration that, without that information, the person wishing to produce such a guide would find it impossible to publish it and offer it for sale. Thirdly, from the fact that such refusal prevented the emergence of a new product for which there was a potential consumer demand, the fact that it was not justified by objective considerations, and was likely to exclude all competition in the secondary market. This last condition relates to the consideration that, in the balancing of the interest in protection of the intellectual property right and the economic freedom of its owner against the interest in protection of free competition, the latter can prevail only where refusal to grant a license prevents the development of the secondary market to the detriment of consumers. Therefore, the denial by an undertaking in a dominant position to allow access to a product protected by an intellectual property right, where that product is indispensable for operating on a secondary market, may be regarded as abusive only where the undertaking which requested the license does not intend to limit itself essentially to duplicating the goods or services already offered on the secondary market by the owner of the intellectual property right, but intends to produce new goods or services not offered by the owner of the right and for which there is a potential consumer demand. In the *IMS* case, the Court eventually held that the refusal to grant a license constituted an abuse of a dominant position within the meaning of Article 82 EC where the following conditions are fulfilled:

(a) the undertaking which requested the license intends to offer, on the market at stake, new products or services not offered by the owner of the intellectual property right and for which there is a potential consumer demand;
(b) the refusal is not justified by objective considerations;
(c) the refusal is such as to reserve to the owner of the intellectual property right the market at stake by eliminating all competition on that market.

The Court confirmed that the application of the essential facilities doctrine to positions dominating the market based on their intellectual property rights requires the supply of a good or service that must be new. In comparison, this condition of novelty must not be fulfilled in those cases where intellectual property rights are not relevant for the essential facility. This additional requirement makes sense from the perspective of the rationale underlying the grant of intellectual property rights, i.e. the promotion of innovative and creative efforts.

The protection of competition in WTO law

Efforts to address anti-trust in international law

The main and overall purpose of the World Trade Organization consists of establishing and securing equal conditions of competition for imported and domestic products and services. In a generic sense, WTO law is about competition and competitive relations. Most of its rules, addressing basic principles of Most Favored Nations (MFN) Treatment, market access in the field of tariffs, non-tariff barriers, trade remedies, services and government procurement, relating to domestic support essentially deal with conditions of competition. General rules, however, have not been extended to competition (anti-trust) rules properly speaking.[48] The 1948 draft Havana Charter entailed important principles relating to competition law. Those principles influenced subsequent developments, but never entered into force. A renewed attempt was made under the auspices of the New International Economic Order in the 1970s, resulting in the 1980 Set of Multilaterally Agreed Equitable Principles and Rules for the Control of Restrictive Business Practices.[49] The United Nations Conference on Trade and Development (UNCTAD) elaborated the International Code of Conduct on the Transfer of Technology in 1980 and a further draft in 1985.[50] In the Organization for Economic Cooperation and Development (OECD), studies resulted in a number of reports and recommendations to Members, but did not result in operational rules.[51] Efforts to establish anti-trust rules, properly speaking, in the WTO, mainly suggested by the European Union after the completion of the Uruguay Round, have not been successful to date, as much as efforts to negotiate common standards on multilateral investment protection have failed. Developing countries

---

[48] Competition law per se is not part of the multilateral trading system and hardly harmonized on a supra-regional level, where rules mainly concern cooperation between competition authorities. This current state of trade law constitutes part of the so-called "Singapore Issues" with which the WTO has to deal. Paragraph 23 of the Doha Declaration recognizes that a multilateral framework could enhance the contribution of competition policy to international trade and development. Para. 25 provides for the Working Group on the Interaction between Trade and Competition Policy to focus on the clarification of: (a) core principles, including transparency, non-discrimination and procedural fairness, and provisions on hardcore cartels; (b) modalities for voluntary cooperation, and (c) support for progressive reinforcement of competition institutions in developing countries through capacity building. However, no substantial progress has so far been made in integrating competition law into the WTO system.

[49] U.N. Gen Ass Res. 35/63. [50] UNCTAD Doc. TD/CODE TOT/47, June 5, 1985.

[51] See OECD, Competition Policy and Intellectual Property Rights, Series Roundtable on Competition Policy, No. 18, DAFFE/CLP(98)18, 1998 (update).

were not prepared to enter negotiations upon completion of the Uruguay Round. They felt that it would be necessary to develop domestic experience in the field of competition policy prior to a process of multilateral negotiations concerning those disciplines. Anti-trust rules can thus be found in WTO only on the margins, in particular in regulating telecommunication under the GATS. The reference paper, incorporated into GATS schedules, obliges Members to adopt appropriate measures with a view to avoid the abuse of dominant positions.[52]

Anti-trust in the TRIPS Agreement

It is most interesting to observe in the present context that the most important agreement pertaining to competition law in the multilateral system is the TRIPS Agreement. Far from separating intellectual property and competition law in the traditions of the inherency doctrine, aspects of competition law are addressed in an attempt to establish an appropriate balance between exclusive rights and competition. The TRIPS Agreement allows Members to pursue competition polices in the field of intellectual property. It provides for carve-outs, protecting Members from being challenged for undue restrictions of intellectual property standards adopted under the TRIPS Agreement.

This implies that the WTO Members remain to a very large extent sovereign to make, implement and enforce competition rules. They therefore keep substantial margin of maneuver and policy space with respect to this legal instrument. This competence is only limited by grounds that could lead to a non-violation complaint according to sub-paragraph 1(b) of Article XXIII of the GATT 1994.[53] WTO Members, therefore, have very

---

[52] Reference Paper on Telecommunications, as incorporated into individual schedules of GATS Commitments of WTO Members. For implications and discussion see the panel report Mexico – Measure affecting Telecommunication Services, WT/DS204/R (April 2, 2004).

[53] Article XXIII:1(b) of the GATT 1994 and Article XXIII:3 of the GATS as well as Article 64:2 of the TRIPS Agreement set forth that a complaint of nullification or impairment of a benefit can also be brought before the Dispute Settlement Body of the WTO if no actual violation under these agreements has occurred. The concept of non-violation complaints is closely related to the principle of good faith and legitimate expectations; see Thomas Cottier and Matthias Oesch, *International Trade Regulation, Law and Policy in the WTO, the European Union and Switzerland, Cases, Materials and Comments*, Berne, London 2005, p. 127, with references to case law, in particular to the Panel report *Japan – Photographic Film and Paper* (WT/DS44/R) dealing with the lack of allegedly appropriate competition law in Japan. According to Article 64:2 of the TRIPS Agreement, sub-paragraphs 1(b) and 1(c) of Article XXIII of GATT 1994 shall not apply to the settlement of disputes under this Agreement for a period of five years from the date of entry into force of the WTO Agreement.

broad flexibilities to legislate against the exercise of intellectual property rights that restrains competition.

Regulation of exhaustion of intellectual property rights is of paramount impact on competition. Article 6 allows Members to choose their own doctrines of exhaustion – national, regional or international – for different forms of intellectual property rights, provided rules are applied on a non-discriminatory basis. This flexibility allows Members to finetune regulations with precepts of competition policy. Members seeking to stress competition will adopt a doctrine of international exhaustion, allowing for parallel imports and thus enhanced competition.[54] Members stressing exclusive rights will operate on the basis of national (or regional exhaustion), thus eliminating competition from parallel trade.

Article 8.2 of the TRIPS Agreement allows the WTO Members to take appropriate measures to prevent the abuse of intellectual property rights by right holders or the resort to practices which unreasonably restrain trade or adversely affect the international transfer of technology. However, these measures must be in compliance with the other provisions of the TRIPS Agreement. The exercise of exclusive rights granted by intellectual property protection legislation may cause market segmentation, e.g. based on licensing practices that can restrain trade. Such a situation is not compliant with the rationale of the TRIPS Agreement. Article 8.2, therefore, entitles the Members to restrict the exercise of intellectual property rights. They have to comply with the principle of proportionality in taking measures since they must be "appropriate" and be confined to "unreasonable" trade restraints.

Article 40 of the TRIPS Agreement specifically deals with the control of anti-competitive practices in license agreements. This provision is closely related to Article 8(2) of the TRIPS Agreement that allows the Members to adopt measures against the abuse of intellectual property rights by right holders or against practices unreasonably restraining trade or adversely affecting technology transfer. Article 40 only covers intellectual property related license agreements to the exclusion of agreements on other transactions such as assignments (transfer of ownership in exclusive rights as opposed to the mere "rental" of such rights under a license agreement). However, this does not exclude taking into account license agreements in the context of corporate transactions such as joint ventures or mergers and

---

[54] It is important to note that the doctrine of regional exhaustion in patent law within the European Community (regional exhaustion) was originally introduced in the context of competition policy (Art. 81 ECT), see joined cases 56 and 58/64, *Consten-Grundig* [1966] ECR 299. Later, it was dealt with as a matter of free movement of goods under Articles 28 and 30 ECT.

acquisitions where a direct or indirect assignment of a license agreement takes place between the parties.[55] Article 40.2 of the TRIPS Agreement provides a non-exhaustive list of licensing practices and conditions that are deemed to be abusive. Licensing practices or conditions, as contemplated under this provision, include, besides the type of agreements and contractual clauses specifically listed (grantback conditions, conditions preventing challenges to validity and coercive package licensing), the refusal to license, the discriminatory grant of licenses and the imposition of discriminatory license terms, as well as restrictive conditions in general.

Perhaps the most important operational provision of the TRIPS Agreement relating to competition is Article 31 defining terms and conditions for compulsory licensing in the field of patents. The provision leaves Members freedom in defining motives for compulsory licensing, but defines in a detailed manner conditions and procedural guarantees which need to be met. In the present context, sub-paragraph (k) is of particular importance. Members are not obliged to comply with the conditions set forth in sub-paragraphs (b) and (k) "where such use is permitted to remedy a practice determined after judicial or administrative process to be anti-competitive." Moreover, the provision entitles the reduction of the amount of remuneration in such cases and the refusal of the termination of such authorization when conditions which led to the compulsory license are likely to recur. The provision thus entitles Members to grant compulsory licenses on the basis of domestic competition law, in accordance with its principles and features. It entitles them to refrain from seeking a compulsory license in the first place in accordance with sub-paragraph (b). Importantly, it allows granting compulsory licensing which need not be limited to predominantly satisfy the domestic market. In may also entail, in other words, exportation of the product.

In the wake of the global HIV/AIDS epidemic and following the obligation to introduce patent protection for pharmaceuticals by 2005, developing country Members of the WTO fought for facilitated access to essential drugs. Negotiations resulted in the successful adoption of a Declaration on the TRIPS Agreement and Public Health at the Doha Ministerial Conference in November 2001.[56] In August 2003, subsequent negotiations

---

[55] For example in the case *Kimberly-Clark* v. *Scott*, case no. IV/M 623, the European Commission ruled that a merger consolidating famous trademarks in a single ownership may lead to a situation of market power which the competition authorities may decide to reduce by ordering the grant of licenses to third parties. See also the case *Henkel* v. *Loctite*, order nos. 4993 C 2641, 9795 C 2641 and 10718 C.   [56] WT/MIN(01)/Dec/2.

within the TRIPS Council resulted in the adoption of the so-called Doha Waiver on essential drugs, the decision on Implementation of Paragraph 6 of the Doha Declaration on the TRIPS Agreement and Public Health.[57] Subsequent negotiations prepared the ground for inserting the substance of the Waiver into the TRIPS Agreement, thus bringing about a permanent regime of *lex specialis* on access to essential drugs in the TRIPS System of intellectual property protection.[58] The decision, to be inserted permanently into the TRIPS Agreement, waived the obligation to limit compulsory licensing essentially for the supply of the domestic market. It allows Members hosting generic producers to grant compulsory licenses for the exportation of cheaper HIV medication to developing countries in need.

From the point of view of competition law, the waiver amounts to a rebalancing of intellectual property rights and conditions of competition. Exclusive rights granted to the research-based pharmaceutical industries were limited with a view to foster competition on export markets. The waiver enhances negotiating powers of national health authorities vis-à-vis the industry. It has contributed to substantial reductions of prices of HIV drugs which the world was able to witness recently. It is submitted that the same effect could also have been brought about by recourse to Article 31 (k) of the TRIPS Agreement, provided that Members of the WTO affected would have developed appropriate disciplines of domestic competition law which also take into account problems of fair and equitable distribution of, and access to, goods under patent protection.[59] Competition policy thus offers an important, but still neglected, avenue to promote access to essential drugs in developing countries.[60] It is of equal importance to lowering high health costs in developed countries alike, in particular by adopting policies of international exhaustion (subject to

---

[57] WT/L/540 (September 2, 2003), including chairman's statement.
[58] Amendment of the TRIPS Agreement, Decision of December 6, 2005, WT/L/641 (December 8, 2005) entailing the following instruments attached: Protocol amending the TRIPS Agreement, Annex to the Protocol amending the TRIPS Agreement (Art. 31*bis*) and Annex to the TRIPS Agreement. These instruments incorporate the legal language of the 2003 Doha Waiver decision, supra note 57.
[59] For a comprehensive analysis see Thomas Cottier, *The Doha Waiver and its Effects on the Nature of the TRIPS System and on Competition Law: The Impact of Human Rights*, NCCR Trade Regulation Working Paper No. 2006/21).
[60] For a discussion on the promotion of public health, in particular regarding the access to essential drugs for the poorer populations in developing countries, based on intellectual property and competition laws and policies, see e.g. Jonathan Berger, "Advancing Public Health by Other Means: Using Competition Policy to Increase Access to Essential Medicines", 2004, UNCTAD-ICTSD, at: www.iprsonline.org/unctadictsd/bellagio/docs/Berger_Bellagio3.pdf.

appropriate trade restrictions) and thus the encouragement of parallel imports. Again, it is a matter of finding a new and more appropriate balance between intellectual property protection and competition rules.

Current trends do not favor this goal. While multilateral progress is stalled, intellectual property protection is reinforced by means of bilateral agreements, without preparing the ground for comparable disciplines in competition law. Bilateral trade negotiations aimed at concluding bilateral investment treaties and bilateral intellectual property agreements are being used by the US and the EU to build more extensive protection for intellectual property than that set out in the TRIPS Agreement to the disadvantage of developing countries (the so-called TRIPS Plus standard). Drahos uses examples of US and EU negotiations with countries such as Nicaragua, Jordan, and Mexico to illustrate how developing countries are being drawn into a highly complex multilateral and bilateral web of intellectual property standards over which they have little control. The author describes, inter alia, how these bilateral agreements are being used to intervene in the detailed regulation of a developing country's economy. Furthermore, he shows how the Most Favored Nation principle within the TRIPS Agreement combines with these bilateral agreements to set and spread new minimum standards of intellectual property faster than would have happened otherwise.[61] Although various bilateral free trade agreements also contain provisions on competition law, the "export" of intellectual property legislation from developed to developing countries generally leads to a more effective implementation of TRIPS Plus standards as compared to the reception of anti-trust rules by these latter countries. As a matter of fact, one can argue that developed countries normally have a stronger interest to widespread higher levels of intellectual property protection than more efficient competition law for obvious international trade considerations. In other words, this issue illustrates the significance of an appropriate combination of, and interplay between, intellectual property and competition law to prevent an abusive exercise of exclusive rights that would damage the interests of competitors, the users and society at large.

Conclusions

The relationship of intellectual property, unfair competition and competition (anti-trust) law is a complex one. All three areas serve the goals of

---

[61] Peter Drahos, "Bilateralism in Intellectual Property", 2001, pp. 2 and 15: www.maketradefair.com/assets/english/bilateralism.pdf.

enhancing welfare by fostering innovation and creativity and to offer due reward for investment and efforts. The three areas may be described as overlapping circles, partly pursuing concurrent goals, partly pursuing specific and sometimes competing goals which need to be balanced. Intellectual property and unfair competition law share many traits in common. The latter often served as a basis for specific forms of protection, and remains important as new technologies and conduct require flexible rules, able to respond to dishonest practices, consumer deception and free riding. The relationship is shaped by the principles of independent application and pre-emption, and may vary from country to country. Unlike in the field of intellectual property rights, the international law of unfair competition has remained rudimentary and untested. It bears a considerable potential which future case law both in international dispute settlement, as well as before domestic courts may exploit more effectively than to date.

The relationship of competition (anti-trust) law and intellectual property protection (as well as unfair competition) is characterized by operational tensions. Despite pursuing shared goals, tensions prevail. The very nature of exclusive rights inherent to intellectual property per se excludes competition to a large extent. Competition policies, at the same time, would unduly undermine intellectual property and requires the operation of exemptions. A proper balance between the two fields needs to be found. It is neither a matter of simply excluding intellectual property from the application of competition policy. Nor is it a matter of giving predominance to competition policy at all costs. The balance needs to be found in shaping the scope of intellectual property rights, the doctrine of exhaustion of rights, and the potential operation of compulsory licenses.

On the level of international law, an appropriate balance between the three areas remains to be found. While intellectual property protection is strongly developed with the TRIPS Agreement, the Paris Convention and the Berne Convention, and further enhanced by means of bilateral agreements, disciplines in the field of unfair competition law are rudimentary, and almost absent in the field of anti-trust rules. Establishing the proper balance with intellectual property obligations is entirely left to unilateral (or regional) domestic regulation. It is submitted that a proper balance cannot be established under such conditions in the long run. Competition law and intellectual property protection go in pair. They need to be addressed on the same level of governance. This is true for domestic law. It is equally true for international law. The current imbalance must be overcome and efforts to bring about shared foundations on global competition law need to be renewed. The experience of the European Union – having jurisdiction in competition law but not in intellectual property rights at the outset – shows that such a constellation is not sustainable. The same is true for the WTO – in an opposite constellation. The balance needs to be sought within the TRIPS Agreement. It should not only entail minimal standards, but also maximal standards which Members must not surpass in the interest of efficiency and workable competition. Secondly, basic disciplines on competition policy need to be inserted in WTO law, complementing domestic competition policies. It is not a matter of prescribing a full set of rules. Members need to retain sufficient flexibility in order to meet the needs of largely divergent economies and levels of development. Anti-trust rules of a developing country will look different from those of the United States or of the European Union. Common interests, however, can be identified. Major needs exist in addressing export cartels and in the field of judicial assistance. All Members of the WTO should carefully assess the gains from global rules on competition and intellectual property in response to globalization and a world economy strongly driven by technological advances and innovation.

Selected bibliography

F. K. Beier, *One Hundred Years of International Cooperation – The Role of the Paris Convention in the Past, Present and Future*, IIC 1984

Georg Hendrik Christian Bodenhausen, *Guide to the Application of the Paris Convention for the Protection of Industrial Property as Revised at Stockholm in 1967*, Geneva 1968

Pierre Régibeau and Katharine Rockett, "The Relation Between Intellectual Property Law and Competition Law: An Economic Approach" (University of Essex and CEPR, Draft June 2004, online: ICSTD)

Gustavo Ghidini, *Intellectual Property and Competition Law. The Innovation Nexus* (Cheltenham, Northampton 2006, Edward Elgar)

Francis Gurry, *Breach of Confidence* (Oxford 1984, reprinted 1998)

Dina Kallay, *The Law and Economics of Antitrust and Intellectual Property. An Austrian Approach* (Cheltenham, Northampton 2004, Edward Elgar)

Massimiliano Gangi, "Competition Policy and the Exercise of Intellectual Property Rights", in *Competition Policy and Intellectual Property Rights Working Papers* (1999) pp. 353–369 (www.archivioceradi.luiss.it/document/archivioceradi/osservatori/intellettuale/Gangi1.pdf)

United Nations Conference on Trade and Development, "Competition Policy and the Exercise of Intellectual Property Rights". Revised report by the UNCTAD secretariat, 19 April 2002, TD/B/COM.2/CLP/22/Rev.1

Carsten Fink and Keith E. Maskus, *Intellectual Property and Development. Lessons from Recent Economic Research* (Washington, New York 2005, World Bank, Oxford University Press)

S. Ricketson, *The Berne Convention for the Protection of Literary and Artistic Works: 1886–1986* (London 1987)

B. Sherman and L. Bently, *The Making of Modern Intellectual Property Law* (Cambridge 1999)

Alan Story, Colin Darch and Debora Halbert, "The Copy/South Dossier. Issues in the Economics, Politics, and Ideology of Copyright in the Global South", May 2006 (Copy, South Research Group: www.copysouth.org)

Martin Khor, "Intellectual Property, Competition and Development", June 2005 (TWN Third World Network)

OECD, *Guidelines for Multinational Enterprises*, chapter IX on Competition, at 26, 53 et seq. (Paris 2000)

UNCTAD Secretariat, "Competition Policy and the Exercise of Intellectual Property Rights", TD/B/COM.2 CLP/22 May 8, 2001

US Department of Justice, Federal Trade Commission, "Antitrust Guidelines for Licensing of Intellectual Property", Washington DC, April 6, 1995

WTO, Report of the Working Group on the Interaction Between Trade and Competition Policy to the General Council of December 8, 1998, WT/WGTCP/2

7

Teaching the economics of intellectual property rights in the global economy

KEITH E. MASKUS

Introduction

Analytical and empirical work in economics is paying increasing attention to the vital questions of encouraging innovation and diffusing information in a world where creativity and knowledge lie at the foundation of economic progress. There are numerous complex and fascinating problems for economists to grapple with in the general area of technical change and growth. These range from deep mathematical treatments of the nature of economic growth in the presence of non-rival knowledge goods, to extensive empirical analysis of the role of information acquisition in economic development, international trade, and public economics.

Inevitably, this attention to the growing importance of the knowledge economy places growing emphasis on the determinants of innovation and learning, especially intellectual property rights (IPR). A burgeoning wealth of economics literature seeks to understand the dynamic incentive effects of IPR, the problems they raise for competition, their significance for international technology transactions, and how they fit into broad strategies for economic development.

In this environment, one would expect that economics departments would begin to offer courses dedicated to studying such issues specifically within the context of IPR. Certainly, the formal study of IPR has become central in law schools and management programs in business administration colleges. However, they have yet to take on a significant role in the curriculum of economics departments in the United States, either at the undergraduate or graduate level.

The reason for this lacuna is not hard to spot. Like anti-monopoly policies, technical product standards, and fiduciary requirements, IPR are business regulations that importantly affect competition, market structure, and other crucial processes. Yet, as regulations, they cut across typical sub-disciplines in economics without themselves rising to the level of uniqueness that would support specific inquiry over a full semester. Put differently, it is common to find IPR covered briefly in both technical analysis and policy discussion in courses on industrial economics, health economics, and (to a lesser degree) international trade and economic development. For example, graduate courses in industrial economics are likely to study dynamic models of innovation, with some emphasis on the importance of patents. However, innovation incentives and effects stem from many factors, and it is unlikely that economists would accord more than a vital complementary role to IPR.

While this emphasis is natural, in my view it leads to a significant risk of misunderstanding, on the part of economists, of the nature and importance of IPR. Economics, as a discipline, is driven by technical approaches emphasizing formal mathematical modeling and sophisticated statistical analysis. To introduce notions of patent or copyright protection into this framework necessarily leads analysts to represent policies in exceedingly simplified ways, often bordering on caricature. For example, patents vary across countries in eligibility standards, examination processes, limitations on scope of claims, access to compulsory licensing, and exhaustion policies, among other elements. Each of these issues could be the focus of substantive formal analysis and, indeed, they sometimes are.[1] However, to bring all of these complexities into a theoretical model is effectively impossible; consequently, economists boil IPR down to a single parameter, such as patent length, in analyzing the incentive impacts and even the optimality of national and international policy.

This approach is inevitable, but it generates two common fallacies among economists. The first is the belief that IPR may be conceived of satisfactorily as simple, one-dimensional policy tools, such that a slight change in the "strength" of a tool will have identifiable impacts on important competitive processes. A good example is the elegant model by Zigic (2000), which asks whether patents and tariffs work together or at cross-purposes as strategic elements of international trade policy. This is an interesting and vital question in light of the fact that membership in the World Trade Organization (WTO) requires developing nations to liberalize trade at the same time as they reform IPR systems. However, patents are treated in the model as a single parameter in determining optimal

[1] For example, Ganslandt and Maskus (2004, 2006) offer close empirical and theoretical analysis of the effects of parallel imports on pricing strategies, Aoki and Nagaoka (2003) study the utility standards in patents, and Samuelson and Scotchmer (2002) consider the economics of reverse engineering.

tariff policy in the strategic setup. The role of patent protection in the model is to raise imitation costs, rather than to facilitate many of the other functions of IPR, including reduced transactions costs in technology trade. Thus, the analytical results are worth contemplating but not generally valid.

A second, and related, problem is that this emphasis on generality discourages virtually all economists from learning the detailed objectives and complexities of an entire system of IPR. Most economists see the role of patents as encouraging investments in research and development, and perhaps to facilitate further innovation through publication of technical details in patent applications, while raising the prospect of monopoly power. They know virtually nothing of the intricate details of IPR systems and how the scope of protection can be enhanced or limited through a multitude of complementary policies. Copyrights, trademarks, geographical indications, plant variety rights, semiconductor design protection, and trade secrecy have been the subject of few formal inquiries, even in terms of a closed economy, let alone in the presence of international trade. Of course, one major reason that economists choose not to understand these intricacies is that required investments of time and effort are significant. Real economic experts in the details of intellectual property policy are scarce and, it seems, could remain so.

The increasing importance of IPR as an economic policy, along with the relative lack of knowledge among economists about how they work, supports the view that there is room for developing courses aimed specifically at learning the subject matter. In this chapter, I sketch an outline of how such a course could be taught. The course I describe is scaled for students at the master's level in economics, international relations, and international business. Further, it has sufficient grounding in practical application and institutions that it would be useful for technical-level policy officials in both developed and developing nations. In my view, there is not much scope for undergraduate courses in IPR per se, though elements of patent and copyright protection might appear in lower-level courses in industrial organization, trade, and economic development.

The perspective I bring to this question is that of an international economist who has undertaken extensive analytical and practical study of IPR as a trade and development issue. While I have taught aspects of IPR in graduate courses in international trade, subject to all of the difficulties mentioned above, I have not yet had an opportunity to teach a full course on the economics of intellectual property. Thus, the approach I set out below reflects my thoughts on how to construct a course *de novo*.

Course objectives and expectations

The first question an economics instructor faces in designing a graduate course in IPR is whether its orientation should be primarily theoretical and model-based, or mix applied theory with empirical work and policy applications. Because the course I describe here would be offered largely to Master of Arts (MA) students in economics and international relations, the emphasis is on practical applications supported by a solid foundation in the economics of IPR. The objectives of this course, which I label "Economics of Intellectual Property Rights in the World Economy," would be as follows.

First, students should understand the basic economic logic of all forms of intellectual property protection. The bedrock issue is that markets for technology and information are imperfect and subject to failure. The various forms of protection have evolved over time with a clear utilitarian purpose in mind in order to address these market difficulties in a way that is generally more efficient than direct government intervention. An important point is that IPR policies are both a stimulus to innovation and an endogenous response to the needs for protection as technologies change. Thus, students should understand that national preferences for IPR regulations vary across countries and evolve over time within countries.

Second, students should gain an appreciation of the ways in which these basic economic principles are implemented in legal rules governing IPR. Thus, essentials of the legal treatment of various forms of IPR, including limitations on scope, should be covered with some attention paid to differences across major jurisdictions, such as the United States, EU and a representative developing country, such as India or Brazil.

Third, students should master the primary elements of the evolving international IPR system. Primarily, this would involve a review of the TRIPS Agreement and its modifications since 1995, but consider also the role of WIPO and the major treaties and conventions it administers. Some attention would be paid as well to bilateral and regional provisions in IPR within the context of trade agreements. An important point to get across in this section is the interrelatedness between trade regulation and intellectual property regulation.

Fourth, a unit on the economic effectiveness of IPR protection in achieving its objectives in the global economy would be a major emphasis of the course. In this context, important studies of the actual role played by patents, copyrights, and trademarks in encouraging innovation and market development would be covered. Central also would be consideration of the role played by intellectual property protection in international technology transfer. Ultimately, the question to be asked is how important IPR are in the processes of economic transformation and growth or, stated more accurately, how should IPR be placed into an overall development context?

Turning to what should be expected of the students, a course of this nature must involve active learning and participation. Thus, while much of the classroom time would be occupied by the instructor's lectures, students would be required to debate issues, make oral presentations of current topics, and undertake research. I would anticipate each student completing two examinations (one mid-term and one final examination) and writing one original term paper, while pairs or groups of students would participate in at least one classroom debate presenting both sides of an important topical issue in the economic development or international trade aspects of IPR. An illustrative list of topics for term papers and policy debates is provided in later sections of this chapter.

Again, the intended audience for a course of this nature would largely be master's students in economics, international relations, and international business, though it could serve as well as a useful supplement in applied doctoral programs. A further important audience would be IPR policy officials in various governments, though the course would presume that students had achieved some prior grounding in economics as a discipline.[2]

Course outline and suggested materials

In a course with such a broad scope, the challenge is deciding what materials to exclude or de-emphasize rather than what subjects to include. In this section, I set out an annotated outline of suggested topics to be covered, along with indications of time to be spent on each. I also list suggested reading materials and include a few relevant illustrations. The course is designed for 13 weeks of classroom meetings, which corresponds to the typical time allocated in an American university. Supposing two classroom meetings per week, this would come to 26 sessions, one of which would be dedicated to a mid-term examination. I also set aside five periods for in-class debates by students, leaving 20 sessions for lecture/discussion times.

---

[2] Those considering a course strictly for such officials presumably would make it shorter, limit the technical economics materials, and perhaps eliminate the mid-term examination in favor of the writing and speaking requirements.

The economics of knowledge, innovation and the need for IPR

The initial subject matter would be an examination of the economic nature of knowledge, how innovation occurs and is encouraged, the need for policy interventions to address problems in markets for information, and the justification of IPR as a critical support for those markets. As indicated in Part 1 of the course outline in the Annex, this inquiry would cover the following essential subjects. First, how do economists conceive of knowledge and information? There are numerous points to be addressed here. One is the distinction between basic knowledge (for example, from scientific research) and marketable information. Next is identification of central failures in markets for information, such as lack of appropriability arising from non-rivalry and non-excludability, uncertainty in long-term investment programs, an inability to signal the legitimate origin and quality of goods to consumers, and problems that interfere with trading technologies.

Second, how do governments deal with such market problems and externalities in order to encourage an optimal path of innovation? Here, attention would be placed generally on innovation systems, which range from educational policies and grants for basic research, to tax incentives for R&D, and encouragements for commercialization of new goods and technologies. This analysis will help set up the importance of IPR as market-based inducements for both innovation and commercialization within competitive economies.

Third, what are the specific aims of various forms of IPR in this context? Here, the material would cover the essential purposes of patents, copyrights, trademarks, plant variety protection, and trade secrets (confidential information). The analysis would discuss both the importance of IPR and reasons for limitations placed on the scope of various forms of protection. The objective within this unit is for students to understand that there are complex trade-offs between providing exclusive rights for developers of new products and cultural goods, on the one hand, and the benefits of wide access of consumers and users to those products. Thus, within any economy, an important balance needs to be struck among these central objectives.

Besides the articles and text chapters listed in that section, simple analytical diagrams would be used to make the basic points about investment, profits from appropriation, and consumer gains from innovation. A standard diagram of that kind is included as Figure 12. In that section, it would be possible also to discuss the economic logic of

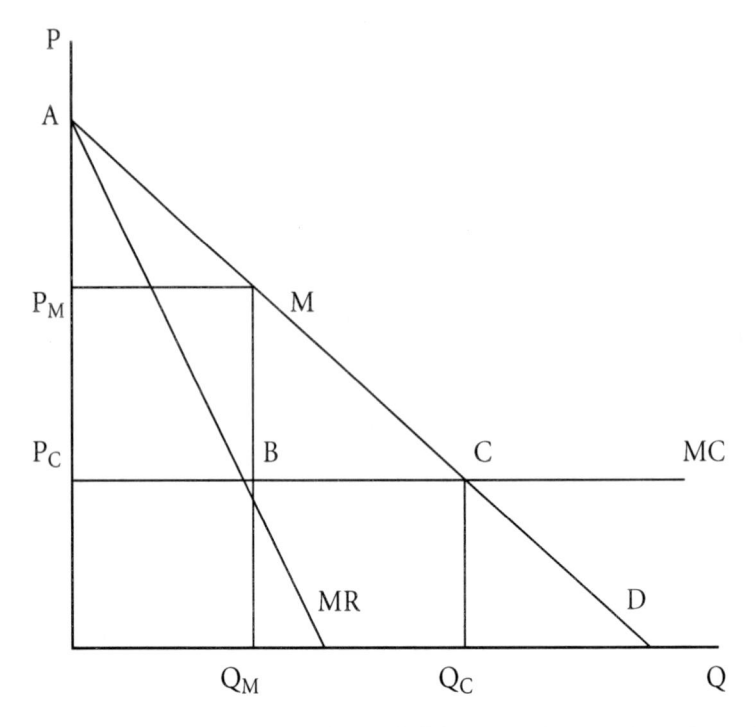

C is a point at which a product should shell for marginal cost. M is a point at which a firm offers the product in case of a monopoly in the product through an intellectual property right. See Keith E. Maskus, *Intellectual Property in the Global Economy*, Institute for International Economics, Washington D.C., August 2000 (ISBN 0-88132-282-2) pages 29 to 31.

Figure 12: Basic access–innovation trade-off in IPRs

such items as the novelty and utility standards in patents, setting the fee structure for patents and trademarks, and the importance of licensing.

The discussion above would lead naturally into a short treatment of variations in policies across countries, and the study of important historical experiences that inform policy today. The discussion would cover international variations in patent rights (and how they are measured) before TRIPS, why they are different, and the historical experiences of the US, Germany, France, and Japan in setting patent regimes. It would also

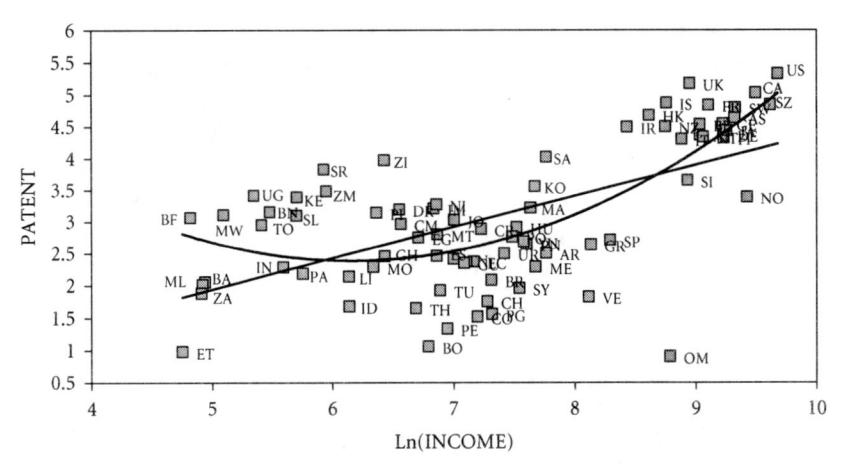

Figure 13: Relationship between patent rights and per-capita GNP

be of interest to overview basic differences in the regimes of key developing countries. A particular graph that visually indicates such differences is included as Figure 13.

Instructors would be free to add current policy variations, such as differences in database protection, patent eligibility, and exhaustion of rights. For example, the EU and the United States differ in their treatments of database protection, while the United States provides stronger patent protection for software and business methods. India's 2005 patent law on pharmaceuticals could be addressed critically in terms of its economic incentives and disincentives. In my view, however, these specific current issues might be better treated in a debate format, as described later.

IPR in international trade agreements

The next general issue that must be addressed is how IPR have been put into international trade agreements and whether such agreements provide effective governance for the use of IPR in the global economy. As noted in the outline, I would envision two sections of discussion. A first subject to understand is the inadequacies of national policy making, the approach taken for centuries, in the global economy. The discussion would approach this question by analyzing the problems that emerge when each national government sets its own IPR policies without considering the spillovers offered into other economies. These spillovers are largely positive, for governments would not ordinarily account for consumer gains and firm profits abroad in setting their own policies. Thus, in a world in which only national policy is made, each country is likely to choose a degree of protection that is weaker than what would be required for a global dynamic optimum. This "policy coordination failure" in information markets provides the essential justification for international agreements in IPR.

Having made the case for coordinated intervention, the discussion would move to a detailed understanding of the TRIPS Agreement at the WTO and how it is supposed to operate.[3] The intention for the instructor would be to consider each of the major policy areas – patents, trademarks, copyrights, plant protection, trade secrets, and enforcement – in terms of the underlying economic problems that coordinated policy is supposed to resolve. An overall assessment of how effective TRIPS is likely to be in this context could be given. This analysis could be extended to consideration of IPR in bilateral agreements as well.

Interregnum: Initial policy debates

At this point, it would be natural to administer a mid-term examination on the basics of IPR and its protection in the global economy. After that, I would envision an initial round of policy debates undertaken by students. In the outline below, I have listed two class sessions, amounting to four debates involving eight students (one on each side of each debate). Students would be expected to read additional literature and develop analytical arguments on either side of an important policy question. An illustrative list of debate topics that could be considered at this stage would be the following:

1. What should be the scope of fair use in developing countries regarding copyrights of digital products?
2. Would implementation of a policy like the US Bayh-Dole Act help spur innovation in developing countries?
3. Are the TRIPS requirements for issuing compulsory licenses sufficiently flexible for effective use? Or is it even economically sensible to use them?
4. For a chosen country, would it be more appropriate to adopt minimum TRIPS standards and take full advantage of available flexibilities in limit-

---

[3] The outline does not anticipate spending much time on WIPO, since I have presumed that that institution would be covered extensively in other courses.

ing the scope of IPR or to move to stronger protection that might promote innovation?

Assessing the economic effectiveness of global IPR policy

The idea in this section would be for students to read and discuss selected empirical studies that consider how IPR seem to affect economic activity. The initial discussion would be aimed at survey and econometric evidence on patent regimes and induced innovation. This will allow the instructor to paint a suitable picture of the complexities and uncertainties involved, leading to the conclusion that the roles of IPR in development and growth are many and sensitive to specific economic circumstances. However, available evidence indicates that, for example, protected and transparent patent rights can generate a growth bonus in middle-income countries that are relatively open to trade and investment.

A second area of inquiry explores this growth claim through the subtle channels of trade and international technology transfer (ITT). There is significant evidence that, for example, patents and trade secrets are important for encouraging trade in high-technology goods (including the development of exports from developing countries), inward foreign direct investment and positive productivity spillovers, and licensing. Further, an important finding is that as global IPR is improved, sophisticated markets for brokering technologies emerge, which has the effect of transferring yet more information to developing economies.

One subtlety that would demand attention is the economic trade-off facing technology importing nations in strengthening their IPR. On the one hand, such a policy change makes it more costly for local firms to imitate international technologies, which would raise the cost of access to information. On the other hand, the greater certainty for firms in their ability to protect technologies encourages more licensing and, ultimately, stronger innovation on a global scale.

Integrating IPR into economic development policy

A final major element of inquiry for the economics of IPR is how patents, copyrights, and the like fit into a broader economic development policy. This is a very broad subject and only components of it can be considered within the timeframe of a single course. Thus, different instructors may have varying views of the importance of what to include.

Listed in the outline shown in the annex below (Part four) are four subjects that fit within this general context. The first is simply to make the case that IPR should properly be considered an important tool in the overall approach to economic development. By themselves, reformed intellectual property rights are not likely to accomplish much for purposes of innovation and growth. Thus, in this first section, there would be a discussion of broader policy approaches that include IPR integrally. Such approaches include human capital development, commercialization incentives, competition maintenance, improvements in capital markets, and other factors. Specific examples of successful development policy could be covered.

A second subject is the relationship of IPR to public health. This is the most controversial issue in the economic arena (and is not solely an economic matter) and requires sound thinking on the part of students. The discussion should cover the benefits and costs of product patents on pharmaceutical innovation and new drug availability and cost, whether price controls are sensible in varying contexts, and the approach to generic entry on the domestic market or from sources overseas.

A third area I have selected is agriculture and IPR. Since many developing countries remain significantly rural, the implications of plant variety protection and patents on new genetic modification technologies are important to understand. A number of developing countries are poised to be significant technology developers, or partners in such development, in agriculture, but the poorer nations are not in that position. Accordingly, students should understand the essential trade-offs for input costs, output variety, and consumer choice of improved IPR protection. Policy questions that could be covered include such items as the form of plant variety protection to provide, patents in living organisms, and whether patents for genetically modified organisms (GMOs) will increase inward technology flows in agriculture. An additional important issue is whether the protection of geographical indications will benefit agriculture.

A final subject listed is centrally important, but not much studied by economists. Specifically, what is the scope for deploying various forms of IPR to encourage small-scale innovation in poor countries? Here the instructor could reinforce the potential gains from utility models, design patents, trademarks, and trade secrets for commercial innovation, and the advantages to local musicians from enforcing copyrights.

There could be other items to consider, of course, and it would be up to the instructor to choose among the many interesting economic questions. A few more elements that might be considered include the economics of collective ownership of property rights (which is relevant for registering traditional knowledge), economic aspects of exhaustion and parallel imports, and the application of competition policy to IPR. There is available literature in each of these areas, though the situation in developing countries has not been sufficiently studied in terms of economic analysis.

Final policy debates

I have reserved the final three classroom meetings in the course outline for six additional policy debates, involving twelve students. These could range across the breadth of items in Parts 3 and 4 or beyond. Following is another list of illustrative debate topics.

1. Are poor countries better off in terms of their access to essential medicines if they follow a policy of international exhaustion or should they restrict parallel trade in such goods in order to facilitate lower domestic prices?
2. Is the TRIPS waiver on compulsory licenses to import medicines in cases of medical needs sufficient to accomplish the tasks of sustaining public health?
3. Are pharmaceutical patents really a difficult problem for access in poor countries or are there other market and infrastructure failures that need to be addressed?
4. Are developing countries likely to achieve significantly more inward technology transfer through improved IPR or are there alternative approaches to achieving this goal?
5. Are countries better off strengthening their IPR at the same time they liberalize restrictions in trade and investment?
6. How important is it for developing nations to develop strong competition policies to check the abuse of IPR?

Term papers

I indicated above that I would expect students to research and write a substantive term paper for the semester. Several of the topics I have listed for policy debates would be relevant in this context as well. But one advantage of a term paper is that it would give students an opportunity to delve deeply into either the IPR policies of a specific country (or regional grouping of countries) or an important global policy question. Thus, for example, someone could write about differences in fair-use provisions in copyrights in the United States, the EU, and a major developing country. Another paper might be devoted to the role of utility models in encouraging agricultural innovation. Yet another topic could be the impact of major recent patent reforms (e.g. in Japan, Korea, and Mexico) on domestic innovation and technology transfer. A final one I could mention is a close analysis of a WTO dispute-resolution panel's findings in an IPR case, such as the Canada patented medicines case. Clearly, the list of potential subjects for inquiry is large.

Concluding remarks

In this chapter I have sketched out a suggested outline for teaching the economics of IPR in a global context. Inevitably, many important aspects of this subject could not be given the emphasis they deserve, and preferences would vary among instructors about how to manage this problem. At the same time, the proposed course outline seems ambitious regarding what students would be expected to master, both in terms of economics and institutions. My hope is that a course structured along these lines would leave students and prospective policy-makers with a deep appreciation for the complexities of the subject and the importance of further analysis.

As stated earlier, the course is set out for a 13-week semester. It could easily be extended to a longer term by adding some materials I mentioned that were ignored here, or by looking into existing topics more fully. Certainly, there is far more literature worth consulting than I have chosen to list here. However, it may be more likely that an instructor would wish to shorten the duration of the course, particularly if it is to be taught to professionals and policy-makers. In that environment, a lesser emphasis on technical economics combined with an overview of empirical work, leaving the central institutional and policy questions intact, would seem advisable.

Ultimately, the intention here is to meet the course objectives listed at the outset of the chapter. Students who take this material seriously and read more widely in preparing debates and a term paper should achieve these goals without question, albeit at the cost of hard work. I hope also that the structure set out here proves appealing to faculty at universities and colleges around the world as they establish their own courses in the economics of IPR.

Selected bibliography

Aoki, Reiko and Sadao Nagaoka (2003), "The Utility Standard and the Patentability of Intermediate Technology," Discussion Paper Series A, No. 437, the Institute of Economic Research, Hitotsubashi University

Ganslandt, Mattias and Keith E. Maskus (2004), "The Price Impact of Parallel Imports in Pharmaceuticals: Evidence from the European Union," *Journal of Health Economics*, vol. 23: 1035–1057

Ganslandt, Mattias and Keith E. Maskus (2007), "Vertical Distribution, Parallel Trade, and Price Divergence in Integrated Markets," *European Economic Review*, vol. 51, no. 4, 943–970

Samuelson, Pamela and Suzanne Scotchmer (2002), "The Law and Economics of Reverse Engineering," *Yale Law Journal*, vol. 111: 1575–1663

Zigic, Kresimir (2000), "Strategic Trade Policy, Intellectual Property Rights Protection and North-South Trade," *Journal of Development Economics*, vol. 61: 27–60

ANNEX

Model syllabus for "The Economics of Intellectual Property Rights in the Global Economy"

Level: This course is designed primarily for students in a master's program in economics, international affairs, and international business management. It would also be useful for technical policy officials in national governments and international organizations.

Required Texts: All students should have access to the following books, which will serve as basic texts:

1. Dominique Foray, *The Economics of Knowledge* (MIT Press, 2004)
2. Keith E. Maskus, *Intellectual Property Rights in the Global Economy* (Institute for International Economics, 2000)
3. Suzanne Scotchmer, *Innovation and Incentives* (MIT Press, 2004)

The readings below are illustrative only. Different instructors may wish to supplement these or develop alternative readings.
Organization of class meeting times and topics for discussion:

Part one: Basic economic issues

Meeting Subject
1–2 The economic conception of knowledge
 Readings:
 – Foray, chapters 1–6.
 – Scotchmer, chapters 1–2.

3 Innovation systems
 Readings:
 – Richard R. Nelson, *National Innovation Systems: A Comparative Analysis*, (1993) chapters 1–2.

4–6   *Basic economics of IPR*
Readings:
- Foray, chapter 7.
- Scotchmer, chapters 3–5.
- Maskus, chapter 3.
- Stanley Besen and Leo Raskind, "An Introduction to the Law and Economics of Intellectual Property," *Journal of Economic Perspectives* (1991) 5: 3–27.
- Roberto Mazzoleni and Richard Nelson, "The Benefits and Costs of Strong Patent Protection: A Contribution to the Current Debate," *Research Policy* (1998) 27: 273–284
- W.M. Landes and Richard Posner, "Trademark Law: An Economic Perspective," *Journal of Law and Economics* (1987) 30: 265–309

7–8   *Variation in policies and historical experiences*
Readings:
- Maskus, chapter 4, 87–109.
- J.C. Ginarte and Walter Park, "Determinants of Patent Rights: a Cross-National Study," *Research Policy* (1997) 26: 288–301
- United Kingdom Commission on Intellectual Property Rights, *Integrating Intellectual Property Rights and Development Policy* (Commission on Intellectual Property Rights, 2002), chapter 1
- B. Zorina Khan, "Intellectual Property and Economic Development: Lessons from American and European History," (2002)
- Janusz Ordover, "A Patent System for Both Diffusion and Exclusion," *Journal of Economic Perspectives* (1991) 5: 43–60

Part two: IPR in international trade policy

9   *Economic problems in international policy coordination*
Readings:
- Scotchmer, chapter 11
- Keith Maskus, "Regulatory Standards in the WTO: Comparing Intellectual Property Rights with Competition Policy, Environmental Protection, and Core Labor Standards," *World Trade Review* (2002) 1: 135–152

10–12   *IPR in Multilateral and Regional Trade Agreements*
Readings:
- Maskus, chapters 2, 6
- Carlos Primo Braga, "Trade-Related Intellectual Property

Issues: The Uruguay Round Agreement and Its Economic Implications" in W. Martin and L.A. Winters (eds.), *The Uruguay Round and the Developing Countries* (Cambridge University Press 1996)
- UK Commission on Intellectual Property Rights, chapter 8
- Maskus, "Intellectual Property Rights in the US–Colombia Free Trade Agreement," in Jeffrey J. Schott (ed.), *The Free Trade Agreement between Colombia and the United States* (Institute for International Economics, 2006)

13   Mid-term Examination

14–15   Policy Debates I: TRIPS and Bilaterals as Trade Policy

Part three: Assessing the effectiveness of global policy

16–17   *IPR, Innovation and Growth*
Readings:
- Maskus, chapter 5
- Keith Maskus, "The Economics of Global Intellectual Property and Development: A Survey," in Peter Yu (ed.) *Intellectual Property and Information Wealth* (Praeger 2006)
- Joshua Lerner, "Patent Protection and Innovation over 150 Years," NBER Working Paper 8977 (2002)
- Wesley M. Cohen, Richard R. Nelson and John P. Walsh, "Protecting their Intellectual Assets: Appropriability Conditions and Why US Manufacturing Firms Patent (or Not)," NBER working paper 7552 (2000).
- David M. Gould and W.C. Gruben, "The Role of Intellectual Property Rights in Economic Growth," *Journal of Development Economics* (1996) 48: 323–350

18–19   *Impacts of IPR on trade and technology transfer*
Readings:
- Maskus, chapter 4, 109–142
- Pamela Smith, "How do Foreign Patent Rights Affect US Exports, Affiliate Sales and Licenses?" *Journal of International Economics* (2001) 55: 411–440
- Bernard Hoekman, Keith Maskus and Kamal Saggi, "Transfer of Technology to Developing Countries: Unilateral and Multilateral Policy Options," *World Development* (2005) 33: 1587–1602

- Ashish Arora, A. Fosfuri and A. Gambardella, "Markets for Technology, IPR and Development," in K. Maskus and J. Reichman, eds., *International Public Goods and Transfer of Technology under a Globalized Intellectual Property Regime* (Cambridge University Press 2005)
- Michelle Connolly and Diego Valderrama, "Implications of Intellectual Property Rights for Dynamic Gains from Trade," *American Economic Review* (2005) 95: 318–323

Part four: Integrating IPR into development policy

20 *The Need for a Broad Policy Approach*
    Readings:
    Maskus, chapter 7.

21 *IPR and public health*
    Readings:
    - UK Commission on Intellectual Property Rights, chapter 2
    - F.M. Scherer and J. Watal, "Post-TRIPS Options for Access to Patented Medicines in Developing Nations," *Journal of International Economic Law* (2002) 5: 913–939

22 *IPR and agriculture*
    Readings:
    - Robert E. Evenson, "Agricultural Research and Intellectual Property Rights," in K. Maskus and J. Reichman, *International Public Goods*
    - Thomas Cottier, "The Case for Protecting Geographical Indications and Traditional Knowledge in Agricultural Trade," manuscript 2003
    - G. Schamel and K. Anderson, "Wine Quality and Varietal, Regional and Winery Reputations," *The Economic Record* (2003) 79: 357–369

23 *Deploying IPR for small-scale innovation*
    Readings:
    - F.J. Penna, Monique Thormann, and J.M. Finger, "The Africa Music Project," in J.M. Finger and P. Schuler (eds.), *Poor People's Knowledge: Promoting Intellectual Property in Developing Countries* (Oxford University Press 2004)
    - K. Maskus, S.M. Dougherty, and A. Mertha, "Intellectual Property Rights and Economic Development in China," in

C. Fink and K. Maskus (eds), *Intellectual Property and Development: Lessons from Recent Economic Research* (Oxford University Press 2004)

24–26   Policy Debates II: Aspects of Global Development Policy

8

Teaching intellectual property in a business school

SUSANNA H.S. LEONG

> Teaching is a social art, necessarily involving a relationship between people; and the success of a teacher in the practice of his art depends upon his possessing that quality or attitude of mind which enables him to make the relationship between himself and his students a reciprocal one. Not all the teaching should be done by the teacher. Not all the learning should be done by the students.
>
> The late Professor Charles I. Gragg in *Teachers Also Must Learn*

Introduction

For many years, business students at the NUS Business School, National University of Singapore, both undergraduates and postgraduates, are taught general principles of intellectual property law together with other business-related law like contract law, company law and the law of sale of goods in one business law module. It is only in recent years that the NUS Business School has started to introduce more specialized intellectual property law modules as electives for the students. As intellectual property law modules are mainly elective modules in the Business School, it is important from a teaching, as well as a long-term sustainability, point of view that students are made to understand and to appreciate the significance and relevance of reading intellectual property law as a subject in the university. To this end, I subscribe to the teaching philosophy of a "student-centered" learning pedagogical model as I strongly believe that courses developed using such a model would best address students' learning needs. I am also of the view that by adopting a "student-centered" learning pedagogical model, students are assured that only the most current and relevant courses are developed and offered by the university and the school.

I begin with a brief introduction to Singapore and the legal infrastructure for intellectual property protection, followed by an overview of the intellectual property law related courses offered by the NUS Business

School. Next, I will discuss the pedagogy and methodology that I have employed in my teaching; the learning outcomes and the modes of assessment adopted. Finally, I conclude with a brief personal reflection of the challenges faced by an intellectual property law teacher in a business school.

Intellectual property protection in Singapore

Singapore is a small Southeast Asian city-state with an area of 648 sq km and a population of almost four million.[1] It is an island city-state without natural resources. However, over the last 40 years, Singapore has achieved remarkable economic success. By 1997, Singapore's per capita GDP was the highest in Asia and fourth highest in the world, after Switzerland, Japan and Norway.[2] This is the result of rapid sustained growth and is derived essentially from the government's efforts in directing Singapore, largely in the last decade, into high value-added, high technology and more capital- and knowledge-intensive economic activities.

The government's general policy to restructure Singapore's economy into a knowledge-based one has also brought about several significant legal reforms over the last few years, particularly in the area of intellectual property laws.

Singapore is a member of the World Trade Organisation (WTO) with the status of an "advanced developing country", and thus was obliged to comply with the Trade Related Intellectual Property Rights Agreement (TRIPS) by 2000. At present, Singapore is also a member of the following conventions:

- Paris Convention for Protection of Industrial Property 1883, as of 23 February 1995;
- The Patent Co-operation Treaty 1978, as of 23 February 1995;
- The Budapest Treaty 1997, as of 23 February 1995;
- The Convention Establishing the World Intellectual Property Organization 1970, as of 10 December 1990;
- The Berne Convention for the Protection of Literary and Artistic Works 1886, as of 21 December 1998;
- Nice Agreement concerning the International Classification of Goods and Services for the Purposes of the Registration of Marks, as of 18 March 1999;

---

[1] Of whom 3.2 million are citizens of Singapore or permanent citizens.
[2] Tim Huxley, *Defending the Lion City – The Armed Forces of Singapore*, Allen & Unwin, 2000, at p. xix.

– Protocol relating to the Madrid Agreement concerning the International Registration of Marks 1989, as of 31 October 2000.

As a result of Singapore's membership in these international conventions and the TRIPS Agreement, numerous legislative changes have since taken place. In 1994, parliament passed its first Patents Act.[3] In February 1998, the Copyright Act was amended, primarily to confer rights on performers, create rental rights for computer programs and sound recordings, expand the remedies for infringement of copyright, and establish border enforcement measures to prevent infringing intellectual property materials from entering Singapore.[4] Within the same year, the Singapore government repealed the old 1939 Trade Marks Act, enacted a new Trade Marks Act[5] and the Geographical Indications Act.[6] In January 1999, the Layout-Designs of Integrated Circuits Act[7] was passed while in August 1999, the Copyright Act was amended again.[8] This time, the amendments dealt specifically with the challenges posed by electronic commerce. On 25 August 2000, the new Registered Designs Act 2000[9] was passed, establishing a new system of registration for industrial designs in Singapore.

In 2003, Singapore entered into a Free Trade Agreement (FTA) with the United States of America, and pursuant to the US–Singapore FTA, intellectual property laws in Singapore have once again undergone radical amendments in 2004. The amendments were wide-ranging, affecting areas such as copyright, trademarks and patents.

Intellectual property law related courses offered by the NUS Business School

Intellectual property laws have become an important component in Singapore's legal infrastructure, and intellectual property awareness is the new buzzword in the market. To increase the level of "intellectual property literacy," the government has expanded resources in the education and training of intellectual property professionals, and undertaken to raise intellectual property awareness in the general public through initiatives and programs by public governmental bodies and institutions of higher-learning. The study of intellectual property is no longer confined

---

[3] Chapter 221, The Statutes of the Republic of Singapore.
[4] Act 6 of 1998 – Copyright (Amendment) Act 1998.   [5] Act 46 of 1998.
[6] Act 44 of 1998.   [7] Act 3 of 1999.
[8] Act 38 of 1999 – Copyright (Amendment) Act 1999.   [9] Act 25 of 2000.

to legal practitioners, legal scholars and law students. In the National University of Singapore, intellectual property has found its way into the curriculum of disciplines such as business, art and social sciences, engineering and computer sciences.

Modules offered at the undergraduate level

At the NUS Business School, intellectual property law courses and intellectual property law related courses are offered to business students both at the undergraduate and the postgraduate level.

For the undergraduate business students, the study of intellectual property laws has always been part of a larger core module offered in the first year – "Legal Environment of Business". In this core module, first year business students are taught basic principles of intellectual property laws, such as the different types of intellectual property, how to obtain protection and the consequences of infringement. As intellectual property law is but one of the several topics covered in this module (like contract law, company law, sale of goods, tort law and credit security law), students are given an introduction to this complex area of law.

Since 2002, two other specialized intellectual property law elective modules have been offered by the NUS Business School to undergraduates: (a) a fourth year elective module under the University's Scholars Program – Management of Intellectual Property; and (b) a general education module – Intellectual Property in Cyberspace. The syllabuses of these two modules are reproduced in Appendix 1.

Management of intellectual property

In 2002, I developed the "UBZ 4001 Management of Intellectual Property" course, a fourth year module for the University Scholars' Program. The main objective of this course is to equip students with the knowledge of the Intellectual Property Rights (IPRs) protection system, its significance as a tool for wealth and value creation in a knowledge-based economy, and the legal, economic and management challenges presented to the IPRs protection system as a result of advancement in science and technology. The uniqueness of this course lies in the exposition of multi-faceted issues in the study of intellectual property rights: legal, economic and management, ethical and public policies issues.

This module is designed with the following learning objectives in mind, and it is hoped that at the end of the module the students will have:

- A good knowledge of the national IPRs protection system and the various categories of IPRs, i.e. copyright; patents; trademarks; trade secrets and registered designs rights.
- A good knowledge of the international IPRs protection system and its implications for business: the impact of trade on IPRs; the impact of the TRIPS Agreement; the relevance of the international conventions and treaties, and issues of dispute resolutions and enforcement of IPRs.
- An in-depth appreciation of the significance of the IPRs protection system as a tool for technology innovation, transfer and ultimately leading to the creation of greater wealth and value for corporations and individuals.
- An in-depth appreciation of the many facets of IPRs protection: legal, economic, management and social issues, and the controversies brought about by advancement in science and technology, particularly in the areas of biotechnology, computer technology and the Internet.

To achieve the above learning objectives, I have introduced the following pedagogical requirements in my module:

Seminar presentations by students

Selected topics in the module are not imparted to the students via the traditional mode of a lecture. Instead, they are introduced to the class through a seminar/case presentation conducted solely by the students. Students reading this module are not only exposed to legal concepts and regulations, but are also introduced to the implications of the legal regime on public policies at large. To provide students with a holistic induction to the many issues both legal and non-legal presented by the intellectual property protection system, I select certain topics such as: biotechnology resources and intellectual property; freedom of expression and intellectual property; intellectual property and the Internet, and so forth. These are taken as topics for seminar presentations undertaken by the students in groups of four to five. Students are normally given a legal case related to each topic and are asked to discuss the case as well as other related questions or issues (see sample Case Presentation attached in Appendix 2). Students must then conduct research on the topic and make a presentation in class. The quality of the learning depends on the input of the students themselves and they in turn learn from each other. There is also greater class participation, as the rest of the students who are not presenting are expected to critique and ask the presenting panel of students questions regarding their presentation.

As the instructor, I facilitate and mediate the classroom interactions and provide assessment and analysis at the end of the presentation. These assessments and analysis are sent to the students electronically. Through these case presentations, the students act as teaching assistants, and I find this occasional shift of the imparting of core knowledge to the students themselves to be novel and intellectually stimulating for everyone. This particular methodology also encourages students to take charge of their own learning and gives them an opportunity to select the issues for discussions that appear most interesting to them.

Online forum

For this module, I have also put in place an online Forum in our university's Integrated Virtual Learning Environment (IVLE) portal. Students make use of this Forum to post questions or comments, and they sometimes continue into cyberspace the discussion that they have left off in class. I also post issues or problems in the Forum for the students to consider and ponder.

Open book assessment and case analysis as the mode of assessment

By adopting an open book assessment as the mode of assessment for the final examinations, I encourage students to spend their time reading as widely as possible on the topics covered in this module. Students are not expected to commit to memory the substantive elements of the law, but are encouraged to understand the principles behind the rules and regulations and to apply these principles to a case analysis on intellectual property issues. To do the case analysis, students must not only have a good grasp of the law but also possess a critical mind to apply these principles to the facts of the case. Sometimes, the issues in the case analysis are complex, as they involve other public interests. In such instances, students are expected to have an opinion on these controversial issues and stand ready to defend their positions with well-crafted arguments.

Independent research on a topic of their choice

Students are expected to complete a 20-page essay individually on a topic of their choice at the end of the module. Typically, these topics have been discussed in class but not in great detail. By researching and writing on the topic of their choice, students are given the opportunity to select a topic that they like and drill deep into the issues at hand. In this way, the module not only provides breadth but also some depth.

Intellectual Property in Cyberspace

The "Intellectual Property in Cyberspace" module is a General Education Module (GEM) of the University. The educational objective of the GEM at NUS is to impart intellectual breadth and foster critical thinking, and hence the dual focus on general knowledge on the one hand, and modes of inquiry on the other. The "Intellectual Property in Cyberspace" module, being a GEM, is offered university-wide to all undergraduate students except law undergraduate students.

This module is inspired by advancements in computer technology, and its impact on the protection of IPRs. Intellectual property is no longer only confined to the "bricks-and-mortar" world but is also found in the new world of cyberspace. Many controversial issues have since surfaced in this complex area of the law. In response to the changes in technology, changes in the laws for the protection of IPRs in cyberspace have also been introduced in Singapore. Major revisions in the law have taken place since the late 1990s. These new changes to the law of trademarks, patents and copyright are analyzed and discussed in this module.

This module is designed with the following learning outcomes in mind:

Domain knowledge

At the end of the module, the students will:
- have a good understanding of the various intellectual property rights and their significance as a tool of wealth creation;
- have an in-depth appreciation of the novel issues related to intellectual property in the digital environment;
- acquire a broad multi-jurisdictional perspective on the subject of intellectual property and the various multi-faceted issues closely linked with it.

Skills and Abilities

At the end of the module, the students will acquire:
- the ability to conduct independent research in areas of their interests;
- the ability to formulate and articulate arguments with clarity of thought and expression;
- the confidence to deliver presentations in class and to engage in questions and answers sessions;
- the ability to assess critically information, arguments and opinions disseminated in class, arrive at conclusions and stand ready to defend the positions taken.

Attitudes and Mindsets

At the end of the module, I expect my students to be individuals who possess the following attributes:
- an inquiring but open mind;
- a willingness to challenge accepted norms;
- the moral courage to defend their views and positions;
- an appreciation that knowledge is never static; and
- the spirit to constantly better themselves in the quest of knowledge.

To achieve the learning outcomes, I employ similar teaching methods and mode of assessment as in the module "Management of Intellectual Property." Besides the methods mentioned above, I also request the students in my GEK 1042 module to complete an Executive Summary of a journal article or chapter in a book assigned to them as reading materials. Students are expected to read at least one assigned journal article or chapter in the book and then write an Executive Summary from the reading. By doing the Executive Summary, the students are required to read the article, summarize pertinent points in the article and finally critique the article. The Executive Summaries are then graded by the instructor and uploaded in the university's IVLE work bin of the module to be shared by the entire class.

The major topics covered in this module include: an overview of intellectual property rights (trade secrets, patents, copyright and trade marks); copyright issues in cyberspace; patents and computer-related inventions; trademarks and domain names; data protection and privacy issues in cyberspace and freedom of expression in cyberspace.

In terms of teaching methodology, this module adopts a seminar style teaching of 3 contact hours a week for a total of 13 weeks. The first 1 hour and 30 minutes of the seminar is typically spent on imparting the basic principles on the subject matter to the students. However, the students must be prepared to interact with the instructor during this session and thus, they must have read the relevant assigned materials before the seminar. The rest of the seminar time is devoted to case analysis and discussions which are prepared and presented by students. These case analyses and discussions are the heart of the module, as it is through careful dissection and systematic presentation of arguments of the issues found in these cases that the students truly learn to appreciate the significance of the issues and to evaluate critically their implications.

The "Intellectual Property in Cyberspace" module is an open book examination module. The students are assessed continuously throughout the semester. Continuous assessment in this module consists of four quizzes, one mid-term written project and ongoing case analysis and presentations. The four quizzes are administered throughout the whole term and carry a weightage of 10%, which is an individual effort assessment. There is also an individual effort mid-term written project in week 11 which carries a weightage of 20%. Students are also expected to do at least one case analysis and make presentations in class. The case presentations are ongoing throughout the module and are done fortnightly. They carry a weightage of 30%; this is a group effort assessment. At the end of the module, the students sit for a Final Examination which consists of one compulsory question. This question takes the form of a case analysis that requires the students to explore a myriad of issues and to formulate cogent arguments in relation to them. The final examination carries a 40% weightage, and it is an individual effort assessment.

Modules offered at the postgraduate level

Between 1998 and 2001, intellectual property courses were offered to business students at the postgraduate level in the Master of Science (Management of Technology) program and the Master of Science (E-Business) program. For students in both of these programs, an elective course entitled "Legal Aspects of Technology Management" was offered to them. For students in the Master of Business Administration program, intellectual property laws are discussed generally in an elective program "Legal Issues in Business". Intellectual property laws are also incorporated into the "International Business and Law" module – one of the 12 core modules in the NUS Business School's Executive MBA (Chinese) program since 1997. This program is conducted entirely in Mandarin and is targeted at senior managers of companies in the Asia Pacific region.

Programs offered to business executives

Ad hoc courses on knowledge management and intellectual property are also being offered to business executives by the Office of Executive Education in our business school throughout the academic year. The duration of such training courses is between one to three days, and the topics discussed vary from time to time.

Teaching methods

Student-centered learning or outcome-based education

A student-centered learning approach is to empower students towards learning on their own with the help of clear and easily accessible learning objectives. In the same way, outcome-based education is a method of curriculum design and teaching that focuses on what the students can actually achieve and do after they have been taught. I have basically adopted the outcome-based education approach in the design of the intellectual property law based modules which I now offer to business, engineering and humanities students in the university. The learning objectives of the intellectual property law related modules are clearly defined in the course outlines which are made available to the students and are posted on the websites of my modules. Multiple instructional (case presentations, lectures and tutorials, role playing and debates, etc.) and assessment (short quizzes, group presentations, project work, written examinations, class participation, etc.) strategies are adopted to meet the learning objectives. The students are also given timely feedback so that assistance may be rendered in time and each student can reach his or her maximum potential. In adopting an outcome-based education method of curriculum design and teaching, I am compelled to review the content of the modules from time to time so as to ensure that the goals of learning are achieved.

Teachers as facilitators[10]

In the advanced module, "Management of Intellectual Property", offered to fourth year students in the University Scholars' Program, I change my

---

[10] See Roger M. Schwarz, *The Skilled Facilitator: The Practical Wisdom for Developing Effective Groups*, San Francisco: Jossey-Bass Publishers (1994); Peter M. Senge, *The Fifth Discipline: The Art and Practice of the Learning Organization*, New York: Doubleday/Currency (1990);

pedagogical approach from instruction to facilitation. As class size is relatively small, approximately 40 to 50 students, I adopt a seminar style. Teaching by facilitation encourages the generation of a greater volume of discussion and debate on the various issues found in the complex subject matter of intellectual property laws. More importantly, through teaching by facilitation, students are constantly challenged to look and re-look at the issues and arguments presented by themselves and their classmates. As a facilitator, the professor exchanges the more traditional role of a "teacher" imparting knowledge to the students for the more interactive roles of a moderator or a discussant of issues and arguments presented in class. I have found that this teaching method encourages students to share their views in class (an ability that is much lacking in Asian students) and to further understand, analyze and integrate the subject matter of intellectual property into their existing assumptions or body of knowledge. Through the discussions in class, intellectual property is transformed from a dry, unpalatable body of laws, treaties and regulations into an interesting and intriguing array of arguments and issues that spur the students to explore further into the subject and to conduct independent research on topics of interest.

Teaching with the case method

In a law-based module, the discussion and analysis of cases (legal judgments) is a useful and helpful teaching tool in this regard. Through an interactive discussion of the cases, students are presented with true to life accounts and real issues of contention. With the help of these cases, students are in a better position to understand the legal principles, appreciate the business or social implications and see the relevance of studying them.

Large class teaching

At the first year undergraduate level, a basic understanding of the legal and regulatory environment of business is important for a holistic business education. Intellectual property laws are introduced to the first year undergraduates in the core module "Legal Environment of Business." As all first year business students must read this core law module, the class

---

and Chris Argyris and Donald A. Schon, *Theory in Practice: Increasing Professional Effectiveness*, San Francisco: Jossey-Bass Publishers (1974).

size is approximately 350 to 400 students. One of the main challenges of teaching in a large class is the ability to engage the students intellectually and to maintain their attention for the entire two-hour duration of the class. A number of strategies may be employed by the professor to effectively conduct an interactive session and avoid a monologue where learning is most passive. These strategies[11] include: (a) personalizing the large class by chatting informally and getting to know the students personally and inviting student feedback at the end of the class; (b) an abundant use of stories drawn from personal experiences and news headlines which help to make the concepts of the lectures vivid and interesting; (c) encouraging students to ask and respond to questions in class. This can be achieved by creating a fun and relaxed atmosphere in the classroom where students are not afraid of being challenged or contradicted.

Small class seminar-style teaching

For undergraduates in their senior years as well as postgraduates, a basic understanding of the legal and regulatory environment of business, coupled with the ability to assess and evaluate the impact of legal judgments in making business decisions, is an important attribute of legal education for business students. In terms of teaching methodology, I recommend teaching by cases in seminars. Students are given a list of cases, textbooks, reference books, journal articles and legislation to read before the seminar. At the seminar, the instructor acts as a facilitator in a "question and answer" learning session. The imparting of knowledge via traditional lecture style is reduced to a minimum. This teaching methodology encourages independent learning and challenges the intellect of the students.

Developing teaching strengths

Domain knowledge

An effective law teacher must be someone who is equipped with strong foundations in his or her domain knowledge. The law, particularly business-related laws like intellectual property, is a body of knowledge that does not remain static but is ever evolving with changing social needs. An effective teacher is one who is able to synergize his/her research

---

[11] Albert Teo, "Interactive Teaching and Learning in Large Class", CDTLink, March 2002 vol. 6 No.1 at p. 5.

output with classroom teaching. I have found that it is useful to share my latest research findings and that of my colleagues with my students. In this way, I ensure that the legal knowledge imparted to my students is the most current in terms of thought leadership, most updated in terms of legal developments and, most importantly, it is information or knowledge that is most relevant and useful to them.

Language of instruction and delivery style

Intellectual property law, like other law subjects, can be extremely technical and uninteresting to students. The ability to capture their attention and to stimulate their interest in the topics is the key to effective classroom teaching. Effective communication skills are very important in the classroom environment. An effective teacher is one who is able to explain and communicate very difficult legal concepts with clarity. However, there is no one best style of teaching, and every professor has his or her own unique manner that appeals to the students.

Using technology as a tool to aid teaching

The advent of the Internet has revolutionized the manner in which information is disseminated and exchanged. To keep abreast with technology, teachers must learn new technologies and apply them in the classrooms. Developing websites for the modules is one good way to allow student to access the teaching and reading materials at a time and place most convenient to them. Learning does not have to be confined to the classrooms; for mature students, they are able to access websites and learn wherever they may be. The website needs to be interactive, and populated with activities which would encourage greater student participation. In this way, learning can also be fun. The electronic medium adds variety to the manner in which information and knowledge may be disseminated and this mode of instruction should be encouraged.

Development of teaching materials and textbooks

Many books in the area of intellectual property laws have been written for practitioners, legal scholars and law students. However, there are few suitable textbooks for non-legal readers, and in this regard, more must be done to generate reading materials to promote general intellectual property awareness.

Organization of teaching materials

An effective teacher is also one who expands resources in the selection and systematic organization of course materials for his/her students. Course materials should be organized in a clear, succinct and systematic manner, as this aids students in their learning processes and ensures accurate transmission of knowledge.

Problems and challenges faced by an intellectual property law teacher in a business school

As a law teacher in a business school, I am presented with the challenge of educating non-legal professionals. The breadth and depth of legal knowledge to be imparted to business students that are not going to be lawyers must be customized according to their needs. The main learning objective is to provide them with adequate legal knowledge so that they are able to appreciate the implications of the law when making business decisions. This is the challenge. I am tasked to make law accessible to these students, but at the same time I must ensure accuracy and correctness of the black letter law imparted to them. The problems that I face are thus associated with "demystifying" the law for non-legal students. In that respect, I have found the "case-method" to be very effective; by learning through cases, students are able to overcome their initial fear and dislike for the subject and subsequently develop a genuine interest in the study of the law.

With regard to teaching intellectual property laws as a subject in a business school, the foremost challenge presented to me is in generating students' interests in the subject. Business students are trained to be generalists, and they must be equipped with a wide range of subject disciplines in order to be ready for the job market. Intellectual property law is not a core discipline in the business curriculum and may be offered only as an elective. If the enrolment of the module is low, the module may not be offered. To overcome this problem, the modules offered must be interesting, useful and relevant to the students. This requires the teacher to constantly update the teaching materials and improve on teaching methodologies.

Conclusion

The teaching and the studying of intellectual property laws in Singapore has indeed grown in scope and importance over the past decade. This is evident from all the education and training initiatives by various institutions, both governmental and non-governmental, and the courses offered at various tertiary institutions. However, intellectual property laws modules are electives in the Business School and they are likely to remain as electives in the business curriculum. These are the realities and they are also the challenges for an intellectual property laws teacher like me in the Business School. The challenge of ensuring that intellectual property laws modules offered will remain relevant and useful to students has encouraged me to undertake constant periodic review of the module contents; to explore new and innovative teaching methodology, and to develop interesting teaching materials. At the Business School, intellectual property laws modules compete with all the other very interesting and useful modules currently offered in the business curriculum for student enrolment and no effort must be spared continuously to inspire students to appreciate the significance and the relevance of reading intellectual property as a subject in the university.

As Singapore aspires to be an intellectual property hub of the region, it is indeed true that only through "a strategy of education, collaboration and communication"[12] among the various stakeholders, that the wider issues of economic, social and cultural benefits of intellectual property protection and its significance to the economy, as the new tool of wealth creation, will be fully appreciated by the public at large. For teachers and researchers working in the field of intellectual property, these are exciting times. I certainly look forward to more opportunities for collaborations and interactions among institutions of higher learning, research centers and governmental bodies both within Singapore and outside of Singapore on this subject of intellectual property law education for the general masses. I am confident that with all the educational initiatives undertaken by the Singapore government and the various institutions, intellectual property will always remain an important subject in our universities' curriculum.

---

[12] *A Model Plan of Action for Intellectual Property Outreach Programmes – Education, Collaboration, Communication*, WIPO.

APPENDIX 1

A. Management of Intellectual Property Module

Course Syllabus

(1) The fundamentals of intellectual property law

- Copyright
- Industrial designs
- Patents
- Trademarks and passing off
- Integrated circuit layout-design protection
- Geographical indication of origin
- Undisclosed information and the protection of personal/institutional knowledge

(2) The international intellectual property system

- International trade and intellectual property
- Organizations and international cooperation
- Sources of law
- Dispute settlement and enforcement issues
- United States of America and Singapore Free Trade Agreement

(3) Intellectual property rights: commercialization and exploitation

- Forms of transfer of technology: licences, assignments and joint-ventures
- Intellectual property and corporate strategies
- Competition and IPRs

(4) Intellectual property rights and technology advancement

- Impact of new technologies on IPRs
- Global electronic commerce and IPRs

(5) Intellectual property rights and public policy issues

- Freedom of information and IPRs
- Biotechnology resources, traditional knowledge and IPRs

B. Intellectual Property in Cyberspace Module

Course Syllabus

Introduction

- What is intellectual property?
- Tangible property vs. intangible property
- "Bricks-and-mortar" world vs. virtual world
- What kind of intellectual property rights are generated in the physical world?
- What is the difference if these intellectual property rights are generated in cyberspace?

Confidential information

- What is confidential information?
- Why is confidential information important or valuable?
- How can confidential information be protected in law?
- What are the implications or consequences if one fails to protect confidential information?
- Confidential information used in cyberspace
- Confidential information and the issues of privacy in the virtual world
- Confidential information and the emerging right of publicity with regard to the protection of famous personal images and other indicia

Data protection and privacy issues in cyberspace

- Data protection laws
- Hacking and computer misuse laws
- Privacy issues and the protection of the law

Patents and inventions

- What is a patent?
- What does a patent protect?
- Why should an inventor apply for a grant of patents for his inventions and innovations?
- How to apply for a patent?

- What are the criteria for grant of a patent?
- What are the exclusive rights conferred upon a patent owner by the law?
- What remedies are available for a patent owner whose patent has been infringed?
- The global market place and the significance of patents

Patents and computer-related inventions

- Can computer programs be patented?
- Can business methods be patented? Should they be protected?

Copyright

- What subject matters are protected by copyright?
- When does copyright subsist in a work?
- What are the exclusive rights of a copyright owner?
- How is copyright protection important and relevant to authors?
- When is copyright infringed?
- What are the consequences of infringement?
- What remedies are available to a copyright owner whose copyright in a work has been infringed?
- The global market and copyright protection

Literary, musical, artistic and dramatic works in cyberspace

- Contract vs. copyright as a form of protection
- Copyright's demise in cyberspace and "Code" as the new form of protection
- The Digital Millennium Copyright Act (United States of America) and its impact
- New laws relating to downloading of copyrighted materials on the Internet and anti-circumvention devices
- Moral rights
- Performers' rights in cyberspace
- Rights management information

Computer programs and copyright

- Are computer programs protected by copyright?
- The protection of designs of circuits and semi-conductor products

- Multimedia works and copyright protection in cyberspace
- Copyright infringement in cyberspace: hyperlinking and framing issues

Databases and factual compilations

- Databases and subsistence of copyright
- The creative originality vs. the "sweat of the brow" or labour investment
- Comparative analysis across jurisdictions: USA, UK, Canada, Australia and Singapore
- The proprietary models: The European Directive on the Legal Protection of Databases; the proposed WIPO Treaty 1996; the proposed Database Investment and Intellectual Property Antipiracy Act of 1996
- The alternative legal model: unfair competition/misappropriation theories

Trademarks and passing off

- What are trademarks?
- How important are trademarks to businesses?
- What is the rationale for protecting trademarks?
- Registrability of trademarks
- Scope of protection and registrability of non-conventional trademarks such as smell marks, sound marks, moving images and so on.
- Well-known marks
- What are the exclusive rights of a registered trademark owner?
- Infringement of registered trademarks
- What remedies are available to a registered trademark owner whose trademark has been infringed?
- Unregistered trademarks – can they be used?
- How to protect unregistered trademarks?

Trademarks and domain names

- What are domain names?
- What is the significance of domain names as an indicator of origin?
- What is cybersquatting?
- Resolution of domain names disputes
- Issues on meta-tagging and other unfair usage of trade marks over the Internet

Freedom of expression in cyberspace

- Regulation of the Internet
- Human Rights Act and its implications on intellectual property rights
- Parodies and other issues

APPENDIX 2

Sample Case Discussion

Discussion 2

Novelty, inventive step and enabling disclosure in patents applications

- *Biogen Inc. v. Medeva PLC [1997] RPC 1, House of Lords*
- George Wei, *Inventions, Genes and Napoleonic Victories*, Vol. 9, March 1997, Singapore Academy of Law Journal, p. 1–34

Format for Discussion:

1. Facts and history of proceedings of the case (5 marks/points)
   - State the facts of the case briefly in your own words. Pick out the salient facts only.
   - State the history of proceedings of the case. What level of judicial proceeding is the case at?
2. Analysis (5 marks/points)
   - Analyze the issues, i.e. what are the questions the court has to decide?
   - Analyze the judgment, i.e. what is the court's decision? State the reasons the court gives for its decision.
3. Issues for discussion (10 marks/points)
   (a) Discuss briefly the recombinant DNA technology.
   (b) The following questions are taken from Abbot, Cottier & Gurry, *The International Intellectual Property System: Commentary and Materials, Part One*, Kluwer Law International 1999, pp. 63–64. Discuss:
      (i) Lord Hoffmann expresses doubt whether there are criteria for an invention other than that a product or process be new, capable of industrial application and involve an inventive step. Can you suggest an added element? The patent system is often justified as a stimulus to inventive activity through enhanced

financial reward (or potential reward). If an invention is achieved by a commercial decision to invest capital in pursuit of a widely identified goal, can the patent grant be said to have stimulated inventive activity? Has it instead stimulated the investment of capital? Is there a difference?

(ii) In the well-known Star Trek science fiction series, people (including alien people) are moved about from one point in space to another by means of the "transporter." The transporter has become so much a part of global culture that most of us likely assume it is only a matter of time (even if a very long time) before people are "beaming" from one place to another. Should the producers of the Star Trek series have filed a patent application on the transporter before they first publicly introduced it?

- When it was introduced, was the concept of the transporter new?[13]
- When it was introduced, was the concept of the transporter capable of industrial application?
- When it was introduced, did the concept of the transporter involve an inventive step?
- If the Star Trek transporter was new, capable of industrial application and involved an inventive step, why should not a patent examiner have recommended the grant of a patent? Could the producers of the Star Trek series have provided an enabling disclosure?

(iii) In 1997, a group of scientists in Scotland announced the successful "cloning" of a sheep named Dolly. A patent application has been filed on this invention. What do you think has been claimed in the patent application? How might the holding in Biogen limit the scope of the claims?

(iv) Lord Hoffmann says that the EPO Technical Board dismissed Medeva's opposition to the Biogen patent without considering the grounds on which the House of Lords invalidates the patent for the United Kingdom. According to Lord Hoffman, what was the substance of the challenge considered by the Technical Board, and what is the additional ground considered by the House of Lords?

---

[13] Staying within the science fiction genre, consider, for example, the teleportation device that played a prominent role in an early science fiction film, *The Fly*, with Vincent Price.

(c) Reflect upon the position in Singapore. Is the phrase "anything under the sun that is made by man can be patented by man"[14] applicable here in Singapore? Explain.

[14] *Diamond* v. *Chakrabarty*, 447 U.S. 305, Supreme Court of United States of America.

APPENDIX 3

Sample Open Book Examination Question

OJIM Ltd – A case analysis of intellectual property issues in business

OJIM Ltd (OJIM) is a Singapore incorporated public listed company. It is a parent holding company of several other subsidiary companies in Singapore and in the region. OJIM's core business is in the manufacturing and selling of life-style health products and supplements for Asian men and women.

OJ-Health Pte Ltd (OJ-Health) is a subsidiary company of OJIM and manufactures a wide range of health supplements and vitamins products for men and women. OJ-Health claims its products are researched and tested for their effectiveness particularly for the Asian market. OJIM, the parent company, has invested a large amount of time, human capital and financial resources in the research and development of OJ-Health's new line of health supplements and vitamins which it claims can help weight loss and increase vitality. OJ-Health's latest product is a range of herbal products called "Lusemfast". It is a whole range of products including dieting pills, health boosters, skin rejuvenating oral supplements, massage cream and others. This range of products is marketed under the trademark "Lusemfast" and OJ-Health has decided to sell their products in a distinctive container in the form of a shapely female human silhouette.

As the health supplements and slimming industry is very competitive, OJIM has invested heavily in a very strong research department that frequently conducts research to develop better and more effective products. The research team is headed by a very talented scientist Dr. Hugh Beh. Dr. Beh and his team of researchers travel far and wide in search of new ingredients and processes for OJ-Health's products. Recently, Dr. Beh has just returned from the deep forests of Borneo and has discovered that a local tribe there has a high number of healthy elderly folks who are mentally active and physically fit even when they are well into their eighties and nineties. Further research reveals that members of this tribe enjoy longevity because a large part of their diet consists of a particular herbal root that is indigenous in that part of Borneo. Dr. Beh has plans to extract the essential ingredient from this herbal root and process it into a health supplement for the Asian market. He has recently completed a long detailed report on the feasibility of this new product including its method of extraction and production. This study is at the embryonic stage and is to be kept under wraps for fear of unauthorized disclosure to OJIM's business rivals.

Recently, OJIM has also ventured into other ancillary businesses such as the fitness business, healthy vegetarian eateries and healthy life-style home furniture. OJIM has invested in the establishment of a one-stop total fitness resort in the nearby Sentosa Island. This new resort is called "Viva Life Fitness Resort Pte Ltd." The resort is equipped with state of the art body-building equipment as well as other slimming and beautifying machines. Above all, OJIM is proud to present to the members of the "Viva Life Fitness Resort" the "Viva Total Wellness Program" specially designed and conducted by the fitness guru Vivienne Voon. Vivienne is a renowned yoga guru and she has developed a special breathing exercise that she claims can effectively control the human mind with regard to the intake of food. In this way, those who practice this breathing exercise have successfully reduced weight and are able to maintain their weight loss. Vivienne claims her unique breathing exercise is a medical breakthrough. However, there is literature to suggest that ancient Chinese monks practiced a similar breathing exercise to focus their minds.

A numbers of issues related to intellectual property rights have arisen recently in relation to OJIM's businesses and its board of directors needs your advice.

Based on the information given to you in the case above and the additional information provided in each of the following questions, answer ALL of the questions citing relevant legislations, cases and policy arguments:

1. OJ-Health Pte Ltd (OJ-Health)

It has come to OJ-Health's knowledge that a business rival in Singapore – Babes & Hunks Pte Ltd ("Babes & Hunks") has started to market an ointment with slimming properties under the brand name "OohSoFast". Babes & Hunks has also decided to use a human silhouette shaped container to market its slimming ointment. The shape of Babes & Hunks' container is not identical but similar to OJ-Health's. The marked difference between the two containers is that OJ-Health's containers are transparent whilst Babes & Hunks' containers are opaque.

(a) Discuss all the possible intellectual property issues that may arise with regard to OJ-Health's new range of herbal products called "Lusemfast" in view of the new information given to you above, specifically with regard to:
  (i) Whether OJ-Health has any rights over the brand name "Lusemfast" and the possible legal action against Babes & Hunks' trade mark "OohSoFast". (10 marks/points)

(ii) Whether OJ-Health has any rights over the shape of its container in the form of a shapely female human silhouette. (10 marks/points)

(iii) The fact that OJ-Health's "Lusemfast" herbal products all possess a distinct smell as a result of the particular herbal ingredients in them. OJ-Health wishes to market its products using this unique smell. Can OJ-Health acquire any monopoly rights over this unique smell? (5 marks/points)

(b) Dr. Beh believes he has made a significant contribution to OJ-Health with his research on the longevity health supplement product. However, he thinks he is not rewarded adequately by OJ-Health. He has the intention of resigning from OJ-Health and to start his own company. Dr Beh knows that the key to effectiveness of the longevity health supplement lies in the brewing method and he has mastered the technique with months of trial and error. Dr. Beh decides to manufacture the health supplement on his own. He has taken all the research reports with him and Dr. Beh intends to publish his findings on this longevity health supplement in a bi-monthly academic scientific journal.

(i) Advise OJ-Health as to its possible causes of action against Dr Beh. (20 marks/points)

(ii) What would be the consequences of a successful publication by Dr. Beh of his findings in the academic scientific journal? Explain. (5 marks/points)

(c) With regard to this new longevity health supplement product, does the community of this local tribe or the government of Indonesia have any rights or claims against OJ-Health or Dr. Beh? (10 marks/points)

2. Viva Life Fitness Resort Pte Ltd

(a) Can a patent be obtained for the unique breathing exercise developed by Yoga guru Vivienne Voon in Singapore or elsewhere in the world? If so, who is the rightful owner of this patent? Explain and discuss. (20 marks/points)

(b) An unhappy customer of Viva Life Fitness Resort Pte Ltd, Will Soo, has set up a website criticizing the service and the programs of Viva Life Fitness Resort Pte Ltd. In particular, he alleges that the Viva Total Wellness Program, which claims to control weight gain or reduce weight loss, employs hypnotic methods which may pose severe psychiatric problems. In fact, he alleges that prolonged reliance of such methods may result in permanent disability of one's sense of smell or taste to food or drinks. In his website, Will Soo quotes large chunks of literature from Viva Life Fitness Resort Pte Ltd's brochures and other marketing materials. Discuss the legal options available to Viva Life Fitness Resort Pte Ltd in relation to:

(i) Will Soo and his website. (5 marks/points)
(ii) The service provider hosting Will Soo's website in Singapore. (5 marks/points)
(iii) With regard to (ii), have the recent changes in the Singapore copyright laws altered the service provider's legal position? Explain. (10 marks/points)

9

Teaching IP practical skills for practitioners and attorneys

HEINZ GODDAR

Introduction

Intellectual Property (IP) covers, in general, many fields of intellectual property rights (IPRs), e.g. how to obtain them, how to enforce them, how to use them for business purposes, whether in technology transfer or in merger and acquisition, etc. Naturally, therefore, a broad variety of experts or professionals with many kinds of educational background and experience work in this business field, all of whom are designated herein by the term "IP professional."

Based on the core of their respective activities, in some fields, one may find persons with a full legal background, i.e. attorneys at law. In other circumstances, such as in business transactions, one may find persons without any formal legal or even technical background, but having received their basic professional education in, e.g. tax matters, accounting, business administration or the like; in other environments, one finds technical experts, both with and without additional legal qualifications.

The author will exemplify the foregoing from his personal viewpoint as a legal practitioner, as a patent attorney, and as a lecturer, at the Munich Intellectual Property Law Center (MIPLC) and at Bremen University, in order to give some insight into the German IP educational world. First, however, taking Germany, the home country of the author, as an example, various kinds of IP professionals active in that country will be described in more detail.

Kinds and education of IP professionals – the German experience

As in many other countries, attorneys at law in Germany are entitled to represent clients and handle matters in all legal fields, including IPRs, their prosecution, enforcement, and business use.

In order to become an attorney at law in Germany one first has to go through full legal studies at a university and the law faculty thereof. The minimum duration of such studies is seven semesters, but normally students need a little bit more, about eight semesters being the average.

Thereafter, a First State Examination takes place, followed by a "Referendarium" of two years, during which the "Referendar" goes through various stages at private law firms, courts, and other governmental and/or international institutions. Thereafter, a Second State Examination takes place – both the First and the Second State Examination comprise written examinations and oral examinations – after which the student/ "Referendar" is given the qualification to practice as a judge, in principle. This entitles her/him to be admitted to the Bar, whereafter, whether as a sole practitioner, or in-house in industry, or as a member of smaller or larger law firms, the attorney at law is entitled to practice all fields of law, including, as stated above, the law in respect to IPRs.

German patent attorneys

The education and training of German patent attorneys is totally different from that of attorneys at law. In order even to be admitted to start the training period for becoming a German patent attorney, the "candidate" has to obtain a full technical degree, i.e., a Diploma, which is only possible after a minimum of eight semesters of studies in science or technology; typical subjects for a Diploma are engineering, physics, chemistry, biotechnology, etc. After the Diploma, the candidate has to work as a scientist/engineer for at least one year in a practical technical field, either in industry or at a university, research institute, or the like. After the practical year, which, in case of doctoral studies, may be integrated into the time preparing a thesis at a research institute, university etc., in science/technology, the candidate may apply to be admitted by the President of the German Patent and Trademark Office, whereafter a legal training period of about three years starts.

In the first two years the trainee works in the office of a German patent attorney, or an equivalent department in industry, under the supervision of a German patent attorney, and is trained on the job.

In parallel to the training at a patent attorney's office and the like, university studies take place at the University of Hagen, in the form of a combination of distance studies, for two years, and live classroom studies, namely two sessions per year lasting one week each. After each year of training, an examination takes place, based on the knowledge acquired by the "candidate" at Hagen University. This examination is independent of the final state controlled examination to become a German patent attorney.

The aforementioned two-year period is followed by about one year of training at the German Patent and Trademark Office, the German Federal Patent Court and, if the trainee so decides, Patent Infringement Courts in Germany. This training period consists of a combination of practical work on the job with, e.g. patent examiners and judges, and lectures plus exercises. After the three years, a German Patent Attorney's Examination takes place, both in writing and orally. The successful candidate will then be qualified as a "Patentassessor," such title and qualification giving her/him the possibility to become admitted as a patent attorney in order to conduct his profession either in industry or in private practice.

The training of the patent attorney, essentially directed to legal matters related to IPRs, comprises the necessary legal background for acting as an IP professional.

European patent attorneys

In order to become a European patent attorney, in other words, a professional representative entitled to represent clients at the European Patent Office, full technical studies must first be passed, subject to examination, as in the case of German patent attorneys.

After such studies, at least three years of supervised work in the office of a European patent attorney or an industry equivalent must be passed. Such training period is regularly accompanied by generally two voluntary training sessions of one week each organized by the Center for International Industrial Property Studies (CEIPI) at Strasbourg.

As an alternative to the compact courses of one week each at Strasbourg, the "candidate" can also choose for a period of two years to have about two hours per week of lectures at Munich, which are also controlled/conducted by CEIPI.

At a time to be chosen by the "candidate," a written examination at the EPO takes place, only in writing, but of remarkable difficulty according to experts, after which the European patent attorney will be registered in the list of European patent representatives and will be entitled to represent clients, both in industry and in private practice. It should be noted that the examination at the European Patent Office requires full knowledge of at least two of the official languages of the EPO, i.e. English, French and German, and sufficient knowledge of the third language enabling the candidate to read and understand prior art documents, etc.

Other professionals

In a country like Germany, IP professionals include not just attorneys at law, German Patent Attorneys, and European patent attorneys, with patent attorneys usually having both the qualification as a German and a European patent attorney, like the author of this chapter. Rather, one finds a variety of other professionals who work in the field of IPRs and their commercial use. For example, big German companies in their patent departments usually employ a large number of technically trained specialists who do not hold the degree of a German or European Patent Attorney, but rather work as "patent engineers" after having been trained on the job. Often, after some years of professional experience, they qualify as patent attorneys, either German or European ones.

Also, if one considers the field of the valuation of IPRs, such as might be connected with technology transfer agreements or merger and acquisition environments, one often finds persons with degrees in economics or business administration, even specialists in tax law and accounting. With their general economics background, they deal with intellectual property in a similar manner to tangible assets, taking the specific characteristics of IPRs into due consideration. All of these "other" individuals cannot be grouped under the umbrella of a uniform training or education experience, but rather should be looked at as "practitioners" able and permitted to work as IP professionals in a very general sense; and, as a matter of course, they must carefully observe the legal restrictions reserving certain rights of professional work in IP to qualified IP professionals, namely attorneys at law and patent attorneys.

The role of patent attorneys in Germany

German patent attorneys in the Federal Republic of Germany (FRG), and the same applies in a similar manner for other Western countries, fulfill a broad spectrum of tasks. These activities can be briefly described below.

Obtaining patents in FRG (German patents)

The most important activity of the patent attorney is naturally to obtain patents. Generally, this involves a client, either an individual inventor or a German company, submitting to the patent attorney a new development, e.g. a new machine with the question as to whether the patent attorney considers this new development to be fundamentally patentable. The patent attorney's evaluation is generally directed at whether so-called "absolute" patentability exists, and not at whether the invention is "relatively" patentable in view of the prior art, because this would involve a (prior?) search for any publications dealing with similar subject matter.

For example, the patent attorney will have to consider whether it is a technical invention, i.e. in which a specific technical problem is solved by advantageously using natural forces. In the case of a positive answer to this question by the patent attorney, he will draft a patent application on the basis of the information supplied to him by the client. The following three criteria must be satisfied by the information required by the patent attorney:

(a) the indication of the prior art on which the new development is based, i.e. what was done technically before the present invention;
(b) the description of those features of the new development which differ from the previously used procedure, i.e. from the predecessor machine; and
(c) the indication of the advantages provided by the novel features according to (b) compared with the prior art according to (a).

The patent attorney then prepares drawings, preferably based on a sketch made available to him by the client, and then drafts claims and a description. This "rough draft" of the application is forwarded to the client and after discussion with him, the final version of the application documents is drafted. The application is then filed at the Patent Office.

According to the German Patent Act, after filing the examination request, the filed application is examined by the Patent Office to establish whether it is inventive in view of the prior art. For this purpose, the Patent Office carries out a search, after which the applicant or patent attorney is supplied with a "first official action" containing various publications which, in the opinion of the Patent Office, make a restriction of the statement of claim necessary.

The patent attorney then discusses the citations with the applicant, possibly followed by an amendment to the statement of claim, which is filed at the German Patent and Trademark Office with a corresponding response. A hearing is also frequently held with the Patent Office Examiner during which the patent attorney and the Examiner discuss the application in view of the prior art, so that frequently at the end of the hearing an allowable set of claims can be drafted. This is followed, after a period of one to three years, by the grant of a patent. If, after patent grant, this is opposed by a third party because, contrary to the opinion of the Examiner, the application is considered, for example, not to contain inventive features, the proceedings are continued before the Patent Division, accompanied once again by an exchange of correspondence and optionally accompanied by a hearing until a final decision is reached by the Patent Office.

The Patent Office decisions can then be reconsidered before the Federal Patent Court in Munich. Throughout these proceedings, the patent attorney acts as the technically versed, legal advisor of the client; he puts the technical content in the form of a new invention or the like worked out by the client into legally manageable language, and contributes to obtaining the patent through discussions with the patent authorities and with the opponent or opponents in any opposition proceedings.

The defense of German patents

Since in the FRG patents can be subject also to an invalidation action after grant, the patent attorney is also responsible for representing the interests of his client in defending the patent if a third party files an invalidation action. It should also be pointed out that, in general, the patent attorney also maintains a watch on the fees (payment of renewal fees) for patents where he has acted as representative. Throughout the life of the patent, the patent attorney is the discussion partner of the Patent Office, which forwards to him invalidation actions of third parties, queries for information regarding special points of the examination proceedings and the like, and he forwards any such information to the client.

Prosecution of and defense against infringements of German patents

Other important activities of the patent attorney are the representation of his clients in infringement litigation. By the very nature of things, in competition, granted patents are not always respected and, instead competitors infringe existing patents of third parties. If the patent attorney is informed by his client, who in this example is the patentee, that a third party is infringing with a particular machine an existing patent of the client, the patent attorney will firstly consider the facts of the infringement in detail, i.e. to establish whether a patent infringement does in fact exist. If this is the case, usually a warning letter will be sent to the infringing party; if the latter does not immediately stop infringing the patent, the patent attorney will file patent infringement proceedings before the appropriate court. The patent attorney will prosecute these proceedings, together with a legal attorney authorized by the particular court. Obviously, the procedure is the same when defending a client who has infringed a patent of a third party and who is warned by the latter, the procedure being reversed.

Obtaining patents outside the FRG (foreign patents)

Whereas patent attorneys deal with obtaining patents within the FRG for German companies, another important field of action for the patent attorney is obtaining foreign patents for German clients. Generally, this involves the client requesting the patent attorney to file a patent application in certain foreign countries.

The patent attorney will then instruct a foreign patent attorney, i.e., a patent attorney practicing in the USA in case of a US application, to file a corresponding foreign application. He will send him the application documents as originally filed in the FRG, and the foreign filing will generally involve the claim of priority in accordance with the Paris Convention for the Protection of Industrial Property. The foreign patent attorney will then act before the Patent Office of the particular country, for example the US Patent and Trademark Office, in the same way as the German patent attorney acts before the German Patent and Trademark Office as described above. The German patent attorney then acts as the German client's intermediary with respect to the foreign patent attorney.

The defense of foreign patents

In a number of foreign countries, it is also possible to attack already granted patents. The foreign patent attorney, in conjunction with the German patent attorney who acts as the intermediary for the client residing in the FRG, then defends the industrial property rights in the same way as described for German patents.

The prosecution of and defense against infringements of foreign patents

Naturally, patents are infringed both by third parties and by the client (of a German patent attorney abroad). In this case, the German patent attorney once again acts as an intermediary between his German client and the foreign patent attorney, who acts before the particular patent offices and represents the interests of the client of the German patent attorney in the same way as described above for the case of patent infringements within the FRG.

The representation of foreigners in patent matters – special factors

The description of the activity of the German patent attorney above largely coincides with the nature of the activity carried out by him when foreigners request him to represent them within the FRG. Thus, for example, a US patent attorney will forward an application text requesting that an application should be filed in the FRG. If the documents are in a foreign language, such as French or English, the German patent attorney will prepare a translation, while revising the text to take account of the special factors governing the German patent proceedings. The application is then filed at the German Patent and Trademark Office and this is followed by the proceedings as described above.

The explanations given for the prosecution and defense of German patents obviously also apply in the case of representing foreigners. One important factor is that on receiving instructions from abroad to file a patent application, the patent attorney does not generally have to draft a complete application text on the basis of the description provided by an "amateur" in the field of industrial property protection. In fact, he is provided with a corresponding arranged application text, subdivided into description and claims, which he can use as a basis for drafting the German application documents. It is also important to note that foreigners must be represented in patent matters in the FRG by a German patent attorney.

Other activities of patent attorneys

As has been stated, the German patent attorney is also able to represent the client in connection with, matters such as utility model, design and trademark questions, as well as patent questions. However, in all these fields of "industrial property protections," the patent attorney works in much the same way as previously described in connection with patents, so that no further explanation is required.

The German patent attorney, usually also having the additional qualification as a European patent attorney entitled to represent clients at the European Patent Office, in this latter capacity is also empowered to represent Germans and foreigners before the European Patent Office. He then acts in much the same way as previously described in connection with the German Patent and Trademark Office, so that once again a more detailed explanation is unnecessary.

Material skills of IP professionals

From a material or factual viewpoint, besides questions of professional training, IP professionals, depending on the specific type of work they are involved in, need to possess a variety of skills, that are dealt with in more detail in the following considerations.

Technical understanding

IP Professionals, except in cases where no technology is concerned, and which in this chapter shall be left out of consideration, must necessarily have a technical understanding of innovations, i.e. patentable inventions as well as technical know-how which can be protected, e.g. as trade secrets, that enables them not only to understand the way in which a certain invention functions, but also to determine its relation both to prior art and potential applications.

Accordingly, at least a basic understanding of technology in a specific field will be a necessary requirement for the education and training of IP professionals. A Bachelor's degree, in Anglo-Saxon education systems, will certainly be the minimum from the author's viewpoint; a Diploma (Master's) degree or even a doctoral degree in complicated technologies such as IT or biotechnology, to name but two, is sometimes advisable.

Legal understanding

IP professionals need to understand the way in which, by law, intellectual property can be protected by IPRs, in which manner IPRs can be enforced, and also, of course, in which manner IPRs can be commercialized.

Accordingly, the fields of law in which IP professionals should be trained comprise all kinds of laws, including: laws concerning property in and remuneration for inventions made by employees, a subject which is of importance, in particular in Germany; contract laws; competition laws; anti-trust laws; and, last but not least, international agreements, like the Paris Convention, the Patent Cooperation Treaty, etc.

A full study of law, entitling a student eventually to practice as an attorney at law in countries like Germany, might not be necessary, since, for example, criminal and family law with regard to IP will only play a role in peripheral areas, notwithstanding the fact that, for instance, anti-piracy procedures have a close relation to some fields of criminal law.

Business understanding

IPRs are the fence, so to speak, surrounding and protecting, at the will of its creator, a certain technology, an "intellectual property," thereby making such intellectual property an intangible asset protectable against unauthorized use by others. Whoever wishes to evaluate IPRs as business instruments must first understand that such exclusive rights have a certain commercial value, not only by giving a competitive edge to their owners, in order to protect their own production, but also providing the possibility of making profits by granting limited or exclusive rights to use such IPRs by means of licensing.

Accordingly, IP professionals should have a thorough knowledge of IPRs as business instruments, i.e. knowing about the exclusivity rights they give. However, they should also understand IPRs as "friendly animals," i.e., vehicles for technology transfer, e.g., by licensing.

In merger and acquisition situations, the valuation of IPRs plays a tremendous role, and accordingly, IP professionals also should be familiar with the usual valuation methods, at least in their basic form, like license analogy based procedures.

Ethics

IP professionals must have a high degree of professional ethics. As an example, in many instances, it will be necessary to keep their own clients' secrets confidential. Also, it will often be necessary to protect confidential information, for instance obtained in certain situations on a confidential basis from a potential client who is asking for representation, secret even against their own client, in case of conflict of interest. Whatever an IP professional during negotiations promises, and not only suggests, to the other side, should always be kept and realized. Nobody in the IP professional world should ever forget about the practically "binding" character of even oral declarations during negotiations. Otherwise, the credibility of an IP professional will be lost.

Also, IP professionals should always put their clients' interest first, their own interests having to be limited to their professional conduct, and no private commercial interest should be mixed into dealings with clients' intellectual property.

Language skills

In a globalized economy, IP professionals have to act internationally. That requires a profound knowledge of the English language, not because English is the mother tongue of certain countries in this world, but because it has developed into the modern "lingua franca," used as a vehicle for communication in technical and legal fields all over the world. An IP Professional who is not fluent in the English language in a practical way cannot do his work satisfactorily, because of the lack of communication possibilities with the "outside" world.

Negotiating skills

The IP world is full of conflicts. Their solution, usually, takes place by settlement. Settlements require negotiations. In negotiations, a deep psychological understanding of their own side, as well as the other side represented in such negotiations, is advisable, combined with basic rhetorical skills. It will be difficult to acquire such skills in specific academic studies during the professional development of an IP professional; particular attention, therefore, should be given to the practical training of such skills "on the job."

Pitfalls for IP professionals that are often observed

In many countries of this world, and certainly in emerging markets only gradually opening to the outside world, particularly with more and more countries entering the WTO, it can often be observed that IP professionals of one or the other kind, being experts in one field of interest, like laws or technology, have a distinct lack of experience in other fields.

Sometimes, one finds technical experts, fully understanding the technologies involved, but without sufficient knowledge either of the English language or of legal matters involved in, for example, licensing, or in both of them. Certainly, by acting in a team, such deficiencies can be balanced to a certain extent, but ideally, a technical expert working in IP should have at least a basic legal background relating to IPRs and laws neighboring this field, as well as a thorough knowledge of the English language.

Another type of "expert" sometimes to be found is the lawyer without technical understanding. Often in these cases one will also find an insufficient knowledge of the English language. Again, team work may help, but lawyers acting in IP should have, even without formal technical studies, a certain "feeling" for technology, and the necessity for English language training is beyond any doubt.

In other emerging markets, particularly in less or least developed countries, one finds language experts, sometimes with an educational background as teachers or interpreters, who speak English fluently, but suffer from a lack of knowledge of technical and/or legal matters. Again, in a team, these persons may work perfectly, but of course their task would much better be fulfilled if they at least had a basic technical and legal knowledge.

Ideal educational profile for IP professionals

In an ideal world, from the author's viewpoint, an IP professional should have a basic technical study, first, enabling the IP professional fully to understand the technology to be dealt with. This requirement may not exist, of course, if "only" trademarks or copyrights are to be handled, but very often these specific IPRs are accompanied by technical ones, which require IP professionals, in order to give full advice to a client, having the ability also to handle technology.

Preferably, from the author's viewpoint, a technical course of study should be at least up to a Bachelor's degree, sometimes, as stated above, going even higher.

During such technical studies, the trainee/student should learn English to the highest possible standard.

Full law studies will not be necessary, but all kinds of law, as dealt above under "Material skills," should be learned. Whether for this purpose a full law degree will be necessary, is doubtful in the view of this author. It might be sufficient that, with the omission of, for example, family law and most fields of criminal law, the legal training covers all fields of law which in a wider sense are related to IPRs.

It is difficult to say to what extent business understanding, including tax law, should be learned by IP professionals in a systematic way. It might be sufficient that an IP Professional, having the necessary technical and legal education, as indicated above, should acquire such additional skills on the job, namely by a number of years of experience in, in addition to prosecution and enforcement of IPRs, technology transfer, merger and acquisition, and, more generally, valuation of IPRs. All this can be done best, in the author's view, by having the forthcoming IP professional working for some years under the supervision of and/or as an assistant to an already experienced IP professional doing such a type of work on a regular basis.

As a final word, once again the necessity of training in language skills should be emphasized. Contracts have to do with communication, and communication necessitates mutual understanding. Mutual understanding is only possible in a common language. Accordingly, all IP Professionals of this world should agree that the ability to use a "lingua franca" fluently is a vital requirement of being a successful, all-round IP professional. It is clear, if unfortunate, that today neither Japanese nor German, to take but two examples, is such a lingua franca, whereas English is and therefore "all of us" have to learn it thoroughly.

Training and education of/in IP at German schools and universities

School system in Germany

Usually, in Germany, children start at an Elementary School at the age of six years. Usually, they stay in such an Elementary School, which may be part of a full-scale school system, for 4 years, after which 8 to 9 years of a High School or "Gymnasium" follow. Germany has essentially no college-like system; rather, after finishing High School, i.e. after 12 to 13 years at school in total, a study at university begins, usually ending with a diploma in, for example, technical science, corresponding, essentially, to a Master's degree in Anglo-Saxon countries, with special provisions for, for example, attorneys at law, as explained above.

During all stages of such education, IP education, though not nearly to a sufficient extent in this author's opinion, is, in principle, available.

IP education at schools

In German schools, sometimes, usually at the private initiative of teachers particularly of "scientific subjects" like biology, chemistry, and/or physics, patent attorneys are invited in order to teach, in order to tell the pupils/students about IP. This usually takes place at most once a year in the last three classes of senior high schools, before students go to university. In elementary schools, no such teaching usually takes place.

IP courses at German universities

"Free" courses

At a number of German universities, there are lectures in IP which are "free" in the sense that there is no obligation for students of any faculty to attend, except as part of regular Master's courses, as indicated below.

For example, the author of this chapter teaches, as far as a "free" course is concerned, at the University of Bremen. The lecture consists of four semesters of patent and other IP subjects, namely (a) Basics of patent law, (b) Advanced and international patent law, (c) Employees' invention law, and (d) Trademark law.

The participants of the courses come from all faculties, equally distributed between graduate and postgraduate students of science subjects and law. Economists also participate, particularly in the course on trademarks.

The students can generally use certificates, based on their participation in the patent and IP law lectures at Bremen University, in order to prove that they have studied for a minimum number of hours in certain "side" subjects, but there is no regular "degree" obtainable through such courses.

In some German universities, through not at Bremen, it is possible to elect IP as a side subject in the first state examination for lawyers, and even in the diploma examination for scientists, for example at the University of Erlangen.

Lectures of the kind that are held in Bremen are available at several German universities, about ten in total.

Master courses for IP

In a number of German universities, it is possible to obtain Master's degrees in intellectual property (LL.M).

These courses, some of which are held in English, some of which are held in the German language, take place at four different locations, namely at the Universities of Düsseldorf, Dresden, Hannover and Munich (MIPLC).

The author of this chapter teaches at the Munich Intellectual Property Law Center (MIPLC). MIPLC is a "joint venture" of the George Washington

University School of Law, Washington, D.C., the Technical University of Munich, the University of Augsburg, and the Max Planck Institute for Intellectual Property at Munich. The course lasts for one year, it ends with an examination, both in writing and orally, and internships at Munich IP firms are integrated into the course. The whole course is held in English.

Generally, admission to these courses at German universities is possible for somebody who has obtained at least a Bachelor's degree in law or science in Germany, or abroad. As far as English language courses are concerned, a certain minimum pass level in the Test of English as a Foreign Language (TOEFL) course, or similar standard, is necessary. The same applies, *mutatis mutandis*, to the German language courses.

A warning should be expressed to somebody who would like to participate in a German language course in Germany. There is a vast difference between studying a science subject, for example physics, which is essentially not language-oriented, in a foreign country, using that country's language, and studying a subject, such as IP Law, which is essentially based on language. Only a nearly perfect control of the language will enable a student to participate fruitfully in such studies.

Staying current with developments in IP and IP-related law

Once an IP professional has "finalized" her/his professional education, whether as a lawyer, specializing in IP, or a European or German patent attorney, or with some other qualification, training and/or education, that IP professional will only remain up-to-date for a very short time (to be counted probably in months rather than in years) with the continuous developments in IP laws and practice. In this regard, one should mention that not only the codified law as such is continuously changing – in a country like Germany, every year at least two or three laws are changed or supplemented, such as the Patent Act, the Trademark Act, or some other regulation, in many instances heavily influenced by EU Directives, and/or Regulations – but, in particular, the case law is also continuously developing, through the Boards of Appeal at the EPO, as well as by courts responsible for patent infringement and validity questions. This can lead to the way in which terms such as "scope of protection", "patentable subject matter", and/or "non-obviousness" are to be interpreted being modified.

Because the situation is constantly changing, probably at a faster rate than any other area of law, except tax law, it is inevitable that IP professionals must keep themselves updated with current developments, since otherwise they can, very simply, no longer reliably do their job. In other words, a "continuing legal education" (CLE) is necessary, which a country like the United States makes available in a compulsory, formalized manner for the "updating" of the knowledge of attorneys at law, and also other professions. In most European countries, and certainly in Europe, such CLE is not formalized, but nevertheless necessary in order to keep the IP professional in a position where she/he is able to give reliable advice.

The first requirement in CLE consists of a continuous reading of IP-related magazines, journals, newspapers and related media. In each of the European countries, and certainly in Germany, a number of specialized magazines and journals of this kind are available, such as in Germany the famous "GRUR", appearing with both a national and an international part, or, on a worldwide level, "Les Nouvelles", a magazine of LES International, a professional IP organization. Many of such specialized magazines and journals are "organs" of professional organizations for IP professionals. It is strongly recommended, too, that IP professionals become members of such professional organizations as AIPPI, LESI, and EPI, the professional organization of the European Patent Attorneys, among others.

Besides a continuous reading and following of case law and legal developments as described in journals, it will also be inevitable that IP professionals in question regularly attend specialized seminars in certain, particularly "hot" areas of their professional field, such as in Germany on employees' inventions. On the European level, one should participate in seminars like those offered by the Patent Academy of the EPO, or, in many countries, in professional education seminars offered by associations like AIPPI, or in Germany GRUR, like LESI, or the European counterpart of AUTM, namely ASTP (Association of European Science and Technology Transfer Professionals). All these organizations offer, not only to their members, but also to outsiders, regular information and training seminars. Beyond that, a variety of professional providers, like FORUM in Germany or FALCONBURY in England, but also many others, offer, on a more "commercial" basis, seminars on specific subjects in IP where professionals can continuously improve and update their skills.

Last but not least, one should not forget Internet-based teaching instruments that are available. "Google", a trademark-protected search machine which offers a wide range of services, makes a broad series of teaching materials available to IP professionals, not only by pointing to seminar possibilities and printed publications, but also by presenting publications on related subjects which may only be available in electronic form. Keywords like "IP watch" may be of help. If an IP professional works with great concentration in a particular technical field, it might also be useful to follow the publications of some patent authorities, like EPO or WIPO, with regard to patent applications published in certain classes of the international patent classification, just in order to keep updated in a technical sense and in a legal sense, in the field of specialization.

Future trends

From the personal experience of the author, and also based on many discussions with IP professionals all over the world, but in particular on the trends in filing and IP litigation numbers observable in Europe, today it appears crystal-clear that whoever decides to become an IP professional can look to a very bright professional future. All over the world, and certainly in Europe, and in countries like China and India, IP is becoming increasingly acknowledged as a business instrument, and accordingly, the numbers of IP professionals needed are steadily increasing.

One can generally say that in practically all fully industrialized countries, but even more in developing countries, there are not enough IP professionals available, particularly in the patent field, where the patent attorney or patent engineer with the necessary technical background is vital in order to "translate" the language of scientists and engineers into a language which can be handled by lawyers and, last but not least, courts.

With the further development of the IP systems in huge countries like China and India, the demand for IP professionals can only increase, not only in those countries, but also in "target" countries – such as Europe and the United States – where applicants from the former countries, and others, may wish to file their patents. Everybody in these countries, and also in many others, should intensify their efforts to train, educate and qualify far more IP professionals.

Concluding remarks

From the viewpoint of the author of this chapter, it would be most advisable if IP education in a country like Germany started much earlier than it currently does such as in elementary schools, at least in a basic form.

In high schools, there should be a regular lecture on IP at least of two hours once per month, during the three last years of high school, since otherwise many students will go into university life without having any chance of a proper choice as to their future profession, because of lack of knowledge about the possibilities the various IP professional careers offer.

In the opinion of this author, it should be compulsory for "technical" students at universities, including science students, to attend during at least one semester a lecture of two hours each week on intellectual property law, particularly patents, in order to get a feeling for the necessity and possibilities of protecting technical innovations by patents. For the professional life of engineers etc., this would be a tremendously valuable asset.

Last but not least: when training IP professionals in countries which do not have a sophisticated IP professional system, one should have in mind the following basic principles.

In many countries of this world, excellent technical experts, for various fields of science and technology, are available. Furthermore, in some countries, one will find excellent attorneys at law. What is missing, however, is a "class" of persons understanding, on the one hand, the language of inventors, i.e. of experts in science and technology, and able, on the other hand, to "translate" the respective facts into a legal language which can be understood by lawyers, patent offices, and judges. The most prominent role of an IP professional, such as a patent attorney or patent agent, in this author's view, is to be a technical translator, able to bridge these two worlds. The goal in the training of IP professionals must therefore be to educate, as much as possible, technically experienced persons in intellectual property matters, so that the interests of inventors, as well as of the public, can be duly represented and taken care of, in administrative and litigious proceedings, as well as in the peaceful commercialization of intellectual property.

10

Teaching intellectual property to non-law students

RUTH SOETENDORP

Introduction and overview

Intellectual property (IP) is a timely and important topic for students graduating from institutions in developing or developed economies, in disciplines as diverse as biotechnology and fashion design. There is international demand for graduates able to capitalize on the knowledge they create. But there is no guarantee that intellectual property education will feature in the curricula of faculties other than law schools. In recent years, academics from across the disciplines have begun to consider the reluctance to teach IP beyond the law school, and to offer suggestions for developing curricula to include it.

Challenges in this subject

This chapter will explore some of the frequently asked questions that occur when academics start to think about including IP in the non-law curriculum.

- **Who** is the audience for IP education?
- **Why** teach IP to non-lawyers?
- **What** does an IP syllabus cover?
- **How** to teach IP to non-lawyers?
- **When** is it best to teach IP?
- **Who** can teach IP?
- **What** if there is only one lecture allocated to IP?
- **Which** resources should be used?
- **What** does the future hold for IP teaching to non-law students?

Who is the audience for IP education?
IP education is relevant to students at all levels, and from all disciplines. Within the university community, it is important to achieve a level of IP

awareness and competence among researchers, faculty members, administrators and technology transfer managers.

Why teach IP to non-lawyers?
The quick and easy answers include: to enable them to protect their creations; to engage effectively with IP professional advisers; to avoid infringing other peoples IP. There are other benefits arising from collaborative interdisciplinary teaching and research.

What does an IP syllabus cover?
Since non-law students are being taught IP in order to produce a level of awareness and competence, rather than produce IP experts or professionals, the syllabus should be designed with that goal in mind.

How to teach IP to non-lawyers?
Teaching IP for non-lawyers fits well with current education theories designed to produce deep learning through problem- or practice-based learning.

When is it best to teach IP?
"Negative" IP education in schools presents pupils with the risks posed by access to downloadable and counterfeit entertainment products. "Positive" IP education, emphasizing its importance in trade and commerce, has a place at any undergraduate or postgraduate level.

Who can teach IP?
One of the biggest barriers to inclusion of IP in non-law programs has been the reluctance of academics to teach a subject that is not their specialty. This has prompted development of interdisciplinary programs, involvement of adjunct professors, and design of self-managed learning opportunities.

What if there is only one lecture allocated to IP?
The important thing is not "how much can the teacher teach?" rather "how much can the learner learn?"

Which resources should be used?
Freely accessible, well-designed Internet resources make realistic the expectation that an IP non-expert could create a useful IP learning opportunity.

What does the future hold for IP teaching to non-law students?
IP learning and teaching for non-law students has expanded rapidly over the past decade. Higher education agendas for problem based and self-managed learning, combined with Government agendas to ensure graduate employability and entrepreneurship, ensure its growing significance.

Identification of a target audience

Who is the audience for IP education?

IP education is relevant to undergraduate students at all levels, and from all disciplines. Inculcating IP awareness at an early point in academic studies ensures future engagement with IP in subsequent stages of a career. Postgraduates and doctoral researchers, especially if they have not previously encountered IP concepts earlier in their education, need to be introduced to the benefits and risks of IP. Within the academic community, post-doctoral professors, and lecturers, as well as resource managers and program administrators, seek opportunities to become familiar with IP concepts.

Three strands now make up the core function of a university: research; learning and teaching; and knowledge exploitation. The latter incorporates commercialization, consultancy, community engagement and technology transfer. IP sits at the heart of exploitation of knowledge arising from research outputs.

Universities no longer look simply to produce graduates who are employable. The current emphasis is on the production of graduates who can operate in an entrepreneurial capacity to increase the potential for enterprise in organizations of all sizes: micro, small and medium, large and transnational. Interest in university spinoff companies has further enhanced interest in IP education.

IP teaching transcends discipline boundaries, and in so doing exposes both students and faculty to an interdisciplinary, or cross-disciplinary, learning and teaching experience.

Why teach intellectual property to non lawyers?

"We need to bring together the programmers and the web publishers, design artists and the film makers and the people who are computer scientists and entrepreneurs and say 'intellectual property is affecting you and you ought to be thinking about how its affecting you.' This is something in which we have to educate people." (Boyle, 2003)[1]

Junghans and Levy (2006) identify the heart of the problem surrounding IP education as "the connection of legal procedure, beyond its mere application, with technological development and the business strategy that drives it." The title of their recent hardcover IP management text *Intellectual Property Management for Scientists, Engineers, Financiers and Managers*,[2] affirms their view of the need for non-lawyers to learn about IP.

One science and technology professor explains the relevance to his students of IP: "The shift in manufacturing and production from high cost to low cost areas of production has pushed companies to look for income generation that stands apart from manufacture and production. This has driven forward changes in company structure. Companies are increasingly aware of protecting the IPR aspects of their assets."[3] Another, determined that "not being able to recognize an invention did not happen to anyone else at the university," wrote a *Basic Workbook in Intellectual Property Management* for the benefit of scientists.[4]

Owning IP implies positive and negative rights. IP offers an incentive to invention and creativity providing right owners an exclusive right for a limited period of time to market goods and services. IP poses challenges, risks and benefits to any operation. If IP is to deliver its true worth to an organization, its value needs to be understood in many different contexts, including buying, selling and investment. Most companies these days will not undertake a new venture without a thorough analytical IP plan. "In the commercial and business world, the development of new tactics and new strategies for deployment of intellectual property rights for commercial advantage has been identified as the next corporate challenge on the battlefields of the knowledge economy" (Rivette and Kline, 2000).[5]

---

[1] J. Boyle, (2003) *Ideas in Cyperspace*, Eversheds Lecture, Royal Society of Arts, London (2003) www.rsa.org.uk/acrobat/james_boyle190303.pdf.
[2] C. Junghans, A. Levy et al., *Intellectual Property Management: A Guide for Scientists, Engineers, Financiers and Managers*, J. Wiley Inc. (2006).
[3] J. Roach and G. Bell, *Intellectual Property Awareness and Project Commercialisation in a University Environment*, www.engsc.ac.uk/downloads/miniproject/ip/Roach-Bell.pdf, (2005).
[4] F. Erbisch, *Institute of International Agriculture ABSP Basic Workbook In Intellectual Property Management*, Agricultural Biotechnology Support Project website, 2005 Michigan State University. www.iia.msu.edu/full_ipr_text%20Erbisch04.pdf.
[5] K. Rivette and D. Klein, *Rembrandts in the Attic*, Harvard (2000).

> ARM Holdings plc (NASDAQ:ARMHY) ranked by Dataquest as the number one semi-conductor intellectual property supplier in the world, emerges as a pre-eminent force in the semiconductor revolution. When ARM pioneered the concept of openly licensable IP for the development of the 32-bit RISC processor-based SoCs in the early 1990s, it changed the dynamics of the semi-conductor industry forever. By licensing, rather than manufacturing and selling cheap technology, the company established a new business model that has redefined the way processors are designed, produced and sold. ARM Holdings plc ARM® technology has shaped a new era of next-generation electronics: ARM Powered® processors are pervasive in electronic products, driving key functions in a diverse variety of applications in key markets. ARM partners have shipped more than 2.5 billion ARM processor-based devices to date.

Figure 14: ARM Holdings PLC pre-eminent global semiconductor IP supplier[6]

From the first day at work, a graduate may be required to sign agreements concerning disclosure, development and ownership of IP, so it is important to hit the ground running. They may be exposed to, and may create, a company's proprietary and confidential information. They need to be aware of the risks and obligations in using someone else's proprietary IP.

Non-law students, including students of business, finance and accountancy, will benefit from learning about IP because of the changing attitudes to IP of banks, financial institutions and the accounting professions. IP formerly had a balance sheet value once it had been traded. Now, the commercial value of IP is more likely to be the most powerful asset a company possesses. IP rights can "command premium selling prices, dominate market share, capture customer loyalty, and represent formidable barriers to competitors."[7]

IP education has not featured as a benchmark or accreditation requirement of professional bodies or institutions. That is slowly changing. In 2004, the UK Engineering Council,[8] in its higher education standards, included in its threshold standards of competence and commitment for

---

[6] www.arm.com/miscPDFs/3822.pdf.
[7] R. Parr, quoted on DIPS resource http://cicel.univ.lu/cours/dips/index2.php.
[8] Engineering Council UK, UK Standard for Professional Engineering Competence, May 2004 www.engc.org.uk/documents/CEng_IEng_Standard.pdf.

chartered engineers the requirement that they "demonstrate an ability to secure necessary intellectual property rights" in the creative and innovative development of engineering technology. The UK Institution of Engineering and Technology (2006) commented recently:

> It is in the institution's experience that newly qualified science and engineering graduates commonly lack an appreciation of IPR. Typically they do not understand the various types of registrable, and unregistrable, IPR; the applicability of each IPR type; corporate and personal ownership distinctions; and the benefits and obligations which IPR bring to an enterprise. This situation is viewed as being to the detriment of the UK's progression to being a knowledge economy. The Institution believes that it would be beneficial if your review brought attention to the desirability that at least tertiary education should include an introduction to, and appreciation of, IPR. Whilst this is considered particularly important in science and engineering undergraduate courses, this should not be exclusive as it is recognised that IPR affects all aspects of creativity, and thus the whole knowledge economy.[9]

Kaplan and Kaplan (2003),[10] US patent attorneys and academics who include intellectual property in their undergraduate engineering classes, suggest that:

> IP knowledge is important for engineers. They should know which IP rights are needed to protect their creations. All of the students have reported that they enjoyed the information and will use the material in the future. The best result came well after the completion of the course. Ms. W returned to thank the professor. Apparently she impressed an interviewer with her knowledge of IP and received an engineering position because of it! Not least, a little IP knowledge can help reduce patent attorney fees. When two Bournemouth University engineering graduates who had studied a half unit in IP, including patenting, went to consult a patent attorney about their latest innovation, the attorney was sufficiently impressed to write to the course leader: "They were so well prepared. Their drawings were excellent, and they were able to describe their invention in language of a patent specification. It saved a lot of time, and money."[11]

---

[9] The Institution of Engineering and Technology www.theiet.org/; Submission to UK Government's Treasury review of IP: The Gowers Review of Intellectual Property (2006) www.hm-treasury.gov.uk/independent_reviews/gowers_review_intellectual_property/gowersreview_index.cfm.

[10] K. Kaplan, and J. Kaplan, "Incorporating Intellectual Property into Engineering Education," paper presented at the 2003 American Society for Engineering Education Annual Conference and Exposition, Nashville, TN, 22–25 June.

[11] Private correspondence between Paul Cole, patent agent and the author.

Chemistry	Business
Industrial Design	Medicine
Engineering	Economics
Bio-Science	Art History
Computing	Education

Figure 15: Faculties involved in interdisciplinary teaching and research

IP for non-lawyers creating opportunities for collaborative interdisciplinary teaching and research

Research undertaken for WIPO[12] (2005) revealed collaborative education and research between IP law and other faculties in a number of universities, worldwide. IP law academics, members of the international Association of IP Teachers and Researchers (ATRIP), responded that they teach IP in a number of disciplines.

Research at the University of Technology, Sydney (McLaughlan et al. 2005),[13] undertaken to explore student and educator beliefs about what engineers need to know about IP, discovered that "to meet the need of [engineering] faculties and students there will need to be a strong contextualisation of IP education." The need to contextualise law content is something with which law teachers are familiar, especially when teaching beyond the law school. Cristudason (2004) writes from her experience of teaching law in the National University of Singapore,

> the teacher's role is not just to assist *(non-law)* students to gain content knowledge. To make students' learning more meaningful and in keeping with the shift in paradigm from teacher-centred to student-centred learning, the teacher should aim to: (i) assist students to apply their knowledge; (ii) inculcate the skills of legal analysis to some extent, so that students can recognise the process and attributes of legal analysis in the context of their likely professions and (iii) help students to assimilate their learning of law subjects with their learning of other subjects and (iv) enable students to see how law subjects are going to be relevant to them in "real life".[14]

---

[12] R. Soetendorp, *Collaboration in Intellectual Property Education & Research*, WIPO International Symposium on Intellectual Property (IP) Education and Research, Geneva 2005, www.wipo.int/academy/en/meetings/iped_sym_05/papers/pdf/soetendorp_paper.pdf.

[13] R. G. McLaughlan, C. P. Killen et al., *Engineering Enterprise through IP Education: What is needed?* Proceedings of the 2005 ASEE/AaeE 4th Global Colloquium on Engineering Education ©2005, Australasian Association for Engineering Education.

[14] A. Christudason, *Challenges of Teaching Law to Non-Law Students*, abbreviated version of a paper presented at the 2004 Society of Legal Scholars Conference, www.warwick.ac.uk: 9080/ukcleadm/directions/issue10/christudason.html.

Additional benefits to IP law academics from engaging in interdisciplinary research or teaching include the fresh perspective gained from presenting IP legal concepts to non-lawyers, and the synergistic research opportunities presented by working across disciplines.

Many of the IP academics surveyed reported being involved in funded research projects that involved collaboration with academics from the other faculties in which they taught. This evidences the suggestions of radical changes in classical approaches to university academic research described by Delanty (2000)[15]: "Massification and democratisation mean that universities are no longer so intimately associated with the production of scientific and professional elites." Forging collaborative cross-faculty partnerships that can undertake "applied industry-oriented research that would produce transdisciplinary knowledge" is a predicted outcome of future academic endeavor. Gibbons et al. (2000)[16] describe the significance of what they term "Mode 2"[17] knowledge, the outcome of research intended to be useful to someone, whether in industry, government or society. Mode 2 knowledge can be produced by coalitions of academics working across disciplines, within the university or with external partners in industry. Where a relationship develops between IP law faculty and non-law faculties, through collaborative teaching or research, there is potential for the non-law faculty to become more adventurous in exploring ways to deliver IP to their students. Non-law students learn their core curriculum, and in addition, how to exploit their innovation. Law students learn their core curriculum, and in addition, can develop a clearer understanding of how the law impacts on their clients' business interests.

Subject matter curriculum

What does an IP syllabus cover?

Designing the IP syllabus for non-lawyers can provide an opportunity for dialogue between different faculties. There is definitely no "one size fits all." This section of the chapter presents a selection of IP teaching content from a number of universities.

---

[15] G. Delanty, *Challenging Knowledge: The University in the Knowledge Society* Buckingham: Open University Press (2001).
[16] M. Gibbons et al., *The New Production of Knowledge*, Sage, London (2000).
[17] As opposed to Mode 1 knowledge, produced as a result of research conducted in the absence of a practical goal (see Gibbons et al., 2000).

At its simplest, syllabus content should answer the question "what does the non-law student need to know?"

IP syllabus design will be influenced by the student's core discipline. Some areas of IP may appear to be irrelevant to some disciplines, e.g. patents for media students or registered designs for biotechnologists. However, it is important that students do not focus solely on the IP right most appropriate to their discipline, e.g. copyright for software programmers, but are encouraged to consider the potential for any innovation to spawn more than one IP right, e.g. trade marks for branding, copyrights for instructions, design rights for packaging. A further factor that influences syllabus design is the amount of time available. Obviously, the more significant the fraction of unit time allocated to IP, the more relevant the discussion between academics and advisers as to how the syllabus should be designed.

The intellectual property tool box

The Intellectual Property "tool box" emerged from discussions between academic lawyers and engineers, with inventors, industrialists and professional advisers[18] as a "model" for bringing together different aspects of intellectual property, as they might impact on the graduate engineer during their studies, or after having left the university. The "tool box" can comprise hard and electronic resources, as well as inputs from academics, professional advisers, managers, lawyers, accountants. It is adaptable for use with graduates of disciplines other than engineering.

The "tool box" contents reflect the fact that while IP is law based, considering only the legal aspects will be insufficient preparation for managing IP in a business context.

It is interesting to note the inclusion in the tool box of other "alternative" regimes. Students may display a residual suspicion about the monopolistic attributes of IP regimes. Sawhney (2002), in research undertaken at MIT, wrote that

> Property rights in scientific research and academic settings have always sparked intense debate about the public vs. commercial nature of research conducted and its impact. Interestingly there are two trends increasingly at play in such settings: a push towards greater commercialization or

---

[18] UK Higher Education Academy Engineering Subject Centre and UK Centre for Learning in Law research project workshop, held Autumn 2005, London, www.engsc.ac.uk/resources/ipminiproj/index.asp.

At a basic level, students should be able to understand

- Intellectual property broadly, rather than deeply
- Awareness of implications surrounding disclosure and confidentiality
- Linkages between IP, innovation and business development
- Awareness of cultural differences between university research and business development
- How not to be taken advantage of in IP matters
- Who to ask for advice
- Where to find patent information
- How to use patent information

At a more sophisticated level, students should be able to understand

- What goes into a patent application and why
- Time scale and costs of patent protection
- Implications of steps to be taken, or avoided, in the patent process
- Relevance of patents
- IP is more than just patents – Trademarks, copyright, design rights
- Application for trademarks
- Application for design registration
- Intellectual property ownership
- Non-disclosure agreements
- National and international intellectual property issues
- Offensive and defensive patent strategies
- IP valuation
- IP ethics
- IP commercialization and exploitation
- Open source licensing and other "alternative" regimes

Figure 16: Contents of the graduate IP tool box

privatization of research through formal IPR mechanisms like patents and copyrights, while there is growing support for greater openness towards academic programs and research through Open Source initiatives.[19]

[19] N. Sawhney, "The sociological nature of Intellectual Property Rights emerging from open collaborative design in university settings," Preliminary analaysis of student projects in MIT Design Studio, PhD draft, 2002, web.media.mit.edu/~nitin/thesis/nitin-iprstudy.pdf.

Devising a syllabus that intentionally disregards the arguments against IP, will be met with suspicion by students. Heverly (2005) suggests the university's role is to present a balanced view to students, and that applies equally to intellectual property. It is important to emphasize that intellectual property protection is not a panacea, and there are alternatives to traditional licensing arrangements. He argues for "universities' responsibility to present students with a full and unbiased picture of intellectual property law, and its options."[20]

International examples of IP syllabus design

Valdosta State University, Georgia, USA

Manning et al. (2001)[21] describe an intellectual property exercise that introduces undergraduate chemistry majors to concepts associated with intellectual property. They write, "This exercise will not be a complete coverage of intellectual property, but serves to familiarize the student with some of the basics. Chemistry students often have a range of career choices possible. In addition to working in industry as a bench chemist, entering professional programs (medical, dental, pharmacy, etc.) and graduate school, students now regularly pursue advanced studies in patent law, enter MBA programs, or become involved in start-up companies." They recognized that there is always too much to squeeze into an IP syllabus, and too little formal contact time in which to teach it. Undergraduate students on the IP course at Valdosta, as part of the laboratory write up, are asked to write a few sentences on each of the topics listed below, where IP and general business topics are inter-mixed. Students are allowed to use any source (web, library, faculty, etc.) to obtain the information.

Osaka Institute of Technology

Osaka Institute of Technology (OIT) has been tasked by the Japanese Government to run an undergraduate program that will meet the need

---

[20] R. Heverly, *Against Indoctrination – Teaching Engineering Students More than just the Doctrines of Intellectual Property Law*, www.engsc.ac.uk/downloads/miniproject/ip/RobertHeverly.pdf.
[21] T. Manning, L. Atwater, A. McRAe, M. Anderson, J. S. Beatty and M. Watson, *Introducing Intellectual Property in the Undergratuate Chemistry Curriculum*, Springer-Verlag New York, Inc. (2000).

Venture Capital	IPO
Angel	Business plan
SBIR contract and federal agencies	Can you patent software?
Going public	Spin off company
NASDAQ	Trademark
Small business development centre	Dow Jones
SEC	Alan Greenspan
SYCE	Paris Cooperation Treaty

Figure 17: Laboratory write up topics at Valdosta

The fundamentals of IP
Related areas in engineering
Venture creation and industrial management
IP prosecution
IP management
IP strategy
International legal affairs
Internship in the IP department of a large company, with an IP attorney
Preparatory search
Thesis search

Figure 18: Osaka Institute of Technology IP Major in intellectual property syllabus

for "para-intellectual property professionals, with an understanding of science." OIT is well aware that the degree in intellectual property will not address the issue of integrating IP teaching in undergraduate non-law disciplines. It will, however, be interesting to monitor the influence of an IP department operating outside a law school and working in close collaboration with science and technology faculties.[22]

Industry and university collaboration, China

In China, a unique collaboration was formed in 2004 between three universities, Renmin, Tsinghua, and Fudan, and a multinational industrial company, Philips Electronic China Group, to deliver a course taught by a team of foreign and local teachers that leads to an award entitled International IP Law in Multinational Companies. The program is designed from a law and business perspective and includes:

[22] www.oit.ac.jp/english/daigakuin/titekizaisankenkyuuka/index.html.

- Introduction and welcome to the intellectual economy
- Trademarks I – subject matter
- Trademarks II – obtaining and enforcing rights
- Trademarks III – infringement
- Design Rights I – subject matter
- Design Rights II – obtaining and enforcing rights
- Copyright I – subject matter
- Copyright II – rights, limitations and relation to the Internet
- Patents I – patentable subject matter and requirements
- Patents II – international procedures
- Patents III – rights and limitations
- Patents IV – European legal aspects
- Trade Secrets – subject matter and rights
- IP litigation in Europe – Guest lectures from European professor
- International IP treaties – TRIPS, Paris Convention, Patent Cooperation Treaty, etc.
- Creating Value with IP

Figure 19: International IP law in multinational companies syllabus (China)

The SPINNOVA project, Europe[23]

Seven European universities[24] have collaborated on a training course designed for researchers at universities and public/private research institutes. The topics covered on the course are:

- Intellectual property rights
- Doing business with existing companies
- Creation of a spin-off company
- Marketing and communication
- Exploitation plan development.

They describe the intellectual property rights component of the course as follows "What is intellectual property? How can you protect it, who owns it, how do you obtain and maintain the intellectual property rights?

---

[23] P. C. van der Sijde and R. Cuyvers, Training Researchers to Commercialize Research Results, Industry & Higher Education, February 2003.

[24] Katholieke Universiteit, Leuven, Belgium; University of Twente, The Netherlands; Katholieke Universiteit Nijmegen, The Netherlands; Westfälische Wilhelms-Universität Münster, Germany; Universität Osnabruck, Germany, Universität Dortmund, Germany; Universidad de Salamanca, Spain.

In Europe, there are differences between countries: in some countries, the person who has carried out the research owns the intellectual property, while in others the university is the owner. It is important that researchers have some knowledge of these issues so that they are aware of the commercial potential of their research and have freedom to operate, and so that the potential for conflict can be reduced" (van der Sijde and Cuyvers 2003).

Tulsa University, USA

In 2000, Tulsa University launched a Certificate Program in Innovation and Product Development.[25] It arose out of the work of an interdisciplinary coalition of faculty members who began working to develop alliances and construct a comprehensive two-year curriculum. The fourteen credit-hour certificate program allows students access to a common core of upper-level interdisciplinary courses in engineering, law, business, and arts and sciences.

It uses an innovation institute concept of theory and practice to provide business, engineering, law, and arts and sciences students the opportunity to interact with others with similar interests. The interdisciplinary curriculum and its faculty assist students with the entrepreneurial evaluation, selection, development management funding and most importantly, the nurturing of promising technological developments. Consequently, the two primary purposes of the program are:

1. To involve interdisciplinary teams in the development of patentable product innovations that could lead to commercialization.
2. To sensitize students from different colleges and disciplines to the fundamental innovation concerns from legal, business, engineering and liberal arts perspectives.

A Tokyo University consortium

In 2001, four major public universities in Japan[26] formed an alliance to deliver a Science and Technology Intellectual Property course. The purpose of the course is to give students an opportunity to understand

---

[25] M. T. Arnold, G. Vozikis, C. Cornell, *The Legal Bridge between Business and Engineering*, proceedings of the NCIIA 9th Annual Meeting. March 17–19, 2005, San Diego, CA.
[26] Tokyo Medical and Dental University, Tokyo University of Foreign Studies, Tokyo Institute of Technology, and Hitotsubashi University, see description of the Science Technology and Intellectual Property undergraduate course, www.valdes.titech.ac.jp/frc-stip/FRC-STIPe.html.

the importance of intellectual property from various viewpoints through attending lectures that present issues of high technology and the theoretical or practical problems surrounding their protection by law. "Though technology and intellectual property have been considered as completely different, students in this course will acquire composite knowledge and can think about technology and intellectual property from both viewpoint of inventor and user or advocate."

Programs that involve students working outside their discipline simulate the inter-professional encounters they will experience in their careers. Research and development alliances in large global enterprises, for example, involve engineers working with different professions, each bringing their expertise to complex problem solving. Graduates need the capacity to cooperate with experts from other fields, to see problems in a complementary way. Employers want flexible multi-skilled graduates open to learning, equipped to respond to the rapidly changing demands of the workplace.

University of Technology, Sydney

An IP law academic has one lecture in which to raise awareness of IP through an introductory lecture; content is delivered within the framework of a series of questions that require the students to consider IP in the context of their future employment:

Approaches and methods to teach in this area (including any problem areas)

How to teach IP (i)

Achieving deep rather than surface learning

Where IP is not part of the core syllabus, the temptation is to expect mere surface learning from the students. Surface learning is concerned with content and the transmission of lots of knowledge. It can involve learning by rote or requiring the regurgitation of facts and the passive acceptance of information, rather than developing critical faculties in students. The UK Centre for Legal Education[27] suggests "it is easy to fall into the trap of

---

[27] UK Centre for Legal Education, *Learning Theory and Legal Research*, www.ukcle.ac.uk/resources/tlr/theory.html.

> - Who owns an invention developed by me at work?
> - Who owns an invention developed by a group of people (including me)?
> - Who owns an invention developed by me outside work (e.g., at home)?
> - Who owns copyright in the technical manual written by me?
> - Who owns the copyright in a technical paper written by me as part of my work?
> - Who owns the copyright in a novel written by me at home?
> - Can I start my own company based on my invention?
> - Will I share in revenues generated by my invention?
> - What are the consequences of talking about an invention to others?

Figure 20: IP questions prospective employees need to consider[28]

merely getting students to jump through particular hoops in order to find pieces of information and, on the way, hoping they pick up some deeper principles of, for example, the use of databases."

Hopefully, the examples in this chapter describe successful opportunities for deep learning. This style of learning is concerned with process. Learners participate in activities, in problem solving, summarizing and digesting new information to change fundamentally the way they think about and use information. Even where the time allocation for IP is minimal, it is possible, with careful attention to their learning needs, to devise learning opportunities which change the way students think about IP.

Experiential learning

Experiential Learning is a cyclical pattern of learning from *experience* through *reflection* and *conceptualization* to *action* and so on to further experience. This process is most widely known through Kolb's learning cycle (Kolb, 1984).

---

[28] B. Childs et al., *Preparing Engineers & Scientists for the 21st Century: A Case for Imbedding an Inherent Awareness of Intellectual Property in Undergraduate Engineering and Science Curricula*, Australian Law Teachers Association, 2006.

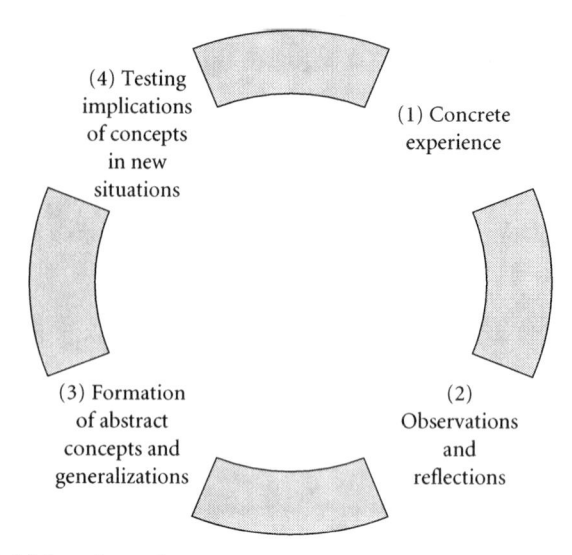

Figure 21: Kolb's learning cycle

The UK Centre for Legal Education[29] describes the principle:

> ideas are formed and re-formed through a cycle of experience. The learning process starts with a concrete learning experience; the learners need time to reflect on what they have learnt by drawing up theories and processing the new ideas through "abstract conceptualisation." During the final stage, "active experimentation," learners use the theories they have drawn up to test and solve problems. Put simply, the learner undertakes a task, reflects/thinks about what they have done, considers whether there are other ways of undertaking the task (an opportunity to compare and contrast) and, finally, tries the task again, but from a position backed by new experience and understanding.

Examples from academic practice

There is no established pedagogy for creating well-planned, integrated, sequenced and cumulative learning experiences to integrate relevant, key material from other disciplines, including intellectual property law, into the core non-law curricula.[30] Hennessey[31] identifies five styles of intellectual property law teaching:

---

[29] The application of learning and teaching theories to the teaching of law can be found on the UKCLE website www.ukcle.ac.uk/resources/tlr/theory.html.

[30] 2005 the UK Higher Education Academy agreed to support a unique interdisciplinary research, funded by the Engineering Subject Centre and the UK Centre for Legal Education.

- The case method
- The problem solving method
- The simulation method
- The clinical method
- (The doctrinal method)[32]

Each may be appropriate, depending on the time available in which to deliver the unit, the background and level of the student, and the intended student learning outcome for the course.

The case method

Open University – Patents in a Forensic Engineering course

Dr. Pete Lewis[33] describes The Open University's two engineering courses with significant intellectual property content. One, Forensic Engineering (T839) is set at postgraduate level and has an annual population of about 100 students, based mainly in commerce and industry. Teaching is based around several case studies of mechanical patents, especially the Catnic lintel, lawnmowers, the Workmate, wheelie bins and residual current devices.[34] Students are given a resource file which includes patents, expert reports and court testimony, and are expected to learn to read a patent and assess the inventive level, given information on the prior art and common general knowledge. The largest Open University undergraduate course, Engineering the Future (T173), presents similar cases, but is taught at an elementary level. Both student groups are given a brief introduction to Registered Designs, Design Right and Copyright, as well as

---

A group of four academics, comprising two lawyers and two engineers, are working together on a model for integrating key but not core concepts across the disciplines, with a focus on intellectual property in the engineering syllabus. Several key barriers to the integration of IP into the engineering curricula have been identified, including engineering academics feeling that IP content is not as important as other engineering content and that the engineering curricula is already overcrowded and could not support any new subjects.

[31] W. Hennessey, "The place of Intellectual Property Teaching in the Curricula or Universities and Technical Institutes," online paper, Franklin Pierce Law Center, Concord NH (1999) www.ipmall.info/hosted_resources/pubspapers/Teaching_IP_Hennessey_99.asp.

[32] The doctrinal method is least appropriate for teaching IP to non-lawyers. It doesn't encourage the student to appreciate the continual evolution of intellectual property law, nor is it designed to equip the student to know where to access up-to-date information, at the appropriate level.

[33] P. Lewis, *Intellectual Property Topics in OU Engineering Courses*, UK Engineering Subject Centre (2005), www.engsc.ac.uk/downloads/miniproject/ip/PeterLewis-OpenUniversity.pdf.

[34] European Patent Office's espacenet database, http://tinyurl.com/2dmnl.

Confidential Information. Students are encouraged to use the Espacenet database as well as the UK Patent Office registered databases, especially as a guide to the state of the art in various product fields. Feedback is excellent, especially as many students, who are mature and combining study with their careers, are themselves patentees (and a smaller number pursuing infringers).

Lewis uses Schneider Patent GB 588 932[35] to teach how it is possible to design around an existing patent. He presents students with the patent's first claim:

> A container for refuse, comprising a body of substantially rectangular cross-section having a cover therefore, a depending flange which extends along one sidewall of the body in the region of an upper edge of said wall and is stiffened by substantially vertically arranged struts connected to the body, and a rib which extends substantially parallel with the body between the body and depending flange; and wherein a reinforcing member is provided for said flange, said member extending along and projecting laterally from said flange and being adapted and arranged to serve as an abutment for said container during emptying thereof.

He then simplifies the first claim:

1. a container for refuse, comprising
2. a body of substantially rectangular cross-section having a cover therefore
3. a depending flange which extends along one sidewall of the body in the region of an upper edge of said wall, and is stiffened by
4. substantially vertically arranged struts connected to the body, and
5. a rib which extends substantially parallel with the body between the body and the depending flange
6. wherein the reinforcing member is provided for said flange, said member extending along and projecting laterally from said flange and being adapted and arranged to serve as an abutment for said container during emptying thereof.

The students are then presented with details of a wheelie bin that was produced without a rib (see 4 above) which was found not to infringe the Schneider patent.

---

[35] European Patent Office espacenet database, http://v3.espacenet.com/textdoc?DB=EPODOC&IDX=GB1588932&F=0.

The refuse container has a rectangular cross-section. The body part is provided with a suspension strip (21), which acts as a stop during tipping, in the region of its upper edge, which is reinforced by struts (23, 24, 29) connected to the body part (20). Attached to the outside of the suspension strip (21) is a reinforcing strip (22) projecting approximately perpendicularly from the latter and integrally connected to the suspension strip. Plate-shaped struts (34) are provided between the reinforcing strip (22) and the suspension strip (21) and extend, with their top edges, beyond the top edge of the projecting rim of the suspension strip. The suspension strip may be exposed to relatively high stresses, it has a longer service life, and its stop function is improved.

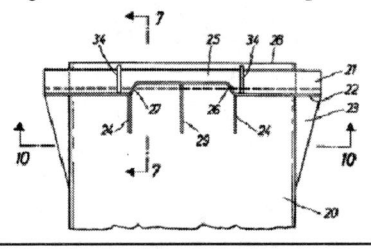

Figure 22: Abstract of patent number GB 1 588 932

The problem solving method

Bournemouth University *(i) Seeing the business issues in patent litigation:* Product design students who have not been taught about IP are invited to suggest the business factors behind a patent dispute. They engage in animated discussion of why they think, for example, Windsurfer International and Tabur Marine[36] found themselves locked in courtroom battle. Asking the students what they would have done if they had been in their place has led to thoughtful contributions. Once the students have considered the business problem aspects of the case, they are more receptive to learning about patent law aspects.

Bournemouth University *(ii) Filing a Patent:* Where a professor has experience of patenting, it is possible to help students to evaluate their "inventions" with a view to filing a patent. Where there is a possibility of successful patenting, the student is supported to make a first filing; students can be supported by involvement of local patent attorneys as adjunct professors or visiting experts.

---

[36] *Windsurfing International* Inc v. *Tabur Marine (Great Britain) Ltd* [1985] RPC 59.

The simulation method

Licence negotiation role-playing gives science and technology students the opportunity to participate in simulations of intellectual property licence negotiation. Such activity is relevant at any stage of an undergraduate or postgraduate program. At Hong Kong University of Science and Technology, engineering students use a standard law faculty teaching tool, "the student moot court."[37] Their moot court debates reinforce student understanding of intellectual property concepts, and reinforce analytic, verbal and reasoning skills.

The clinical method

Law students and non-law students as adviser and client

The "advice letter" is one way to present non-law students with intellectual property learning in a way that does not make excessive demands on their resources or time. Nor does it require intellectual property expertise from their tutors or professors. Instead, the "advice letter" involves the engineers in a self-managed learning exercise. The non-lawyers present their innovative project work to student IP lawyers, who in turn provide a letter containing IP advice. The IP lawyer's advice can be quite wide-ranging, determined to some extent by the information provided by the non-lawyer.

Advice can be provided about national and international commercial exploitation. Non-law students are advised that the legal rules concerning employees' patentable inventions do not apply to undergraduate project work (that is, so long as there has been no additional undertaking that someone funding the project has rights).

When the most recent cohort of engineers completed their feedback sheet, there was overwhelming support for repeating the "advice letter" exercise with the following year's graduating class. Most of the engineers had had more than one email contact with their IP lawyer. If anything, the engineers were asking for more contact with their IP advisers earlier in the project cycle, and for more contact. They found the information in the advice letter useful, and would use it in compiling the design report they are expected to produce for their project work.

---

[37] O. Lee, *Engineering Students' Moot Court Debates the Question: Is Software Patentable?* Journal of Information Technology & Law, No. 1 (2002), www2.warwick.ac.uk/fac/soc/law/elj/jilt/2002_1/lee/.

> Bournemouth University: IP law students write one assignment as an IP Adviser to a design engineering student "client." The IP students must advise the design engineers on the intellectual property potential of their final year projects. The assignment tests the IP students' ability to identify appropriate advice and apply it. While the text of the advice letter must be intelligible to the design engineer, the IP students are expected to submit a full appendix of the legal authority on which their advice has been based. The exercise has benefits for both groups of students in enhancing graduate employability skills. The IP lawyers get clinical experience of drafting advice. The design engineers receive intellectual property information they would not otherwise have had as well as receiving clinical experience of presenting their ideas in dialogue with a professional adviser. This assignment helps reduce plagiarism because the advice has to be tailored to the client's needs.

Figure 23: The IP law student and non-law student client advice letter

Benefits of working in partnership with a law student, rather than seeking advice from other sources, are clear. By having to describe the project to the law student, the engineer student rehearses the process of articulating his work to a non-engineer. There is the opportunity to test "consumer" aspects of the project work. There is also the opportunity for the first time to describe his work to a professional adviser. Following the "advice letter" assignment, two engineers decided to approach a patent agent with a view to pursuing a patent for their invention. The patent agent wrote to their professor, "It was such a pleasure to meet these two. They were able to describe their work in words and drawings. It took much less time for me to formulate my advice to them. Being able to communicate so well saved me time, and them money!"

How to teach IP (ii)

Introducing IP into the non-law curriculum

The biggest challenge facing an academic who wants to introduce IP into the non-law curriculum will be the reluctance of fellow academics who argue that the syllabus is too crowded; there is not the expertise.[38] This section challenges those reluctant responses with strategies and resources for delivery.

(i) An IP undergraduate curriculum map

The development of curricula designs and instructional techniques that allow knowledge and understandings from other disciplines to be integrated into the engineering curricula has been the work of Dr. Rob McLaughlan at the University of Technology, Sydney. This has involved learning designs for online role play-simulations and debates as well as pedagogies for sustainability and safe design,[39] commissioned by the Australian National Occupational Health and Safety Commission.[40] He has recently applied those principles to curriculum design for introducing IP education for Engineers.[41] The UK Royal Academy of Engineering Ethics Working Group produced a curriculum map,[42] for the teaching of ethics. The work of both McLaughlan and The Royal Academy influenced the design, of an undergraduate IP curriculum map (see Figure 24), together with implementation guidelines and schedule.

The map can be extended to cover input to the curriculum of postgraduate and research programs, continuous professional development and lifelong learning programs.

(ii) Implementation of the curriculum map

Implementation team

The strategy for embedding intellectual property in the undergraduate curriculum to achieve awareness and competence in graduating students should be undertaken in a comprehensive manner. When the University of Tulsa team developed their Certificate in Innovation and Product Development, they did so having first obtained "the approval of the

---

[38] B. De La Harpe, A. Radloff, J. Wyber, "What do Professional Skills Mean for Different Disciplines in a Business School?", in *Improving Student Learning through the Disciplines*, OCSLD, 2000.

[39] R. McLaughlan, Department of Engineering, University of Technology, Sydney consultant to the ASCC(2006), *Safe Design for Engineering Students*, Australian Safety and Compensation Council, ISBN 0 642326 029.

[40] R. McLaughlan, Department of Engineering University of Technology, Sydney, consultant to Australian National Occupational Health and Safety Commission (2003–2004).

[41] McLaughlan et al., note 13 above.

[42] www.raeng.org.uk/news/releases/pdf/Ethics_Curriculum_Map.pdf.

president of the University of Tulsa and the deans from the Colleges of Law, Business Administration, Engineering and Natural Sciences, and Arts and Sciences." Ideally, there should be support from the central offices of the university for implementing intellectual property across the disciplines of the different faculties. In such cases, the institution may invest centrally in electronic resources and a parallel staff development program. At faculty, department and program levels, implementing the map will require a level of commitment to ensure the suggested amendments to current curricula and syllabi survive the academic democratic processes that have a default tendency to preserve the status quo, rather than to innovate.

McLaughlan's suggestions[43] for the implementing team have been adapted for the purpose of integrating IP. The implementing team should have the support, if not the membership, of the Faculty Head and should include Head of Learning & Teaching, together with program leaders, at least one of whom would be a committed IP competence supporter of the introduction of IP to programs. An IP competence champion will be required to ensure that syllabus changes take place, which conform to course documentation and accreditation requirements. The IP competence champion will also be instrumental in ensuring that staff development opportunities are in place to enable colleagues to develop subject content and produce IPR-related learning resources.

Another level of implementation may be at the subject coordinator, "grass-roots" level. An IP subject co-ordinator can work ad hoc across the faculty without the need for a widespread, systematic and planned implementation. There are a range of options (levels) available depending upon the suitability of the subject and the capacity of an educator to integrate IP within their environment. The design and delivery of IP teaching within any particular syllabus will depend on a number of factors including learning outcomes and resources. The IP lecturer will be involved in a series of decisions, including what aspects of IP to focus on, including legal, financial, ethical, commercial, strategic, and risk, as well as when and how students will best learn about intellectual property.

It is unlikely that a faculty team, especially one with no IP expertise, will be able to achieve integration of IP into the learning and teaching of

---

[43] McLaughlan et al., note 13 above 2005, Australasian Association for Engineering Education.

	Aims & Objectives	Delivery point	Learning outcomes	Content Topics	Practical suggestions
U/grad Year 1	Understanding of what IP is: Substantive IP rights and Quasi IP rights Nature of Rights and Monopolies	Induction Modules Personal Development Portfolio PDP	Student should be able to Identify circumstances in which IP is created Recognise that IP situations are legal situations Identify other peoples' IP	National IP or Patent Office website IP Rights & Confidentiality Plagiarism/ethics of copying, including copying other people's IP	Students present an 'IP' case from Press for group discussion Guest lecture or masterclass from IP professional Why me? Relevance of IP in particular industry/profession – students choose successful artefact – case study of successful use of IP in relevant industry Replace an existing case study for teaching e.g. ethics, engineering management that uses a non-IPR topic (e.g. sustainability) with a case study that uses IPR as context Guided self-managed learning from an online IP resource (e.g. POwww!) followed by an online quiz
Year 2	Critique appropriateness of IP protection Reflect on IP as an element of enterprise and sustainability	Modules Placement or Show preparation PDP Employability Placement	Choose which IP rights are appropriate to their work Demonstrate the initial steps to protecting their IP Use database to locate	IP in the inventive/ innovative/ creative process Patent specifications & Patent	Study the University's IP policies Arrange student briefing meeting with University Technology Transfer office Integrate criteria relating to IP into criteria for summative assessment work

Level	Modules	Learning outcomes	IP content	Activities
Final 3/4	Final Show preparation PDP Employability Optional IP/enterprise module	Anticipate and/or resolve legal problems Appreciate the usefulness of legal advice Specialist study	patent/trademark/design information Trademark use Copyright Design protection Alternatives to IP – trade secrets; open source licenses	Identify case studies that illustrate failure to use IP, ask students to discuss and propose alternative course of action. Self-managed learning – research the Internet to find examples of alternatives to IP protection: e.g. open source, trade secrets Placement: include evaluation of the placement company's IP portfolio management policy in the placement report
		Distinguish between IP professional advisers Plan a presentation of their work to an IP adviser Evaluate critically IP at different stages of innovation/invention/creativity process	Cost of IP protection IP Ownership: at university, employment, freelance Commercial exploitation of IP: capital investment; licensing	Self-managed learning – research the financial press for case studies of IP valuation, IP exploitation and present for small group seminar discussion Seminars with one or more of IP professionals, University Technology Transfer office; inventors; entrepreneurs Integrate criteria relating to IP into criteria for summative assessment work Audit the IP in final year project work

Figure 24: An undergraduate IP curriculum map

students across programs without external assistance. The IP implementing team should bring in someone with expertise in the teaching or practice of IP management, from the, e.g., university's Technology Transfer Office, Business or Law faculty, local Patent Attorney or IP lawyer, or National IP or Patent Office. Assistance with the design of staff development activities as well as learning and teaching resources would be valuable.

Staff Development

Opportunities for staff to develop IP management skills will increase their confidence in working with students. It should also enhance their professional abilities.

The Library and Learning and Teaching support staff should be briefed to be prepared for intellectual property queries from faculties other than law. They should be able to locate useful recent hard copy acquisitions or electronic additions to resources.

Workshops on curriculum development, involving colleagues from different faculties, will be useful, as will interdisciplinary groups to develop case studies and to discuss interdisciplinary assessment tasks and placement opportunities. Developing a cross-faculty group to share good practice via a virtual learning environment would eventually build into a valuable resource.

Assessment

Summative assessments (for which the mark/grade achieved goes towards a named award) and formative assessments (from which the learner receives formative feedback) are both appropriate means of reinforcing intellectual property learning.

Summative assessments could include:

Awarding a proportion of marks/grades in a technical assignment to:
- An evaluation of the intellectual property inherent in an innovative project work;
- A review of patents that relate to the technology;
- A review of design right or design patent that protect individual character;
- An outline of steps to be taken to protect copyright in a creative work;
- A critique of a media report of an IP-based business decision or dispute; and
- Drafting a patent specification (or design or trade mark specification) for assigned work.

Formative assessments could include:

- Small group analysis of the intellectual property in a well-known consumer item, followed by database search to identify registered IP;
- Class discussion of Internet research of an IP policy issue;
- Research and presentation of an IP issue receiving media attention; and
- Report of patent search.

Learning outcomes

Skilful use of learning outcomes in the design of a program can provide the framework within which intellectual property awareness and competence can be learned as an outcome of professor-led or self-managed student learning. The scope of an independent learning outcome is determined by the proportion of study time allocated to the topic, and the level of the student.

The language of learning outcomes can be challenging. Bloom (1956)[44] identified six levels within the cognitive domain, from the simple level of being able to recall or recognize facts, to the highest level of ability to evaluate complex combinations of fact and information. Below is a suggested range of verbs to employ when drafting learning outcomes. Incorporating an IP-related learning outcome in the learning outcomes for a module or program clarifies its significance to teachers and learners alike.

IP, and patents in particular, should not be taught uncritically. Heverly[45] argues for "balanced" teaching of IP. Some universities include IP in the ethics module of a non-law course. Leeds and Koppelman(2002) state:

> There is a good chance that students will not have given much thought to issues concerning credit and intellectual property. Interdisciplinary collaboration and technological advances have made this topic more controversial. Technological advances raise questions about whether tangible, material property can be treated the same as technological property or whether new moral or legal laws are needed. Interdisciplinary collaboration and the incredible growth of science and engineering have raised such questions as who counts as author and who should get credit for dual discoveries. This section is designed to give pedagogical advice for getting students to think deeply about these issues.[46]

---

[44] Bloom's Taxonomy, see www.officeport.com/edu/blooms.htm.
[45] See Heverly, note 20 above.
[46] M. Leeds and E. Koppelman, *Teaching the Individual Engineer about Fair Credit and Intellectual Property*, The Online Ethics Centre for Engineering and Science at Case Western Reserve University (2004), http://onlineethics.org/edu/credit.html.

> 1. **Knowledge**: arrange, define, duplicate, label, list, memorize, name, order, recognize, relate, recall, repeat, reproduce state.
> 2. **Comprehension**: classify, describe, discuss, explain, express, identify, indicate, locate, recognize, report, restate, review, select, translate,
> 3. **Application**: apply, choose, demonstrate, dramatize, employ, illustrate, interpret, operate, practice, schedule, sketch, solve, use, write.
> 4. **Analysis**: analyze, appraise, calculate, categorize, compare, contrast, criticize, differentiate, discriminate, distinguish, examine, experiment, question, test.
> 5. **Synthesis**: arrange, assemble, collect, compose, construct, create, design, develop, formulate, manage, organize, plan, prepare, propose, set up, write.
> 6. **Evaluation**: appraise, argue, assess, attach, choose, compare, defend, estimate, judge, predict, rate, core, select, support, value, evaluate.

Figure 25: Bloom's Taxonomy

Students need to appreciate that applying for a patent is not always the most appropriate course of action. National patent offices, and the European Patent Office, should not shy away from discussing shortcomings of the patent system. Learning outcomes should focus on a mixture of attitude, competence and knowledge captured in this matrix[47]:

At the University of Technology, Sydney, an IP law academic, Bill Childs, is invited to a presentation lecture of an overview of IP law as a component of an enterprise module of a capstone subject. Here Childs[48] describes one such occasion,

> The lecture explored the relevance to engineers of patents, trademarks, copyright and confidential information. The initial phase of the lecture was uneventful. The students' level of interest was commensurate with the lecturer's expectations of final year students generally. The students engaged with the material and asked intelligent questions. However, towards the end of the lecture, the concept of confidentiality, and the

---

[47] Adapted by R. McLaughlan, from the UK Health & Safety Executive Board of Moderators Guideline (appendix C) core curriculum framework, see www.learning-hse.com/hse/infor_frameset.phtml.   [48] See Childs et al., note 28 above.

Attitude	Ability to: appreciate the ethical view; recognise that intellectual property is integral to an engineer's work, that awareness of intellectual property rights is everyone's responsibility.
Competence	Ability to: implement initial steps to protect; know who to consult for further advice, and when; identify the context in which IP rights are being used or created.
Knowledge	Ability to: understand the legal frameworks governing IP rights and their commercial exploitation; fulfil responsibility of managing an intellectual property portfolio; appreciate the human resource issues and recognise the benefits of learning from history.

Figure 26: Devising Learning Outcomes for IP in a non-law course

consequences of inadvertent release of confidential information were introduced.

The academic illustrated his point on confidentiality with statistics illustrating US business losses in 2002 of $53–59 billion. Those statistics "were catalysts that transformed the lecture from an interesting session about IP into something that was perceived by the students to be extremely relevant to their immediate futures." He posed the question: "What will you do when (in the very near future) your prospective employer insists that you sign a contract of employment giving up your intellectual property and requiring absolute confidentiality?" Evidence of the deep learning that had taken place during the lecture was evidenced by one student's question: "Why haven't we been made aware of something as important as this much earlier in our course?"

When an academic with little or no IP experience is requested to create a meaningful IP learning experience, in an hour or two "slot," it can be daunting. Here is one suggestion, developed at Bournemouth, which makes use of freely available Internet resources.[49] It was developed for use with product design engineer students who were allocated only one two-hour period for IP. The lecturer responsible for the class had no intellectual property expertise and was unsure how to get the

[49] www.engsc.ac.uk/resources/ipminiproj/index.asp.

most out of the session. It was felt that if she prepared a two-hour lecture, it would be impossible to cover all the information sources and the ways in which it could be used. The learning outcome for the students was that they should be able to "locate and apply intellectual property information."

The UK Patent Office website was chosen as an ideal resource to deliver a focused, deep learning experience where the teacher is not an expert in the field. It is a very well thought out resource which has been constructed to meet the needs of IP novices, as well as IP professionals. Through introduction in class to the website, the students became aware of the different substantive IP rights (patents, copyrights, trademarks and designs) and could see how they are recognized and protected. They could also see how much it costs to apply for and maintain patents, trademarks and registered designs, and how the IP rights work together in respect of any particular innovation. This exercise has been used subsequently with other classes and similar positive feedback.

By being introduced to the databases of registered rights, i.e. patents, registered trademarks and registered designs, the student understands the importance of undertaking research before investing time in "reinventing the wheel."

Patent databases in particular are valuable sources of technical information. They are increasingly becoming recognized as an indispensable tool in the engineer's "tool kit." Drafting a learning outcome to include "the student will be able to search a patent database" or "the student will be able to prepare a report of relevant patent applications," provides the student with an opportunity to explore, e.g. the European Patent Office's database, Espacenet. Students respond positively to working in this way with an Internet resource.[50]

What if there is only one lecture allocated to IP?

In many universities, in a number of programs, the challenge will be to move from zero IP teaching to an agreement for one lecture slot to be allocated. The two examples above illustrate how a meaningful, deep learning experience can be created in a minimum amount of time. In such circumstances, it is important to remember that it is not how much a teacher can teach in one hour that counts, rather it is how much, in one hour, the student can learn.

---

[50] R. Soetendorp, "Food for Engineers", Intellectual Property Education for Innovators, Industry & Higher Education, December 2004.

Required: student Internet access

Intended Learning Outcome: at the end of the hour, students will know where to locate IP information and appreciate the relevance of IP to their work.

Introductions:

Ask students to consider the following statements:

(1) Your project work may lead to IPR which ought to be protected.
(2) A future employer may ask what you know about IPR.

What would you do?

Activity

(1) Log on to the Patent Office website www.patent.gov.uk (or your national IP website).
(2) Read the Home page introduction.
(3) Click the buttons describing "Trade Mark," "Patent," "Copyright," and "Design."
(4) List the different IPRs that apply to your innovation.

Question

(5) What are the first two steps you would take to protect your IPR at work?

Feedback responses from tutors

(i) I had very little knowledge of IPR.
(ii) They responded well to the interactive demo on the Patent Office website.
(iii) The visit to the Patent Office website was useful as they tried to get an idea of how to answer the questions.
(iv) They liked the website organization and I noticed that they found the information easily.

From students:

(i) I would advise my employer to research into IPR on the Internet and maybe look at the patent website www.patent.gov.uk.
(ii) I would advise the company to research into all the Intellectual Property Rights by going onto the Patent website and also take part in the exercise we have just done, because many companies will be surprised with what is protected and what is not.
(iii) By the way, this was very useful! Thank you!

Figure 27: A time-limited introduction to intellectual property

When is it best to teach IP?

There is no prescribed place in the non-law undergraduate course to introduce students to IP. There are advantages of including IP in the final year before graduation, or in the year preceding a placement, internship or *stage*. The student's mind is attuned to workplace issues, and receptive to IP concepts. Introducing IP at the beginning of the undergraduate program raises student awareness of IP's significance from the start of studies. Then, ideally, IP concepts can be integrated into assessed project work at every level of the undergraduate program. Here is an example of a three year cycle of implementing IP into a non-law program.

A three year cycle for implementation

Embedding IP into the curriculum takes time. It will not happen overnight, nor as a result of a big bang. Here is how it might work over a three-year period in an engineering faculty where there had previously been no IP education and where the faculty is committed to incremental development of IP education within the syllabus.[51]

First Year of implementation:

Level I: Induction – an introduction to intellectual property – draw on students personal experience (e.g., ask them to see how much IP they can identify in their cellphone).
Guest lecture from IP professional.
Introduction to national office website.
Review IP in a consumer item.

Level II Search patent database for patents similar to the students' technical assignment.

Level III Review confidentiality and non-disclosure arrangements for final year exhibition or show.

Second Year of implementation

Level I Include IP references in learning and teaching materials, module handbooks, case studies, etc.

---

[51] Modelled on the UK Health & Safety Executive Board of Moderators Guideline (appendix C) core curriculum framework see www.learning-hse.com/hse/infor_ frame set. phtml.

Level II   Review patents and trademarks policy of placement company, or major industry player.
Use case studies with IP references.
Level III   Review IP policy of the university and discuss how it impacts on student work.

Third Year of implementation

Level I   As in first and second years.
Level II   Draft a patent specification for technical assignment.
Include IP references in learning and teaching materials, module handbooks, case studies, etc.
Level III   IP Management optional module available.
Core module includes reference to intellectual property recognition and protection.
Final Year dissertation to include IP reference.

(iii) Integrating IP through adapting an existing syllabus[52]

Level I: Adapt existing unit design, with minimal changes:

Replace an existing case study for teaching about, e.g., ethics, management, economics that uses a non-IPR topic (e.g., sustainability, quality) with one that uses IPR as a context.
Insert a risk identification activity into a subject, e.g. where IP has not been recognized or protected, to raise awareness of IP.
Educate the students about the fundamental principles of IP by providing them with a self-guided activity involving provided reading, or Internet locations, and asking them to complete an online quiz.
Introduce IP aspects into formative or summatively assessed activities, e.g. search *espacenet* (the European Patent Office database www. http://ep.espacenet.com) to find at least *one* patent related to current work.

Level II: Adapt existing subject and materials

Integrate IP into an existing activity by providing student support through IP lectures or other input delivery, concepts, principles and tools.

[52] With reference to McLaughlan and Royal Academy Engineering, note 42 above.

Adapt materials to draw out stronger linkages between core discipline and IP.

Level III: Integrate IP into learning outcomes, assessment and activities

Integrate desired IP-related learning outcomes into subject learning outcomes.
Build in deeper linkages through adapting the package case studies and activities for the subject and/or developing further context-specific IP-related materials.
Modify an assessable design task in the subject to incorporate a requirement for IP competence, and integrate criteria relating to IP into the assessment criteria for the task.

Who can teach IP?

There is no definitive answer to the question "who should be teaching IP?" It is suggested that one of the inhibitors to the growth of IP teaching to non-law students has been uncertainty as to who should be teaching it. Engineering academics, asked in 2003, why their students were not being taught IP, provided a range of reasons.

It is not one person's responsibility.
I shouldn't have to teach this.
I don't know how to teach this.
If the students were any good, they wouldn't need to be taught it.
It would be seen as a "soft" subject rather than "hard" engineering.
The awareness of IP's importance is not there yet.
It's only relevant for those in industrially related research.
It's a subject that ought to be taught by experts.
If a colleague really wanted to teach it, maybe time would be found.
The syllabus is too crowded to include IP.
There are more important things an engineer needs to know about, e.g. standards, safety, etc.

Figure 28: Reasons for reluctance to teach IP to non-lawyers[53]

---

[53] R. Soetendorp et al., (2005) *Engineering Enterprise through Intellectual Property Education – Pedagogic Approaches,* Proceedings of the 2005 WSEAS International Conference on Engineering Education, Vouliagmeni, Athens, Greece.

These findings are born out by Hennessey (1999),[54] who suggests that there are three barriers to the inclusion of IPR in the non-law curriculum:

(i) the engineering curriculum at most engineering and technical institutes is very concentrated and focused on acquisition of the knowledge and professional skills needed to become licensed as engineers;
(ii) professional engineering organizations do not require an understanding of IP as an area of knowledge within the engineering discipline;
(iii) the absence of a member of the faculty who is qualified to teach the subject.

The foregoing responses echoed findings from similar research undertaken at Curtin University, Australia.[55]

Where IP is being taught to non-lawyers, the teacher can be any of the following:

- University law academic[56]
- Technology transfer office staff
- Adjunct professor – patent attorney, or IP lawyer
- Visiting lecturer – IP professional, lawyer or attorney, local business person
- IP law academic
- Knowledge transfer academic
- Entrepreneurship academic
- Engineering academic, with some experience of patenting.

The Tokyo Science Technology and Intellectual Property undergraduate course[57] describes its faculty thus: "since science technology changes rapidly and internationally, we will provide many lectures by patent attorneys, lawyers and company directors whose major responsibility is protection of technology intellectual property, and who will be able to refer to examples based on latest technology developments."

Materials, references, cases and other sources of assistance

What resources to use

It is never too soon to introduce people to IP. This was illustrated charmingly at the 2005 WIPO High Level National Seminar on Intellectual

---

[54] Hennessey, note 31 above.   [55] De La Harpe, Radloff and Wyber, note 38 above.
[56] See Soetendorp, note 12 above.   [57] See note 26 above.

Property held in Foshan, China.[58] The Guangdong region educators demonstrated their commitment to the introduction of IP education to primary age pupils, by the motto "Educate one student, influence one family and activate society." A class of 10-year olds put on an authoritative and very engaging presentation about trademarks and their relevance to business.

At the European Patent Office in Vienna, a volunteer team has been working on *five2twelve*.[59] This is a program by which they hope to inspire young Europeans between the ages of 5 and 12 to take a closer look at the fascinating and exciting world of patents. The UK Patent Office launched its Think Kit®[60] in 2005. It is aimed at high school students and uses contemporary case studies, including Adidas®, Pop Idol® and Virgin®, to illustrate how IP is used in business. The UK Patent Office is currently working on a version of Think Kit® for use with undergraduates. The case studies will feature student innovations that are enjoying commercial success due to their IP being recognized and protected. Singapore[61] has designed an engaging site that captures the fun elements in IP with cartoons and comics specifically designed for youngsters. IP Australia's InnovaTed[62] site is designed for teachers, aimed at helping them to uncover their students' creativity and imagination. Ippy's Big Idea is an interactive game featuring a video game icon. IP Professor[63] is a resource for the tertiary sector, which includes lecture material and other resources suitable for university use.

As a result of these initiatives, year on year more students will arrive at university with some awareness of IP. This will greatly influence curriculum design and choice of resources to use in IP education.

National IP or patent office websites

There has been a rapid growth in the number of national patent or IP offices preparing freely available, well designed IP resources aimed at school students. The European Patent Office and the US Patent and Trademark Office both have comprehensive patent databases. National offices are developing databases for registered designs and trademarks.

---

[58] WIPO High Level National Seminar on Intellectual Property Education in China, Foshan, China 2005.   [59] Reported in Epidos news 3/2004 October, 2004.
[60] www.patent.gov.uk/about/marketing/thinkkit/index.htm.
[61] http://app.ipos.gov.sg/iperckidz/index.asp.
[62] www.innovated.gov.au/innovated/html/i02.asp.
[63] www.ipaustralia.gov.au/ipprofessor/index_js.htm.

The WIPO website has much useful information, and especially its collection of case studies, which can be easily adapted for use in teaching or assessment.

Commercial websites

The websites of law firms and accountancy practices, banks and financial service advisers are a good source for focused IP education. Designed to attract clients, and to inform them, the material they contain can be easily adapted for classroom use.

Interactive packages and books

There are many products available to license for academic use. Any list would be swiftly out of date, similarly with books, a trawl of amazon.com will reveal new additions and old favorites.

Examples from popular culture

Learning and teaching materials for copyright, designs and trademarks can readily be drawn from national media reports of disputes between companies, often settled out of court. Trade journals provide a good source of context-appropriate case studies for students to work with. Even strip cartoons can provide a useful resource.

What does the future hold for IP teaching to non-law students?

Universities are being pushed by governments to produce entrepreneurial, enterprising graduates. In such an environment, IP teaching is relevant and significant. By involving students and academics from engineering or technology with academics and students from business, finance, management or law, both groups are encouraged to think along "enterprise" lines. IP teaching fits with contemporary pedagogic theory, with its emphasis on self-managed, deep learning. IP teaching creates opportunities for innovative learning, teaching and research projects. Such encounters offer ways to understand how innovation, through wise and informed management of IP, can be most beneficial to individuals, companies, and society.

11

Using the new technologies in teaching intellectual property (distance learning)

PHILIP GRIFFITH

Introduction

There are many subjects and topics that can be taught within the broad field of intellectual property. There are many different kinds of organizations wishing to deliver teaching or training in some aspect of the field, and many different audiences for those courses. The courses themselves can be delivered in a great variety of ways. Digital communication technologies have permeated almost all aspects of modern life. These electronic communication technologies, and in particular the Internet, have revolutionized the way people work, play and relax, and the kind of entertainment they access. They now provide a range of tools to use in the delivery of teaching programs.

There is an ongoing discourse about the manifold implications of using electronic technologies in education.[1] This chapter, however, is primarily concerned with providing some basic description of the options available and sharing some practical advice about designing, preparing and delivering courses using available technology. This chapter does not attempt to provide models of particular IP courses, although one example is described.

Just as there can be many different kinds of courses, teachers and student groups, there are many ways to use the technology and differing levels in the way it can be employed. For the sake of discussion, however, it may help to contemplate three broad levels of increasing sophistication.

Basic level

At a fairly simple and straightforward level, some organizations and teachers may wish to use technology to provide access to course documentation

---

[1] Some suggested readings can be found at the end of the chapter.

(like course outlines and class lists) and teaching materials (like readings, extracts of documents, tutorial topics and so on) as an aspect of a traditional face-to-face course.

A further step at this level might be to provide lectures through audio or video recordings. Traditional distance learning programs would provide taped lectures in cassette form, or more recently through the medium of the compact disk (CD). These would usually be posted to students with workbooks and learning exercises and a timeline for completion of modules and tasks. However, the cassettes or CDs can be hard to update. Entire tapes or CDs would therefore have to be rerecorded to incorporate new material. Providing lectures through audio or video conferencing is a possible alternative to recordings but there can be difficulties in organizing students in differing time zones. The Internet allows the delivery of sound and/or video recordings for copy or download, or through what is currently referred to as "podcasting."[2] The main focus for people using technology at this level is on the technology and administration.

Intermediate level

An intermediate level, involving more complexity and sophistication, uses technology, primarily the Internet, to provide communication tools to allow students to raise concerns, obtain clarification, and perhaps to engage in discussion relating to subject materials and to learning activities. The great advantage gained is the possibility of more flexible communication between teacher and student. The major issue that will arise for teachers and organizations employing technology at this level is the effective and efficient management of student expectations and demands.

A more sophisticated level

At the most sophisticated level, the organization and teachers wish to use the technology to deal with every aspect of administration and delivery of the course. There is a possibility to use technology as the primary means of engaging students from enrolment to completion of the program including every aspect of learning and assessment. For teachers at this level, the major issues relate to adapting the traditional face-to-face teaching and learning activities to an online context, designing and incorporating new

---

[2] For a useful discussion of the nature and uses of "podcasting" see the Wikipedia entry at http://en.wikipedia.org/wiki/Podcasting.

features which the technology facilitates, and designing and implementing an effective online assessment system.

The objective is to create an educational conversation within a secure and well managed electronic environment. This environment must assist students to:

- become involved with the narrative of the subject;
- acquire the relevant information and knowledge base;
- acquire and practice the skills needed to analyze and update the material;
- adapt to the knowledge and relate it to the learning objectives of the subject;
- interact with the material, the teacher and with other students;
- reflect upon the significance and possible uses of the subject matter under discussion; and
- demonstrate a sufficient level of understanding and mastery of the subject matter.

The focus of this chapter

While it is possible to use new technologies in courses and training programs of all kinds, the emphasis in this chapter is upon:

- online courses,
- delivered by an ongoing educational institution or training college,
- at a tertiary level or level which requires sophisticated learning and critical thinking,
- where the course will be conducted over a substantial teaching period like a semester,
- where there are established learning objectives

and where the major vehicle for :

- administrative contact,
- course instructions and announcements,
- delivery of course content,
- access to materials,
- teacher and student discussion,
- discussion between students,
- coursework,
- final assessment, and
- assessment feedback,

will be electronic technologies accessed through the Internet.

Why use the new technology?

Teachers should consider why they are choosing to use an online teaching strategy. The title of this chapter refers to "Distance learning", and one of the great advantages of using electronic communication technologies in teaching is the capacity to reach distance students. If a course is to be taught through a website accessed via the Internet, the students, and indeed the teachers, can be anywhere in the world.

However, the use of these technologies should not be seen as a form of second best compromise forced upon teachers trying to communicate with distance students. These technologies provide teaching and learning opportunities that have possible advantages for all students, including local students who are able to attend face-to-face classes.

The Internet, and associated technologies, if properly used, can have a number of advantages. After initial set up costs, it can be relatively cheap and easy to use for teacher and student, is often attractive to students, can access resources in different media, can access resources in a wide range of collections and sources, can interlink with resources and useful material in other subject areas, can be designed to facilitate collaborative work, and allows interaction to incorporate text, graphics, sound, video, either stand alone or as interactive multimedia.

Furthermore, delivering courses online can permit high levels of organization, and facilitate standardization of administrative support, announcements, content distribution, and assessment tasks. It can also be used to create a very strong learning environment with considerable interaction between teachers and students and a cooperative learning exchange between students.

It does, however, require correspondingly high levels of organization, and investment in time, resources, infrastructure and support, the acquisition of new teaching, technical and administrative skills, and adaptation of existing skills.

A particular possible advantage of Internet teaching is that many students like the opportunity to be able to access course materials and content at a time that suits them rather than according to a timetable that may be determined by nothing more than room availability in a building. If students can access lectures and discussion boards at any time, they can choose the time which best suits their needs and preferences. Further, many students report that they like being able to access a lecture and listen to it repeatedly, or revisit parts as often as is needed to grasp the material being presented.

An online course can provide a very wide range of materials for a student. The course website could contain sound lectures, multimedia presentations, photographs, scanned documents, lecture guides, supplementary notes, collections of essential materials, reading guides electronically marked up to link to major legal databases of legislation, cases, intellectual property office decisions, law reports, government policy papers, statistics or processes, "frequently asked question" lists, past exam papers, practice questions, and so on.

The website can also cater to different levels of student interest, involvement and sophistication. The site might present the core material that all students should address, but also provide a wide range of additional materials for students who wish to pursue areas of special interest. The student can access everything needed to pursue the course at the depth at which they are comfortable.

Online teaching environments can provide a particularly effective opportunity for creating, supporting and monitoring cooperative learning between the students. This is especially useful in postgraduate courses or courses where at least some of the students have particular knowledge and expertise which can be usefully shared with other students and provide the teacher with opportunities to expand course content. Discussion boards are useful tools to foster cooperative learning.

It must also be acknowledged that electronic teaching methods do not suit all students and indeed do not suit all teachers.[3] Most teachers and students regard education as an essentially social activity and derive great satisfaction from personal interaction. One of the challenges of using new technologies to teach courses is finding a way to create an interactive sense of social connection, not only between teachers and students, but in particular between the students in the course.

A well-designed course should seek to create what has been described as an "online learning community."[4] It may be that online teaching provides greater opportunities for engagement and interaction between students relating to the subject matter than traditional face-to-face teaching programs. Educators seeking to design and

---

[3] G. Moore, K. Winograd and D. Lange, (2001) *You Can Teach Online*, New York, McGraw-Hill Higher Education p. 11.3.

[4] K. Shelton and G. Saltsman, "Tips and Tricks for Teaching Online: How to Teach Like a Pro!" www.itd.org/journal/Oct_04/article04.htm; J.V. Boettcher and R.M. Conrad (1999), *Faculty Guide for Moving Teaching and Learning to The Web*, Mission Viejo, CA: League for Innovation in the Community College.

deliver an online course must at least address the issue of the social style they wish to create within the course,[5] and decide upon strategies to facilitate the kinds and levels of engagement they consider are desirable.

It is also possible that student attitudes and perceptions about online teaching will be shaped by the teacher's underlying ideas about teaching and learning in general, and teaching online in particular. It should be made clear to students why the course is being delivered in the way that it is. While there are many issues to think about in using new technologies, the most important issues remain the general questions about teaching and learning.

Delivery vehicle

When deciding to create a new web-based teaching resource, it is important to consider the delivery vehicle.

In some cases, all that may be required is the setting up of a simple website providing for the use of email and provision of a syllabus and reading guide, and a list of resource reading documents. Going one step further, this level of website could actually provide the full text of essential documents.

A more complex site will, in addition to the features listed in the first level, allow access to documents and materials available in electronic form on other sites, like the WIPO Worldwide Academy Library or the United States Patent Office electronic collection, or the various university data bases. These websites will provide a suggested order of reading and hyperlinks to materials available elsewhere.

Another variation is to provide a site that contains a mix of text and links but also incorporates some form of search engine. Many combinations are possible.

However, at the other end of the spectrum is the kind of delivery vehicle needed for a large institution like a university delivering courses that require close interactive contact and a system of assessment and a requirement to manage, not merely content, but also student interaction and administration.

---

[5] K. White, "Face to Face in the Online Classroom" in K. White and B. Weight (eds.), *The Online Teaching Guide*, Needham Heights, MA, Allyn and Bacon (2000), pp. 7–12.

Commercial electronic interface products

When creating a major course online with full interactive facilities, it is not advisable to start from scratch and attempt to design and program a new vehicle.[6] There are educational software firms that specialize in creating products of this kind.[7] Products will allow for:

- the registration of students,
- sorting them into class lists,
- establishing common course notice boards, particularly the Announcement Panel,
- putting up lecture notes and class materials,
- tutorial lessons and other teaching content,
- an archive of frequently asked questions and the answers given,
- references and links to other material held on other sites,
- tutorial class chat rooms,
- student discussion boards,
- threaded discussion and monitoring tools,
- feedback channels in which teacher responses can be directed to an individual student, any subset or subsets of students or all students in the classes,
- a facility for putting up assessment material and automatically controlling the timing and range of its availability,
- electronic drop boxes where students submit work,
- automatic marking of multiple question type assessments,

---

[6] If for some reason an organization decides to attempt to create their own delivery vehicle from first principles, there are some basic design and structure tips and tricks to be found at www.fcs.iastate.ed/computer/tips/gooddesign/.htm.

[7] There is a variety of well known systems and portals (e.g. WebCT, Blackboard, Lotus LearningSpace, Moodie, CBTS systems, Docent etc.) The major characteristics (learning and pedagogical resources organization, enrolments system, user profiles, testing methodology, tools) of 17 platforms and 10 e-learning portals can be compared using an online tool at www.edutools.info/course/compare/index.jsp. (This information derived from N. Talavera, E. Álvarez, P. Mondelo, F. Terrés, *Capturing Requirements for E-learning Systems Design*, Proceedings of International Conference on Computer-Aided Ergonomics and Safety. Maui, Hawaii, USA, July 29–August 1, 2001). For information about one of the most popular products viz Blackboard, see: http://company.blackboard.com/docs/cp/orientation/pcmag.pdf; http://company.blackboard.com/docs/cp/orientation/ASP.wp.pdf.

See also LAMS, an open source *Learning Activity Management System* that allows teachers to create a wide range of learning activities. The system manages the group of learners with feedback to the teacher who can then respond according to the teaching strategy of the course, www.lamsfoundation.org/

– result and feed back channels,
– capacity to interact with other student administration databases within the university or organization.

Student expectations

Online teaching has changed student expectations.[8] Students, even those with sophisticated experience in using the Internet for normal research or recreational activities, may not automatically understand how to participate in online courses.[9] But students do come to online learning with strong expectations that there will be clear and specific detail concerning "course structure, assignments activities and evaluation, and concise instructions for navigating the online environment."[10] They also expect close individual attention, and feedback. Teachers designing or delivering an online course must recognize these student expectations, and adopt strategies to manage them. The most important implication is that online courses require increased levels of communication[11] between teachers and students, and that communication must be clear and must be easily accessible.

Preliminary issues

A really basic issue is ensuring that the institution has the necessary hardware, sufficient capacity to accommodate expected user traffic, and a technical support person to maintain the server. Equally important is ensuring that someone has expertise in the creation of a website or skill in the use of a commercial courseware package.

Course designers must consider a number of preliminary issues. There are some basic commonsense guidelines relating to preparing for Internet-based teaching, including that designers should provide:

– a good user interface;
– a consistent design style within the subject website;
– effective navigational tools;

---

[8] J. Van Sickle, *Making the Transition to Teaching Online: Strategies and Methods for the First Time Online Instructor*, Morehead, KY: Morehead State University (ERIC Document Reproduction Service No. ED479882 (2003).
[9] K. Shelton and G. Saltsman, note 4 above.
[10] J. Perrine, *Developing an Interaction-Centred Evaluation Tool for Distance Education* (2003), Masters of Science Thesis Oregon Health and Science University, citing L. Lansdell, *Distance Learning Environment* (2001) http://people.uis.edu/rschr1/onlinelearning/archive/2002_09_01_archive.html.   [11] White, note 5 above.

- a package of information available to students about how to use the website and any other technologies employed within the subject;
- references to frequently asked questions (FAQs) about technical problems;
- the possibility of, and contact information for, access to advice and support about technical glitches or problems that can, and assuredly will, arise;
- structured lesson material;
- course materials provided in full within the website; and
- reading lists or links to material not directly provided by the website.

Designers should also consider when access to the website and its course content, discussion forums and other resources will be closed off to students. Students may need to have access and communication channels with teachers and the website after completion of assessment to discuss grades, to communicate about extensions of time, supplementary or alternative examinations or appeals about grade. But at some time the subject website must close.

Developing an online teaching course requires significant planning and organization[12] well before the first class.

Establish the educational goals and design a content syllabus

The first task is to design the academic content and syllabus of the course. Then it is possible to think about how the course can be delivered online or to distance students.

This is a simplification. It would be nice to think that developing a curriculum or training materials could be achieved by a clear logical step by step process. But most teachers and course designers find that in real life not only is it not a logical process, it tends not to be a particularly orderly or sequential process. Somehow teachers have to work out aims and objectives, perspectives, topics to be addressed, teaching techniques and styles, reading materials and resources and assessment regimes. Most teachers have an intuitive idea of the sort of course they would like to teach based on their personalities and experience, their existing knowledge of the field, their strengths as teachers, the needs of the overall program in which the subject will be taught and so on. Or the content is

---

[12] E. Brewer, J. DeJonge and V. Stout, *Moving to Online: Making the Transition from Traditional Instruction and Communication Strategies*, Thousand Oaks, CA: Corwin Press Inc. (2001).

essentially driven by some outside factor like regulations establishing educational requirements or proficiency in a knowledge base required for professional registration, or the acquisition of specific kinds of knowledge or skills to perform a particular role or office, like patent or trademark examiner.

Teachers then sit down to juggle with the assets and resources they have, or think they can acquire, and the constraints imposed upon them. As they do so, they will probably work on all of the various elements of the process more or less simultaneously. As the various topics are considered and fitted into a syllabus, course designers may end up adjusting the aims and objectives, altering the perspectives of the course as a whole, choosing different teaching methods or a different assessment system. Or having decided that one objective is to introduce, say, a law and economics approach to students, they search for a topic that will provide a suitable vehicle and that may cascade through the design elements again.

In online teaching, just as in face-to-face teaching, the actual mode of delivery is a tool used to provide an opportunity for students to acquire information, skills, competencies and perspectives – it is not an end in itself. Do not start with the technology. Start with deciding the content and perspectives and skills that the students need to engage, and then think about ways of using the technology to achieve those goals. Once the basic approach to using technology to achieve the learning goals has been established, it is possible to think about where the technology may provide advantages and then to adjust the syllabus and design accordingly.

Intellectual property rights

When compiling materials to be made available in online teaching programs, either in full on the website, or through hot links, the designers must respect the exclusive economic and moral rights of the owners of intellectual property rights in the material to be used. Some jurisdictions have enacted a system of statutory license to allow educational institutions to use works and other subject matter, including material available in digital form, in defined ways on payment of equitable remuneration. In other jurisdictions, collecting societies representing authors offer voluntary licenses on terms. In some cases, the materials can be sourced from collectives or associations, such as "Creative Commons" offering access under some modification of normative copyright or neighboring rights standards. Some material may be available in the public domain. Use of some material may be justified by doctrines of fair use or fair dealing. In some cases, permissions cannot be obtained and the material should not be used. It is the responsibility of teachers and course designers to inform themselves about intellectual property implications of their course and the restrictions, or the conditions for access, to the material. Teachers should also pay particular attention to moral rights. The basic moral rights relating to proper attribution and to the integrity of the work should, in any event, be met by a person engaged in normal ethical scholarly practice.

Use of modules

Traditional distance education often employed modular design; in online teaching, it is advantageous after having designed a course syllabus in the usual way to then see whether it can be presented in clear interlinked modules. The nature of computer files and courseware products makes it technically easy to provide content in modules, but division of intellectual content into modules is not necessarily easy or conceptually satisfying because topics to be learned are often not of equal length, complexity or weight.

However, using modules can assist students. Students may find that they have a clearer idea of the material they should be addressing. Students may also have a sense that the course is clearly organized and structured, which can provide a greater sense of security in being an online student. One of the dangers in any educational program, but particularly in online programs, is that participants may not keep up with the content and then try to cram material at the end of the course. Modules can be used to provide clear timelines about the expected progress through the material particularly if each module or cluster of modules has an assessment task attached. Modules also assist in establishing clear topics for use in discussion boards. This promotes the possibility of coherent interaction in the discussion forums.

Modularization is generally easier and most effective in training courses where the goals are to assist in the acquisition of a defined knowledge base, or mastery of technical content, or to provide training in a specific set of tasks.

Modularization can, however, have educational disadvantages. It may suggest a series of neat boundaries in the content, or broader conceptual framework, which either do not really exist, or which if they do exist, are nothing like as neat or clear as the module structure suggests. Teachers designing online courses that use modules should also consider how students can be encouraged to see overarching themes and connections and perspectives, and to think outside the modules. This can be done through explicit teaching in lectures and classes, but also in discussion boards and through carefully designed analytical research essay-type assessment items.

Information about Administration of the Course

One common mistake of teachers who are creating an online course is they do not provide sufficient information to students about the administration and operation of the online subject.[13] Students must receive clear information about:

- use of the technology,
- orientation aids or activities,
- contact methods with the teacher and the responsible education provider,
- subject codes or identifiers,
- subject content description,
- subject learning objectives,
- workload expectations,
- activity requirements,
- the course schedule, including all relevant and significant dates required by administration, student rules and the educational timetable, (e.g., dates of commencement of teaching, any dates relevant to enrolment, withdrawal, application for special consideration, etc.),
- the dates of any online quiz to be used,
- due dates for assignments,
- examination dates,
- release of results dates,
- dates for appeal procedures,
- the assessment regime,
- marking scales,
- communication policies and etiquette, and
- the date at which the website will be closed to students at the end of the course.

---

[13] S. Ko and S. Rossen, *Teaching Online: A Practical Guide*, 2nd edition, Boston: Houghton Miffin (2000).

Expect problems

It is sensible to expect that problems will arise. Some students may be unable to log onto the website, be unable to use their email, have a computer malfunction during a timed online quiz or any number of difficulties. Teachers need to be flexible and have a strategy or plan to respond to these difficulties. Some problems can be dealt with by having an FAQ file relating to common technical problems and having an appropriately trained technical support person available to respond to student enquiries.

Example of a common problem: non-receipt of work claimed to be submitted

In courses where examination or assignment scripts can be submitted through an online "drop box", it sometimes happens that a student claims to have written the script and submitted it online but the teacher is unable to find it in the drop box. This can be the result of the student making a mistake using the submission tool or might involve some technical difficulty or mistake at the receiving end. Most of the major commercial software packages have some form of student tracking facility. Nonetheless, students could be instructed to make back up files of all material submitted on line. This includes not only assignments, essays, quizzes or examination answers and scripts to be submitted, but also contributions to be posted to discussion boards or forums. Teachers should plan to check all material submitted online as soon as the submission date/time has expired and submissions checked off against the student class list. Some commercial courseware programs provide a tool to monitor and match submissions to a class list. A student whose work is missing can then be contacted by telephone or email and advised that the work has not been received. If the student claims to have done the work, a teacher could request the student to submit the back up file as an attachment to an email either immediately, or within a reasonable period of time, and the work could be accepted either with or without penalty depending upon the circumstances.

Equity in experience

It may sometimes happen that a course or subject is being delivered on campus through face-to-face delivery and also off campus as a distance education online course. There is a danger that the online cohort or the face-to-face cohort, or both, may come to believe that the other cohort of students is obtaining some advantage that they are not. Teachers need to consider a strategy to provide each cohort equal treatment and to try to make the experience of each group consistent and equitably balanced so that students do not feel that another student group is receiving a benefit not available to them, or more favorable treatment.

One possibility would be to give both cohorts access to the online material and delivery system, and record all face-to-face lectures and classes and put them on the website. Individual circumstances will differ, but teachers should consider the equity of access issue, and be aware of the possibility of student resentment that could interfere with successful student learning experiences and satisfaction with the course.

Online etiquette

Where an online course involves interaction between student and teacher, and particularly between student and student, it is sensible to establish some principles of online etiquette. Most teachers and students are aware of the common courtesies and customs of the teacher and student relationship, the student-to-student relationship and acceptable classroom behavior, but have less experience or appreciation of Internet courtesies and customs.[14]

It is important that online classes be conducted in an atmosphere of mutual respect. Teachers should be careful to safeguard a student's personal and confidential information, and to adopt practices which do not involve risk of embarrassing or shaming students. Before copying any communication with an individual student to others, and particularly to the wider class community, teachers should consider whether it contains information or comment that could cause embarrassment or should not be communicated to others.

Teachers should remind class participants that when involved in discussion boards and threaded conversations, they must not disparage the contributions of other students. Disagreement and lively debate and exchange of opinion enhance educational goals, but sarcasm, irony or angry argument seldom assist learning.

---

[14] For a listing of various articles on Internet communication etiquette see: www.onysd.wednet.edu/internet_etiquette.html.

Communication policies

It has already been noted that students come to online teaching with high expectations and demands. Students in online courses work through email and discussion boards to connect themselves to the teacher and the course, and they often expect that they will receive instant feedback or responses from their teachers. The demands for attention are much greater than in traditional face-to-face classes; if the teacher were to attempt to respond to every communication from students, the task would quickly dominate the teacher's time. Teachers with even a modest class size can find themselves inundated with emails and be faced with substantial and complex discussion threads to monitor.

Email

Where possible, students should be asked to use a standard email address. This should preferably be their standard student email address issued to them by the educational institution they attend and accessed through the mail facility in the commercial courseware package being used to deliver the subject. Teachers can utilize the tools and settings available on the mail program they will use to receive student emails related to the course to assist them to manage the flow. One useful mechanism is to require students to put a standard identifier, perhaps the subject identifying number for the teaching period, in the subject box of their emails and the mail program can be instructed to automatically sort all incoming mail from students in the course into a dedicated mailbox. Mail from each individual student can be sorted to a separate sub-folder for that student.

Teachers should realistically appraise how quickly they can respond to student emails and how much time they are able to allocate to the task. Teachers must decide how they are going to manage this demand and, from the outset, publish in course instructions clear guidelines setting out expectations and responsibilities for students and teachers concerning the use of email. These practices should be reinforced. The teacher should strive to apply them consistently throughout the course.

Teachers are not advised to immediately send an email response to a student request,[15] even if it is possible to do so, unless there is a

---

[15] C. Jamon, *Strategies for Developing Effective Distance Learning Experience in Teaching at a Distance: A Handbook for Instructors*, Mission Viejo CA League for Innovation in the

compelling and urgent reason to reply immediately. It is better to establish a specific time for sending replies to emails from students. Teachers can draft replies to emails at any time and keep them in a draft email outbox to be sent out at the agreed time. Shelton and Saltsman[16] provide the useful tip that teachers might read their mail in reverse order so that the newest posting from a student is accessed first. In some, perhaps many cases, students solve their own problem, particularly if a relevant answer is available on an FAQ listing, and the earlier questions no longer require a reply.

It is also useful to create an archive of emails received and sent. Most of the commercial courseware packages provide a facility for this but it is also easy to create on most email programs. It also makes sense to create a Frequently Asked Question (FAQ) file with standard answers to commonly asked email questions, and to place this on the front page of the website.

Discussion boards or forums

A similar approach can be taken to managing, monitoring and responding to postings on teaching discussion boards. Teachers should set aside specific times to monitor discussion boards and to make interventions, in the discussions where necessary. Teachers may monitor at any convenient opportunity and draft responses or interventions, but it is sensible management practice to have a consistent timetable for the release of those responses and interventions. In courses with sufficient personnel resources, it is helpful to have a teaching assistant or cyber tutor maintain regular close attention to discussion board postings and to alert the teacher to anything that requires a response, intervention or feedback.

As with emails, it is most useful to maintain archives of discussion board postings. Creating a Frequently Asked Question (FAQ) file is also very valuable for use in discussion boards. Often, a number of students have the same type of question about the learning content of the subject; if the subject is offered again in the next teaching or training period, the same sorts of questions are likely to arise. It is possible to develop FAQs for each module or topic. Commercial courseware packages provide the

---

Community College (1999), pp. 1–14. J. Boettcher and R. Conrad, *Faculty Guide for Moving Teaching and Learning to the Web*. Mission Viejo, CA: League for Innovation in the Community College. Both quoted with approval in K. Shelton and G. Saltsman, note 4 above.   [16] Ibid.

necessary tools for creating archives. It is sensible to maintain the archives and the FAQ files at the end of each course for use in forthcoming courses.

Participation requirements

Teachers must determine what sort of participation requirements they will set for online students. Teachers providing a course at the basic or intermediate level may be content to provide the student with the materials and an explanation of the assessment requirements, and allow the student to work through at a pace and level of engagement of their own choosing.

However, a teacher wishing to engage students in an online "learning community" must take a more structured and proactive approach. Education or training through an online "learning community" approach is predicated upon students interacting and contributing to the discussion of materials, topics and information, and exchanging ideas, opinions and perspectives and helping each other learn.[17] Students who do not participate in the process not only deprive themselves of the benefits of the course educative environment, they also detract from the experience and learning opportunities of the other students. Teachers need to determine which activities all students must participate in, and contribute to and set clear instructions and requisites in the course syllabus and student requirement information.[18]

If students are required to carry out an activity that they must work to fulfill, and their work reveals the level of their understanding of course content and has value for others in the program, there should be some reward for fulfilling the task and some disadvantage suffered if the activity is not performed. In online courses, it is likely that if the activity is not included in or clearly linked to the assessment regime, many students will not participate.[19]

Typically, the most important "learning community" activity is participation in the online discussion forum. Teachers can set discussion topics and require each student to contribute according to a defined schedule. This might be to contribute to certain topics, or to all topics, weekly or fortnightly or monthly. To be able to contribute effectively, students must keep up with the relevant materials, lectures and readings, and are less

[17] J. Boettcher and R. Conrad, note 15 above.
[18] R. Palloff and K. Pratt, *Building Learning Communities in Cyberspace: Effective Strategies for the Classroom*, San Francisco: Jossey–Bass (1999), p. 28.
[19] S. Ko and S. Rossen, note 13 above.

likely to allow their work schedule to fall behind or become disorganized. If contribution to the discussion boards and forums is graded, students should not be allowed to submit late postings and receive marks for that contribution.

Course commencement

The commencement of the course provides an opportunity to set the tone of the online experience.[20] Teachers wishing to create a "learning community" with a sense of cohesion should pay particular attention to the opening week.

Most online teachers start by delivering a welcome message to all students and introducing themselves. This can be done by an announcement on the Course Announcement box on the front page of the course website, or by sending a group email, or both. The initial posting by the teacher can provide a model of the online communication style. Students should be asked to read all of the documentation, student information, policies, protocols and instructions and the academic syllabus.

Students should also be encouraged to introduce themselves; it is helpful to have a discussion board available for this process. Teachers should pay particular attention to the postings by which each student introduces himself or herself. It is good teaching practice to make a conscious effort to treat online students as individuals with personalities and to pay attention to the matters disclosed by students in their introductions and throughout their postings of emails or discussion board contributions. Teachers can learn enough to personalize their individual communication with that student. Just using a student's preferred name sends a message about respect and attention that can be beneficial.

Some teachers will use the commencing session to engage students in a form of "icebreaker" activity to encourage students to reveal aspects of their personalities and encourage the beginnings of a sense of group or class identity. There are a number of icebreaker activities available on the Internet.[21]

---

[20] Ibid.
[21] E.g. V. Varvel, *Icebreakers*, The Illinois Online Network: Instructional Resources: Pointers and Clickers Article, www.ion.illinois.edu/resources/pointersclickers/2002_01/index.asp; S. Thiagarajan, *Virtual Games for Real Learning: A Seriously Fun Way to Learn Online*, www.work911.com/cgi-bin/links/jump.cgi?ID=4362, or the questionnaire at *Vark a Guide to Learning Styles*, www.vark-learn.com/english/index.asp.

Course materials

Course materials might consist of lectures as sound or video files, text documents, work book exercises, instructions to read text materials available on the website, or in text books set as readings, lists of readings, graphics, video or audio files or non-lecture material, and links to materials available online.

In IPR courses, it is useful to be able to provide either the text or links to the legislation, patent office guidelines or manuals, practice notes and the reasons for decisions by superior courts, as well government and NGO reports and learned articles. The capacity to show graphics is useful in showing diagrams of the technology in patents, the actual appearance of a registered mark and the alleged infringing mark in trademarks, the registered design and how it appears when applied to an article.

Students should be provided with a suggested order in which the learning materials should be accessed and timelines for covering the materials.

One of the potential advantages of online courses is that teachers can provide access to so much material. The course website can provide a wide range of material, access to archives of previous material, and links to external material. Students with differing levels of interest and learning capacity can access differing amounts and types of materials. However, students should not be left to wade among the materials without guidance. It is useful to identify clearly the core reading materials and to link that core material in a structured way to the lesson structure or learning modules of the course. Students will be assisted by information rating the relevance, importance and weighting of materials in relation to the stated learning aims and objectives of the course and the assessment regime. Students should be informed about what core materials they are expected to have accessed, read, considered and understood. Teachers can provide a key to inform students whether, in the teacher's opinion, particular materials are essential building block materials, extremely important core materials, useful but not essential materials, further examples of materials already covered in the essential readings, esoteric or frivolous or marginally related materials in the context of this course, etc. This can be particularly important where the website provides extensive lists of externally accessed material and can be done by a symbol system, or by using background colors for documents if the software allows, or by an index system.

It is also worth noting that a useful class participation task or exercise is to have students review, analyze and comment upon the materials and literature on a topic. These contributions can be monitored, edited and consolidated and over time built up into a very useful teaching resource which can then be provided online and linked to topics or learning modules.

Discussion boards

A well-designed e-learning course should make use of a discussion board or discussion forum which requires all students to participate by posting contributions to teacher selected and monitored discussion points, topics and questions. Discussion boards allow teachers to set or elicit useful learning topics, and require all students to contribute within a timeframe. The list of questions and discussion topics can match the learning objectives for each module or topic of the subject. The teacher can monitor the general level of knowledge of the topic within the class as a whole, can monitor every contribution and provide additional comment and feedback, correcting errors or misconceptions where necessary, supervise threads of discussion, and monitor each individual, or any subset of the class.

A teacher may use a technique where each student makes a contribution and comment available to everyone else in the class. This can be used not only as a tool by which the teacher elicits student responses, monitors their discussion and gathers an impression of the overall group understanding of a given topic, but also as an excellent vehicle to allow students to exchange useful information, and equally importantly, explore and exchange their views and perspectives about the topic at hand. Discussions can be extremely valuable learning experiences for all concerned, including the teacher.

Teachers must learn to facilitate and review the discussions, but at the same time allow them to evolve and not just permit, but assist, the students to explore the topic or discussion subject as much as possible. Teachers used to traditional face-to-face teaching with limited classroom time to cover large amounts of information and content may feel they need to control or dominate the discussion board conversation. In online discussion boards, the technology allows students an equal opportunity to express their views and provide information or knowledge. Teachers used to a high level of control may consider it risky to allow students this freedom and could find it difficult to adapt their style to the new environment.

Teachers should encourage students to consider the discussion board as their meeting space, where they can genuinely participate and express their views, while feeling confident that there is a "safety net" because they are aware that the teacher is monitoring the discussion and will not allow it to fall into error or become misleading or counterproductive.

There is also a discussion about the advantages of linear as opposed to threaded discussions.[22] Linear discussions, as the name suggests, list all contributions in the order of their posting. Threaded discussions, however, group the postings as responses to an initial message. Threaded discussion tools allow asynchronous responses to be coherently grouped together. Teachers will discover their own preferences through use of each model and student response can be sought.

Sometimes senior teachers can make use of teaching assistants or "cyber tutors" to monitor the discussion and report back with summaries and suggestions about ways to make use of the line of analysis or commentary. It is also possible to create "group leaders" or obviously competent and experienced senior students to work with the teaching assistant.

Teachers should provide comment and feedback in the discussion forum. In particular, they should be ready to intervene and stimulate when a discussion appears to have become stuck. They should provide guidance and correction if discussion involves too many errors of fact, or is pursuing an irrelevant or erroneous path based upon faulty understanding of the material. Teachers should not intervene too hastily, or with too detailed an assertion of the correct path. In some cases, students will themselves recognize the issue and suggest a more appropriate or considered approach which the teacher can then recognize and support. In other cases, it may be possible to get the discussion into more fruitful pathways, not by setting out the teacher's views, but by asking judicious questions, or by asking students to go back to particular materials and then reconsider an aspect of the discussion.

A possible strategy to develop participation and confidence in student use of the discussion board forum is to start as early as possible with a relatively simple, clear and discrete task, with all students being required to submit a contribution. This task could be as simple as asking students to review the course syllabus and provide a summary and comment upon what the course is going to cover. It might involve requiring students to

---

[22] K. Peters, *Creative Use of Discussion areas, Pt 1* www.webct.com/OTL/ViewContent?contentID=898084; L. Assaf and P. Platt, *Threaded Discussions in TeachNet* Learning Technology Center, University of Texas at Austin, www.edb.utexas.edu/teachnet/discussions.php; *Creative Use of On-line Discussion Areas*, http://tlt.its.psu.edu/suggestions/ discuss/; DiscusWare Support Centre *Threaded vs. Linear Discussion Format*, http://support.discusware.com/center/resources/essays/thread.html.

summarize and critique an article which provides an introductory overview of the area to be studied in the course. Teachers should be actively involved in this discussion providing feedback and comment, and, wherever possible, positive reinforcement relating to students contributions but not allowing themselves to become the dominant voice. After the initial week, as students are participating, the teacher can start to pose more challenging questions and stimulate responses by asking such things as "Why do you think that?", "Is there a counter argument to that position?", "What if . . . .?"

Where a student does not participate, this should be noticed and prompted.[23] In the early weeks at least, the student should be contacted by email or telephone and asked if there is some problem or reason why he or she has not submitted, and if they require assistance. Successive tasks can become progressively more sophisticated.

While all students may be required to participate in the central teaching discussion board for the subject, teachers can also create private discussion forums for subset learning groups so that they can interact among themselves without the whole class seeing their discussions. Each topic can have its own discussion forum. Sensitive or highly controversial topics can be put into a discussion board that allows anonymous listings to encourage a free exchange of opinion. Discussion boards can also be used to practice and work though past examination questions. Students tend to be interested in this type of practice and can learn a great deal if they believe that participation will assist them when it comes to the final assessment task.

It can be useful to have several discussion boards for different purposes on the website. One, a general "getting to know you" site where students introduce themselves, provide personal details and engage in social conversation; one which allows general discussion about any topic which is broadly connected to the subject matter of the course; and one which is focused closely upon the syllabus of the course. Discussion boards can be used in many ways and developing skills with this tool will greatly assist online teaching.

Groups

Some teachers like to use group teaching and group work assignment and marking techniques. This can be adapted to an online environment.

---

[23] B. Bischoff, "The Elements of Effective Online Teaching", in K. White and B. Weight (eds.), *The Online Teaching Guide*, Needham Heights, MA: Allyn and Bacon (2000), p. 70.

Commercial courseware programs make it easy to separate the student cohort into groups of any size and based upon a wide variety of criteria. It is then possible to use the various teaching and communication tools with each group. The practical implication is that there is often more work associated in dealing with a number of small groups rather than with one. Where a teacher does wish to use groups, it is suggested that teachers choose the group rather than allow students to self select. The postings in which students describe and introduce themselves could provide clues that certain students might work well together.

Each group can work through its own discussion board as well as contributing to the common central discussion.

It is also possible to use "wiki"[24] technology to allow all members of the group to work on a single document on line. All members of the group have equal access and can contribute to edit and change the document. It can be used to collaborate on a single group assignment document, or to collate the data from each individual researcher, etc. While this can be a very flexible electronic tool, it requires that the teacher have some skill in group work and is able to set clear guidelines to the group about individual responsibilities to contribute and to act responsibly within the group. "Wiki" technology can be used by teaching staff as well. They can use the technology to collaborate on the creation of the syllabus and course material documents.

Online assessment

Just as most traditional teaching methods can be adapted to be used in an online course, most forms of assessment can be adapted to be used in online courses.

If the examiners wish to assess student competence through a traditional research essay model, it is a simple task to post the essay topics and questions on the Assessment Panel in the website and make an announcement in the Announcement Panel indicating that they have been posted. Students could be instructed to email the essays back to the teacher but the amount of material being sent could result in the teacher's normal email account exceeding its limit and becoming blocked or inaccessible. Commercial courseware packages contain an electronic "drop box" facility. The student

---

[24] For some explanations of the "wiki" technology, discussions of its use in education and examples of courses in a number of disciplines using "wiki" technology in online teaching see: S. Mather, *Using Wiki in Education*, www.scienceofspectroscopy.info/edit/index.php?title=Using_wiki_in_education and the range of resources at the Home Page.

uses a tool on the website to submit a file. The time of submission is electronically recorded and attached to the file, and the student is sent an electronic receipt.

A similar approach can be used to adapt the traditional formal sight unseen examination. The examination paper can be made available on the website at a programmed time and students given a time limit to submit an answer script through the drop box. Teachers should consider how much time can be allowed for submission of answers. Traditional exams tended to be two or three hours long with students writing in examination books by hand. Teachers may consider that different levels of keyboard skills amongst the student group require a longer time.

It is unlikely to be practical to arrange for online distance examinations to be supervised or proctored. Teachers can do a number of things to enhance the integrity of the examination system. Firstly, from the commencement of course, the teachers should make it clear to students that they expect responsible, honest and ethical behavior. The examination paper should specifically remind students that they are expected to contribute their own work and that any breach of normally understood academic practices will carry penalties if discovered. More particularly, examiners should design examination papers recognizing the realities of online courses. Questions should not require discussions of general topics in ways which will encourage or tempt students simply to search for, copy or adapt material they can find in books or materials or online. Questions which require analysis of hypothetical fact problems require the student to produce their own work. An examination question used in one teaching period should not then be used in examinations in subsequent offerings of the course, but can be used as practice questions in the next teaching session.

Commercial courseware programs offer a range of tools which can be used in assessment. They provide for setting online quizzes or short answer tests. These can be conducted in real time with all students in a teaching group being required to complete them "live" online, (which reduces the likelihood of use of external resources) or as tests set to be submitted by a specified date and time. Courseware programs also include facilities to create short answer tests where the teacher can set answers and the tests are automatically graded by the software program. While these automatic marking tools have their uses, there can also be problems due to typographical errors, faulty spacing, inconsistent or unrecognized abbreviations and so on.

Some online teachers like to provide a lot of study drill questions in their courses and also run regular short answer tests in order to encourage students to keep moving through the course subject matter.

Where possible, there are advantages in being able to use a combination of assessment items. These can include short on line tests, submission of assignments, essays and projects, participation in discussion boards, a reflective journal (which can be created as an online "blog"[25]) and online examination.

Examiners need to consider how much of their time they are able to devote to marking and how they will deal with the material submitted. Few teachers are entirely comfortable with reading and marking dense and reasonably lengthy essays or examination answers on screen. An alternative is to print out the work submitted and mark it in the traditional way, and then provide feedback or comments online. This requires that someone download the material, staple answers together, check submissions against the class list and contact students where work has apparently not been submitted.

Plagiarism in online assessment

In recent years, it seems that the issue of plagiarism in student assessment tasks is more prevalent and the availability of the Internet is obviously a contributing factor. There are now computer programs which can detect plagiarism;[26] where a student is submitting work in digital file formats online, it is easy to use these programs to check the work. Teachers who suspect plagiarism from outside sources can use a search engine, like Google to search for phrases and if matches are found compare the works. This is often effective but is not as efficient as a dedicated program. With a dedicated program, it is possible to compare student work with all material available online and to compare two or more student works to detect collaboration. The software will give readings of the degree of overlap and pinpoint the sources. These programs are not foolproof and should be used as a tool to inform a final consideration by the examiner.[27] Plagiarism detection software can also be used

---

[25] http://en.wikipedia.org/wiki/Blog
[26] The best known is Turnitin, www.turnitin.com/static/home.html. For a listing of other well known plagiarism detection programs see: R. Gaither, Plagiarism Detection Services www.lib.umich.edu/acadintegrity/instructors/violations/detection.htm.
[27] Bedford Martins, *Turnitin.com, A Pedagogic Placebo for Plagiarism*, www.bedfordstmartins.com/technotes/techtiparchive/ttip060501.htm.

as a teaching tool with students taught to use the facility to check their own work and improve their scholarly writing research and referencing practices.

Example of courses in IPR delivered online

What follows is a description of a program of subjects being run at a university providing educational qualifications for people wishing to register as patent or trademark professionals. This is a full suite of subjects in a course directed to the theory and the detailed systemic requirements and the practical skills of professional activity. The course focuses on providing candidates with an understanding of the core concepts and skills, and addresses applications for registration of rights, maintenance of registration, management of rights and litigation to protect rights. Course designers considered that current doctrinal details of the law and practice were important, but that they would change. The important educational aim was considered to be that a graduate acquired not only familiarity with the narrative of the law and its particular topics, but more importantly the skills to keep abreast of changing detail and a conceptual framework to allow them to assess their significance and importance to the development of the field from doctrinal, theoretical and practical perspectives.

The course is presented at Masters level and consists of nine subjects designed for patent professionals There are two introductory subjects One is *Legal Process and Overview of Intellectual Property* which introduces the legal system and legal skills concerned with statutory interpretation, case analysis, legal research and legal writing techniques. The other is *Professional Conduct*. There are three subjects teaching the general doctrinal content of the substantive law relating to *Patents, Trade Marks* and *Industrial Designs*. Then two subjects dealing with the national and international systems for acquisition and maintenance of patents and trademarks called *Patent Systems* and *Trade Marks Practice*. The final two subjects are concerned with high level professional skills for patent professionals, one entitled *Validity and Infringement of Specifications* and other the *Drafting of Patent Specifications*.

Trademarks professionals can complete a subset of the Masters program to obtain a Graduate Certificate which involves *Legal Process, Professional Conduct, Trademarks Law* and *Trademarks Practice*.

A crucial stage in the design of this program was determining the learning needs of the potential student cohort and working out the goals and objectives of the overall program and each individual subject, and then designing a manageable course syllabus and content. Modes of delivery, electronic resources, web-based learning and so on were considered to be just tools. The real issue is what message the teachers are trying to share. What do teachers want the student to learn? What are the teachers' strategies for helping students to acquire the skills of learning in this subject and then how to develop familiarity with the content? And once students have some familiarity with the content, what do teachers want them to be able to do with it? In this case, the professional competency objectives and knowledge base had been established by government. The university had to devise a structure and set educational goals for its program of subjects.

The university undertook with the government that it would deliver the subjects everywhere in the national jurisdiction, and the only practical way to do that was through a course designed around web-based "online" teaching.

Students are required to have access to a computer with web browsing capacity. Each subject has its own website. The university has an institution wide policy using a major commercial courseware product and sufficient hardware and network resources to support the course. Training programs are available to assist teaching staff to develop capacity to use the tools provided by the software.

The individual subject website is secure and can only be accessed by students who are properly enrolled in the course by the university. Students who enroll in the subject are given password access and log in details to the website. Each student is also given an email account which operates from within the website.

In the earliest days of this course, the starting point was normal face-to-face lecture and tutorial classes on the university campus. Every class was taped using a digital tape recorder. Every student question or comment was taped using a separate digital microphone. Every note or diagram or graphic put on the whiteboard, every Powerpoint slide or overhead projector transparency was digitally captured.

At the end of the class all of this material was uploaded to the subject website. The lectures were available as sound files and the students could listen to them at any time. The graphics were available in various formats. The students could listen to the full lecture, or any part of the lecture, as often as they wished.

As the course coordinators have become more experienced, different teachers now use different ways to get lecture material online. Some still want to teach face to face and use the first technique. One teacher pre-records 16 two-hour lectures. Sometimes the teacher has an audience of one or two postgraduate research students to provide a focus for the lecture performance. For a number of semesters, the lecture series was then "burnt" as a CD and sent to students before the semester began. In more recent semesters, the lectures have been placed as audio files which can be downloaded from the subject site. The lectures are now recorded direct to computer before loading them to the website. The lectures are recorded using a readily available program which creates a file format which allows them to be "podcast". If there is an important development or decision, it is easy to record some additional material and make it available on the website. Other teachers are experimenting with not using lectures at all and teaching though a full text and document-based system. One teacher has structured a subject around the authoritative practitioner's manual in the subject. One teacher is delivering a subject through a detailed series of teacher-directed questions requiring students to carry out their own research.

Because at different times, different topics or cases are of greater interest than at others, the subject coordinator keeps an archive of past lectures and additional recorded material which can be accessed on line.

Where the teacher does use lectures, the website includes an accompanying set of notes on the topic discussed and explained in the lecture. These notes are not the content of the lecture in printed form. They are usually far more detailed and structured notes. The detailed complex information is available in the notes, while the lectures provide a framework and a perspective.

Another feature of the resources available to students is the electronic reading guide. There is a carefully structured reading guide which is organized to fit the lecture schedule. The references in the reading guide have been automatically marked up by a particular mark-up program and linked to a publicly available, free-to-use legal materials database. The database contains the full text of all relevant legislation, regulations, case law, Patent and Trademark Office decisions, Patent and Trademark Office Examiners Manuals and a variety of electronically available articles. If a student clicks on a reference in the reading guide, or in the accompanying notes, and that material is available on the database, it will be displayed on screen. Any reference within the text on screen can then also be accessed. The database itself contains a number of very powerful search and referencing tools. It provides immediate access to all relevant primary legal materials.

If, for example, a student clicks on the reference to a section in the Patents Act, the text of the legislative section will be displayed. The text itself may contain terms which are defined in the legislation and they are highlighted. Clicking on the highlight will give the reference or definition. The student may then hit the "note up" button. That will list every cross-reference to the section. This may consist of references to associated sections, regulations, case law, commentary in the Patent Office Examiners Manuals or in the course accompanying notes. Selecting any reference will bring it up on screen, and it too will have been marked up so that all of the references to other legislative sections, cases regulations and so on can be accessed; furthermore, it is possible to obtain another list of every case which has referred to that case.

Now, however "high tech" this might sound, in the end teaching and learning is a social human activity. The teachers found that they wanted to give students a sense of connection with the teachers and with each other as classmates. The course coordinators made a decision to try to create virtual "learning communities." They introduced a number of discussion boards. A "getting to know you" discussion board for exchange of personal information. A general broad discussion board for a free ranging discussion on any intellectual property topic that was of interest to anyone in the class. Finally, a problem solving discussion board where each week a problem or hypothetical was posted and students were required to submit answers, analysis and comment. Participation in this discussion board is included in the assessment system.

The assessment system is also operated online. Examination or assignment papers are made available on the website at a precise time. Students are given time to answer and then submit a file to the electronic drop box. This will record the time of submission to the second. Teachers can organize the papers alphabetically, or by class, or tutorial group, or anonymously – whatever they choose. Examination answers can be marked on screen or they can be downloaded and marked as paper. Grades, results and feedback can all be provided online through the course website. Grades can be sent to each individual as a private communication, or as a public document or announcement, or as an entry in a grade book all students can see.

The course coordinators have introduced a "cyber tutor" for each subject teacher who wants one. The cyber tutor will put up notices, monitor the discussion boards, add comments and direct discussion, and alert the professor if there is a question or an issue that needs to be responded to in an expert fashion or where there is an especial teaching opportunity. Furthermore, there is at least one technical assistant to deal with the server and some administrative assistance to deal with electronic enrolment and student records.

The University is pleased with the levels of cooperation involved in the design, development and delivery of this online program. The University is cooperating with government, with the Patent and Trademark and Designs Offices, with the statutorily established professional regulatory body, with the professional practitioner organizations, with the firms, with senior practitioners, with university academics, with students and with technicians and administrators.

What is being done in this program is still evolving and developing. The teachers are constantly learning, changing and discovering new educational issues. New teachers are joining the teaching staff for the program and some teachers are leaving, and so the approaches and experiments change with them.

Final comment

The technology is malleable. In the end, the real issues in online teaching are about students and student learning. Readers are urged to take the view that technology is merely a tool, it is never an end in itself. They are also urged not to be afraid of trying to use the technology and experimenting for themselves and their students.

Some suggested further reading

Books

Bates, A. and Poole, G. (2003) *Effective Teaching with Technology in Higher Education*, San Francisco: Jossey-Bass

Collis, B. and Moonen, J. (2001) *Flexible Learning in a Digital Age*, London: Kogan Page

Laurillard, D. (2002) *Rethinking University Education: A Conversational Framework for the Effective Use of Learning Technologies*, 2nd edition, London: Routledge Falmer

Ryan, S., Scott, B., Freeman, H. and Patel, D. (2000) *The Virtual University: The Internet and Resource-based Learning*, London: Kogan Page

Stephenson, J. (ed.). (2001) *Teaching and Learning Online: Pedagogies for New technologies*, London: Kogan Page

Chapters

Alexander, S. and Boud, D. (2001) "Learners Still Learn From Experience When Online", in Stephenson, J. (ed.). *Teaching & Learning Online: Pedagogies for New Technologies*, London: Kogan Page

Biggs, J. (2003) Chapter on "Educational Technology" in *Teaching for Quality Learning at University*, 2nd edition, Buckingham: SRHE Open University Press

Papers

Sfard, A. (1998) "On Two Metaphors for Learning and the Dangers of Choosing Just One", *Educational Researcher*, 27(2)

Steel, J. and Hudson, A. (2001) "Educational Technology in Learning and Teaching: The Perceptions and Experiences of Teaching Staff", *Innovations in Education & Teaching International*, Vol. 38 Issue 2

Government Report

Department for Education and Skills. (2003) "Towards a Unified e-learning Strategy", available at www.dfes.gov.uk/consultations

12

Teaching current trends and future developments in intellectual property

CHARLES R. MCMANIS

Introduction

This chapter proceeds on the assumption that the ultimate goal of intellectual property law teaching – and legal education generally – is not simply to impart knowledge of the law, but rather to inculcate in students the necessary analytical skills to apply the law to new factual situations. Thus, one of the most important, and challenging, tasks for the intellectual property law teacher is helping law students develop the ability to identify emerging legal issues and predict future legal developments in intellectual property law and policy.

The challenge has become particularly daunting for intellectual property law teachers because of the increasingly dynamic nature of the subject matter. This dynamism is the product of rapid global developments in three overlapping fields: international law, technology, and commerce.

Until 1994, for example, the field of international intellectual property law was largely governed, as it had been for the past century, by the Paris Convention for the Protection of Industrial Property ("Paris Convention")[1] and the Berne Convention for the Protection of Literary and Artistic Works ("Berne Convention").[2] The modest goals of these two conventions were (1) to ensure that foreign nationals were provided "national [i.e. non-discriminatory] treatment" with respect to whatever intellectual property protection a member chose to grant its own nationals; (2) to establish an international priority system for industry property; and (3) to establish some initially modest international minimum standards for the prevention of unfair competition and the protection of

---

[1] Available at www.wipo.int/treaties/en/ip/paris/index.html.
[2] Available at www.wipo.int/treaties/en/ip/berne/index.html.

literary and artistic works. In 1967, the administration of these two conventions was vested in a new international agency, the World Intellectual Property Organization (WIPO), which was also to promote the protection of intellectual property throughout the world.[3] In 1994, however, the field of international intellectual property law underwent a tectonic shift with the promulgation of the Agreement on Trade-related Aspects of Intellectual Property Rights (TRIPS),[4] one of a bundle of agreements that were to be administered by the newly established World Trade Organization (WTO).[5]

The TRIPS Agreement essentially thrust the protection of intellectual property into the heart of international trade law by obligating all Members of the WTO to comply with a detailed set of international minimum standards for intellectual property protection and enforcement, and provided that any disputes concerning alleged violations of intellectual property rights by a Member were to be submitted to the WTO dispute settlement process. Suddenly, the WIPO, which had unsuccessfully sought to develop a consensus among its Member States on international minimum standards for intellectual property protection, found itself cast in a new international role as the international agency responsible for keeping pace with rapid technological developments, identifying emerging intellectual property law issues, and developing appropriate international law and policies to deal with those emerging issues. WTO, on the other hand assumed the role of obtaining compliance with the TRIPS international minimum standards for intellectual property protection and enforcement.[6]

The two technology fields that have offered the most significant challenges for international intellectual property policy development are digital technology and biotechnology. For example, even as the TRIPS Agreement was being finalized, the Internet and biotechnology revolutions were gathering force, leading many commentators to criticize the TRIPS Agreement as an essentially backward-looking document that largely failed to address emerging technologies and associated intellectual

---

[3] See Convention Establishing the World Intellectual Property Organization, Article 3, available at www.wipo.int/treaties/en/convention/index.html.
[4] Available at www.wto.org/english/docs_e/legal_e/27-trips_01_e.htm.
[5] For the Agreement Establishing the World Trade Organization and related agreements to be administered by the WTO, see www.wto.org/english/docs_e/legal_e/legal_e.htm.
[6] See generally Agreement Between the World Intellectual Property Organization and the World Trade Organization, December 22, 1995, available at www.wipo.int/treaties/en/agreement/trtdocs_wo030.html.

property issues. TRIPS did, of course, specify that: 1) computer programs are to be protected as literary works under the Berne Convention; 2) databases which by reason of the selection or arrangement of their contents constitute intellectual creations are to be protected as such; 3) microorganisms and microbiological processes are patentable subject matter; and 4) plant varieties are to be protected either by patents or by an effective *sui generis* system or by any combination thereof. At the same time, however, the TRIPS Agreement left unanswered many of the emerging intellectual property questions being spawned by the digital and biotechnology revolutions.

Just two years after the TRIPS Agreement was adopted, for example, the WIPO found it necessary to convene an international conference to address the digital revolution by drawing up a new pair of treaties, the WIPO Copyright Treaty[7] and the associated WIPO Performances and Phonograms Treaty.[8] The WIPO Copyright Treaty made it clear that computer programs are literary works under the Berne Convention, recognized an exclusive rental right for computer programs, cinematographic works and works embodied in phonograms, and explicitly recognized an exclusive right to authorize communication to the public of a copyright work by wire or wireless means. It also imposed two new "para-copyright" obligations against circumvention of effective technological measures to prevent unauthorized use of copyright works and to provide effective remedies against the knowing removal or alteration of any electronic rights management information (including terms and conditions of use of the work) without authorization. The WIPO Performances and Phonograms Treaty created similar "para-copyright" obligations with respect to phonograms. WIPO also considered, but ultimately decided not adopt, a proposed database protection treaty modeled on the European Union Database Directive, which mandates the creation of a new *sui generis* form of intellectual property protection for databases.

Meanwhile, on the international trade front, WTO by 1999 found itself confronting the unruly phenomenon of globalization and its discontents, as its Ministerial Conference in Seattle collapsed amidst violent and teargas beclouded anti-globalization protests. This reversal stimulated the issuance of the Doha Declaration in 2001,[9] in which WTO conceded that it needed to be more sensitive to the needs and interests of developing

[7] Available at www.wipo.int/treaties/en/ip/wct/index.html.
[8] Available at www.wipo.int/treaties/en/ip/wppt/index.html.
[9] Available at www.wto.org/english/thewto_e/minist_e/min01_e/mindecl_e.htm.

countries. Specifically, the Doha Declaration stressed that the TRIPS Agreement was to be interpreted in a manner supportive of public health, by promoting access to existing medicines and research and development into new medicines, as spelt out in a separate declaration acknowledging the gravity of the public health problems afflicting many developing and least developed countries. Eventually, that separate WTO Declaration on the TRIPS Agreement and Public Health[10] led to the first modification of the TRIPS Agreement, relaxing Article 31's strict limitations on compulsory licensing to enable one Member to supply another Member with patented pharmaceuticals without the authorization of the patent holder.[11] In addition, at the urging of developing countries, the Doha Declaration specifically directed the TRIPS Council to examine the relationship between the TRIPS Agreement and the Convention on Biological Diversity (CBD), as well as the protection of traditional knowledge and folklore. Notwithstanding the issuance of these two declarations, and the ambitious goals set for the Doha Round of multilateral trade negotiations, however, the accomplishments thus far have been modest, and the negotiations are in danger of deadlocking on agricultural subsidies and access to the agricultural markets in the industrialized world, and consequently imperiling implementation of the TRIPS Agreement in the developing world.

These, then, represent some of the emerging international intellectual property issues that intellectual property teachers will need to address. The objective of this chapter is to suggest how intellectual property teachers can best do that.

One option, of course, is to include in each course devoted to a specific field of intellectual property law (patents, copyrights, trademarks, etc.) a component that specifically deals with emerging issues, particularly those issues involving international intellectual property law. If the experience of the author of this chapter is any guide, however, both emerging intellectual property issues and international intellectual property law tend to get short shrift in basic introductory intellectual property courses, particularly if they are tacked on as the final two topics to be covered in the course. A skilled teacher may be able to touch on one of these two topics in an introductory course, but seldom is there time to cover both adequately, particularly if the particular introductory course also covers an

---

[10] Available at www.wto.org/english/thewto_e/minist_e/min01_e/mindecl_trips_e.htm.
[11] See WTO Press Release 426, December 6, 2005, available at www.wto.org/english/news_e/pres05_e/pr426_e.htm.

ancillary field of intellectual property or unfair competition law, such as utility models, industrial designs, trade secrets, semiconductor chip design or plant variety protection. The challenge is still more daunting in a general introductory intellectual property course seeking to offer an across-the-board introduction to patent, copyright and trademark law.

On the other hand, conceptualizing courses devoted exclusively to emerging intellectual property law issues or to international intellectual property law presents its own challenges, as such courses can be unworkable or unwieldy as a practical matter. A teacher offering a course devoted exclusively to emerging intellectual property law issues will need to develop his or her own teaching materials, and will probably need to require students to have taken one or more introductory intellectual property courses as a prerequisite. Even then such a course may be unworkable, as students will not necessarily have the same grounding in the same areas of basic intellectual property law. Teachers of international intellectual property law courses may likewise need to develop their own materials and establish prerequisites for the course. Here, too, the course may prove to be unworkable or unwieldy, particularly if the objective of the course is to provide students with a comprehensive introduction to all of the existing international intellectual property agreements.

However, the twin challenges of teaching emerging intellectual property issues and teaching international intellectual property law offer the potential for a single integrated solution to both challenges. The basic hypothesis that will guide the discussion in the remainder of this chapter is that a workable approach to teaching emerging intellectual property issues is to utilize these issues as organizing themes or topics to give focus to a basic international intellectual property law course or seminar. Specifically, this chapter will describe a basic international intellectual property course that the author has successfully taught in a variety of contexts to a wide range of students, many of whom had no prior background in intellectual property law.[12] The educational objective of this course is to introduce students to intellectual property law generally and

---

[12] In addition to teaching the course as a basic introductory intellectual property law course to rising second year students at Washington University, the author has also taught the course to a combination of US and European law students enrolled in two different summer law programs in Europe – the University of San Diego 2001 London Institute on International and Comparative Law; and the 2006 Summer Institute for Global Justice, jointly sponsored by Washington University School of Law in St. Louis, Case Western Reserve University School of Law, and Utrecht University (see http://law.case.edu/summer-institute).

international intellectual property law in particular, while at the same time helping students identify and analyze emerging intellectual property law issues.

Organizing the course

The course is organized around a number of topics and sub-topics, beginning with the general topic, intellectual property and international trade, followed by an examination of the specific legal issues raised by digital technology and biotechnology, respectively. The reading for the course consists entirely of primary international legal materials and selected secondary sources, most of which can be accessed online, and examples of which will be provided in footnotes throughout this chapter.[13] The two primary pedagogical methods to be employed in the course are: 1) engaging in a close reading and analysis of basic legal texts; and 2) utilizing these texts to identify and analyze specific emerging issues of international intellectual property law.

Topic I: Intellectual property and international trade

The initial objective is to introduce students to the TRIPS Agreement and the intellectual property issues that it addresses, particularly those identified in the Doha Declaration.[14] Indeed, the TRIPS Agreement and the Doha Development Agenda provides the basic legal anatomy for the course as a whole.[15]

For example, Article 1.2 of TRIPS offers students a working definition of what constitutes "intellectual property" for purposes of the TRIPS Agreement and simultaneously introduces students to the basic anatomy of Part II of TRIPS, which specifies the international minimum standards concerning the availability, scope, and use of seven discrete types of intellectual property and the control of anti-competitive practices in contractual licenses. From these structural elements in the TRIPS

---

[13] For a comprehensive set of online materials that can be employed to teach the course described in this chapter, see the Final Report of the Commission on Intellectual Property Rights, *Integrating Intellectual Property Rights and Development Policy* (2002) (hereinafter IPR Commission Final Report), and accompanying study papers and other documents, available at www.iprcommission.org/.

[14] See supra notes 9–11 and accompanying text.

[15] In addition to the TRIPS Agreement itself, reading materials for this segment of the course could consist of Chapter 1, "Intellectual Property and Development," of the IPR Commission Final Report, supra note 13.

Agreement, the teacher should be able to help students develop a matrix, or chart, for use throughout the course, integrating the various types of intellectual property law and the three basic phases of intellectual property practice (acquisition, enforcement, and licensing or transfer of rights). Across the top of the chart is the spectrum of intellectual property and related rights (copyrights and related rights, trademarks, geographical indications, industrial designs, patents, layout-designs of integrated circuits, and undisclosed information). Down the side of the chart are the three phases of intellectual property practice, which can be subdivided as follows:

1. Acquisition of rights:
   (a) subject-matter protected, and
   (b) substantive and procedural requirements for obtaining protection.
2. Enforcement of exclusive rights:
   (a) Scope and term of exclusive rights, and
   (b) prima facie infringement (including ownership of rights, directly infringing acts, active inducement, contributory infringement and vicarious liability); defenses; and remedies.
3. Licensing and Transfer of rights:
   (a) Licensing (voluntary and compulsory), and
   (b) Assignment (sale, gift, testamentary transfer).

In short, this "IP Law and Practice" matrix offers a way for students to examine the law and practice of intellectual property as a whole and to fit the particular provisions of the TRIPS Agreement into a larger mosaic.

For example, an examination of the table of contents of the TRIPS Agreement will make it clear that, in addition to establishing minimum standards for the protection of intellectual property in Part II, the TRIPS Agreement also establishes minimum enforcement standards in Part III, minimum administrative and procedural standards for the acquisition and maintenance of intellectual property rights in Part IV, and at the same time establishes a system for international dispute settlement among its Members in Part V, while addressing various transitional and institutional arrangements in Parts VI and VII. Article 2, in turn, makes reference to Parts II, III and IV of the TRIPS Agreement, as it offers the opportunity to introduce students to the primary pre-existing intellectual property agreements – the Paris Convention, the Berne Convention, and the Rome Convention – and thus provides the teacher with the opportunity to identify the basic subject matter protected by these Conventions, as suggested by their full titles in footnote 2 (i.e. industrial property, literary and artistic works, and "neighboring rights" with respect to performances, phonograms, and broadcasts).

Likewise, Article 2, taken together with Articles 3, 4 and 5, offers an opportunity to introduce students to the concepts of national (or non-discriminatory) treatment and most-favored-nation treatment, and to WIPO. This discussion, in turn, will enable the teacher to distinguish the limited objectives of the Paris, Berne, and Rome Conventions with the more ambitious objectives of the TRIPS Agreement. Examining Articles 2–5 of the TRIPS Agreement will also provide a springboard for introducing the role of WIPO in administering the Paris, Berne, and Rome Conventions, as well as related supplementary treaties, such as the Patent Cooperation Treaty (PCT), the Madrid Agreement and Protocol on the International Registration of Marks, the Lisbon Agreement for the Protection of Appellations of Origin and their International Registration, etc.[16]

The foregoing introduction will also lay the groundwork for an initial foray into Part II of the TRIPS Agreement, where Articles 9 and 10, respectively, offer an example of an intellectual property topic TRIPS specifically declines to address (i.e. moral rights of authors), thus deferring to the exclusive competence of WIPO, and an example of a more interventionist TRIPS provision, which specifies that computer programs, whether in source or object code, are to be protected as literary works under the Berne Convention. It is worth pointing out to students that the latter provision amounts to a *de facto* "amendment" of the Berne Convention – an amendment that is given *de jure* status with the promulgation of the WIPO Copyright Treaty in 1996. The teacher can also ask students to consider why the TRIPS Agreement is deferential on the topic of moral rights, but not on the protection of computer programs, thus highlighting the fact that not all intellectual property issues are "trade-related."

A comparative analysis of the substantive international minimum standards for intellectual property protection contained in Part II, Sections 1–7 of the TRIPS Agreement, in turn, should enable the students to see that each section is organized in accordance with the "IP Law and Practice" matrix described above – i.e. each section enumerates the subject matter and standards for protection first, followed by articles specifying the scope, term, and limitations of exclusive rights, and concluding with any relevant articles concerning licensing and assignment,

---

[16] For the texts of the 23 treaties administered by WIPO, see www.wipo.int/treaties/en/.

as further qualified by section 8's single article permitting WTO Members to control anticompetitive licensing practices. Likewise, an examination of Part III should provide the students with a basic understanding of the international minimum procedural and remedial standards for intellectual property protection.

With the completion of this basic introduction to the TRIPS Agreement and to international intellectual property law generally, the students are now equipped to consider some of the interpretive disputes that might be raised in the WTO dispute settlement process, incorporated by reference in Part V of the TRIPS Agreement, over the meaning of various TRIPS provisions. At this point, the teacher may ask students to read selected WTO dispute settlement decisions, as these decisions are readily accessible online.[17] Once the students have gotten a general overview of the types of disputes that have already been submitted for WTO resolution, the course can then turn to the first of two general categories of emerging legal issues to be considered in the remainder of the course – namely those generated by digital technology.

Topic II: Digital technology

As suggested above, an initial foray into Part II of the TRIPS Agreement will immediately confront students with a concrete example of a fundamental copyright issue arising as a result of the emergence of digital technology – namely whether computer software in all of its forms should be classified and protected as literary works. The protection of computer programs is an ideal place to begin a discussion of emerging IP issues, as it offers a good example of a "hybrid" subject matter that might be protectable under more than one form of intellectual property law.[18]

---

[17] See www.wto.org/english/tratop_e/dispu_e/dispu_subjects_index_e.htm#trips.
[18] For possible introductory readings on this topic, see Chapter 5, "Copyright, Software and the Internet," IPR Commission Final Report, supra note 13; Charles R. McManis, "Taking TRIPS on the Information Superhighway: International Intellectual Property Protection and Emerging Computer Technology," 41 *Villanova L. Rev.* 207 (1996) (hereinafter McManis, Taking TRIPS on the Information Superhighway). For a discussion of what industries will benefit most and least from the TRIPS Agreement, see Charles R. McManis, "Intellectual Property and International Mergers and Acquisitions," 66 *U. Cincinnati L. Rev.* 1283 (1998). For a discussion of the challenges confronting the WIPO and WTO in regulating intellectual property rights in the information age, see Pamela Samuelson, "Challenges for the WIPO and the TRIPS Council in Regulating Intellectual Property Rights in the Information Age," [1999] *Eur. I.P. Rev.* 578.

After all, a computer program in source-code (i.e. human-readable) form clearly appears to qualify as a copyright literary work, but that same program in object-code (i.e. machine-readable) form seems to perform more like a machine part, and when embedded in an integrated circuit, even looks more like a machine part than a literary work. Likewise, a computer program can be widely distributed in object-code form, while closely guarded as a trade secret in source-code form. Were trade secret law the only form of protection available for computer programs, it would clearly seem to be permissible to reverse engineer a publicly distributed computer program, as reverse engineering of publicly distributed products is a well-established permissible means of acquiring the trade secrets of others, but reverse engineering of software also amounts to reproducing, or at least translating, the program, which violates one or more of the exclusive rights conferred by copyright law. Finally, a computer program not only gives instructions to a machine, but also generates separate works on a computer screen, and those works, in turn, may be literary works, pictorial, graphic, or motion picture works, and may also be accompanied by musical works that are also generated by the computer program. Some elements of these screen displays may be so highly distinctive as to constitute trademarks; some elements may be highly functional (e.g. icons), and all are arguably a digital form of trade dress, in addition to being copyright subject matter.

If the teacher wishes to provide students with a comparative, as well as an international, introduction to intellectual property law, while exploring specific intellectual property issues that have been generated by digital technology, this may be accomplished by comparing the US and European approaches to three specific controversies involving digital technology – namely 1) the interoperability debate; 2) the mass-market (shrink-wrap and click-wrap) licensing debate; and 3) database protection debate. For example, the teacher may ask students to examine the EC Directive on the Legal Protection of Computer Programs[19] and assign readings that compare the US and EU approaches to the software reverse engineering and interoperability debate.[20] Students may also be asked to read materials comparing the US and EU approaches to mass-market

[19] Available at http://wiretap.area.com/Gopher/Gov/Other/copyrigh.ec.
[20] For possible introductory readings on this topic, see Charles R. McManis, "Intellectual Property Protection and Reverse Engineering of Computer Programs in the United States and the European Union," 1993 *High Tech. L.J.* 25; McManis, Taking TRIPS on the Information Superhighway, supra note 18.

licensing of computer programs.[21] Finally, the students may be asked to read the EU Database Directive,[22] which creates a new *sui generis* form of intellectual property protection for the non-copyright contents of databases, and read materials comparing the US and EU approaches to database protection.[23]

This final topic offers a particularly good opportunity to explore the difference between "national treatment" and "material reciprocity," as the EU Database Directive contains a material reciprocity provision, limiting *sui generis* database protection to nationals or habitual residents of EU member countries, businesses having a registered office and ongoing and genuine business links to an EU member country, and those foreign nationals of countries that extend comparable protection to databases of nationals or habitual residents of EU member countries.[24] Whether and to what extent Members of the WTO and/or members of the Paris or Berne Conventions can condition *sui generis* intellectual property protection for non-nationals on the basis of material reciprocity is an important (albeit abstruse) international intellectual property issue that the TRIPS Agreement itself does not explicitly address.[25]

With the emergence of the Internet, whole new congeries of trademark and copyright issues were generated, as savvy web page developers learned to attract "hits" (or develop opportunities for arbitrage) by registering and utilizing the marks of others as domain names ("cybersquatting"). They have also utilized the marks of others as metatags to attract the attention of Internet search engines, constructed web pages that "frame" other web pages, and have even adopted domain names consisting of well-known misspellings of the marks or domain names of others

---

[21] For possible introductory readings on this topic, see McManis, Taking TRIPS on the Information Superhighway, supra note 18; Pamela Samuelson and Kurt Opsahl, "Licensing Information in the Global Information Market: Freedom of Contract Meets Public Policy," 1999 *Eur. I.P. Rev.* 386; Catherine L. Mann, "Balancing Issues and Overlapping Jurisdictions in the Global Electronic Marketplace: The UCITA Example," 8 *Wash. U.J.L. & Pol'y* 215 (2002), available at http://law.wustl.edu/journal/8/p215Mannbookpages.pdf.
[22] Available at http://europa.eu.int/ISPO/infosoc/legreg/docs/969ec.html.
[23] For possible introductory readings on this issue, see Charles R. McManis, "Database Protection in the Digital Information Age," 7 *Roger Williams U. L. Rev.* 7 (2001) (hereinafter, McManis, Database Protection); F.W. Grosheide, "Database Protection – The European Way," 8 *Washington U.J.L. & Ploy's* 39 (2002), available at http://law.wustl.edu/journal/8/ p39Grosheidebookpages.pdf.
[24] See Directive 96/9/EC of the European Parliament of March 11, 1996 on the Legal Protection of Databases, Article 11 and recital 56.
[25] For a discussion of this issue, see McManis, Taking TRIPS on the Information Superhighway, supra note 18, at 258–259, and authorities cited therein.

("typosquatting"). Posing a hypothetical fact situation of the latter sort will provide the teacher with a good opportunity to introduce the distinction between consumer confusion as to the source of goods or services (the classic harm that trademark law seeks to prevent) and "initial interest" confusion, which merely imposes unwanted initial search costs on the consumer.[26]

The teacher may also wish to ask students to consider whether cybersquatting could be said to "dilute" famous marks, and whether, in extending the scope of Article 6*bis* of the Paris Convention, Article 16.3 of the TRIPS Agreement does or does not require WTO Members to protect famous marks against dilution.[27] Another way to explore international domain name controversies, while at the same time introducing students to the technology generating these issues, is to assign a cybersquatting research assignment, requiring students to examine online actual domain name controversies decided by the WIPO Arbitration and Mediation Center.[28]

This would also be an appropriate point in the course to conduct a detailed study of the WIPO Copyright Treaty,[29] and explore national implementation of its two provisions on digital rights management, requiring members to provide adequate legal protection and effective legal remedies against (1) the circumvention of effective technological measures designed to protect access to or copying of a copyrighted work, and (2) persons knowingly removing, altering or deleting electronic rights management information, including terms and conditions of use of the work. It is important for students to understand how these requirements can operate in conjunction with mass-market licensing provisions prohibiting reverse engineering, etc., to create what might be called "paracopyright," or "electronic trade secret protection" for authors of digital works, thus making much of conventional copyright law simply irrelevant

---

[26] See, e.g. *Electronic Boutique Holdings Corp. v. Zuccarini*, 2000 WL 1622760, 56 U.S.P.Q.2d 1705, E.D.Pa., October 30, 2000 (finding sufficient consumer injury where a consumer mistakenly types a misspelled domain name and is "mousetrapped," i.e. subjected to a barrage of advertising windows which cannot be exited without clicking through the entire succession of advertisements.

[27] For possible introductory readings on this issue, see Daniel Gervais, *The TRIPS Agreement: Drafting History and Analysis* (1998); J. Thomas McCarthy, "Dilution of a Trademark – European and United States Law Compared," 94 *Trademark Rep.* 1163 (2004); Paul J. Heald, "Mowing the Playing Field: Addressing Information Distortion and Asymmetry in the TRIPS Game," 88 *Minn. L. Rev.* 249 (2003).

[28] Available at http://arbiter.wipo.int/domains/decisions/index.html.

[29] For a possible introductory reading on the WIPO Copyright Treaty, see Thomas C. Vinje, "The New WIPO Copyright Treaty: A Happy Result in Geneva," 1997 *Eur. I.P. Rev.* 230.

in a digital environment.[30] This particular proprietary approach to the distribution of digital content can also be compared with the burgeoning "open-source" software development model, and implications of the two models for developing countries can be discussed.[31] Introducing the concept of "open-source" technology development as a feasible alternative wherever consumers of intellectual property are also innovators, is particularly useful at this point, as it will lay the groundwork for explaining the "common heritage" approach to agricultural innovation that is embodied in the "Multilateral System" established by the Food and Agricultural Organization's new International Treaty for Plant Genetic Resources for Food and Agriculture[32] – a potential topic of discussion in the second half of the course, as the focus of the course shifts from digital technology to biotechnology and the associated fields of biodiversity, traditional knowledge protection, and public health.

Topic III: Biotechnology, biodiversity, traditional knowledge protection, and public health

As noted earlier, the 2001 WTO Ministerial Conference, in its Doha Declaration, specifically directed the TRIPS Council to examine the relationship between the TRIPS Agreement and the CBD, as well as the protection of traditional knowledge and folklore.[33] Likewise, in 2000, WIPO established an Intergovernmental Committee on Intellectual Property and Genetic Resources, Traditional Knowledge and Folklore (IGC),[34] to facilitate discussion of intellectual property issues that arise in the context of access to genetic resources and the fair and equitable sharing of benefits arising out of the utilization of same, as well as the protection of traditional knowledge, innovations, creativity, and expressions of folklore. As these actions by WTO and WIPO illustrate, a second fundamental emerging

---

[30] For possible introductory readings on this point, see McManis, Taking TRIPS on the Information Superhighway, supra note 18; McManis, Database Protection, supra note 23.
[31] For a possible introductory reading on this point, see Chapter 5, "Software Protection and the Internet," IPR Commission Final Report, supra note 13; Chapter 4: "Free and open-source software: Implications for ICT [information & communications] policy and development," in United Nations Conference on Trade and Development, E-Commerce and Development Report 2003 (hereinafter UNCTAD E-Commerce Report), available at www.unctad.org/ecommerce/.
[32] International Treaty on Plant Genetic Resources for Food and Agriculture (hereinafter FAO Treaty), available at www.fao.org/ag/cgrfa/itpgr.htm, discussed infra notes 51–62 and accompanying text.   [33] See supra text following note 11.
[34] See www.wipo.int/tk/en/igc/.

legal issue in international intellectual property law is the growing interface with international environmental law. Similarly, the separate WTO Declaration on the TRIPS Agreement and Public Health highlights the growing interface between international intellectual property and public health law. Finally, the TRIPS requirement that WTO Members protect plant varieties either by patents or by an effective *sui generis* system or some combination thereof, together with the recent promulgation and entry into force of the FAO International Treaty on Plant Genetic Resources for Food and Agriculture, highlights the growing interface between international intellectual property and agricultural law. One or more of these emerging issues could provide a thematic focus for a third and final component of a basic international intellectual property law course or seminar.

One unfortunate consequence of the resort by the industrialized world to the rhetoric of "piracy" in the push to strengthen intellectual property protection in the developing world was that it stimulated a countervailing outcry in the developing world and elsewhere over what has come to be known – and vilified – as "biopiracy." Biopiracy has been defined as the "appropriation of the knowledge and genetic resources of farming and indigenous communities by individuals or institutions seeking exclusive monopoly control (patents or intellectual property) over these resources and knowledge."[35] One response to the concern over biopiracy was the promulgation of the CBD, the objective of which was to affirm national sovereignty over genetic resources and promote the conservation, sustainable use, and facilitated access to, and fair and equitable sharing of, the benefits arising from utilization of genetic resources and any associated traditional knowledge.[36] Ironically, the practical effect of the CBD has been to inhibit, rather than to facilitate, access to genetic resources in the developing world, thus heightening the urgency of developing a more equitable system of benefit-sharing if medical and agricultural biotechnology is to continue to have access to genetic resources as a starting point for research and development.

---

[35] See www.etcgroup.org/text/txt_key_defs.asp. This is the definition of the ETC Group (formerly known as RAFI – the Rural Advancement Foundation International), an advocacy organization that believes that "intellectual property is predatory on the rights and knowledge of farming communities and indigenous peoples." Ibid.

[36] For possible readings on traditional knowledge protection and the relationship between TRIPS and the CBD, see Chapter 4, "Traditional Knowledge," IPR Commission Final Report, supra note 13; Charles R. McManis, "The Interface Between International Intellectual Property and Environmental Protection: Biodiversity and Biotechnology," 76 *Washington U.L.Q.* 255 (1998), available at http://law.wustl.edu/WULQ/76-1/761-18.html.

The biopiracy controversy has produced a number of specific proposals on the part of developing countries to modify the existing intellectual property regime to make it more responsive to developing country needs and interests, and particularly to promote more equitable benefit-sharing. In response to these proposals, the Doha Declaration directed the TRIPS Council to examine the relationship between the TRIPS Agreement and the CBD, as well as the protection of traditional knowledge and folklore, and WIPO established the IGC.[37]

The specific intellectual property proposals that have surfaced in international discussions thus far can be divided into three categories: (1) proposals to provide more effective defensive protection of public domain genetic resources and traditional knowledge by expanding the definition of "prior art" and/or creating and improving access to documentation of public domain genetic resources and traditional knowledge in online databases and digital libraries; (2) proposals to promote a more fair and equitable sharing of the benefits of genetic resources and associated traditional knowledge, as mandated by the CBD, by requiring disclosure of the origin of any relevant genetic resources and associated traditional knowledge and evidence of prior informed consent of the providers of same as a condition either for filing a patent application or for enforcing an otherwise valid patent; and (3) proposals to create a new *sui generis* form of affirmative intellectual property protection for traditional knowledge. One or more of these specific proposals, together with the threshold question whether and to what extent existing intellectual property and unfair competition law in fact provides defensive and/or affirmative protection for traditional knowledge, could be the focus of a specific class assignment or research problem.[38] Asking students to compare the potential impact of a disclosure of origin and evidence of

---

[37] For a possible reading on these developments, see Charles R. McManis, "Intellectual Property, Genetic Resources and Traditional Knowledge Protection: Thinking Globally, Acting Locally," 11 *Cardozo J. Int'l & Comp. L.* 547 (2003).

[38] For possible readings on these proposals, see Charles R. McManis, "Fitting Traditional Knowledge Protection and Biopiracy Claims into the Existing Intellectual Property and Unfair Competition Framework," in *Intellectual Property and Biological Resources* (Burton Ong, ed) (2004); Nuno Pires de Carvalho, "From the Shaman's Hut to the Patent Office: In Search of a TRIPS-Consistent Requirement to Disclose the Origin of Genetic Resources and Prior Informed Consent," 17 *Washington U.J.L. & Pol'y* 111 (2005) (hereinafter Carvalho, From the Shaman's Hut to the Patent Office), available at http://law.wustl.edu/Journal/17/p111%20Carvalho%20book%20pages.pdf; Sabine Sand, "Sui generis Laws for the Protection of Indigenous Expressions of Culture and Traditional Knowledge," 22 *U. Queensland L.J.* 188 (2003); Angela R. Riley, "'Straight Stealing': Towards An Indigenous System Of Cultural Property Protection," 80 *Wash. L. Rev.* 69 (2005).

prior informed consent requirement, based on whether it is imposed as a condition for acquiring a patent or as a condition for enforcing a patent, provides an opportunity to examine practical aspects of the patent acquisition and enforcement process. As a practical matter, imposing such a requirement as a condition for acquiring a patent would impose a crushing burden on patent offices lacking any expertise to judge the sufficiency of the disclosure, whereas imposing such a requirement as a condition for enforcing an otherwise valid patent would focus the patent system on those few biotechnology patents sufficiently valuable to be worth enforcing, and thus capable of generating benefits.[39]

As we have seen, a second emerging issue with respect to intellectual property protection for medical biotechnology, and pharmaceutical products more generally, is the concern over TRIPS and public health.[40] This issue starkly reveals the inherent tension in a system for stimulating innovation through incentives based on the temporary grant of exclusive intellectual property rights.[41] The incentives provided by the patent system are arguably the most efficient means for promoting modern medical biotechnology and pharmaceutical research and development. At the same time, however, without some modification of the exclusive rights provided by the patent system, the benefits of modern medical biotechnology and pharmacology will be beyond the financial reach of much of the developing world. For that reason, one of the most controversial provisions in TRIPS is its requirement that patent protection be extended to pharmaceutical products.[42] Although Article 31 of the TRIPS Agreement in theory permits WTO Members to resort to government-mandated compulsory licensing as a permissible response to a public health emergency, this tool has remained out of reach for developing countries that lack a domestic industrial capacity to respond to the health crisis, as compulsory licensing under Article 31(f) of TRIPS is permissible only where it is "predominantly for the supply of the domestic market of the Member authorizing such use." Recognition of this shortcoming in Article 31 has produced the first modification in

---

[39] See generally Carvalho, From the Shaman's Hut to the Patent Office, supra note 38.
[40] See supra notes 10–11 and accompanying text.
[41] For a possible reading on this point, see Chapter 6, "Patent Reform," IPR Commission Final Report, supra note 13.
[42] This requirement can be extrapolated from Article 27.1, which requires that patent protection be available for any inventions, whether products or processes, in all fields of technology, and from Article 65.4, extending the transitional period for developing countries as set out in Article 70.8. For a possible reading on this point, see Chapter 2, "Health," IPR Commission Final Report, supra note 13.

the TRIPS Agreement,[43] which was designed to make permanent the Decision of August 30, 2003, waiving the foregoing limitation on compulsory licensing.[44] Examination of the online materials tracing the negotiations that led to this modification thus offers an opportunity to study the role of the WTO's TRIPS Council in developing international intellectual property policy.[45]

A third emerging biotechnology-related international intellectual property issue involves agricultural biotechnology and plant variety protection.[46] While Article 27.3 of the TRIPS Agreement permits WTO Members to exclude from patentability plants and animals other than micro-organisms, and essentially biological processes for the production of plants and animals other than non-biological and microbiological processes, it includes a proviso specifying that plant varieties are to be protected either by patents or by an effective *sui generis* system or by any combination thereof.

The proviso in Article 27.3 clearly does not require WTO Members to adhere to the latest (1991) revision (or for that matter any other version) of the International Convention for the Protection of New Varieties of Plants (UPOV),[47] but it does require WTO Members to provide "effective" plant variety protection of some sort. A number of developing countries opted to adhere to the earlier and more limited 1978 revision of UPOV, and they were allowed to join UPOV just before UPOV 1978 was superseded by UPOV 1991.[48] However, because UPOV 1991 has superseded UPOV 1978, it could be argued under TRIPS Article 27.3 that UPOV 1978 does not in fact provide "effective" *sui generis*

---

[43] See Amendment of the TRIPS Agreement, Decision of December 6, 2005, available at http://docsonline.wto.org/DDFDocuments/t/WT/L/641.doc.

[44] See Implementation of paragraph 6 of the Doha Declaration on the TRIPS Agreement and Public Health, Decision of August 30, 2003, available at www.wto.org/english/tratop_e/trips_e/implem_para6_e.htm.

[45] See generally WTO Doha Development Agenda: Negotiations, Implementation and Development, available at www.wto.org/english/tratop_e/dda_e/dda_e.htm.

[46] For a suggested reading on this topic, see Chapter 3, "Agriculture and Genetic Resources," IPR Commission Final Report, supra note 13.

[47] Available at www.upov.int/en/publications/conventions/index.html.

[48] For the members of UPOV 1978 and 1991, see www.upov.int/en/about/members/pdf/pub423.pdf. UPOV 1991 entered into force on April 24, 1998. See UPOV Press Release No. 30, available at www.upov.int/en/news/pressroom/30.htm. Under Article 37(3) of UPOV 1991, no instrument of accession to UPOV 1978 may be deposited after the entry into force of UPOV 1991. Apparently, developing countries that had begun the process of joining UPOV prior to the date of the entry into force of UPOV 1991 were allowed to adhere to UPOV 1978.

protection for plant varieties, thus suggesting a potential dispute as to what does and does not constitute "effective" *sui generis* plant variety protection.

Another potential dispute that could arise under TRIPS Article 27.3 stems from the fact that at least some developing country WTO Members have interpreted Article 27.3 to permit the exclusion of "the whole or part of natural living beings and biological materials found in nature, or isolated therefrom, including genome or germplasm of any natural living being."[49] That interpretation is likely to be challenged by industrialized WTO Members as inconsistent with Article 27.1 and submitted to the WTO dispute settlement process for eventual resolution.[50]

Also relevant to the protection of agricultural biotechnology and plant varieties is the recently adopted FAO International Treaty on Plant Genetic Resources for Food and Agriculture,[51] which will govern access to most materials in national and international germplasm collections (more than 6 million accessions in some 1300 collections around the world) as well as to *in situ* and on-farm sources.[52] The FAO International Treaty was negotiated with the understanding that it would be in harmony with the CBD, and is similar to the CBD in its overall objectives to promote the conservation, sustainable use, and equitable sharing of benefits arising out of the use of plant genetic resources for food and agriculture, as well as associated traditional agricultural knowledge, for sustainable use and food security. However, the FAO Treaty also goes well beyond the CBD, in that it builds on an existing national and international system of *ex situ* germplasm collections of genetic resources for food and agriculture, namely the Consultative Group on International Agricultural Research (CGIAR),[53] and creates a formal "Multilateral System" – i.e. a system of "common-pool goods" – in 36 genera of crops and 29 genera of forages, designed to provide "facilitated" (i.e. free or low cost) access to these genetic resources,

---

[49] See Brazilian Patent Law Article 10.1X, Law 9,279 (1996), cited in Carlos Correa, *Intellectual Property Rights, the WTO and Developing Countries: The TRIPS Agreement and Policy Options* 54 (2000).

[50] For a possible reading on this issue, see Charles R. McManis, "Patenting Genetic Products and Processes: A TRIPS Perspective," Chapter 5, in *Perspectives on Properties of the Human Genome Project* (F. Scott Kieff, ed) (2003).   [51] See FAO Treaty, supra note 32.

[52] See Cary Fowler, "Accessing Genetic Resources: International Law Establishes Multilateral System," 51 *Genetic Resources and Crop Evolution* 609 (2004).

[53] See www.cgiar.org/.

and to ensure an equitable sharing of the benefits derived from any commercialized product that incorporates materials from the Multilateral System.[54]

A critical feature of the "facilitated access" that the FAO Treaty seeks to promote is that recipients of genetic plant genetic resources covered by the Multilateral System are not to "claim any intellectual property or other rights that limit the facilitated access to the plant genetic resources for food and agriculture, or their genetic parts, or components, in the form received from the Multilateral System."[55] The FAO Treaty also pays lipservice to the concept of "farmers' rights"[56] as well as to a corresponding farmers' privilege to save and sell farm-propagated seeds.[57] How the foregoing provisions are to be reconciled with the TRIPS requirement that all WTO Members provide "for the protection of plant varieties either by patents or by an effective *sui generis* system or by any combination thereof,"[58] is not specified. However, the prohibition against claiming intellectual property rights is restricted to plant genetic resources, or their

[54] See Stephen B. Brush, "Protecting Traditional Agricultural Knowledge," 17 *Washington U.J.L. & Pol'y* 59 (2005) (hereinafter Brush), available at http://law.wustl.edu/centeris/Confpapers/index.html).   [55] See FAO Treaty, supra note 32, Article 12.3(d).

[56] Ibid. Article 9.1–9.2. The concept of "Farmers' Rights" was originally embraced in a 1989 FAO resolution, appended as an annex to the FAO's 1983 International Undertaking on Plant Genetic Resources, available at www.fao.org/ag/cgrfa/IU.htm. The concept of "farmers' rights" represented a political reaction to another FAO resolution, also appended as an annex to the Undertaking, that first purported to recognize plant genetic resources as a "common heritage" of mankind to be preserved, and to be "freely available" for use, for the benefit of present and future generations, but then acknowledged that plant breeders' rights, as provided for by UPOV, supra note 47, were not incompatible with the Undertaking. The concept of "farmers' rights" was thus apparently conceived of as an analogous and offsetting affirmative legal right that farmers should be able to assert against plant breeders, just as plant breeders could assert the *sui generis* plant breeder's right against farmers (subject, of course, to any "farmers' privilege" recognized in the relevant plant variety protection legislation). Article 9.1 of the FAO Treaty, however, merely states that the responsibility for realizing farmers' rights "rests with national governments." For a detailed discussion of farmers' rights, see Brush, supra note 54, at 85–93.

[57] Ibid. Article 9.3, which merely states that "Nothing in this Article shall be interpreted to limit any rights that farmers have to save, use, exchange and sell farm-saved seed/propagating material, subject to national law and as appropriate." For members of UPOV, however, this farmer's privilege must be spelled out in the member's plant variety protection legislation as a limit on the *sui generis* plant breeder's right. Article 15(2) of UPOV 1991 makes clear that recognition of a farmer's privilege is optional, not mandatory, and that any such privilege is to be limited to permitting farmers to use for propagating purposes, on their own holdings, the product of the harvest they obtain by planting a protected variety or an essentially derived version thereof on their own holdings. This privilege is substantially narrower than the privilege alluded to in Article 9.3 of the FAO Treaty.   [58] TRIPS Article 27.3(b).

genetic parts, or components, "in the form received from the Multilateral System," suggesting that plant variety protection can be sought for varieties derived from these starting materials. Moreover, the FAO Treaty specifies that germplasm from the Multilateral System is to be available under the terms of a standard material transfer agreement (MTA), which is to include provisions for benefit sharing in the event of commercialization of products developed using genetic resources received from the Multilateral System.[59] This, too, suggests that plant variety protection may be sought for plant varieties derived from genetic resources received from the Multilateral System, though subject to the Treaty's benefit-sharing requirements. In this respect, the FAO Treaty seems somewhat analogous to the "open-source" approach to software development, which requires source (i.e. human-readable) code to be distributed with the open-source software itself, but permits a programmer to modify the software and release the modified version under terms that are proprietary.[60]

The stronger the intellectual property protection provided for plant varieties (including those varieties developed by innovative farmers), the more market-produced economic benefits there will likely be available to share under the FAO Treaty's benefit sharing provisions. Conversely, the broader the definition of any legally recognized "farmers' right" or "farmers' privilege" in plant variety protection legislation, the more likely it is that the benefits emanating from the Multilateral System will consist primarily of the publicly improved plant varieties as such.[61] In any event, the ultimate success or failure of benefit-sharing provisions of the FAO International Treaty will depend in significant part on the ability (and willingness) of participating germplasm collections to enforce benefit sharing terms in applicable MTAs and the ability of the Governing Body responsible for administering the Treaty to reach a consensus as to the level, form, and manner of payment of an "equitable" sharing of monetary benefits.[62]

[59] FAO Treaty Articles 12.4 and 13.2(d)(ii).
[60] See generally UNCTAD E-Commerce Report, supra note 31, at 100, which distinguishes between "open-source" software and software distributed under the "copyleft" terms of the GNU General Public License, which requires any redistribution of GPL software to be released only under the GPL to prevent the "closing" of the code and deter its use in a proprietary commercial development environment.
[61] For a discussion of how farmers' rights have been implemented at the national level, see Brush, supra note 54, at 93–98.
[62] Article 13.2(d)(iii) of the FAO Treaty specifies that the "Governing Body shall, at its first meeting, determine the level, form and manner of payment" of any monetary benefits, "in line with commercial practice." The first meeting of the Governing Body took place on June 12–16, 2006. For the draft provisional agenda and other documents for this meeting, see www.fao.org/ag/cgrfa/gb1.htm.

In any event, a comparative study of the FAO International Treaty, UPOV, and the TRIPS Agreement, offers a good opportunity to compare several alternative systems for promoting agricultural innovation, ranging from "free" to "open-source" to purely proprietary systems, and will thus put in broader perspective the question as to what constitutes "effective" protection of plant varieties within the meaning of the TRIPS Agreement. Such a study also offers the opportunity to conclude the course with a comparative examination of the dynamics of software and plant innovation.

Conclusion

This chapter has sought to demonstrate that one effective way to introduce students to current trends and future developments in intellectual property law is by studying these trends and developments in the context of an introductory international intellectual property course organized around three general themes or topics: (1) intellectual property and international trade; (2) digital technology; and (3) biotechnology, biodiversity, traditional knowledge, and public health. There are a number of advantages to this approach. First, it will enable the teacher to focus on emerging issues of intellectual property law throughout a single introductory course, rather than addressing these issues in separate introductory patent, copyright, and trademark courses. Second, the course can be offered as an introductory course, without any need to require prerequisite courses. Third, the course can be taught using materials that are largely, if not entirely, available online. Fourth and finally, it will provide a policy-based focus for the study of international intellectual property law.

INDEX

abuse of dominant position 147n, 150–1, 155, 158
adjunct professors 6–7
African Regional Intellectual Property Organization (ARIPO) 17, 28, 120
Agreement on Trade-Related Aspects of Intellectual Property Rights *see* TRIPS Agreement
Agreement on Trade-Related Investment Measures (TRIMS) 14
American Institute of Architects 99
Andean Pact 19, 28
anti-trust law *see* competition law
applied arts 37, 50, 58
architects
  professional organizations 99
architectural works 50, 125
art works
  deformation 138–9
  works of applied arts 50
  works of fine arts 50
Association for the Advancement of Teaching and Research in Intellectual Property Law (ATRIP) 2, 65, 236
attorneys *see* European patent attorneys; German patent attorneys
audio-visual recordings 269
  see also distance learning
audio-visual works 49–50
  see also performers' and phonogram producers' rights
Australia
  University of Technology, Sydney 244

Bangui Agreement on the Creation of an African Intellectual Property Organization (OAPI) 17, 28, 120
Benelux Designs Office 120
Berne Convention for the Protection of Literary and Artistic Works 33, 34, 36, 38, 39, 40, 299–300, 305, 306
  broadcasting rights 45
  computer programs 301, 306
  folklore 42
  industrial design 125, 127–8
  management systems 48
  moral rights 139
  Singapore 186
bilateral agreements 99, 162, 163, 174
biodiversity
  Convention on Biological Diversity (CBD) 148, 302, 311, 312, 313, 316
  plant genetic resources 311–18
biopiracy 312
biotechnology 21–2, 300–1, 304
  plant varieties protection 18, 19, 131, 176, 301, 303, 312, 315–19
block exemptions for licensing of IP 153
Brazil 3, 20, 30, 169
broadcasting right 41, 44–5, 46, 50–1
  moral rights and 138–9
broken line drawing practice 123–4
Budapest Treaty on the International Recognition of the Deposit of Microorganisms for the Purposes of Patent Procedure 1977 18, 22, 186
business school
  business executive programs 194
  case method 190, 193, 195

sample case discussion 205–7
challenges faced by teachers 198
delivery style 197
domain knowledge 191–2, 196–7
generally 4, 9, 11, 185–6
language of instruction 197
large classes 195–6
materials 197, 198
open book assessment 190, 193
  sample examination question 208–11
outcome-based education 194
postgraduate modules 193
small class seminar-style teaching 189–90, 193, 196
student-centered learning 194
teachers as facilitators 194–5
teaching methods 189–90, 193, 194–6
technology as aid to teaching 197
textbooks 197
undergraduate modules 188
  case analysis 190, 193
  continuous assessment 193
  Final Examination 193
  independent research 191
  Intellectual Property in Cyberspace 191–3, 201–4
  Management of Intellectual Property 188–9, 200–1
  online forum 190
  open book assessment 190, 193, 208–11
  student seminar presentations 189–90, 193

cable transmission rights 45
Cartagena Agreement 38
case method of teaching 11
  business school 190, 193, 195
  sample case discussion 205–7
  non-law IP students 247–9
  patents 27–8
  trademark law 78
Chicago School 153
China 228
  IP education 5, 241–2, 266
  patents 3, 17, 20, 30

cinema
  trademark law and 81–2
clinical teaching method 250–1
Community Design registration system 117–19, 127, 128
comparative advantage theory 135
competition 13
  intellectual property rights and 37–8, 132
competition law
  abuse of dominant position 147n, 150–1, 155, 158
  anti-trust guidelines 153
  block exemptions for licensing of IP 153
  concerted practices 149–50
  effect 132
  essential facilities doctrine 153–6
  generally 130, 132–3
  horizontal agreements 150
  inherency doctrine 152, 158
  intellectual property rights and 151–6
  international law, anti-trust in 157–62
  merger control 150–1
  objectives 132, 149–51
  parallel conduct 49–50
  principles 149–51
  restrictive agreements 149–50
  TRIPS Agreement, anti-trust in 158–62
  unfair competition law and 137–8
  WTO law 157–62
  see also unfair competition law
computer programs
  Berne Convention 301, 306 *see also* Berne Convention for the Protection of Literary and Artistic Works
  business models for development and use 46
  copyright 46, 308
  databases 46, 50
  EU Computer Programs Directive 46, 308
  generally 50
  open-source software development 34, 43, 46, 50, 51, 311, 318–19

computer programs (cont.)
  reverse engineering 34, 46, 308, 310
  see also digital technology;
    information technology
concerted practices 149–50
continuing legal education (CLE) 227
Convention on Biological Diversity
  (CBD) 148, 302, 311, 312, 313,
  316
Convention Establishing the World
  Intellectual Property Organization
  (WIPO Convention) 16, 186
copyright and related rights
  architectural works 50, 125
  audiovisual works 49–50
  Berne Convention 33, 34, 36, 38, 39,
    40, 42
  broadcasting right 41, 44–5, 46, 50–1
  cable transmission rights 45
  case law 37, 38, 47
  civil law system 43
  collective management 43, 45, 46,
    47–9, 51, 56
  common law system 43
  competition and 37
  computer programs see computer
    programs
  contracts and 43, 49, 50, 51, 55–6
  corroborative systems 34
  damages for infringement 52
  database protection 46
  developing countries 34, 41–3, 54, 59
  digital rights management 46, 47, 51
  digital technology 39–40, 46–7
  dispute settlement 39, 49
  dramatic and dramatico-musical
    works 49
  economic importance 52
  economic rights 33, 40, 41, 47, 50
  enforcement of rights 43–4, 51–2, 57
  exceptions 53–4
  exercise of rights 51
  folklore 34, 41–3, 54
  free dissemination 51
  future trends 52, 59
  generally 33–5
  globalization trends 56–7
  government, role of 49
  human rights and 34, 35, 36–7, 53
  individual exercise of rights 43, 45
  individual licensing 51
  industrial design and 38–9, 57–9,
    103, 104, 105–6, 125
  information technology and 46–7,
    131
  interface with other disciplines,
    theories and principles 52–3
  international treaties 38
  Internet 7, 46–7
  Internet Treaties 33, 38, 39, 42, 46
  legal sources 38
  liability of service providers 47, 51
  limitations 53–4
  literary works 49
  "making available" right 40, 44–6,
    47, 48, 49
  moral rights 33, 36, 40, 41, 50
  multimedia productions 50
  musical works 49
  national laws 38
  networked environment and 39–40,
    47
  p2p systems and 47
  performing/communication rights
    44–6
  photographic works 50
  piracy 33
  postgraduate programs 44–52
  in practice 49–52
  public interest 34
  regional rules 38
  rights management information
    (RMI) 46, 47
  role in economic, social and cultural
    development 35–6
  Rome Convention 33, 38, 39, 40
  simulcasting 45–6, 49
  Singapore 187
  social importance 52
  special courses 44–52
  summaries 40–1
  technological protection measures
    (TPMs) 46, 47, 49
  three-step test 37, 39, 41
  traditional cultural expressions
    (TCEs) 41, 42, 54

TRIPS Agreement *see* TRIPS
    Agreement
undergraduate course 35–44
web-pages 50
webcasting 45–6, 49
WIPO Copyright Treaty (WCT) 33,
    34, 39–40, 45, 46, 301, 306,
    310
  database protection 46
WIPO Internet Treaties 33, 38, 39,
    42, 46
WIPO Performers and Phonograms
    Treaty (WPPT) 33, 34, 39–40,
    45, 301
  works of applied arts 50
  works of fine arts 50
  YouTube 7
court hearings
  attending 27
cultural development
  role of copyright 35–6
current trends and future
    developments
  biotechnology 300–1, 304, 312,
    314–16
  copyright and related rights 52, 59
  course organization 304–19
  digital technology 307–11
  generally 299–304
  industrial design law 127–8
  international trade 304–7
  IP professionals 226–8
  non-law IP students 232, 267
  patents 30
  plant genetic resources 311–18
  plant varieties protection 301, 303,
    312, 315–19
  trademark law 82
  traditional knowledge 302, 311–13
  TRIPS Agreement 301–2, 304–7
cyberspace 191–3, 201–4
cybersquatting 309, 310

damages
  copyright infringement 52
  patent infringement 26
databases
  Database Directive 46, 301, 309
  protection 41, 46, 50, 173, 203, 301,
    308, 309
  as resource 124, 245, 248, 260, 266,
    295
  see also digital technology;
    information technology
delivery style 197
developing countries 15
  access to drugs 160–1
  copyright
    folklore 34, 41–3, 54
    future trends 59
    preferential treatment 34, 41–3
  Doha Declaration 2001 24, 157n,
    160–1, 301–2, 304, 311
  HIV/AIDS epidemic 160–1
  IP standards and 162
  WTO and 167
digital technology
  copyright and 39–40, 46–7
  current trends and future
    developments 307–11
  digital rights management 46, 47, 51
  generally 300
  reproduction right and 47
  rights management information
    (RMI) 46, 47
  technological protection measures
    (TPMs) 46, 47, 49
  see also computer programs;
    databases; information
    technology
dispute settlement
  copyright 39, 49
  unfair competition law 142, 148
  WIPO Mediation and Arbitration
    Center 148
  WTO system 39, 142, 307
distance learning
  access 271, 272, 275, 276, 286, 290,
    295–6
  audio-visual recordings 269
  basic level 268–9
  commercial electronic interface
    products 274–5
  communication policies 282
  content syllabus design 276–7
  course commencement 285

distance learning (*cont.*)
  delivery vehicle 273
  discussion boards or forums 190, 276, 278, 280, 283, 285, 287–9
  educational goals 276–7
  email 282–3
  equity in experience 280–1
  example 293–7
  Frequently Asked Question (FAQ) file 283–4
  generally 11, 197, 268
  groups 289–90
  information to students 279
  intermediate level 269
  learning community 272, 284, 285
  materials 269, 271–2, 273, 276, 277–8, 286–7
  modules 278–9
  online assessment 290–2
    plagiarism 292–3
  online etiquette 281
  participation requirement 284–5
  patents 30
  plagiarism 292–3
  preliminary issues 275–6
  problems 280
  reasons for using 271–3
  sophisticated level 269–70
  student expectations 275
  use of materials 277–8
  WIPO facilities 11, 273
  see also Internet
DNA sequences 13, 14, 22, 27–8
doctrine of equivalence 26
Doha Declaration 2001 24, 157n, 160–1, 301–2, 304, 311
downstream benefit-sharing 8, 11, 51
dramatic and dramatico-musical works 49

economic development
  monitoring 15
  role of copyright 35–6
economics of IPR
  course objectives 169–70, 178
  course outline 170
    economic effectiveness of global IPR policy 175
    economics of knowledge, innovation and need for IPR 171–3
    integrating IPR into development policy 175–7
    international trade agreements 173–4
    model syllabus 180–4
    policy debates 170, 174–5, 177
    term papers 170, 177–8
  generally 166–8
  materials 170
email
  distance learning and 282–3
employee
  service invention 22, 220, 225, 227, 250
Erythropoietin (EPO) 28
essential facilities doctrine 153–6
Eurasian Patent 28
Eurasian Patent Convention 1994 17
European patent attorneys 214
European Patent Convention 1973 (EPC) 16, 18, 28
  entitlement to patent 22
  extent of protection 25
  patentability 19, 20, 21
  procedures 23
European Patent Office (EPO) 3, 21, 214, 266
  Boards of Appeal 23
European Union
  block exemptions for licensing of IP 153
  Community Design registration system 117–19, 127, 128
  Computer Programs Directive 46, 308
  Database Directive 46, 301, 309
  Directive on the Legal Protection of Biotechnological Inventions 1998 19, 22
  Information Society Directive 40, 49
  Satellite and Cable Directive 45
SPINNOVA project 242–3
"exchange-for-secrets" rationale 134–5
exhaustion of IPR 24, 159

INDEX

exhibitions of new products at trade shows 101
experiential learning 245–6

field trips 80–1
first-to-file system 20, 22
first-to-invent system 20, 22
folklore 34, 41–3, 54, 311, 313
  see also traditional cultural expressions; traditional knowledge
Food and Agriculture Organization (FAO)
  International Treaty on Plant Genetic Resources for Food and Agriculture 312, 316–19
foreign direct investment (FDI) 13, 175
foreign patents
  defense 218
  German patent attorneys and 218–19
  holders 13
  infringement litigation 218–19
  obtaining 218
France 125
  copyright 125
  industrial designs 100, 108, 112, 125
  patents 17, 27, 173
  university-level education 5
free riding 132, 137, 145–9
future developments *see* current trends and future developments

General Agreement on Services (GATS) 14, 158 *see also* World Trade Organization (WTO)
General Agreement on Tariffs and Trade (GATT) 14, 102, 106, 111, 158 *see also* World Trade Organization (WTO)
genetic resources 311–18
genetically modified organisms (GMOs) 176
Geneva Act of the Hague Agreement Concerning the International Registration of Industrial Designs 88, 99, 102, 107–11, 112, 127, 128
  national systems and 116–17

geographical indications 72, 77, 131, 140, 141–2, 144, 168, 176
  TRIPS Agreement 145–6
German patent attorneys
  defense of patents 217
  foreign patents 218
foreign patents
  defense 218
  infringement litigation 218–19
  obtaining 218
  generally 213–14, 219–20
  infringement litigation 217–18
    foreign patents 218–19
  obtaining patents 215–17
    foreign patents 218
  role 215–17
Germany
  extent of patent protection 25, 28
  inventive step 20–1
  patent attorneys *see* German patent attorneys
  patent system 15, 27, 173
globalization 2, 301
  copyright and related rights 56–7
  harmonization and 56–7

Harare Protocol on Patents and Industrial Designs 17
Havana Charter 157
historical development approach
  patents 16–17
HIV/AIDS epidemic 160–1
homologous recombination 28
horizontal agreements 150
human genes
  patenting 27
human rights
  copyright and 34, 35, 36–7, 53
  property rights 134

India 3, 30, 169, 173, 228
Industrial Design Alliance 98
industrial design law
  ARIPO registration system 120
  basket 85–6
  Benelux regional system 120
  broken line drawing practice 123–4
  chair 86–7

325

industrial design law (*cont.*)
  concept introduction 93, 98
  copyright law and 38–9, 57–9, 103, 104, 105–6, 125
  EU Community Design system 117–19, 127, 128
  examples 87–93, 94–8
  exhibitions of new products at trade shows 101
  future trends 127–8
  generally 84–5
  industry-related laws 126
  infringement
    broken line drawing practice 123–4
    generally 120
    partial product design protection 123–4
    primarily functional features 120–1
    resources 124
    substantially identical industrial designs 121–3
  integrated circuit designs 106
  international agreements
    foreign applications 100–1
    generally 99–100
    Geneva Act 88, 99, 102, 107–11, 112 *see also* Geneva Act of the Hague Agreement Concerning the International Registration of Industrial Designs
    integrated circuit designs 106
    local products 105–6
    national perspective 107
    national treatment 101
    Paris Convention 99, 100–2, 103–4
    protection right 105
    resources 111–12
    TRIPS Agreement 99, 100, 102–7
  international registration 107–11
    deferred two-dimensional design 110
  national registration systems
    generally 112–13
    Geneva Act interactions 116–17
    history 112–13
    types 113–16
  OAPI registration system 120
  Paris Convention 16, 17, 28
  partial product design protection 123–4
  patent or utility model compared 85–7, 93, 98, 100–2
  primarily functional features
    exclusion 85–6, 87, 93, 104, 105, 113
    infringement analysis 120–1, 122, 123
  purpose 131
  resources 98–9
    EU Community Design system 119
    industry-related industrial design laws 126
    registration infringement 124
    treaties and agreements 111–12
  scissors 87
  Singapore 187
  textile designs 87, 103, 106, 110, 111, 112, 117
  trademark law and 124–5
  TRIPS Agreement 58
  unfair competition law and 125
Industrial Designer Society of America 99
Information Society Directive 40
information technology
  copyright and 46–7, 131
  liability of service providers 47, 51
  "making available" right 47
  p2p systems 47
  right of reproduction in the digital environment 47
  rights management information (RMI) 46, 47
  technological protection measures (TPMs) 46, 47, 49
  see also computer programs; databases; digital technology; Internet
inherency doctrine 152, 158
injunctions 26, 51

integrated circuit designs 106, 126, 131, 135, 187, 308
Integrated Circuit Treaty 106, 107, 124, 126
Intergovernmental Committee on Intellectual Property and Genetic Resources, Traditional Knowledge and Folklore (IGC) 43, 311, 313
International Code of Conduct on the Transfer of Technology 157
International Convention for the Protection of New Varieties of Plants (UPOV) 18, 315–16 *see also* plant varieties protection
International Council of Societies of Industrial Design 98
International Covenant on Economic, Social and Cultural Rights 134
International Trademark Association (INTA) 65
International Treaty on Plant Genetic Resources for Food and Agriculture 312, 316–19
International Union of Architects (UTA) 99
Internet
  copyright 7, 46–7
  cyberspace 191–3, 201–4
  cybersquatting 309, 310
  materials and references 10–11, 197, 266–7
  online forum 190
  webcasting 45–6, 49
  weblogs 79–80
  websites 10–11, 50, 197, 266–7
  WIPO Internet Treaties 33, 38, 39, 42, 46
  YouTube 7
  see also distance learning; information technology
inventive step 20–1
  mosaic method 21
Inventors Statute 1474 17
IP professionals
  business understanding 221
  continuing legal education (CLE) 227
  current trends and future developments 226–8
  ethics 221–2
  European patent attorneys 214
  generally 212, 228–9
  Germany 224–6
  ideal educational profile 223–4
  language skills 222, 223, 224
  legal understanding 220–1
  Master's degrees 225–6
  material skills 220–4
  negotiating skills 222
  patent engineers 215
  pitfalls 222–3
  school 224–5
  technical understanding 220, 223
  university 225–6
  see also German patent attorneys
Italy 17

Japan 3, 178, 186
  language 224
  partial product design protection 123–4
  patents 17, 20, 25, 173
  unfair competition law 125
  university-level education 5
    Osaka Institute of Technology 240–1
    Tokyo University 243–4

Korea *see* Republic of Korea

language of instruction 197
licensing
  compulsory 17, 42, 152, 153
  HIV/AID epidemic 160–1
  Paris Convention 101–2
  TRIPS Agreement 24, 159–62, 302, 314–15
  copyright and related rights 51
  patents 26
lifelong IP education 9, 252
Lisbon Agreement for the Protection of Appellations of Origin and their International Registration 144n, 306
literary works 49

LL.M programs 4, 5, 15
Locarno Agreement 110, 118

Madrid Agreement concerning the International Registration of Marks 1989 187, 306
Madrid Agreement for the Repression of False or Deceptive Indications of Source on Goods 144n
Madrid Protocol 108
"making available" right
  copyright and related rights 40, 44–6, 48, 49
  information technology 47
material transfer agreements (MTAs) 318
materials and references 10–11
  business school 197, 198
  databases 124, 245, 248, 260, 266, 295
  distance learning 269, 271–2, 273, 276, 277–8, 286–7
  economics of IPR 170
  examples from popular culture 267
  interactive packages and books 267
  non-law IP students 231, 265–7
  patents 28–9
  textbooks 28–9, 197
  trademark law 78–82
  websites 10–11, 197, 266–7
medicines
  compulsory licence to import 160–1, 177
merger control 150–1
methods of teaching *see* teaching methods
Mexico 3, 30
monopoly 13, 38
"monopoly-profit-incentive" thesis 134
moral rights 33, 40, 41, 306
  architectural works 50
  Berne Convention 139
  educational use of materials 277, 278
  natural rights 135
  patents and 22
  unfair competition law and 138–9
mosaic method 21

most favored nation treatment principle 38, 157, 162, 306
multimedia productions 50
musical works 49

natural rights 134, 135
Netherlands 27, 120
New International Economic Order 157
new IP paradigm 7–9
new world economic order 14–15
newly industrialized countries 15
Nice Agreement 186
non-law IP students
  case method of teaching 247–9
  challenges 230–1
  clinical method 250–1
  collaborative interdisciplinary teaching and research 236–7
  experiential learning 245–6
  future 232, 267
  generally 230
  identification of target audience 232–7
  IP undergraduate curriculum map 251–64
  problem solving method 249
  reasons for teaching IP to 231, 232–6
  resources 231, 265–7
  simulation method 250
  subject matter curriculum 237–8
  syllabus 231, 237–8
    international examples 240–4
  teachers 231, 264–5
  teaching methods 231, 244–51
  "tool box" 238–40
North American Free Trade Association (NAFTA) 28, 38, 146n
Norway 186
novelty 20, 28

online teaching *see* distance learning
open book assessment 190, 193
  sample examination question 208–11
Organization for Economic Cooperation and Development (OECD) 157

Osaka Institute of Technology 240–1
outcome-based education 194

p2p systems
  copyright and 47
  parallel conduct 49–50
Paris Convention for the Protection of Industrial Property 1883 16, 17, 28, 99, 100–2, 103–4, 299–300, 305, 306
  compulsory licensing 101–2
  dilution of famous marks 310
  Singapore 186
  unfair competition 140–3, 146, 147
    bad faith 144
    protection against dishonest practices, confusion and false allegations 143–4
    traditional knowledge 146
partial product design protection 123–4
passing off 137, 203
Patent Cooperation Treaty 1970 (PCT) 16, 22, 23, 28, 108, 186, 306
patent engineers 215
Patent Law Treaty (PLT) 18
patents
  anti-trust law and 13
  applications 3
  approaches to teaching 26–8
  assignment 26
  biotechnological inventions 21
  blocking effects 13
  case method of teaching 27–8
  challenges in teaching patents 14–15
  claims drafting 22–3
  competency of the courts 26
  compulsory licences 24
  databases 260, 266
  disclosure of invention in application 21
  distance learning courses 30
  DNA sequences 14
  doctrine of equivalence 26
  economic policy and 17
  economics of the patent system 14
  effect of patent right 24
  entitlement to protection 13, 22
  equivalents 25
  "exchange-for-secrets" rationale 134–5
  exhaustion of patent right 24
  experimental use purposes 24
  extent of protection 24–5, 28
    extending 25–6
  farmers and 24
  first-to-file system 20, 22
  first-to-invent system 20, 22
  foreign *see* foreign patents
  foreign direct investment and 13, 175
  future trends 30
  generally 13–14
  historical development approach 16–17
  human genes 27
  identification of target audience 15–16
  as incentives to invention 13, 14, 134
  industrial designs compared 85–7, 93, 98, 100–2
  infringement 26
  international aspects 16
  international protection 13
  international treaties 17, 18
  interrelationship with other IPR 17
  invention 20
  inventive step 20–1
  jurisdiction 26
  licensing 26
  materials 28–9
  mosaic method 21
  nature 13, 14, 23
  novelty requirement 20, 28
  patentability 18–22
  plant varieties protection 18
  prior art 21
  prior users 24
  "product-by-process" claim 23, 28
  purposive patent claim construction 26
  references 28–9
  regional treaties 17–18
  remedies for infringement 26
  Singapore 187
  sources of applicable law 18

patents (cont.)
  subject matter curriculum 16–26
  teaching methods 26–8, 30
  technology transfer and 13
  undisclosed information 131
  worldwide applications 2
performers' and phonogram producers' rights 41, 45, 50
  audio-visual works 49–50
  collective management 46, 48, 49
  webcasting and simulcasting 45
  WIPO Performers and Phonograms Treaty (WPPT) 33, 34, 39–40, 45, 301
Phonograms Convention 38
photographic works 50
piracy 33
plant genetic resources 311–18
plant varieties protection 18, 19, 131, 176, 301, 303, 312, 315–19
postgraduate education 4
  business school 193
  copyright and related rights 44–52
practitioners see IP professionals
prior art 21
problem-solving method of teaching 11, 249
"product-by-process" claim 23, 28
professionals see IP professionals
public health
  compulsory licence to import medicines 160–1, 177
  developing countries' access to drugs 160–1
  Doha Declaration 2001 24, 157n, 160–1, 301–2, 304
  IPR and 176, 183
  TRIPS Agreement 160–1, 177, 314–15
purposive patent claim construction 26

references see materials and references
Republic of Korea 3, 178
resources see materials and references
restrictive agreements 149–50
reverse engineering 34, 46, 308, 310
"reward-by-monopoly" theory 134
rights management information (RMI) 46, 47

Rome Convention 33, 38, 39, 40, 305, 306
  broadcasting rights 45

Satellite and Cable Directive 45
Satellites Convention 38
Semi-Conductor Chip Protection Act (US) 107
seminar-style teaching 189–90, 193, 196
service invention 22, 220, 225, 227, 250
Set of Multilaterally Agreed Equitable Principles and Rules for the Control of Restrictive Business practices 157
simulation teaching method 250
simulcasting 45–6, 49
Singapore
  Free Trade Agreement with USA 187
  IP protection 186–7
  NUS Business School 185–211
small class teaching 189–90, 193, 196
social development
  role of copyright 35–6
software see computer programs
SPINNOVA project 242–3
Statute of Monopolies 1623/24 17
student-centered learning 194
subject matter curriculum 16–26
Switzerland 138, 186
syllabus 9–10
  distance learning 276–7
  economics of IPR 180–4
  non-law IP students 231, 237–8
  international examples 240–4
  Osaka Institute of Technology 240–1
  Valdosta State University 240

target audience
  identification 15–16
teachers as facilitators 194–5
teaching materials see materials and references
teaching methods 11
  business school 189–90, 193, 194–6
  case method see case method of teaching
  clinical method 250–1

court hearings 27
distance learning *see* distance learning
experiential learning 245–6
field trips 80–1
large classes 195–6
non-law IP students 231, 244–51
outcome-based education 194
patents 26–8, 30
problem-solving method 11, 249
simulation method 250
small class seminar-style teaching 189–90, 193, 196
student-centered learning 194
teachers as facilitators 194–5
trademark law 78–82
technological protection measures (TPMs) 46, 47, 49
Technology Licensing Office (TLO) 4
textbooks 28–9, 197
textile designs 87, 103, 106, 110, 111, 112, 117
Tokyo University 243–4
trade shows 101
trademark law
  approaches to teaching 78–82
  case method of teaching 78
  challenges in teaching trademark law 66–8
  the cinema 81–2
  complexity 67–8
  conceptualization problem 67–8
  criminal enforcement agencies 74
  exploitation 70–1
  field trips 80–1
  future trends 82
  general public 75–6
  generally 63–6
  housekeeping 71
  identification of target audience 68–76
  industrial design 124–5
  judiciary 73–4
  litigation 70
  materials 78–82
  official materials 79
  over-familiarity with subject matter 66–7
  passing off 137, 203
  police 74
  prosecution work 69–70
  purpose 131
  randomly selected materials 81
  schoolchildren 75
  Singapore 187
  strategists 71
  students 74–5
  subject matter of the curriculum 76–7
  teaching methods 78–82
  teaching and training compared 68
  trademark ancillary service providers 73
  trademark legal practitioners 69–72
  trademark owners 72
  trademark system administrators 72–3
  unfair competition and 138
  weblogs 79–80
traditional cultural expressions (TCEs) 41, 42, 54
  see also folklore
traditional knowledge 54, 302, 311–13
  registering 177
  unfair competition law 146, 147–8
"tragedy of anti-commons" 134
"tragedy of commons" 134
TRIPS Agreement
  anti-trust 158–62
  compulsory licensing 24, 159–62, 302, 314–15
  copyright and related rights 33, 34, 36, 38–9, 40, 43, 58
    broadcasting rights 45
    enforcement 43
    human rights and 36
    industrial property rights 38–9, 58
    most-favored-nation treatment principles 38
    national treatment principles 38
    three-step test 37, 39, 41
  criticism 300–1
  current trends and future developments teaching 301–2, 304–7
  databases 46

TRIPS Agreement (cont.)
  dilution of famous marks 310
  Doha Declaration 2001 24, 157n, 160–1, 301–2, 304, 311
  effect of patent right 24
  exhaustion of IPR 24, 159
  free riding, protection against 145–7
  generally 2, 14, 16, 18, 28, 133
  geographical indications 145–6
  industrial design 58, 99, 100, 102–7
  mandatory international standards 19
  most-favored-nation treatment principle 38, 157, 162, 306
  public health 160–1, 177, 314–15
    Doha Declaration 2001 24, 157n, 160–1, 301–2, 304
  rationale underlying 135
  Singapore 186, 187
  unfair competition 140, 141–2
TRIPS Plus standards 162
Tulsa University 243

UNESCO
  folklore 42–3
unfair competition law
  as basis for codification of intellectual property 140
  competition law and 137–8
  free riding, protection against 132, 137, 145–9
  generally 130–2, 133
  independent application 138–9
  industrial design and 125
  intellectual property protection and 138–40
  international law
    bad faith 144
    dispute settlement 142, 148
    foundations 140–3
    Paris Convention 140–4, 146, 147
    protection against dishonest practices, confusion and false allegations 143–4
    traditional knowledge 146, 147–8
    TRIPS Agreement 140, 141–2, 145–7
  moral rights and 138–9

pre-emption 139–40
principles and objectives 131–2, 135–8
United Kingdom
  extent of patent protection 25, 28
  inventive step 20–1
United Nations Conference on Trade and Development (UNCTAD) 157
United States 3
  adjunct professors 6–7
  Anti-Trust Guidelines 153
  Chakrabarty decision 19
  Chicago School 153
  "essential facilities" doctrine 153–6
  extent of patent protection 25
  first-to-invent system 20, 22
  Free Trade Agreement with Singapore 187
  inherency doctrine 152
  inventive step 20–1
  Lanham Act 139
  licensing of intellectual property 153
  partial product design protection 123–4
  patents 17, 19, 113, 173
  prior rights 21
  Rural v. Feist 35
  Semi-Conductor Chip Protection Act 107
  Tulsa University 243
  university-level education 5, 15, 240, 243
  Valdosta State University, Georgia 240
  Vessel Hull Design Protection Act 107, 128
United States Patent and Trademark Office (USPTO)
  inventive step 21
  Utility Examination Guidelines 21
Universal Declaration of Human Rights 36, 134
university-level education 3–5, 30
  adjunct professors 6–7
  Australia 244
  basic law degree programs 4
  business schools 4, 9

challenges facing universities 5–7
China 5, 241–2
Germany 225–6
Japan 5, 240–1, 243–4
LL.M programs 4, 5, 15
postgraduate 4
  business school 193
  copyright law 44–52
private-sector participation 8
role of TLO 4
science and engineering faculties 4, 11
specialized degree programs 4
SPINNOVA project 242–3
teaching methods 11
United States 5, 15, 240, 243
WIPO Symposium 5–6
UPOV *see* International Convention for the Protection of New Varieties of Plants (UPOV)

Valdosta State University 240
Vessel Hull Design Protection Act (US) 107, 128

webcasting 45–6, 49
weblogs 79–80
websites
  copyright and related rights 50
  materials and references 10–11, 197, 266–7
  see also distance learning; Internet
works of applied arts 50
works of fine arts 50
world economy 2–3, 14–15
World Intellectual Property Organization (WIPO)
  broadcasting rights 45
  Convention establishing 16, 186
  copyright and industrial property rights 58
  Copyright Treaty (WCT) 33, 34, 39–40, 45, 46, 301, 306, 310
  database protection 46
  Databases Treaty 46
  developing countries 59
  Development Agenda 42
  enforcement of copyright 43
  filing system 108, 109, 110
  folklore 42–3
  generally 2, 300
  globalization and 56
  industrial design registration 88
  international registration 108, 109, 110
  International Symposium on IP Education and Research 5–6, 12
  Internet Treaties 33, 38, 39, 42, 46
  Mediation and Arbitration Center 148
  Performers and Phonograms Treaty (WPPT) 33, 34, 39–40, 45, 301
  proposed Treaty on the Protection of Broadcasting Organizations 45, 46
  teaching materials 11
  traditional knowledge protection 148
  website 10, 11
  WIPO Convention 16
  Worldwide Academy 4, 5
    developing countries 59
    distance learning facilities 11, 273
    global network of IP Academies 9
    website 10
World Trade Organization (WTO)
  anti-trust rules 157–8
  competition, protection of 157–62
  copyright and industrial property rights 58
  developing countries 59
  dispute settlement system 39, 307
  Dispute Settlement Understanding 142
  GATT 14, 102
  generally 2, 133
  globalization and 56–7
  Ministers Conference 2001 24
  Paris Convention and 142
  "Singapore Issues" 157
  see also TRIPS Agreement

YouTube 7